Step-By-Step
Legal Forms and Agreements

Step-By-Step
Legal Forms and Agreements

Charles B. Chernofsky

Griffith G. deNoyelles, Jr.

Round Lake Publishing

Round Lake Publishing Co.
31 Bailey Avenue
Ridgefield, CT 06877

Printed in the United States of America

098765432

ISBN 0-929543-10-6

Acknowledgements

Our thanks to the legions of attorneys and judges who have preceded us and whose fine tuning of language have made many provisions of these and other legal forms standards for the profession.

Special thanks to attorney Paula Walter, Professor of Law at Baruch College in New York City, who rechecked our forms and instructions to ensure their accuracy.

Most of all, we want to express our appreciation to our "forms widows," Adrianne Chernofsky and Judith Levin, for their understanding and support when, in the toil of our labor on this book, we worked late, missed meals and sometimes whole weekends.

Contents

Brokerage Agreements

Buying and Selling a Residence

Contract Clauses for Sale of Residence

Mortgages

Easement

Leases

Chapter 3 BUYING AND SELLING GOODS

Selling Personal Property

Selling and Leasing—Business

Assignments and Licenses

Chapter 4 BORROWING AND LENDING MONEY

Promissory Notes

Loan Agreements and Letters of Credit

Guaranties

Demands

Assignments

Financing

Chapter 5 STARTING A BUSINESS

Partnerships and Joint Ventures

Corporations

Chapter 6 OPERATING A CORPORATION

Chapter 7 BUYING AND SELLING A BUSINESS

Chapter 8 GENERAL CONTRACT CLAUSES

Chapter 9 EMPLOYEES AND REPRESENTATIVES

What This Book Can Do for You

This book is designed help you deal effectively with many situations you encounter in your personal and business life. It will help you write a will or a living will, rent a house or apartment (either as tenant or landlord), sell your car or borrow money. It will also help you start (or sell) a business, prepare an employee contract, appoint someone to act for you or write a consulting agreement. In fact, there are more than 160 forms covering a great many situations individuals and business people experience.

What makes the book so unique and helpful are the step-by-step instructions accompanying each form, explaining *exactly what to put in each blank*, in language that is concise and easy to follow.

While no book can be a substitute for an attorney, many of the forms in this book cover basic situations and may not necessarily require an attorney's involvement. Others, of a more complex nature, can be completed by you but should be reviewed by an attorney. Still others cover technical areas and are included primarily for informational purposes. In these cases, an attorney should prepare the forms, but you will have the advantage of knowing what should be included.

Be sure to read the next section, "How to Use this Book," before starting to use the forms. It contains helpful advice and information you should have to help you in their preparation.

How to Use This Book

The format

Each form in this book is introduced by a brief explanation of how to use it and when it is to be used. Any necessary warnings follow. *Pay particular attention to these warnings—they were designed to protect the user.*

The form is shown on the right side of the page, with step-by-step instructions on how to fill it in immediately to the left. When a form continues beyond one page, a notation appears below the form:

(Document continued on next page)

Be sure to read and use the entire form.

Filling in the blanks

Each blank in the form is numbered to correspond to an instruction. The numbers in the blanks are in brackets:

EXAMPLE: I, _____[1]_____, residing at

In some forms, the legal language *of the form itself* contains numbers. These numbers are in parentheses:

EXAMPLE: upon three (3) days' notice

When the blanks get filled in, the underlines and bracketed numbers are to be deleted. *The numbers in parentheses are NOT to be deleted since they are part of the form.*

Be sure to fill in all the blanks. If some blanks are not filled in, the form will be open to interpretation.

Deleting or changing sections

When the instructions call for a section of the form to be deleted or changed, that section appears in italics preceded by a bracketed number corresponding to the instruction:

EXAMPLE: *[6]The Creditor shall*

Delete or change the italicized text and remove the bracketed number.

Making choices

Sometimes the instructions ask the user to choose between two or more alternatives. When this occurs, the choices in the form are in italics, separated by ***OR*** so that they are easily seen:

EXAMPLE: The apartment *[8][is]* ***OR*** *[is not]* to be vacated

Choose only one of the alternatives and *delete the others* and the bracketed number. Of course, the word ***OR*** must also be deleted.

Signing the forms

If the person signing the form is an individual or the sole owner or proprietor of a business, he is acting for himself and should sign the form in his own name. The instructions state where individuals are to sign.

Any other form of business—such as a corporation, partnership or joint venture—is a "created" entity which cannot act by itself. It can only act through people such as officers, directors, managers or others authorized to act for the business. In those cases, the signer should *follow the instructions for signing by corporations.*

IMPORTANT NOTES

State and local laws

The forms in this book were designed to be usable in 49 states. The one exception is Louisiana, whose laws are based on French rather than English law. However, a number of the forms caution that local or state law must be checked, since that particular form's requirements vary by locale.

This is particularly true for the real estate forms; the reader should check his local and state housing authorities or a local attorney to be sure of meeting the necessary legal requirements.

The use of "he" and "him"

The use of the masculine gender throughout the instructions in this book is for the sake of clarity and simplicity.

If you don't understand a form

If you don't understand the purpose of a particular form or how to fill it in, *don't use it!* Instead, seek advice from an attorney.

Wills and Gifts 1

The forms in this chapter provide a method for voicing and preserving for posterity a person's wishes concerning his property and body, both during his lifetime and when he can no longer express those wishes himself.

Wills A Will protects the maker of the Will and his heirs by preserving the wishes of the maker regarding the orderly distribution of his property. Without a Will, the state decides the distribution, based on formulas that typically leave the property to relatives. The forms in this section provide simple Wills for the most common situations.

Living Wills The Living Will preserves the voice of the maker by addressing medical decisions to be made when he is unable to speak for himself as a result of medical incapacity. The Durable Power of Attorney provides for the appointment of another person to make decisions on behalf of the maker.

Gifts An Anatomical Gift establishes in writing a person's wish to donate his body parts or organs after his death. The Gift to a Minor contains the elements necessary to establish, primarily for tax purposes, a gift to a minor while the maker of the gift is still alive.

Personal Records This form organizes the detailed record of a person's assets and liabilities as well as important personal information. It can also be used as a checklist to ensure that a person's affairs are in order.

INTRODUCTION TO WILLS

The basic purpose of a Will is to speak for its maker (also known as the Testator) after his death and to provide for the distribution of the Testator's assets upon his death. In addition, a Will should clearly revoke any earlier Wills or Codicils (supplements to a Will). Typically, the Will provides for 1) the payment of debts, funeral expenses and estate taxes and 2) naming of an Executor (the person who will apply to the court for probate of the Will, and who will administer the estate) and Successor Executor. The Executor will be responsible for gathering the deceased's assets, paying the deceased's bills and the estate's bills and estate taxes, and distributing whatever remains in accordance with the Will. Since the Executor assumes personal liability, most jurisdictions provide that he or she is entitled to a statutorily determined commission or fee, payable out of the deceased's estate.

WARNINGS

As far as the wording of a Will is concerned, the only requirement is that the Will be clear as to the deceased's intention. However, one of the few absolutes in the law relates to the proper *signing* of Wills. Since a Will speaks for the deceased after he is no longer able, the courts must be absolutely satisfied that the document claiming to be the deceased's Will in fact is his Will. This is accomplished by having Witnesses to the signing of the Will who can later testify that the deceased had asked them to Witness the signing of his Will and that the deceased did, in fact, sign the Will in the presence of all of the Witnesses together; in short **THE WILL MUST BE SIGNED BY THE TESTATOR ONLY IN THE PRESENCE OF THE WITNESSES.** The Witnesses will then sign the Will as well.

While most states require that a Will be witnessed by only two people, the use of three is strongly recommended because it increases the odds that the Executor will be able to locate at least two. No state requires more than three Witnesses.

Anyone of majority age can act as a Witness to the signing of a Will, with one exception: most states prevent a beneficiary of a Will from serving as a Witness to the Will's execution. The person named as the Executor or Trustee can act as a Witness, unless that person is also a beneficiary.

It is also strongly urged that each page of the Will be signed by the Testator along the left margin or at least initialled on either the lower left or right corner.

A final caveat: some states require that if more than one Will is signed, all must be found and admitted to probate. The technology of photocopiers has become so good that it is frequently impossible to tell which document is an original and which is the copy. To avoid confusion, it is strongly recommended that *no* photocopies be made *after* signing.

The question of where to store a Will inevitably arises. A Will that has been lost or mistakenly destroyed is the same as no Will at all. It is strongly urged that the Will be maintained in a safe but accessible place with other important personal papers where it will be found by the Executor. The Will should NOT be stored in a safety deposit box because the box may be sealed upon the death of the Testator.

SIMPLE WILL—ALL TO SPOUSE (1-01)

This Will should be used when the desire of the Testator (the person making the Will) is to leave all assets remaining (after the payment of his debts, funeral expenses and expenses of administration of his estate and federal and state estate taxes) to one's spouse.

Many states mandate, by statute, that spouses shall not disinherit one another, and the states assign a percentage share of the estate to a surviving spouse (the percentage varies with each state) that must be left to that spouse. Most jurisdictions do not have laws preventing the Testator from disinheriting his surviving children.

1. The name of the Testator (the person making the Will.)

2. If the Testator is or has been known by any other name (or has assets in another form of his name such as the use of his middle name), insert this other name. If not, delete the words "also known as ________[2]________."

3. The Testator's address.

4. The city in which the Testator resides.

5. The county in which the Testator resides.

6. The state in which the Testator resides.

SIMPLE WILL—ALL TO SPOUSE

LAST WILL AND TESTAMENT OF
________________[1]________________

___________[1]_________, *[also known as ___________[2]__________,]* presently residing at ________________[3]_____________, in the City of ______[4]_____, County of ______[5]_____ and State of ______[6]______, being of sound and disposing mind and memory do hereby make, publish and declare this to be my Last Will and Testament.

FIRST: I hereby revoke all former Wills and Codicils heretofore made by me.

SECOND: I direct that my Executor pay and discharge all of my just debts, including the expenses of my last illness, funeral and administration expenses as soon as shall be practicable. I further direct that any and all federal, state, foreign or other estate, transfer, inheritance, succession, legacy and similar taxes, including interest and penalties thereon, if any, imposed upon or with respect to any property required to be included in my gross estate under the provisions of any such tax law, and whether passing hereunder or by any codicil hereto or otherwise, or upon or with respect to any person with respect to any such property, shall be paid out of my residuary estate as an expense of administration and shall not be equitably prorated or charged against the gifts provided herein.

THIRD: I give, devise and bequeath all of the rest, residue and remainder of my property, real, personal and mixed, of whatsoever kind and nature and wheresoever situated, of which I shall die seized or possessed, and all property over or with respect to which I shall have any

(Document continued on next page)

7. The name of the spouse.

8. The spouse's address.

9. The name of the Executor.

10. The Executor's address.

11. The name of the Successor Executor (who may act in the event of the death or refusal of the Executor to act).

12. The Successor Executor's address.

13. The date of signing the Will.

14. The Testator's name printed directly below the line, with the Testator to sign above the line.

15. The number of pages of the Will.

power of appointment, remaining after the payment of my debts, funeral and administration expenses and any taxes which may be payable, absolutely and forever to my spouse __________[7]_________, presently residing at ____________[8]______________, irrespective of whether there are any children born of our marriage after the date of execution of this Will. I make no specific provision for any children born of our marriage since I am confident that my spouse will make provision for them.

FOURTH: I nominate, constitute and appoint __________[9]________, presently residing at ___________[10]____________, as the Executor of this Will. In the event of (his)(her) death or resignation or failure or refusal to act in said capacity, I nominate, constitute and appoint __________[11]__________, presently residing at ___________[12]____________, as the Successor Executor of this Will.

FIFTH: I direct that no bond, security or other undertaking shall be imposed upon or required at any time or in any jurisdiction of any individual named herein for the faithful performance of his duties.

IN WITNESS WHEREOF, I have set my hand and seal this __[13]__ day of ________, 19__.

___________________(L.S.)
[14]

The foregoing consisting of __[15]__ pages inclusive of this page, the original of which was signed or initialled by the above named Testator

(Document continued on next page)

16. The date of signing by the Witnesses (which should be the same date as in No. 13).

17. The name of each Witness printed directly below the line, with each Witness to sign above the line.

18. The address of each Witness.

prior to the execution thereof, was signed, published and declared by said Testator as and for his Last Will and Testament, in our presence and hearing and we thereupon, at his request, and in the presence of each other subscribed our names as witnesses this __[16]__ day of ________, 19__.

________________ residing at ____________________
[17] [18]
____

________________ residing at ____________________
[17] [18]
____

________________ residing at ____________________
[17] [18]
____

SIMPLE WILL—ALL TO SURVIVING SPOUSE AND ALTERNATIVE BEQUEST TO ADULT CHILD(REN) (1-02)

This Will should be used when the Testator (the person making the Will) has a spouse and one or more adult children. It provides that all assets remaining after the payment of the Testator's debts, funeral expenses and expenses of administration of the estate and federal and state estate taxes go to the surviving spouse. In the event that the spouse dies before the Testator, all assets remaining go to the Testator's adult child or children in equal share.

The term "per stirpes" at the end of paragraph 3 means that while all of the Testator's children will receive equal shares if they survive the Testator, if any of the Testator's children were to die before the Testator but have children of their own, the pre-deceased child's children would split only their parent's share. Suppose, for example, the Testator had 3 children and Child No. 1 had no children of his own, Child No. 2 had two children and Child No. 3 had three children. If Child No. 2 and Child No. 3 died before the Testator, upon the death of the Testator, Child No. 1 would inherit one-third, Child No. 2's children would split No. 2's one-third such that each would inherit one-half each of the one-third share of Child No. 2 (which is one-sixth of the total), and Child No. 3's children would split No. 3's one-third share such that each would inherit one-third each of the one-third of Child No. 3 (which is one-ninth of the total).

If, on the other hand, the term "per capita" is substituted for "per stirpes," using the same example, the Testator's Child No. 1 and the Testator's five grandchildren (two by Child No. 2 and three by Child No. 3) would all share equally such that each would receive one-sixth of the total.

If "per capita" is desired, change the last word at the end of the THIRD paragraph to "capita."

Note that this form assumes that if any of the Testator's children should die before the Testator, it would be the Testator's wish that any children of that child (the Testator's grandchildren) would inherit that parent's share. If this is not what the Testator wishes, the word "surviving" should be inserted in front of the word "issue" before blank #9 in the document, and the words "per stirpes" at the end of that paragraph should be deleted.

SIMPLE WILL—ALL TO SURVIVING SPOUSE AND ALTERNATIVE BEQUEST TO ADULT CHILD(REN)

1. The name of the Testator (the person making the Will).

2. If the Testator is or has been known by any other name (or has assets in another form of his name such as the use of his middle name), insert this other name. If not, delete the words "also known as _______[2]_______."

3. The Testator's address.

LAST WILL AND TESTAMENT OF

__________________[1]__________________

____________[1]__________, *[also known as ____________[2]____________,]* presently residing at ______________[3]_____________, in the City of

(Document continued on next page)

4. The city in which the Testator resides.

5. The county in which the Testator resides.

6. The state in which the Testator resides.

7. The name of the spouse.

8. The spouse's address.

9. The name of the person (a child, not necessarily a minor, of the Testator) who will inherit in the event that the spouse has died before the Testator.

10. The address of the child named in No. 9.

11. The name of the Testator's second child (Note: this form assumes that the Testator has a spouse and two children; if the Testator has only one child, delete "and __[11]__, presently residing at ___[12]___ in equal shares per stirpes."

12. The address of the child named in No. 11.

13. If the Testator has more than two children, add "and ___[11]___, presently residing at ___[12]___" for each additional child.

______[4]_____, County of _____[5]_____ and State of ______[6]_____, being of sound and disposing mind and memory do hereby make, publish and declare this to be my Last Will and Testament.

FIRST: I hereby revoke all former Wills and Codicils heretofore made by me.

SECOND: I direct that my Executor pay and discharge all of my just debts, including the expenses of my last illness, funeral and administration expenses as soon as shall be practicable. I further direct that any and all federal, state, foreign or other estate, transfer, inheritance, succession, legacy and similar taxes, including interest and penalties thereon, if any, imposed upon or with respect to any property required to be included in my gross estate under the provisions of any such tax law, and whether passing hereunder or by any Codicil hereto or otherwise, or upon or with respect to any person with respect to any such property, shall be paid out of my residuary estate as an expense of administration and shall not be equitably prorated or charged against the gifts provided herein.

THIRD: I give, devise and bequeath all of the rest, residue and remainder of my property, real, personal and mixed, of whatsoever kind and nature and wheresoever situated, of which I shall die seized or possessed, and all property over or with respect to which I shall have any power of appointment, remaining after the payment of my debts, funeral and administration expenses and any taxes which may be payable, absolutely and forever to my spouse, ________[7]_______, presently residing at ___________[8]___________. Should my spouse _______[7]______ fail to survive me, I give, devise and bequeath all of my said property to my issue, _________[9]________, presently residing at ___________[10]____________, *and* ________*[11]*_______*, presently residing at* ___________*[12]*_________*, [13]* in equal shares *per stirpes.*

FOURTH: In the event that any of the legatees under this Will shall die with me in a common accident or disaster, or under such circumstances as make it impossible or difficult to determine which of us died first or in the

(Document continued on next page)

14. The name of the Executor.

15. The Executor's address.

16. The name of the Successor Executor (who may act in the event of the death or refusal of the Executor to act.)

17. The Successor Executor's address.

18. The date of signing the Will.

19. The Testator's name printed directly below the line, with the Testator to sign above the line.

20. The number of pages of the Will.

21. The date of signing by the Witnesses, which should be the same date as No. 18.

22. The name of each Witness printed directly below the line, with each Witness to sign above the line.

23. The address of each Witness.

event that any such legatee shall die within sixty (60) days of my death, regardless of the circumstances, it shall be conclusively presumed that such legatee shall have predeceased me and deemed not to have survived me.

FIFTH: I nominate, constitute and appoint _________[14]________, presently residing at ___________[15]__________, as the Executor of this Will. In the event of (his)(her) death or resignation or failure or refusal to act in said capacity, I nominate, constitute and appoint _________[16]_______, presently residing at ___________[17]____________ as the Successor Executor of this Will.

SIXTH: I direct that no bond, security or other undertaking shall be imposed upon or required at any time or in any jurisdiction of any individual named herein for the faithful performance of (his)(her) duties.

IN WITNESS WHEREOF, I have set my hand and seal this __[18]_ day of __________, 19__.

________________________(L.S.)
[19]

The foregoing consisting of __[20]__ pages inclusive of this page, the original of which was signed or initialled by the above named Testator prior to the execution thereof, was signed, published and declared by said Testator as and for his Last Will and Testament, in our presence and hearing and we thereupon, at his request, and in the presence of each other subscribed our names as witnesses this __[21]__ day of ________, 19__.

_________________ residing at ______________________
[22] [23]
____

_________________ residing at ______________________
[22] [23]
____

_________________ residing at ______________________
[22] [23]
____

SIMPLE WILL—ALL TO SURVIVING SPOUSE AND ALTERNATIVE BEQUEST TO CHILD(REN) WITH SIMPLE TRUST IF ANY CHILD IS A MINOR (1-03)

This Will should be used when the Testator (the person making the Will) has a spouse and one or more children. It provides that all assets remaining after the payment of the Testator's debts, administration expenses of the estate and federal and state estate taxes go to the surviving spouse. In the event that the spouse dies before the Testator, all assets remaining go to the Testator's child or children in equal share.

This Will also provides that if, at the time of the Testator's death, any beneficiary is a minor, that beneficiary's share is not to be given outright to that beneficiary but is to be held in Trust. Many states define the age of majority as eighteen. However, some states provide that minority ends only on reaching the twenty first birthday.

Note that this form provides that any Trust shall terminate and the property then held in Trust shall be paid out when the beneficiary reaches the age of 21. The Testator may, if he so desires, provide that the Trust will not terminate until some later age. However, if the Trust is to terminate at some later age, the Testator should be aware that some states recognize the so-called "Rule Against Perpetuities" which, simply stated, prohibits holding property in Trust for a period longer than a "life in being plus 21 years" when measured from the date of the Testator's death (and *not* from the date of making the Will). This means that while the Testator is free to provide for any termination date he wishes for any minor beneficiary who is alive at the time of his death, the Trust for that beneficiary must terminate not later than the date upon which the Testator's grandchild (born after the death of the Testator) reaches 21. Suppose for example, that one of the Testator's children is, at the time of the Testator's death, only 17 years old—that child's share would go into Trust. Further suppose that this child married at 19, had a child of his or her own and died thereafter, but before reaching the age of 21 (and the termination of the Trust). That child's share would go to his child (the Testator's grandchild) but would be held in Trust for the grandchild since the grandchild is also a minor. The Rule Against Perpetuities holds that the Trust must terminate on the date that this grandchild reaches 21.

The term used here, "per stirpes," means that while all of the Testator's children would receive equal shares if they survive the Testator, if any of the Testator's children were to die before the Testator but have children of their own, the pre-deceased child's children would split only their parent's share. Suppose, for example, the Testator had 3 children and Child No. 1 had no children of his own, Child No. 2 had two children and Child No. 3 had three children. If Child No. 2 and Child No. 3 died before the Testator, upon the death of the Testator, Child No. 1 would inherit one-third, Child No. 2's children would split No. 2's one-third such that each would inherit one-half each of the one-third share of Child No. 2 (which is one-sixth of the total), and Child No. 3's children would split No. 3's one-third share such that each would inherit one-third each of the one-third of Child No. 3 (which is one-ninth of the total).

If on the other hand, the term "per capita" were substituted for "per stirpes," using the same example, the Testator's Child No. 1 and the Testator's five grandchildren (two by Child No. 2 and three by Child No. 3) would all share equally such that each would receive one-sixth of the total.

SIMPLE WILL—ALL TO SURVIVING SPOUSE AND ALTERNATIVE BEQUEST TO CHILD(REN) WITH SIMPLE TRUST IF ANY CHILD IS A MINOR *continued*

If "per capita" is desired, change the last word at the end of the THIRD paragraph to "capita."

This form assumes that if any of the Testator's children should die before the Testator, it would be the Testator's wish that any children of that child (the Testator's grandchildren) would inherit that parent's share. If this is not what the Testator wishes, the word "surviving" should be inserted in front of the word "issue" before blank #9 in the document, and the words "per stirpes" at end of that paragraph should be deleted.

SIMPLE WILL—ALL TO SURVIVING SPOUSE AND ALTERNATIVE BEQUEST TO CHILD(REN) WITH SIMPLE TRUST IF ANY CHILD IS A MINOR

1. The name of the Testator (the person making the Will).

2. If the Testator is or has been known by any other name (or has assets in another form of his name such as the use of his middle name), insert this other name. If not, delete the words "also known as ________[2]________."

3. The Testator's address.

4. The city in which the Testator resides.

5. The county in which the Testator resides.

6. The state in which the Testator resides.

LAST WILL AND TESTAMENT OF
____________________[1]____________________

__________[1]__________, *also known as* __________*[2]*__________, presently residing at ____________[3]____________, in the City of ________[4]_______, County of _____[5]_____ and State of _______[6]_____, being of sound and disposing mind and memory do hereby make, publish and declare this to be my Last Will and Testament.

FIRST: I hereby revoke all former Wills and Codicils heretofore made by me.

SECOND: I direct that my Executor pay and discharge all of my just debts, including the expenses of my last illness, funeral and administration expenses as soon as shall be practicable. I further direct that any and all federal, state, foreign or other estate, transfer, inheritance, succession, legacy and similar taxes, including interest and penalties thereon, if any, imposed upon or with respect to any property required to be included in my gross estate under the provisions of any such tax law, and whether passing hereunder or by any Codicil hereto or otherwise, or upon or with respect to any person with respect to any such property, shall be paid out of my residuary estate as an expense of administration and shall not be equitably prorated or charged against the gifts provided herein.

THIRD: I give, devise and bequeath all of the rest, residue and remainder of my property, real, personal and

(Document continued on next page)

SIMPLE WILL—ALL TO SURVIVING SPOUSE AND ALTERNATIVE BEQUEST TO CHILD(REN) WITH SIMPLE TRUST IF ANY CHILD IS A MINOR *continued*

7. The name of the spouse.

8. The spouse's home address.

9. The name of the person (a child, not necessarily a minor, of the Testator) who will inherit in the event that the spouse has died before the Testator.

10. The address of the child named in No. 9.

11. The name of the Testator's second child (Note: this form assumes that the Testator has a spouse and two children; if the Testator has only one child, delete "and __[11]__, presently residing at __[12]__ in equal shares per stirpes."

12. The address of the child named in No. 10.

13. If the Testator has more than two children, add "and __[11]__, presently residing at __[12]__" for each additional child.

mixed, of whatsoever kind and nature and wheresoever situated, of which I shall die seized or possessed, and all property over or with respect to which I shall have any power of appointment, remaining after the payment of my debts, funeral and administration expenses and any taxes which may be payable, absolutely and forever to my spouse, ________[7]________, presently residing at __________[8]__________. Should my spouse _______[7]______ fail to survive me, I give, devise and bequeath all of my said property to my issue, ________[9]________, presently residing at ___________[10]____________, *and ________[11]________, presently residing at __________[12]__________, [13] in equal shares per stirpes.*

FOURTH: Despite the foregoing, if any property becomes payable or distributable under this Will to a person who is then under the age of twenty-one (21) years, such property shall not vest in such person but shall be set apart and held by my Trustee, hereinafter named, in Trust, for the following uses and purposes:

(a) To hold, manage, invest and reinvest the said property, to collect and receive the income therefrom, and to pay the net income, in quarter-annual installments to such child until the termination of the Trust herein created.

(b) In addition to the said payment of net income from said Trust, my Trustee is authorized to pay from the principal of the Trust, at any time or from time to time, such portion or portions of the principal as my Trustee, in his sole and uncontrolled discretion may determine to be in the best interests of such child in order to provide for the health, education and general welfare of such child.

(c) When such child attains the age of twenty-one (21) years, one-half (1/2) of the then principal of the Trust shall be paid over and distributed absolutely and forever to such child, and when such child attains the age of twenty-five (25) years, the remaining principal of the Trust then held shall be paid over and distributed absolutely and forever to such child together with any and all undistributed income and the Trust herein created shall cease and terminate. In the event that such child shall die before the termination of the Trust as herein provided but shall leave issue surviving, my Trustee shall divide the remaining principal then held in Trust for such child together with any

(Document continued on next page)

14. The name of the Executor.

15. The Executor's address.

16. The name of the Successor Executor (who may act in the event of the death or refusal of the Executor to act.)

17. The Successor Executor's address.

18. The name of the Trustee of the Trust(s) created if any beneficiary is a minor at the time of the Testator's death. Note: DO NOT name the Testator's spouse as Trustee because under this form, the Testator's children inherit only if the spouse had died before the Testator. The Trustee and the Executor can be the same person.

19. The Trustee's address.

undistributed income into such number of equal shares as shall provide one share for each of such child's issue and shall thereupon be held in Trust by my said Trustee in accordance with the provisions of the Trust herein created, except that each such separate Trust shall cease and terminate upon the attaining of the age of twenty-one (21) years by each such issue of such child. In the event that such child shall die before the termination of the Trust as provided herein and shall leave no issue surviving, the Trust herein created shall cease and terminate on the date of such child's death and the remaining principal then held, together with any undistributed income, shall be paid absolutely and forever to those persons who would have been my heirs at law had I died intestate on the date of such child's death.

FIFTH: In the event that any of the legatees under this Will shall die with me in a common accident or disaster, or under such circumstances as make it impossible or difficult to determine which of us died first or in the event that any such legatee shall die within sixty (60) days of my death, regardless of the circumstances, it shall be conclusively presumed that such legatee shall have predeceased me and deemed not to have survived me.

SIXTH: I nominate, constitute and appoint ________[14]________, presently residing at __________[15]__________, as the Executor of this Will. In the event of (his)(her) death or resignation or failure or refusal to act in said capacity, I nominate, constitute and appoint ________[16]________, presently residing at __________[17]__________, as the Successor Executor of this Will. I nominate, constitute and appoint ________[18]________, presently residing at __________[19]__________, as the Trustee of any Trust herein created.

SEVENTH: I direct that no bond, security or other undertaking shall be imposed upon or required at any time or in any jurisdiction of any individual named herein for the faithful performance of (his)(her) duties.

(Document continued on next page)

SIMPLE WILL—ALL TO SURVIVING SPOUSE AND ALTERNATIVE BEQUEST TO CHILD(REN) WITH SIMPLE TRUST IF ANY CHILD IS A MINOR *continued*

20. The date of signing the Will.

21. The Testator's name printed directly below the line, with the Testator to sign above the line.

22. The number of pages of the Will.

23. The date of signing by the Witnesses, which should be the same date as No. 20.

24. The name of each Witness printed directly below the line, with each Witness to sign above the line.

25. The address of each Witness.

IN WITNESS WHEREOF, I have set my hand and seal this __[20]__ day of __________, 19__.

____________________(L.S.)
[21]

The foregoing consisting of __[22]__ pages inclusive of this page, the original of which was signed or initialled by the above named Testator prior to the execution thereof, was signed, published and declared by said Testator as and for his Last Will and Testament, in our presence and hearing and we thereupon, at his request, and in the presence of each other subscribed our names as witnesses this __[23]__ day of ________, 19__.

__________________ residing at ______________________
[24] [25]
____

__________________ residing at ______________________
[24] [25]
____

__________________ residing at ______________________
[24] [25]
____

CODICIL TO WILL (1-04)

A Codicil is a written supplement, alteration or modification of a Will and is typically used when the proposed modifications are deemed to be minor and not of enough importance to justify rewriting the entire Will, or when time constraints prohibit rewriting the entire Will. A Codicil does not supersede a prior Will. Rather it alters, modifies or explains the prior Will. For this reason, it is regarded as part of the Will and the Will and the Codicil are read as one document. A Codicil is considered to ratify and republish those parts of the prior Will that are ***not*** specifically altered or modified by the Codicil. Because a Codicil does not supersede, revoke or modify the entire prior Will but only specific portions, care must be taken as to those portions of the Will that are to be modified and those that are to remain. The same is true of second or subsequent Codicils.

A Codicil must be signed and witnessed with the same formality as a Will. See "Introduction to Wills" at the beginning of this chapter.

WARNING

Despite the foregoing, the authors have found that any time savings achieved by preparing a Codicil versus a new Will are minimal. They believe that the wiser practice is to avoid the use of Codicils. The authors strongly recommend preparing a new Will even when changes are slight.

CODICIL TO WILL

____[1]____ CODICIL TO LAST WILL
AND TESTAMENT
OF
________[2]________

________[2]________, *[also known as ________[3]________,]* presently residing at __________[4]__________, in the City of _____[5]_____, County of _____[6]_____ and State of _____[7]_____,

(Document continued on next page)

1. Identify the Codicil as "First," "Second" and so forth.

2. The name of the Testator (the person making the Codicil).

3. If the Testator is or has been known by any other name (or has assets in another form of his name such as the use of his middle name), insert this other name. If not, delete the words "also known as _____[3]_____."

4. The Testator's address.

5. The city in which the Testator resides.

6. The county in which the Testator resides.

7. The state in which the Testator resides.

being of sound and disposing mind and memory do hereby make, publish and declare this to be the ____[1]____ Codicil to my Last Will and Testament dated _________[8]________ *[9][and the ____[10]____ Codicil thereto dated ________[11]________.*

[12]FIRST: I give devise and bequeath absolutely and forever to ________[13]________, presently residing at _________[14]__________, the sum of ________[15]________ Dollars ($____[15]____).

[16]SECOND: I give, devise and bequeath absolutely and forever to ________[17]________, presently residing at __________[18]__________, my ___________________[19]__________________.

8. The date of the Will being modified.

9. If this is the first Codicil to the Will, delete the words "and the___[10]___Codicil thereto dated ___[11]___" and skip to No. 12.

10. The number of the most recent Codicil to the Will.

11. The date of the most recent Codicil to the Will.

12. Use this paragraph for adding to a Will a bequest for a certain amount of money. Otherwise delete this paragraph, skip to No. 16, and renumber the remaining paragraphs.

13. The name of the person receiving the bequest.

14. The address of the person named in No. 13.

15. The amount of the bequest, in words and numbers.

16. Use this paragraph for a bequest of a specific asset such as shares of stock of a specific corporation, a painting, a piece of jewelry or the like. Otherwise delete this paragraph, skip to No. 20, and renumber the remaining paragraphs.

17. The name of the person receiving the specific asset.

18. The address of the person named in No. 17.

19. A specific description of the asset. (The more specific you are, the more likely you are to avoid a fight between the heirs.)

(Document continued on next page)

20. Use this paragraph to modify, by either enlarging or reducing, the amount of a bequest in the Will. Otherwise delete this paragraph, skip to No. 25, and renumber the remaining paragraphs.

21. The name of the person whose prior bequest is being modified.

22. The address of the person named in No. 21.

23. The amount of the modified bequest, in words and numbers.

24. The specific number of the article or paragraph of the Will being modified.

25. Use this paragraph to revoke a prior bequest. Otherwise delete this paragraph, skip to No. 30, and renumber the remaining paragraph.

26. A description of the bequest being revoked.

27. The name of the person whose bequest is being revoked.

28. The address of the person named in No. 27.

29. The specific number of the article or paragraph of the Will being modified.

30. Use this paragraph for changing the Executor named in the Will. Otherwise delete this paragraph and skip to No. 34.

31. The name of the person now chosen to be the Executor.

32. The address of the person named in No. 31.

33. The name of the former Executor.

[20]THIRD: I give, devise and bequeath to ________[21]________, presently residing at __________[22]__________, the sum of ________[23]________ Dollars ($____[23]____) in lieu of and in place of and not in addition to the bequest made to him by Article __[24]__ of my Last Will and Testament dated ________[8]________.

[25]FOURTH: I hereby revoke in all respects the legacy of ______________[26]________________ given to ________[27]________, presently residing at __________[28]__________ made to him by Article __[29]__ of my Last Will and Testament dated ________[8]________.

[30]FIFTH: I nominate, constitute and appoint ________[31]________, presently residing at __________[32]__________, as the Executor of my Last Will and Testament dated ________[8]________in place of ________[33]________ and I hereby revoke the

(Document continued on next page)

34. The date of signing the Codicil.

35. The Testator's name printed directly below the line, with the Testator to sign above the line.

36. The number of pages of the Codicil.

37. The date of signing by the Witnesses (which should be the same date as No. 34).

38. The name of each Witness printed directly below the line, with each Witness to sign directly above the line.

39. The address of each Witness.

nomination of ________[33]________ as the Executor of my Last Will and Testament dated ________[8]________.

IN WITNESS WHEREOF, I have set my hand and seal this __[34]__ day of ________, 19__.

______________________________(L.S.)
[35]

The foregoing consisting of __[36]__ pages inclusive of this page, the original of which was signed or initialled by the above named testator prior to the execution thereof, was signed, published and declared by said Testator as and for the ____[1]____ Codicil to his Last Will and Testament dated ________[8]________, in our presence and hearing and we thereupon, at his request, and in the presence of each other subscribed our names as witnesses this __[37]__ day of ________, 19__.

__________________ residing at ______________________
[38] [39]
____

__________________ residing at ______________________
[38] [39]
____

__________________ residing at ______________________
[38] [39]
____

AFFIDAVIT OF DECEDENT'S DOMICILE (1-05)

An Affidavit of Decedent's Domicile (a person's legal address) is used by the representative of a deceased person in connection with a transfer of the deceased's property. The representative may be an Executor (who is acting under the authority of a Will) or an Administrator (someone appointed by a court when the deceased left no Will). Or it can be someone acting as a surviving tenant (the survivor of two or more people who own property jointly) with authority to act in a specific situation.

An Affidavit of Decedent's Domicile is usually provided by a bank or stock transfer agent; the instructions presented here can be used as a guide to filling it out.

This form must be signed before a Notary Public.

AFFIDAVIT OF DECEDENT'S DOMICILE

STATE OF ______[1]______)
COUNTY OF _____[2]______) ss.:

________[3]________ being duly sworn, deposes and says:

My residence address is __________[4]_________. I am the *[5][______[6]_____ of ________[7]________, a corporation duly organized under the laws of the State of _____[8]_____,]* *[9][Executor]* ***OR*** *[Administrator]* ***OR*** *[Surviving Tenant]* of the Estate of ________[10]________

(Document continued on next page)

1. The state where the Affidavit is signed.

2. The county where the Affidavit is signed.

3. The name of the person giving the Affidavit.

4. The residence address, including street address, city, state and zip code of the representative (the person whose name is given in No. 3).

5. If the person making the Affidavit is not an officer or director of a corporation, bank or the like, delete the words "___[6]___ of ___[7]___, a corporation duly organized under the laws of the State of _____[8]______."

6. The corporate title of the person named in No. 3, i.e. President, Secretary or the like.

7. The name of the corporation.

8. The state of incorporation of the corporation named in No. 7.

9. Choose one.

10. The name of the deceased person.

who died at __________[11]__________ on ________[12]_______.

At the time of *[13][his]* ***OR*** *[her]* death, decedent's domicile (legal residence) was at ________[14]_________, in the County of _____[15]_____, State of _____[16]____. The decedent resided at such address for ____[17]_____ years, *such residence having commenced on ________[18]________.*

Decedent last voted in the year __[19]__ at _________[20]________, in the County of _____[21]_____, in the State of _____[22]____.

Decedent's principal place of business at the time of [23][his] ***OR*** *[her] death was at*

(Document continued on next page)

11. The place of death (the street address if available, and the city and state).

12. The date of death, including month, day and year.

13. Choose one.

14. The residence address (number and street) of the deceased person named in No. 10 on the date of death.

15. The county in which the deceased resided on the date of death.

16. The state in which the deceased resided on the date of death.

17. The number of years, in numbers, the deceased lived at the address given in No. 14.

18. If known, the day, month and year that the deceased began living at the address at which he lived on the date of death. Otherwise delete, beginning with "such residence" to the end of the line.

19. If known, the year in which the deceased last voted. Otherwise delete the paragraph and skip to No. 23.

20. If known, the street address at which deceased last voted. Otherwise delete "at _____" through the end of the paragraph and skip to No. 23.

21. The county in which No. 20. is located.

22. The state in which No. 20 is located.

23. Choose one.

24. The address where the deceased worked on the date of death, or last place of business if not working at time of death. If not known, or if the deceased did not work, delete this paragraph and skip to No. 27.

25. The county in which No. 24 is located.

26. The state in which No. 24 is located.

27. Choose one.

28. The address of the deceased as stated on the deceased's most recently filed federal income tax return.

29. The county in which No. 28 is located.

30. The state in which No. 28 is located.

31. The name or names of such other states in which the deceased resided in the three years prior to his death, and the dates of residence in those states. If the deceased had no other residences within the three year period prior to his death, delete "except as follows."

32. The name of the person giving the Affidavit printed directly below the line, with that person to sign above the line.

33. A Notary Public fills in the date and signs and seals the form by affixing his stamp or seal.

__________*[24]*__________*, in the County of* _____*[25]*____*, in the State of* _____*[26]*_____.

Decedent's most recent federal income tax return shows *[27][his]* ***OR*** *[her]* legal residence as __________[28]__________, in the County of _____[29]_____, in the State of _____[30]_____.

Within three years prior to death decedent was not a resident of any other state *[31][except as follows:]* ____.

Any and all debts, taxes and claims against the estate have been paid or provided for; this affidavit is made for the purpose of securing the transfer or delivery of property owned by decedent at the time of decedent's death to a purchaser or the person or persons legally entitled thereto under the laws of decedent's domicile and that any apparent inequality in distribution has been satisfied or provided for out of other assets in the estate.

____
[32]

Sworn to before me this

__[33]__ day of ________, 19__.

__________[33]__________
Notary Public

LIVING WILL (1-06)

A Living Will is used by an individual to express his desires regarding medical treatment in the event he becomes unable to participate in making such decisions. It is called a Living Will because it is to be given force and effect during that person's life (unlike a regular Will which has no effect until after death). Most states now recognize an individual's right to refuse medical treatment and to request the care that the individual desires. This form can and should be made to conform with the individual's personal wishes as suggested in the instructions below.

Copies of the Living Will should be given to all people likely to be involved in providing medical care or making decisions relating to such care. The form should note the location of the original Living Will. The original Living Will should be kept with other important papers; however, the authors recommend that the original Living Will be kept in a safe deposit box *only* if the person making the Living Will is not the sole person who has access to the box.

WARNINGS

The law regarding the validity of a Living Will varies from state to state. A particular state may have specific rules regarding the length of effectiveness, requirements for witnesses and the like. The reader is cautioned to verify with the state in which he lives what constitutes compliance with that state's requirements for a Living Will. The language provided here is general, setting forth the individual's directions and desires. However, even where a state has no legislation specifically recognizing a Living Will, this form still will be clear evidence of the individual's desires.

The Living Will only states the wishes of the person making the Living Will. It does not name any one person to be the "voice" of that person. The person making the Living Will should use the Durable Power of Attorney which follows to designate his "voice." Some states require (and the authors strongly urge) that the Living Will be used **only** in conjunction with a Durable Power of Attorney.

1. The name of the person making the Living Will (the "Declarant").

2. If the Declarant has been known by any other name, insert this other name. If not, delete the words "also known as ______[2]______."

LIVING WILL
of
__________[1]__________
[Also Known As ___________[2]___________]

TO MY FAMILY, MY PHYSICIAN, MY ATTORNEY AND ANY MEDICAL FACILITY IN WHOSE CARE I MAY COME OR HAPPEN TO BE AND ALL OTHERS WHO MAY BE RESPONSIBLE FOR MY HEALTH, WELFARE OR AFFAIRS:

If the time comes when I can no longer take part in decisions for my own future, let this statement stand as an expression of my wishes and direction while I am still of sound mind.

If I should be in an incurable or irreversible mental

(Document continued on next page)

3. The language in this section can be changed to conform to the Declarant's wishes.

4. If applicable, insert other instructions. Otherwise delete this text.

5. The language in this paragraph can be changed to conform to the Declarant's wishes.

or physical condition so that there is no reasonable anticipation of my recovery from severe physical or mental incapacity, I direct that I be permitted to die and I do not want to be kept alive by medications, artificial means, or so-called "heroic measures." I request and direct that treatment, including medication, water and fluids be mercifully administered to me to alleviate pain and suffering so as to keep me comfortable even though this may shorten my remaining life.

These instructions are set forth after careful thought and are in accordance with my clear convictions and beliefs. I want the wishes and directions here expressed carried out to the extent permitted by law unless I have rescinded them in a new writing or by clearly indicating that I have changed my mind. Those concerned with my health and welfare are specifically asked to take whatever action necessary, including legal action, to realize my wishes and instructions. I hope that those to whom this document is directed will regard themselves as morally bound to abide by its contents if and to the extent that the provisions of this document are not legally enforceable.

[3][If at any time there is no reasonable expectation of my recovery from extreme physical or mental disability, I feel especially strong about, and specifically refuse the following measures of artificial life support:

(a) Electrical or mechanical resuscitation of my heart when it has stopped beating.

(b) Nasogastric tube feeding when I am paralyzed or unable to take nourishment by mouth.

(c) Mechanical respiration when I am no longer able to sustain my own breathing.]

[4][My other personal instructions are:]

[5][I would like to live out my last days at home rather than in a hospital if it does not jeopardize the chance of my recovery to a meaningful and sentient life and does not impose an undue burden on my family.]

(Document continued on next page)

6. The Declarant's name printed directly below the line, with the Declarant to sign above the line.

7. The date of signing the Living Will.

8. The name of the Witness printed directly below the line, with the Witness to sign above the line.

9. The date of signing by the Witness.

10. The Witness's complete address.

11. The Witness's telephone number.

12. The Notary Public completes this section and affixes his stamp or seal.

13. The specific location of the Living Will.

14. The address of the location of the Living Will.

Signed:____________________ Date:_______[7]______
[6]

Witness: ____________________ Date:_______ [9]______
[8]
Address:______________[10]________________
Tel. No.:______________[11]________________

Witness: ____________________ Date:_______ [9]______
[8]
Address:______________[10]________________
Tel. No.:______________[11]________________

STATE OF ____[12]____, COUNTY OF____[12]____, ss:

On ________[12]________, 19__, before me personally came ________[12]________
to me known, and known to me to be the individual described in and who executed the foregoing LIVING WILL, and duly acknowledged to me that (s)he executed the same.

____
Notary Public

The ORIGINAL Living Will is in the ______[13]______, located at __________[14]_________.

(Document continued on next page)

15. The name of each person who has a copy of the Living Will.

16. The address of each person who has a copy of the Living Will.

COPIES of this Living Will have been distributed to:

_______[15]______ residing at ________[16]________

____

_______[15]______ residing at ________[16]________

____

_______[15]______ residing at ________[16]________

____

DURABLE POWER OF ATTORNEY (1-07)

A Durable Power of Attorney is used by an individual (the Declarant) to express in writing, while he is capable of making decisions, his desires to appoint another person (the attorney-in-fact) to make health care or medical treatment decisions in the event he becomes unable to participate in the making of such decisions. The attorney-in-fact is empowered to make decisions based on the Declarant's wishes as well as specific instructions which have been conveyed.

Copies of the Durable Power of Attorney (together with the Living Will) should be given to all people likely to be involved in providing medical care or making decisions relating to such care. The form should note the location of the original of the Durable Power of Attorney (and the Living Will). The original Durable Power of Attorney (and the Living Will) should be kept with other important papers; however, the authors recommend that the original Durable Power of Attorney, like the Living Will, be kept in a safe deposit box *only* if the person making the Living Will is not the sole person who has access to the box.

WARNINGS

This form should be used in conjunction with the form immediately preceding, the Living Will.

As with the Living Will, the law regarding the validity of a Durable Power of Attorney varies from state to state. A particular state may have specific rules regarding the length of effectiveness, requirements for witnesses and the like. The reader is cautioned to verify with the state in which he lives what constitutes compliance with that state's requirements for a Durable Power of Attorney. The language provided here is general, setting forth the individual's designation of a person to act. However, even where a state has no legislation specifically recognizing a Durable Power of Attorney (and Living Will), this form will still be clear evidence of the individual's desires.

The Durable Power of Attorney only designates who the maker of the Durable Power wishes to act as his "voice." By itself it does not express any evidence of what that "voice" should say. That is the function of the Living Will. Some states require (and the authors strongly urge) that the Living Will be used **only** in conjunction with a Durable Power of Attorney.

DURABLE POWER OF ATTORNEY

I, ________[1]________ *[, also known as ________[2]________,]* hereby designate ________[3]________, presently residing at __________[4]__________, to serve as my attorney-in-fact for the purpose of making health care and medical

(Document continued on next page)

1. The name of the person making the appointment (the Declarant).

2. If the Declarant has been known by any other name, insert this other name. If not, delete the words "also known as ____[2]____."

3. The name of the person being appointed (the attorney-in-fact).

4. The address of the person being appointed at the time of the signing of the Durable Power of Attorney.

5. This section can be changed to conform to the Declarant's wishes.

6. The Declarant's name printed directly below the line, with the Declarant to sign above the line.

7. The date of signing the Durable Power of Attorney.

8. The name of the Witness printed directly below the line, with the Witness to sign above the line.

9. The date of signing by the Witness.

10. The Witness's complete address.

11. The Witness's telephone number.

treatment decisions *[5][, including decisions to withhold or withdraw life-support,]* on my behalf. Unless I have rescinded this appointment in a new writing, this power of attorney shall remain effective in the event that I become incompetent or otherwise unable to make or communicate such decisions for myself.

Signed:____________________ Date:_______[7]_______
[6]

Witness: ____________________ Date:_______ [9]______
[8]
Address:_______________[10]__________________
Tel. No.:_______________[11]__________________

Witness: ____________________ Date:_______ [9]______
[8]
Address:_______________[10]__________________
Tel. No.:_______________[11]__________________

(Document continued on next page)

12. The Notary Public completes this section and affixes his stamp or seal.

13. The specific location of the Durable Power of Attorney.

14. The address of the location of the Durable Power of Attorney.

15. The name of each person who has a copy of the Durable Power of Attorney.

16. The address of each person who has a copy of the Durable Power of Attorney.

STATE OF ____[12]____, COUNTY OF____[12]____, ss:

On ________[12]________, 19__, before me personally came ________[12]________
to me known, and known to me to be the individual described in and who executed the foregoing DURABLE POWER OF ATTORNEY, and duly acknowledged to me that (s)he executed the same.

____
Notary Public

The ORIGINAL Durable Power of Attorney is in the ______[13]______, located at _________[14]_________.

COPIES of this Durable Power of Attorney have been distributed to:

_______[15]______ residing at ________[16]________
____

_______[15]______ residing at ________[16]________
____

_______[15]______ residing at ________[16]________
____

STATEMENT OF ANATOMICAL GIFT MADE BY A LIVING DONOR (1-08)

This form is to be used by an individual to evidence an intent, made while living, to donate some or all of his organs or body parts upon his death. This form speaks for the individual, while he is still living, of a gift which does not take effect until his death. The gift can be revoked or modified at any time prior to death.

The intent to make a gift of organs or body parts can be included in a Will but this separate form is strongly recommended since the normal delays associated with locating a Will or the probate of a Will may be such that the value or usefulness of an organ will be lost and the intent of the person making the gift (the Donor) may be thwarted. If the Donor resides in a state which makes reference to organ donation on its driver's license, the organ donation portion of the license can be filled out to indicate the location of this form.

ANATOMICAL GIFT
by
__________[1]__________
[Also known as ________[2]________]

1. The name of the person making the gift (the Donor).

2. If the Donor has been known by any other name, insert this other name. If not, delete the words "also known as ____[2]____."

3. Choose one.

4. If it is the Donor's intent to donate only certain organs or body parts, insert the names of those specific organs or body parts.

5. Choose one and fill in the specific name and address.

6. If it is the Donor's intent to donate specific organs or body parts to specific, but different, physicians or institutions, fill in this section, including the names and the addresses of the physicians or institutions. Otherwise delete this section.

I, __________[1]__________ *[, also known as ________[2]________,]* state that I am over the age of eighteen (18) years and I am of sound and disposing mind.

I hereby make the following ANATOMICAL GIFT to take effect upon my death: *[3][any needed organs or part(s).]* ***OR*** *[ONLY the following organs or part(s): ______________________[4]______________________.]*

The foregoing ANATOMICAL GIFT(S) are made to: *[5][the physician in attendance at the time of my death.]* ***OR*** *[the hospital where I am physically located at the time of my death.]* ***OR*** *[the following named physician: ____________________________.]* ***OR*** *[the following named hospital/medical or teaching school/storage facility or other medical institution:______________________.]*

[6][I hereby make the following ANATOMICAL GIFT(S) to the following to take effect upon my death:

Organ/Body Part	Recipient
____________________	____________________
	____________________
____________________	____________________
	____________________
____________________	____________________
	____________________]

(Document continued on next page)

STATEMENT OF ANATOMICAL GIFT MADE BY A LIVING DONOR *continued*

7. Choose one.

8. The Donor's name printed directly below the line, with the Donor to sign above the line.

9. The date of signing the Statement of Anatomical Gift.

10. The name of the Witness printed directly below the line, with the Witness to sign above the line.

11. The date of signing by the Witness.

12. The Witness's complete address.

13. The Witness's telephone number.

The foregoing ANATOMICAL GIFT(S) are made *[7][without limitation and for any purpose authorized by law.]* ***OR*** *[for transplantation.]* ***OR*** *[for medical research/ education.]*

It is my specific wish and desire that my relatives, friends and other interested physicians honor the foregoing ANATOMICAL GIFT(S) and not interfere with this purpose and intent.

Signed:____________________ Date:_______[9]_______
[8]

Witness: ____________________ Date:______ [11]______
[10]
Address:______________[12]________________
Tel. No.:______________[13]________________

Witness: ____________________ Date:______ [11]______
[10]
Address:______________[12]________________
Tel. No.:______________[13]________________

(Document continued on next page)

STATEMENT OF ANATOMICAL GIFT MADE BY A LIVING DONOR *continued*

14. The Notary Public completes this section and affixes his stamp or seal.

15. The specific location of the Statement of Anatomical Gift.

16. The address of the location of the Statement of Anatomical Gift.

17. The name of each person who has a copy of the Statement of Anatomical Gift.

18. The address of each person who has a copy of the Statement of Anatomical Gift.

STATE OF ____[14]____, COUNTY OF____[14]____, ss:

On ________[14]________, 19__, before me personally came ________[14]________ to me known, and known to me to be the individual described in and who executed the foregoing STATEMENT OF ANATOMICAL GIFT, and duly acknowledged to me that (s)he executed the same.

____
Notary Public

The ORIGINAL Statement of Anatomical Gift is in the _______[15]______, located at _________[16]_________.

COPIES of this Statement of Anatomical Gift have been distributed to:

_______[17]_______ residing at ________[18]________

____

_______[17]_______ residing at ________[18]________

____

_______[17]_______ residing at ________[18]________

____

GIFT TO A MINOR (1-09)

Lifetime gifts to minors may serve as an important element of a person's estate planning. Under the "Uniform Gifts to Minors Act" (which most states have adopted) an adult can make an irrevocable gift to a minor of money, securities (including stocks, bonds, notes and the like, either registered or unregistered), life insurance policies or annuity contracts. Gifts to minors may also be made in one's Will, a so-called testamentary disposition. The purpose of this form is only for a gift made during the lifetime of the person making the gift (the Donor). The person receiving the gift is called the Donee. In order for a gift to be effective, the law requires (a) donative intent—unequivocal evidence of the Donor's intent to make the gift, and (b) delivery of the gift to the person receiving the gift (the Donee) or in the case of a minor, to a custodian. This form provides written evidence of the donative intent by the maker of the gift (the Donor) and delivery of the gift by acknowledgement of receipt by the custodian.

WARNINGS

A gift to a minor under the "Uniform Gifts to Minors Act" is **irrevocable**. Once made (meaning upon delivery with donative intent), the gift cannot be undone or unmade, and the Donor can no longer exercise any ownership rights. Also, since the gift is irrevocable, when the minor Donee attains the age of majority, the Donee has the absolute right to claim physical control and ownership of the property in his own name. In states where 18 is the majority age, the Donor may wish to specify that full transfer of the property be deferred until the age of 21.

Your tax planner should be consulted regarding the subject of a gift, the age of majority in your state and the tax consequences to the minor as well as to the adult Donor.

GIFT TO A MINOR

I, __________[1]__________, hereby deliver to __________[2]__________ as custodian for __________[3]__________ under the _____[4] _____ Uniform Gifts to Minors Act, the following property:
________________________[5]________________________
____.

1. The name of the adult making the gift (the Donor).

2. The name of the person who will be the custodian. In some cases the Donor may be the custodian and in other cases the custodian must be an adult other than the Donor, as when the gift is an unregistered security. The custodian also may be a bank.

3. The name of the minor to whom the gift is being made (the Donee).

4. The state where the gift is being made.

5. A thorough description of the property being delivered to the custodian.

(Document continued on next page)

6. The name of the Donor printed directly below the line, with the Donor to sign above the line.

7. The date of delivery of the gift.

8. The name of the custodian printed directly below the line, with the custodian to sign above the line.

Note: in addition to the use of this form, the simplification of gifts to minors under the Uniform Gifts to Minors Act permits making a gift by transferring ownership simply by delivering the property and registering it in the name of the custodian by use of the words "As custodian for ___(name of Minor)___ under the __(name of state)__ Uniform Gift to Minors Act." This is usable for a gift of money, an insurance policy, or a registered security provided that the requirements of the specific financial institution for the registration of ownership are followed.

____
[6]

________[2]________ hereby acknowledges receipt of the above described as custodian for the above minor under the _______[4] ______ Uniform Gifts to Minor Act.

Dated: ________[7]______

____
[8]

RECORD OF PERSONAL AND BUSINESS INFORMATION (1-10)

This form is a personal record of the diverse information that is a part of every person's life—but which most people do not have in one place. The purpose of this document is to help focus one's thinking in assembling this information so that it is complete and available if needed by someone in his absence. Once done, the form should be reviewed periodically and updated if necessary (because of moving, job change, birth of a child or the like).

The form is self explanatory. Add or delete categories as appropriate.

RECORD OF PERSONAL
AND BUSINESS INFORMATION

Name ____________________ Date of Birth___________

Social Security Number___________ Passport No._______

Address: ____

Phone No. Home:_____________ Business:_____________

Occupation and Place of Business: ___________________
____

Military History, if any ____________________________

If Married:

Date ________ Place of Marriage ____________________

Spouse's Name ________________ Date of Birth________

Social Security Number_________ Passport No._________

Address ____

Phone No. Home:_____________ Business:_____________

Occupation and Place of Business: ___________________
____

Military History, if any ____________________________

If Divorced:

Name(s) of Former Spouse (s):
____

Date(s) of Divorce _________________________________

(Document continued on next page)

If any children:

Name of child	Date of Birth	Address
_______________	_______________	_______________
_______________	_______________	_______________
_______________	_______________	_______________
_______________	_______________	_______________

Other relations (parents, siblings, grandparents)

Name & Relationship	Date of Birth	Address
_______________	__________	_______________
_______________	__________	_______________
_______________	__________	_______________
_______________	__________	_______________
_______________	__________	_______________

ASSETS

A. BANKING:

1. Checking Accounts:

Name and address of Bank	Account No.	Joint Owner
____________________	__________	__________
____________________	__________	__________
____________________	__________	__________
____________________	__________	__________

(Document continued on next page)

2. Savings Accounts (including IRA accounts):

Name and address of Bank	Account No.	Joint Owner
____________________	__________	__________
____________________	__________	__________
____________________	__________	__________
____________________	__________	__________

3. Certificates of Deposit (including IRA accounts):

Name and address of Bank	Account No.	Joint Owner
____________________	__________	__________
____________________	__________	__________
____________________	__________	__________
____________________	__________	__________

4. Mortgages, Loans, Notes:

Name of Lender	Amount of Loan	Monthly Payment	Maturity Date
______________	$______	$______	______
______________	$______	$______	______
______________	$______	$______	______

5. Safe Deposit Box(es)

Location	Joint Owner
________________	__________
________________	__________

(Document continued on next page)

B. REAL ESTATE:

Owned:

Location	Estimated Value	Mortgage
____________	______________	$_______
____________	______________	$_______

Leased:

Location	Expiration Date	Annual Rental
____________	____________	____________
____________	____________	____________

C. STOCKS (exclusive of own business) AND BONDS

1. Brokerage Accounts:

Name and Address of Brokerage Firm	Account Number	Tel. Number
________________	_____________	__________
________________	_____________	__________

2. Stocks:

Name of Stock	No. of Shares	Date Purchased	Purchase Price
____________	_____	________	$______
____________	_____	________	$______
____________	_____	________	$______
____________	_____	________	$______

(Document continued on next page)

3. Bonds:

Description of Bond	Face Value	Date Purchased	Purchase Price
____________	______	_________	$______
____________	______	_________	$______
____________	______	_________	$______
____________	______	_________	$______

D. INSURANCE (Life and otherwise):

Company	Policy No.	Amount	Beneficiary
a) Owned by you on your life:			
____________	_________	$______	__________
____________	_________	$______	__________
b) Owned by others on your life:			
____________	_________	$______	__________
____________	_________	$______	__________
c) Owned by you on life of others:			
____________	_________	$______	__________
____________	_________	$______	__________
d) Group Life Insurance (paid for by your company):			
____________	_________	$______	__________
____________	_________	$______	__________

(Document continued on next page)

e) Property and
Liability Insurance:

__________ __________ $_____ __________

__________ __________ $_____ __________

f) Accident &
Health Insurance:

__________ __________ $_____ __________

__________ __________ $_____ __________

g) Disability Insurance:

__________ __________ $_____ __________

__________ __________ $_____ __________

E. MISCELLANEOUS PROPERTY

1. Personal Property (e.g. Autos, boats, jewelry, art collection, stamp collection, professional equipment, patents, trademarks or copyrights, contract rights)

Description Of Item	Location	Est. Value
_______________	__________	$________
_______________	__________	$________
_______________	__________	$________
_______________	__________	$________
_______________	__________	$________
_______________	__________	$________
_______________	__________	$________

(Document continued on next page)

2. Interests in Estates and Trusts

Will or Trust	Interest
____________	____________
____________	____________

3. Interests in Pension, profit sharing, stock bonus or other retirement plan(s):

Name and Address of Plan	Description	Beneficiary
____________	____________	____________
____________	____________	____________
____________	____________	____________

F. MISCELLANEOUS BUSINESS INTERESTS

Description	Location
____________	____________
____________	____________
____________	____________
____________	____________

(Document continued on next page)

LIABILITIES

Debts, including mortgages, credit card obligations, loans against life insurance, obligations under divorce agreements:

Total Amount of Debt	Monthly Payment	Lender
$______________	$________	________
$______________	$________	________
$______________	$________	________
$______________	$________	________
$______________	$________	________
$______________	$________	________
$______________	$________	________

MISCELLANEOUS INFORMATION

Name and Address of Physician: ____________________

____

Name and Address of Dentist: ____________________

____

Name and Address of Attorney: ____________________

____

Name and Address of Accountant: ____________________

____

(Document continued on next page)

5. Credit Cards Held:

Credit Card	Account No.	Line of Credit
______________	__________	____________
______________	__________	____________
______________	__________	____________
______________	__________	____________
______________	__________	____________

6. Gifts and Transfers (over $10,000) During Lifetime:

Name of Recipient	Amount of Gift	Date of Gift
__________________	$__________	___________
__________________	$__________	___________
__________________	$__________	___________
__________________	$__________	___________
__________________	$__________	___________
__________________	$__________	___________

WILL

Names and addresses of Executors	Name and Address of Attorney
________________________	____________________
________________________	____________________
________________________	

Special Instructions

____

____

Buying, Selling and Leasing Real Estate 2

Real estate is as old as the Earth itself and transactions relating to the land are almost as old. Real estate transactions are perhaps the most common of all transactions, since everyone has or will come in contact with real estate, whether as owner or renter.

Option to Purchase a Residence An Option is an agreement to sell real estate at some future time, at a price agreed upon in the present, if the buyer elects to do so by exercising the Option. These forms easily can be adapted for commercial transactions or even for unimproved land (land with no buildings on it).

Brokerage Agreements Every present and would-be home owner is likely to encounter a real estate broker and his brokerage agreement. These forms set forth the most commonly used types of agreements and explain the important distinctions between them.

Buying and Selling Real Estate The most significant financial transaction in most people's lives is the purchase or sale of a home. These forms provide a basic contract and a menu of common provisions that can be added to the basic contract and can serve as a checklist of issues to consider when buying or selling a home.

Mortgages A mortgage is security for a loan made by a lender to a borrower to enable the borrower to purchase real estate. The mortgage and associated forms will help the borrower or lender understand the provisions that are typically included in such documents.

Leases An alternative to owning real estate outright is to "borrow" the use of it for a period of time and for an agreed upon price—to lease. This section presents forms for both residential and commercial leases and for the transactions associated with leases, such as applications, renewals and sub-leases.

OPTION TO PURCHASE REAL ESTATE (2-01)

An Option to Purchase Real Estate is a contract in which the owner of real estate (the OPTIONOR) gives to another (the OPTIONEE) the exclusive right for a specified period of time to purchase the property on the terms agreed upon. In a Contract of Sale, both the seller and the buyer are bound. In an Option, the owner of the property (as proposed seller and OPTIONOR) cannot normally revoke the Option and is bound to sell the property as agreed. On the other hand, the holder of the Option (the OPTIONEE) can elect to purchase or not.

1. The date of the Option.

2. The name of the owner of the property giving the Option (the OPTIONOR).

3. The name of the person purchasing the Option (the OPTIONEE).

4. If the OPTIONOR is an individual, identify by inserting the words "residing at __________" and fill in the address. If the OPTIONOR is a corporation, insert the words "a corporation formed and existing under the laws of the State of ________ and maintains its principal office at __________" and fill in the state in which incorporated and the address of the corporation.

5. A short description of the property such as the street address. In addition, it is recommended that on a separate sheet, headed "Schedule A," the so-called "metes and bounds" be set forth that describe the property by feet and compass direction—which is the best description of the property. This description is typically found in the property's original deed. The information should be copied from that deed EXACTLY.

OPTION TO PURCHASE REAL ESTATE

OPTION to purchase granted _______[1]_______,19__, by ________[2]_______ (hereinafter, the "OPTIONOR") to ________[3]________ (hereinafter, the "OPTIONEE").

1. THE PARTIES

1.1 OPTIONOR _________[4]_________.

(a) OPTIONOR is the owner of certain real property improved by a building located at ____________[5]____________ (the "Property") and more particularly described in Schedule A attached.

(b) OPTIONOR is desirous of granting to OPTIONEE an Option to purchase the Property.

(Document continued on next page)

6. If the OPTIONEE is an individual, insert the words "residing at __________" and fill in the address. If the OPTIONEE is a corporation, insert the words "a corporation formed and existing under the laws of the State of ____________ and maintains its principal office at ________" and fill in the state in which incorporated and the address of the corporation.

7. The dollar amount, in words and in numbers, being paid for the Option. Note that this is for the purchase of the Option itself, not for the purchase of the property.

8. The time of day at which the Option expires, for example: 12 Noon, 5:00 P.M. or the like.

9. The date on which the Option expires.

10. Insert the method of exercising the Option. The example given is for exercise by mailing, which is the recommended method as it provides a means of getting a delivery receipt via Certified Mail—Return Receipt Requested.

11. The recommended procedure is for a complete proposed contract to be annexed to the Option with each page of the proposed contract initialled (but not signed) by the parties. If so, insert the words "as annexed." If the complete form cannot be attached, the terms of the purchase agreement should be stated as completely as possible.

1.2 OPTIONEE __________[6]__________.

(a) OPTIONEE is desirous of purchasing from OPTIONOR an Option to purchase the Property.

2. GRANT OF OPTION

2.1 OPTIONOR, in consideration of the payment of the sum of ________[7]________ Dollars ($____[7]____) (the "Option Price"), the receipt of which is hereby acknowledged, grants to the OPTIONEE, the exclusive Option to purchase the Property.

3. OPTION PERIOD AND EXERCISE OF OPTION

3.1 This Option, if not exercised in accordance with the terms and conditions, shall expire and terminate at ____[8]____ on ________[9]________.

3.2 *[10][This Option may be exercised at any time during the option period and prior to the expiration of this Option only as follows: by giving written notice of exercise of the Option sent by certified or registered mail, return receipt requested, sent to OPTIONOR at the address set forth above (or such other address as OPTIONOR may have previously in writing designated).]*

4. CONTRACT OF SALE/TERMS OF PURCHASE

4.1 The contract of sale to be entered into by the parties shall be _______[11]_______.

5. FAILURE TO EXERCISE OPTION

5.1 If OPTIONEE shall fail to exercise this Option either in strict accord with the terms and conditions contained herein or within the time provided herein, the consideration paid for this Option shall be retained by OPTIONOR and neither party shall have any further rights or claims against the other by reason of this Option.

6. BROKER

6.1 OPTIONOR and OPTIONEE each represent to the other that such party has not dealt with any broker or person or entity acting on behalf of any broker *other than*

(Document continued on next page)

12. The name of the real estate broker involved who brought the parties together or who assisted either party. If there is no broker involved, delete "other than" through the remainder of the sentence, delete all of paragraph 6.2, renumber paragraph 6.3 as 6.2, and skip to No. 14.

13. The party who will be paying the broker.

14. If the right to purchase the property may not be assigned by OPTIONEE to another, insert "not" and delete the space after "OPTIONEE."

15. If the OPTIONEE has only a limited right to assign, insert any limitations after "OPTIONEE."

16. The name of the OPTIONOR if a corporation. Otherwise delete the line.

17. If the OPTIONOR is an individual, delete "BY" and print the OPTIONOR's name directly below the line, with the OPTIONOR to sign above the line. If the OPTIONOR is a corporation, print the name and title of the individual acting for the corporation directly below the line, with that person to sign above the line.

18. The name of the OPTIONEE if a corporation. Otherwise delete the line.

19. If the OPTIONEE is an individual, delete "BY" and print the OPTIONEE's name directly below the line, with the OPTIONEE to sign above the line. If the OPTIONEE is a corporation, print the name and title of the individual acting for the corporation directly below the line, with that person to sign above the line.

________[12]________ in connection with this transaction.

6.2 ________[13]________ shall pay the commission of such broker pursuant to a separate agreement. The broker shall not be deemed a third-party beneficiary of this provision.

6.3 This Section 6 shall survive the closing.

7. ASSIGNMENT

7.1 The Option granted herein may *[14]* be assigned by the OPTIONEE ________*[15]*________.

IN WITNESS WHEREOF, the parties have signed this agreement as of the date first above written.

__________*[16]*__________

*BY*______________________
[17]

__________*[18]*__________

*BY*______________________
[19]

NOTICE OF EXERCISE OF OPTION TO PURCHASE REAL ESTATE (2-02)

An Option Agreement will typically state the method for exercising the Option which must be followed exactly. The holder of the Option (the OPTIONEE) who ignores the specific terms of the Option does so at his peril since a possible result may be that the OPTIONOR will refuse to recognize the exercise of the Option. Even if not specifically required, it is recommended that Notice of Exercise of Option be in writing.

Note: this form assumes that the proposed Contract of Sale will have been attached to the Option Agreement and is complete in all of its terms. If so, it can and should be signed by the OPTIONEE and returned together with the Notice of Exercise.

1. The name and address of the OPTIONOR (the owner of the property giving the Option).

2. The date of the Option Agreement.

3. A brief description of the property such as the street address.

4. Delete if the terms of the contract do not provide for the payment of a deposit (sometimes referred to as "earnest money") upon delivery of the contract to the OPTIONOR.

5. The time of day for the closing.

6. The date for the closing.

7. The location for the closing.

8. The date of signing the Notice of Exercise.

9. The name of the OPTIONEE if a corporation. Otherwise delete the line.

10. If the OPTIONEE is an individual, delete "BY" and print the OPTIONEE's name directly below the line, with the OPTIONEE to sign above the line. If the OPTIONEE is a corporation, print the name and title of the individual acting for the corporation directly below the line, with that person to sign above the line.

NOTICE OF EXERCISE OF OPTION TO PURCHASE REAL ESTATE

__________[1]__________
____
____

This will confirm that the undersigned, as OPTIONEE of the Option Agreement made by you as OPTIONOR dated ________[2]________ for the purchase of the property located at ___________[3]___________, hereby elects to exercise the Option to purchase.

Two (2) copies of the form of Contract of Sale as signed by the OPTIONEE are enclosed *[4][together with a check in the form payable and in the amount specified in the Contract of Sale]*.

Please sign and return one (1) copy of the Contract of Sale to the undersigned.

Further, the undersigned designates __[5]__, on ________[6]________ at ___________[7]___________ for the closing of the purchase in accordance with the terms and conditions stated in the Option Agreement.

Dated: ________[8]________

__________*[9]*__________

*BY*______________________
[10]

EXTENSION OF OPTION TO PURCHASE REAL ESTATE (2-03)

An Extension of Option to Purchase Real Estate is a contract in which the owner (OPTIONOR) agrees with another (OPTIONEE) to extend a previously agreed upon right to purchase the property for an additional specified period of time.

1. The date of the Extension.

2. The name of the owner of the property giving the Extension (the OPTIONOR).

3. The name of the person receiving the Extension (the OPTIONEE).

4. If the OPTIONOR is an individual, insert the words "residing at ________" and fill in the address. If the OPTIONOR is a corporation, insert the words "a corporation formed and existing under the laws of the State of ________ and maintains its principal office at ________" and fill in the state in which incorporated and the address of the corporation.

5. If the OPTIONEE is an individual, insert the words "residing at ________" and fill in the address. If the OPTIONEE is a corporation, insert the words "a corporation formed and existing under the laws of the State of ________ and maintains its principal office at ________" and fill in the state in which incorporated and the address of the corporation.

6. A short description of the property such as the street address.

7. The expiration date of the Option.

8. The dollar amount, in words and numbers, being paid for the Extension.

EXTENSION OF OPTION TO PURCHASE REAL ESTATE

OPTION EXTENSION AGREEMENT made ______[1]______, 19__, by ________[2]________ (hereinafter, the "OPTIONOR") and ________[3]________ (hereinafter, the "OPTIONEE").

1. THE PARTIES AND THE OPTION

1.1 OPTIONOR __________[4]__________.

1.2 OPTIONEE __________[5]__________.

1.3 The parties acknowledge that OPTIONOR, as the owner of real property located at ___________[6]___________ (the "Property"), for consideration the receipt of which is acknowledged, has given to OPTIONEE an Option to purchase the Property which expires on ________[7]________.

2. EXTENSION OF OPTION

2.1 In consideration of the payment to OPTIONOR by OPTIONEE of the sum of ________[8]________ Dollars ($____[8]____) simultaneously with the signing of this Agreement, the receipt of which is acknowledged, the Option will be

(Document continued on next page)

9. The time of day at which the extended Option will expire, for example: 12 Noon, 5:00 P.M. or the like.

10. The date on which the extended Option will expire. Note: if the parties do not agree to additional extensions, paragraphs 2.2 and 2.3 should be deleted, and 2.4 and 2.5 should be renumbered 2.2 and 2.3 respectively, then skip to No. 21.

11. The dollar amount, in words and numbers, being paid for any additional extension.

12. The time of day at which the payment for any additional extension must be delivered.

13. The date on which the payment for any additional extension must be delivered.

14. The time of day at which the additional extended Option will expire.

15. The date on which the additional extended Option will expire.

16. The dollar amount, in words and numbers, being paid for any further additional extension.

17. The time of day at which the payment for any further additional extension must be delivered.

18. The date on which the payment for any further additional extension must be delivered.

19. The time of day at which the further additional extended Option will expire.

20. The date on which the further additional extended Option will expire.

extended and terminate and expire at __[9]__ on ________[10]________.

2.2 *Upon payment to OPTIONOR by OPTIONEE of an additional sum of ________[11]________ Dollars ($____[11]____) not later than __[12]__ on ________[13]________, the Option will be further extended and then terminate and expire at __[14]__ on ________[15]________.*

2.3 *Upon payment to OPTIONOR by OPTIONEE of an additional sum of ________[16]________ Dollars ($____[16]____) not later than __[17]__ on ________[18]________, the Option will be further extended and then terminate and expire at __[19]__ on ________[20]________.*

2.4 The Option shall terminate and expire at the time and date of the extension period for which OPTIONEE has made payment.

2.5 Any extension of the Option upon payments as set forth in the paragraph shall be an extension of the expiration of the Option only and all other terms and conditions in the Option shall remain in force and effect.

(Document continued on next page)

21. If the OPTIONEE (purchaser) will be given a credit at the closing of the sale for the Option and extension payments, delete both blanks. Otherwise insert "not" in both places.

22. The name of the OPTIONOR if a corporation. Otherwise delete the line.

23. If the OPTIONOR is an individual, delete "BY" and print the OPTIONOR's name directly below the line, with the OPTIONEE to sign above the line. If the OPTIONOR is a corporation, print the name and title of the individual acting for the corporation directly below the line, with that person to sign above the line.

24. The name of the OPTIONEE if a corporation. Otherwise delete the line.

25. If the OPTIONEE is an individual, delete "BY" and print the OPTIONEE's name directly below the line, with the OPTIONEE to sign above the line. If the OPTIONEE is a corporation, print the name and tile of the individual acting for the corporation directly below the line, with that person to sign above the line.

3. PURCHASE PRICE

3.1 The payment for the Option and any payments for extension of the expiration of the Option shall _*[21]*_ be applied towards the purchase price of the Property and OPTIONEE shall _*[21]*_ receive a credit at the closing equal to the amount(s) paid for the Option and any extension.

IN WITNESS WHEREOF, the parties have signed this agreement as of the date first above written.

__________*[22]*__________

*BY*________________________
[23]

__________*[24]*__________

*BY*________________________
[25]

ASSIGNMENT OF OPTION TO PURCHASE REAL ESTATE (2-04)

An Assignment of an Option to Purchase Real Estate is a contract in which the holder of the Option (the OPTIONEE) agrees as ASSIGNOR with another (the ASSIGNEE) to assign his Option so that the ASSIGNEE would have the right to purchase the property on the same terms and conditions as the OPTIONEE. In short, the ASIGNEE would "stand in the shoes" of the OPTIONEE.

ASSIGNMENT OF OPTION TO
PURCHASE REAL ESTATE

ASSIGNMENT OF OPTION made _______[1]_______, 19__, by ________[2]________ (the "ASSIGNOR") and ________[3]________ (the "ASSIGNEE").

1. THE PARTIES

1.1 ASSIGNOR __________[4]__________.

1.2 ASSIGNEE __________[5]__________.

1.3 The parties acknowledge that ASSIGNOR is the holder of an Option to purchase real property located at ____________[6]____________ (the "Property") which

(Document continued on next page)

1. The date of signing the Assignment of the Option.

2. The name of the holder of the Option (referred to in the original Option agreement as OPTIONEE and now known as the ASSIGNOR) who is selling his rights to the Option.

3. The name of the person receiving the Assignment of the Option (the ASSIGNEE).

4. If the ASSIGNOR is an individual, insert the words "residing at __________" and fill in the address. If the ASSIGNOR is a corporation, insert the words "a corporation formed and existing under the laws of the State of __________ and maintains its principal office at ________" and fill in the state in which incorporated and the address of the corporation.

5. If the ASSIGNEE is an individual, insert the words "residing at __________" and fill in the address. If the ASSIGNEE is a corporation, insert the words "a corporation formed and existing under the laws of the State of __________ and maintains its principal office at ________" and fill in the state in which incorporated and the address of the corporation.

6. A short description of the property such as the street address.

expires at ___[7]___ on ________[8]________ (the "Option"), a copy of which is annexed.

1.4 ASSIGNOR as OPTIONEE of the Option represents to ASSIGNEE that the Option has not expired and that it is assignable.

2. ASSIGNMENT OF OPTION

2.1 In consideration of the sum of ________[9]________ Dollars ($____[9]____) paid by ASSIGNEE to ASSIGNOR, the receipt of which is acknowledged, ASSIGNOR assigns to ASSIGNEE all of ASSIGNOR's right, title and interest in and to the Option.

IN WITNESS WHEREOF, the parties have signed this agreement as of the date first above written.

__________*[10]*__________

*BY*______________________
[11]

__________*[12]*__________

*BY*______________________
[13]

7. The time of day at which the Option will expire, for example: 12 Noon, 5:00 P.M. or the like.

8. The expiration date of the Option.

9. The dollar amount, in words and numbers, being paid for the Assignment of the Option.

10. The name of the ASSIGNOR if a corporation. Otherwise delete the line.

11. If the ASSIGNOR is an individual, delete "BY" and print the ASSIGNOR's name directly below the line, with that person to sign above the line. If the ASSIGNOR is a corporation, print the name and title of the individual acting for the corporation directly below the line, with that person to sign above the line.

12. The name of the ASSIGNEE if a corporation. Otherwise delete the line.

13. If the ASSIGNEE is an individual, delete "BY" and print the ASSIGNEE's name directly below the line, with that person to sign above the line. If the ASSIGNEE is a corporation, print the name and title of the individual acting for the corporation directly below the line, with that person to sign above the line.

INTRODUCTION TO REAL ESTATE BROKERAGE AGREEMENTS

An OWNER wishing to sell his real estate may try to sell the PROPERTY himself by placing a "for sale" sign on the PROPERTY or by placing his own advertisement in the newspaper. The more likely scenario is that the owner will use a real estate broker. The BROKER will probably ask that the OWNER sign a commission agreement. Three of the most common types of Brokerage Agreements follow.

WARNINGS

Every state requires that real estate brokers be licensed and that any person seeking a commission for procuring or obtaining a buyer must be a licensed real estate broker. **Any use of this or the following real estate brokerage forms for any purpose other than providing information may violate the laws of your state.** The purpose of these forms is solely to educate the OWNER as to the most common forms of Brokerage Agreements so the OWNER will understand what he is agreeing to by signing a Brokerage Agreement. Neither the authors nor the publisher nor any seller of this work will assume responsibility or be liable for any use of these forms for other than informational purposes.

Brokers may use other forms or different language from that which is supplied here. Brokerage Agreements are negotiable. Discuss the terms of any Agreement *before* signing any document and if your BROKER refuses to accept your terms, talk to another BROKER.

Generally, the law states that unless a written Agreement provides otherwise, the BROKER is entitled to a commission when the BROKER has produced a buyer who is "ready, willing and able" to meet the OWNER's terms—even if the PROPERTY is not actually sold. Therefore, an Agreement should provide that the commission will be earned only after the real estate transaction has closed.

An important point that should be agreed to in advance is whether the OWNER who sells the PROPERTY on his own will be required to pay the entire commission or a portion of it to the BROKER. Although under any Brokerage Agreement, other than the "Exclusive Right to Sell" type of Agreement, the OWNER is permitted to sell the PROPERTY on his own without paying the commission, most BROKERS are reluctant to forgo a significant portion of that commission since money has been spent for advertising and marketing the property. This issue should be negotiated carefully between the OWNER and the BROKER prior to signing the Brokerage Agreement.

Negotiate and enter into a written Brokerage Agreement *before* the BROKER brings any prospective buyers.

"OPEN LISTING" REAL ESTATE BROKERAGE AGREEMENT (2-05)

The most common type of Brokerage Agreement is the so-called "Open Listing" whereby the OWNER as the seller agrees to pay a brokerage commission to the BROKER only if the BROKER can demonstrate that he produced the buyer. The listing is "Open" in that the OWNER is free to list the PROPERTY with other brokers or sell the PROPERTY himself. If the Agreement does not state or imply "Exclusive" it is probably an "Open Listing."

WARNING

Every state requires that real estate brokers be licensed and that any person seeking a commission for procuring or obtaining a buyer must be a licensed real estate broker. **Any use of this or the following real estate brokerage forms for any purpose other than providing information may violate the laws of your state.** The purpose of this and the following forms is solely to educate the OWNER as to the most common forms of Brokerage Agreements so the OWNER will have knowledge as to what he is agreeing to by signing a Brokerage Agreement. Neither the authors nor the publisher nor any seller of this work will assume responsibility or be liable for any use of these forms for other than informational purposes.

"OPEN LISTING" REAL ESTATE
BROKERAGE AGREEMENT

1. The date of signing the Agreement.

2. The name of the OWNER of the PROPERTY.

3. The OWNER's address.

4. The name of the licensed real estate broker (BROKER).

5. The address of the BROKER.

6. The address of the PROPERTY to be sold.

7. The period of time the BROKER will have to procure a buyer (usually between three and six months, but may be shorter or longer).

8. A short statement of the terms the OWNER will accept, especially the price, but also terms such as whether the OWNER will take a purchase money mortgage or the like. (A purchase money mortgage means that the seller is willing to furnish the mortgage for the PROPERTY he is selling.)

AGREEMENT made __________[1]__________, between ________[2]________ of ____________[3]____________ ("OWNER"), and ________[4]________ of ____________[5]____________ ("BROKER").

1. OWNER REPRESENTATION. OWNER represents that he is the owner in fee simple of the property located at ____________[6]____________ (the "PROPERTY") and agrees to convey THE PROPERTY if it is sold to a person procured by BROKER on the terms and conditions set forth.

2. EMPLOYMENT. OWNER grants to BROKER a non-exclusive agency to sell the PROPERTY for a period of ______[7]______ from the date of this agreement.

3. TERMS OF SALE.
________________________[8]________________________
____.

(Document continued on next page)

"OPEN LISTING" REAL ESTATE BROKERAGE AGREEMENT *continued*

9. The commission that the OWNER agrees to pay and the BROKER agrees to accept—usually set forth as a percentage of the purchase price but may be stated as a dollar amount.

10. The name of the BROKER.

11. The name of the individual acting for the BROKER printed directly below the line, with that person to sign above the line.

12. The name of the OWNER printed directly below the line, with the OWNER to sign above the line.

4. COMMISSION. BROKER shall be entitled to a commission of __[9]__ percent of the purchase price if BROKER procures a purchaser for THE PROPERTY upon the terms stated, which commission shall be earned, and payable out of the purchase price, when, as, and if and in the event title shall actually close.

IN WITNESS WHEREOF, the parties have signed this agreement as of the date first above written.

__________[10]__________

BY______________________
[11]

____
[12]

"EXCLUSIVE AGENCY" REAL ESTATE BROKERAGE AGREEMENT (2-06)

Under the "Exclusive Agency" type of Brokerage Agreement, the OWNER as seller agrees to pay a commission to a particular BROKER as the sole and exclusive agent of the OWNER. If the OWNER sells the PROPERTY, he must pay the agreed upon commission to this BROKER even if the buyer was procured by another BROKER. The only exception to this is if the OWNER sells the PROPERTY himself in which case the "Exclusive Agency" is terminated and the OWNER is not liable for the BROKER's commission.

The key language to look for in this type of Brokerage Agreement is "Exclusive Agency."

WARNING

Every state requires that real estate brokers be licensed and that any person seeking a commission for procuring or obtaining a buyer must be a licensed real estate broker. **Any use of this or the preceding or following forms for any purpose other than providing information may violate the laws of your state.** The purpose of these forms is solely to educate the OWNER as to the most common forms of Brokerage Agreements so the OWNER will have knowledge as to what he is agreeing to by signing a Brokerage Agreement. Neither the authors nor the publisher nor any seller of this work will assume responsibility or be liable for any use of these forms for other than informational purposes.

"EXCLUSIVE AGENCY" REAL ESTATE
BROKERAGE AGREEMENT

AGREEMENT made __________[1]__________, between ________[2]________ of ____________[3]____________ ("OWNER"), and ________[4]________ of ____________[5]____________ ("BROKER").

1. OWNER REPRESENTATION. OWNER represents that he is the owner in fee simple of the property located at ____________[6]____________ (the "PROPERTY") and agrees to convey the PROPERTY if it is sold to a person procured by BROKER on the terms and conditions set forth.

2. EMPLOYMENT. OWNER grants to BROKER an exclusive agency to sell the PROPERTY for a period of _____[7]_____ from the date of this agreement.

1. The date of the Agreement.

2. The name of the OWNER of the PROPERTY.

3. The OWNER's address.

4. The name of the licensed real estate broker (BROKER).

5. The address of the BROKER.

6. The address of the PROPERTY to be sold.

7. The period of time the BROKER will have to procure a buyer (usually between three and six months, but may be shorter or longer).

(Document continued on next page)

8. A short statement of the terms the OWNER will accept, especially the price, but also terms such as whether the OWNER will take a purchase money mortgage or the like. (A purchase money mortgage means that the seller is willing to furnish the mortgage for the PROPERTY he is selling.)

9. The commission that the OWNER agrees to pay and the BROKER agrees to accept—usually set forth as a percentage of the purchase price but may be stated as a dollar amount.

10. The name of the BROKER.

11. The name of the individual acting for the BROKER printed directly below the line, with that person to sign above the line.

12. The name of the OWNER printed directly below the line, with the OWNER to sign above the line.

3. TERMS OF SALE.

______________________[8]______________________

____.

4. COMMISSION. BROKER shall be entitled to a commission of __[9]__ percent of the purchase price if BROKER procures a purchaser for THE PROPERTY upon the terms stated, which commission shall be earned, and payable out of the purchase price, when, as, and if and in the event title shall actually close.

IN WITNESS WHEREOF, the parties have signed this agreement as of the date first above written.

__________[10]__________

BY______________________

[11]

____

[12]

"EXCLUSIVE RIGHT TO SELL" REAL ESTATE BROKERAGE AGREEMENT (2-07)

Under the "Exclusive Right to Sell" type of Brokerage Agreement, the OWNER agrees to pay a commission to one particular BROKER if the PROPERTY is sold—regardless of who procured the buyer (even if the OWNER has sold the PROPERTY himself).

For this reason, the "Exclusive Right to Sell" Brokerage Agreement typically provides that the BROKER is entitled to a commission even if the PROPERTY is taken off the market during the term of the Agreement. This form of Agreement also typically provides that the BROKER is entitled to his commission even if the PROPERTY was sold after the expiration of the Agreement to a buyer the BROKER procured during the term of the Agreement. This effectively prohibits the OWNER from defeating the BROKER by taking the PROPERTY off the market or refusing other offers until after the expiration of the contract and then selling to another party, since the BROKER will still be entitled to his commission.

The key language to look for in this type of Brokerage Agreement is "Exclusive Right to Sell," "Sole Right to Sell" and references to a prohibition from removing the PROPERTY from the market.

WARNING

Every state requires that real estate brokers be licensed and that any person seeking a commission for procuring or obtaining a buyer must be a licensed real estate broker. **Any use of this or the preceding forms for any purpose other than providing information may violate the laws of your state.** The purpose of these forms is solely to educate the OWNER as to the most common forms of Brokerage Agreements so the OWNER will have knowledge as to what he is agreeing to by signing a Brokerage Agreement. Neither the authors nor the publisher nor any seller of this work will assume responsibility or be liable for any use of these forms for other than informational purposes.

"EXCLUSIVE RIGHT TO SELL" REAL ESTATE BROKERAGE AGREEMENT

1. The date of the Agreement.
2. The name of the OWNER of the PROPERTY.
3. The OWNER's address.
4. The name of the licensed real estate broker (BROKER).
5. The address of the BROKER.
6. The address of the PROPERTY to be sold.

AGREEMENT made __________[1]__________, between ________[2]________ of ____________[3]____________ ("OWNER"), and ________[4]________ of ____________[5]____________ ("BROKER").

1. OWNER REPRESENTATION. OWNER represents that he is the owner in fee simple of the property located at ____________[6]____________ (the "PROPERTY").

2. EMPLOYMENT. OWNER grants to BROKER the sole and exclusive right to offer for sale or

(Document continued on next page)

sell the PROPERTY for a period of _____[7]_____ from the date of this agreement.

3. TERMS OF SALE.

________________________[8]________________________
____.

4. COMMISSION. BROKER shall be entitled to a commission of __[9]__ percent of the purchase price if BROKER procures a purchaser for THE PROPERTY upon the terms stated, which commission shall be earned, and payable out of the purchase price, when, as, and if and in the event title shall actually close.

5. WITHDRAWAL OF PROPERTY/SALE AFTER TERMINATION. If, during the term of the agreement, OWNER shall remove or withdraw the PROPERTY from the market or otherwise prevent or interfere with BROKER from selling the PROPERTY, BROKER shall nevertheless be entitled to the commission at the rate set forth herein. If, after termination of this agreement, the PROPERTY shall be sold to or on behalf of a buyer initially procured by BROKER, BROKER shall nevertheless be entitled to the commission at the rate set forth herein.

IN WITNESS WHEREOF, the parties have signed this agreement as of the date first above written.

__________[10]__________

BY______________________
[11]

____
[12]

7. The period of time the BROKER will have to procure a buyer (usually between three and six months, but may be shorter or longer).

8. A short statement of the terms the OWNER will accept, especially the price, but also terms such as whether the OWNER will take a purchase money mortgage or the like. (A purchase money mortgage means that the seller is willing to furnish the mortgage for the PROPERTY he is selling.)

9. The commission that the OWNER agrees to pay and the BROKER agrees to accept—usually set forth as a percentage of the purchase price but may be stated as a dollar amount.

10. The name of the BROKER.

11. The name of the individual acting for the BROKER printed directly below the line, with that person to sign above the line.

12. The name of the OWNER printed directly below the line, with the OWNER to sign above the line.

OFFER TO PURCHASE REAL ESTATE (2-08)

An Offer to Purchase Real Estate is just that—an offer. It is not binding on either the buyer (PURCHASER) or the SELLER until signed by the SELLER. It may be revoked in writing by the PURCHASER at any time before the Seller signs the form. However, on signing an Offer to Purchase, the PURCHASER has immediately obligated himself to the terms of the Offer. The PURCHASER does not pay any money until the Offer is accepted.

WARNING

This form is recommended only for very simple real estate transactions in which all of the essential terms of the agreement can be spelled out. For more complex transactions, it is recommended that the "Offer" be made in the form of a full Contract of Sale, which follows, containing all terms and conditions.

OFFER TO PURCHASE REAL ESTATE

________[1]________ ("PURCHASER") offers to purchase from ________[2]________ ("SELLER") the real

1. The name of the PURCHASER. If the PURCHASER is an individual, add the words "residing at __________" and fill in the address. If the PURCHASER is a corporation, add the words "a corporation formed and existing under the laws of the State of __________ and maintains its principal office at ________" and fill in the state in which incorporated and the address of the corporation.

2. The name of the SELLER. If the SELLER is an individual, add the words "residing at __________" and fill in the address. If the SELLER is a corporation, add the words "a corporation formed and existing under the laws of the State of __________ and maintains its principal office at __________" and fill in the state in which incorporated and the address of the corporation.

(Document continued on next page)

3. A short description of the property such as the street address. In addition, it is recommended that on a separate sheet, headed "Schedule A", the so-called "metes and bounds" be set forth that describe the property by feet and compass direction—which is the best description of the property. This description is typically found in the property's original deed. The information should be copied from that deed EXACTLY.

4. The dollar amount, in words and numbers, being offered for the property.

5. The dollar amount, in words and numbers, of the down payment.

6. The dollar amount, in words and numbers, representing the balance of the purchase price. (Note: make certain that the amount of the down payment and the amount of the balance equal the total amount being offered.)

property located at ____________[3]____________ and which is more fully described in Schedule A attached, together with all rights, privileges, easements and all improvements, buildings and fixtures in their present condition as are now on or attached to the property (collectively, the "PROPERTY") on the following terms:

1. PURCHASE PRICE - PURCHASER agrees to pay to SELLER for the PROPERTY the sum of ________[4]________ Dollars ($____[4]____) as follows:

(a) down payment (earnest money) in the amount of ________[5]________ Dollars ($____[5]____) to be paid in accordance with the terms of this offer and to be deposited in escrow to a special or trust account and

(b) the balance of ________[6]________ Dollars ($____[6]____) to be paid at the closing of title in cash, bank check or certified check to the order of the SELLER.

2. TITLE - SELLER shall give a warranty deed conveying such title as a reputable title insurance company would insure, free and clear of liens or encumbrances and with rights of dower, if any, released except:

(a) Restrictions of record and easements, reservations, conditions and laws and governmental regulations affecting the use and maintenance of the PROPERTY, provided they are not violated by any improvements on or to the PROPERTY,

(b) zoning ordinances, if any,

(c) encroachments or projections, if any, of record,

(d) taxes and assessments not yet due and payable.

3. APPORTIONMENTS - The following shall be apportioned as of midnight of the day before the closing: rents as and when collected; interest on existing mortgages; premiums on insurance policies if transferred; taxes, water charges and sewer rents, fuel oil or gas.

4. POSSESSION - SELLER shall deliver possession of the PROPERTY to the PURCHASER on the date of the closing. If the PROPERTY or any part is damaged or destroyed before the closing, PURCHASER shall have the

(Document continued on next page)

7. The name and address of the Escrow Agent.

8. The time of day of the closing, for example: 12 Noon, 5:00 P.M. or the like.

9. The date of the closing.

10. The address of the closing.

11. The time of day at which the Offer expires.

12. The date on which the Offer expires.

right either (a) to receive any insurance proceeds or (b) to cancel and revoke this Offer and to the return of all money previously paid or deposited.

5. ESCROW AND CLOSING - The down payment shall be deposited with and held in escrow by ________[7]________ within five (5) days of receipt of this Offer as accepted by SELLER. The closing will take place at ___[8]___ on ________[9]________ at ____________[10]____________ at which time PURCHASER shall pay the balance of the purchase price and SELLER shall present the deed in recordable form, all keys and any occupancy permits required by law.

6. DEFAULT - The parties agree that if PURCHASER shall default in paying the balance due at the closing, SELLER shall be entitled to retain the down payment as liquidated damages and if SELLER shall default, PURCHASER shall be entitled to specific performance by SELLER.

6. ACCEPTANCE - PURCHASER may IN WRITING revoke this Offer at any time prior to its acceptance. Unless an accepted copy of this Offer is delivered to PURCHASER on or before __[11]__ on ________[12]________ this Offer will expire and neither party will have any obligation to the other. Upon acceptance and payment of the down payment by PURCHASER, this Offer will become a binding agreement containing all material terms and conditions necessary and

(Document continued on next page)

13. The name of the PURCHASER if a corporation. Otherwise delete the line.

14. If the PURCHASER is an individual, delete "BY" and print the PURCHASER's name directly below the line, with the PURCHASER to sign above the line. If the PURCHASER is a corporation, print the name and title of the individual acting for the corporation directly below the line, with that person to sign above the line.

15. The PURCHASER's address and telephone number.

16. The name of the SELLER.

17. The name of the SELLER if a corporation. Otherwise delete the line.

18. If the SELLER is an individual, delete "BY" and print the SELLER's name directly below the line, with the SELLER to sign above the line. If the SELLER is a corporation, print the name and title of the individual acting for the corporation directly below the line, with that person to sign above the line.

there being no additional conditions, representations, warranties or the like, either written or oral.

__________*[13]*__________

*BY*______________________
[14]

Address: _________[15]__________

_________[15]__________

Telephone Number: _________[15]__________

ACCEPTANCE OF OFFER

_________[16]_________ ("SELLER") acknowledges that he is the owner of the PROPERTY, consents to the deposit of the down payment in escrow with ____________________[7]____________________ and accepts the Offer to purchase the PROPERTY on the terms and conditions of this Offer.

__________*[17]*__________

*BY*______________________
[18]

CONTRACT FOR SALE OF RESIDENCE (2-09)

This form contains the basic terms of a Contract for Sale of Residence. It is complete as it exists; however it is suggested that you carefully examine each contract clause that follows in this chapter and include those that are appropriate to your transaction.

WARNINGS

The use of several methods of identifying the property to be sold is very important, even though it may seem redundant. It is vital that the property be identified precisely and without ambiguity or confusion so that the Seller is selling neither more nor less than he intends to sell and so that the Buyer knows exactly what he is buying. For this reason, the authors strongly urge the use of several methods of identifying the property as indicated in this form.

Further, the authors strongly urge that the Seller carefully examine his deed (the document the Seller received when he purchased the property) and use exactly the same property description as the deed contains.

The authors also strongly urge that the Seller give only the same type of deed as the Seller himself received (see Instruction No. 30 below).

1. The date of signing the agreement.
2. The name of the Seller.
3. The address of the Seller.
4. The name of the Buyer.
5. The address of the Buyer.
6. Delete if the sale is for land only.
7. The city in which the property is located.
8. The county in which the property is located.
9. The state in which the property is located.

Note: the information for Nos. 10 through 20 is typically found on the Seller's deed or the tax map of the property located in the office of the local tax authority.

10. Delete through No. 15 if your locale does not use a "block and lot" system of identifying property.

CONTRACT FOR SALE OF RESIDENCE

WARNING: NO REPRESENTATION IS MADE THAT THIS CONTRACT FOR THE SALE AND PURCHASE OF REAL PROPERTY COMPLIES WITH THE SO-CALLED "PLAIN ENGLISH" LAWS OF THIS STATE

CONTRACT OF SALE made _______[1]_______, between ________[2]________, __________[3]________ ("Seller"), and _______[4]_______, __________[5]_______ ("Buyer").

1. AGREEMENT - Seller agrees to sell and Buyer agrees to purchase the real property *[6][including all buildings and improvements on and to said property]* located in the City of _____[7]_____, County of _____[8]_____, State of _____[9]_____, *[10][identified on the Tax Map of*

(Document continued on next page)

_____[11]_____, dated ________[12]________ as Section ___[13]___, Block ___[14]___, Lot(s) ___[15]___], known by the street address _______[16]_______ and intended to be the same property conveyed to Seller by Deed recorded in the Office of ______[17]_____ at *[18][Liber]* ***OR*** *[Reel]* __[19]__, Page __[20]__, (the "Premises") and more particularly described *[21][on Schedule A annexed to and made part of this Contract]* ***OR*** *[as follows: beginning at a point ____]*

2. STREET RIGHTS - This sales includes all the right, title and interest, if any, of the Seller in and to any land lying in the bed of any street, or highway opened or proposed, in front of or adjoining the Premises, to the center line thereof. It also includes any right of the Seller to any unpaid award by reason of any taking by condemnation and/or for any damage to the Premises by reason of change of grade of any street or highway. The Seller will deliver, at no additional cost to the Buyer, at the closing, or after the closing, on demand, any document which Buyer may require to collect the award and damages.

3. PURCHASE PRICE - The purchase price is ________[22]________ Dollars ($_____[23]_____) payable as follows:

(Document continued on next page)

11. The name of the town, county or district where the tax map referred to is filed.

12. Identify the specific tax map by the date it was filed.

13. The Section in which the property being sold is located.

14. The Block in which the property being sold is located.

15. The Lot(s) being sold.

16. The address of the property.

17. The title of the city, county, district or state office responsible for recording deeds.

18. Choose one (see No. 19 for explanations).

19. The number of the "Liber" (book) or "Reel" (microfilm) where the Seller's deed was actually recorded.

20. The page number of the Liber or Reel where the Seller's deed was actually recorded.

21. Choose one, and on either a separate page headed "Schedule A" or after the words "beginning at a point" insert the legal description (the so-called "metes and bounds") of the property. Note: this is the best description of the property. It is typically found in the property's original deed. The information should be copied from that deed EXACTLY.

22. The purchase price, in words.

23. The purchase price, in numbers.

By check on the signing of this contract, subject to collection, to be held in escrow $_____[24]_____

[25][By allowance for and subject to Seller's existing mortgage in principal amount remaining $_____[26]_____]

[27][By a purchase money mortgage and note given by Buyer as Mortgagor to Seller as Mortgagee $_____[28]_____]

Balance due and payable at closing $_____[29]_____

All money payable for other than the purchase price shall be paid by cash or personal check of Buyer not to exceed $500.00. All money payable toward the purchase price shall be paid by cash not to exceed $500.00, certified check of Buyer, or official check of any bank, savings bank, trust company, or savings and loan association having a banking office in the State of ____[9]____, payable to the order of the Seller, or the order of the Buyer duly endorsed to the order of the Seller in the presence of the Seller.

4. VIOLATIONS - Seller shall comply with all notices of violations of law or municipal ordinances, order, or requirements noted in or issued by any governmental department having authority as to lands, housing, buildings, fire, health and labor conditions affecting the premises as of the date of this Contract, and the Premises shall be conveyed free of them. This provision shall survive closing. The Seller shall furnish Buyer with such authorization necessary to make any searches.

5. LIEN OF BUYER - All money paid on account of this contract and the reasonable expense of examination of the title to the Premises and of any survey and survey inspection charges are by this contract made liens on the Premises and are collectable out of the Premises. Any such lien shall not continue after default in performance of this contract by the Buyer.

6. BUYER'S CREDIT - Seller shall have the option to credit the Buyer, as an adjustment to the purchase price, with the amount of any unpaid taxes, assessments, water charges and sewer rents, together with any interest and pen-

24. The amount of the deposit, in numbers, due on signing the contract (which is negotiable, and customarily, though not necessarily, 10% of the purchase price).

25. Delete through No. 26 if the Seller is not assigning his present mortgage to the Buyer. Note: even if the parties are willing, such an assignment will probably require the written approval of the lender holding the Seller's mortgage.

26. The amount, in numbers, of the Seller's present mortgage being assigned by the Seller and assumed by the Buyer.

27. Delete through No. 28 if this sale is "all cash to the Seller"—that is, if the Seller will receive the entire sale price in cash at the closing. Note: a sale is "all cash to the Seller" even if the Seller must use part of the proceeds of the sale to satisfy or pay off the Seller's existing mortgage.

28. The amount, in numbers, of the purchase money mortgage the Buyer will pay. (A purchase money mortgage is a loan given by the Seller, as opposed to one given by a bank, to the Buyer to enable the Buyer to purchase the property. The loan is secured by a mortgage.)

29. The balance, in numbers, due and payable at the closing. Note that regardless of how the transaction is structured, the amounts inserted at No's 24, 26, 28 and 29 *must* equal the total purchase price inserted at No. 22.

(Document continued on next page)

30. The type of deed being given by the Seller, for example: "Quit Claim," "Bargain and Sale Deed without Covenants," "Bargain and Sale Deed with Covenants." Note that the Seller should give only the exact same type or form of deed that the Seller himself received when he purchased the property.

alties, to the closing date, if any official bills, computed to that date, are produced at closing. If there is anything else affecting the sale which is the obligation of Seller to pay or discharge at closing, Seller may use any part of the balance of the purchase price in payment or discharge. If the title insurance company engaged by Buyer will nevertheless insure title free and clear of such matter or insure the Premises against enforcement of such matter against the Premises, Seller shall also have the option to deposit money with the title insurance company engaged by Buyer to assure such payment or discharge. Upon request made within a reasonable time before closing, Buyer agrees to provide separate certified checks as may be requested by Seller to assist in clearing these matters.

7. DEFAULTS - If the Seller shall be unable to convey title in accordance with the terms of this contract, the sole liability of the Seller will be to refund to Buyer any amounts paid on account of this contract, including amounts expended or charges incurred for examination of title, searches, survey and survey inspections and the like made under this contract. Upon such refund and payment this contract shall be deemed cancelled, and neither Seller nor Buyer shall have any further rights against the other by reason of this contract.

If Buyer shall willfully default in the performance of any of the terms and conditions of this contract imposed upon Buyer, Buyer shall forfeit and Seller shall have, without limitation or exclusion of any other rights, the right to retain the entire deposit previously paid by Buyer upon signing of this contract as liquidated damages.

8. DEED - The deed shall be the usual ______[30]______ deed in proper statutory form for recording. The deed shall be duly signed and acknowledged in such form as to convey to Buyer the Premises in fee simple, free and clear of

(Document continued on next page)

31. The location where the closing will be held.

32. The time of day of the closing.

33. The day, month and year scheduled for the closing.

any encumbrances except as may be permitted by this contract.

9. CLOSING - As used in this contract, the term "closing" means the settlement of the obligations of Seller and Buyer to each other under this contract. Closing includes the payment of the purchase price to the Seller and the delivery to the Purchaser of the deed.

If Seller is a corporation, Seller will deliver to Buyer at closing a resolution of its Board of Directors authorizing the sale and delivery of the deed, and a certificate of the Secretary or other authorized officer of the Seller certifying the resolution and stating the facts showing that the transfer is in conformity with the requirements of the laws of the state of incorporation of such corporation. The deed will contain a recital sufficient to establish compliance with such state law.

The closing will take place at
__________[31]__________, at ___[32]___, on
__________[33]__________.

10. TRANSFER AND RECORDING TAXES - Seller will deliver a certified check at the closing payable to the order of the appropriate State, City or County officer in the amount of any applicable transfer tax, recording tax, or both, payable by reason of the sale of the Premises, the delivery or recording of the deed, together with any required tax return. Buyer agrees to duly complete the tax return and to cause the check and the tax return to be delivered to the appropriate officer promptly after closing.

11. ENTIRE AGREEMENT - All prior understandings and agreements between Buyer and Seller are merged in this contract, which alone fully and completely expresses their agreement. This contract is entered into after full investigation, neither party relying upon any statement or representation, not set forth in this contract, made by anyone else.

12. MODIFICATION OF CONTRACT - This contract may not be changed or terminated except in writing.

13. BINDING EFFECT/BENEFIT - This contract shall also bind and be for the benefit of the heirs, executors, administrators, successors, distributees, and assigns of the respective parties.

(Document continued on next page)

34. The name of the Buyer if a corporation. Otherwise delete the line.

35. The name of the Witness to the signing of the contract printed below the line, with the Witness to sign above the line.

36. If the Buyer is an individual, delete "BY" and print the Buyer's name directly below the line, with the Buyer to sign above the line. If the Buyer is a corporation, print the name and title of the individual acting for the corporation directly below the line, with that person to sign above the line.

37. The name of the Seller if a corporation. Otherwise delete the line.

38. If the Seller is an individual, delete "BY" and print the Seller's name directly below the line, with the Seller to sign above the line. If the Seller is a corporation, print the name and title of the individual acting for the corporation directly below the line, with that person to sign above the line.

14. CONSTRUCTION - Any singular word or term in this contract shall also be read as in the plural whenever the sense of this contract may require. Any masculine terms in this contract shall also be read as in the feminine whenever the sense of this contract may require.

IN WITNESS WHEREOF, this contract has been duly executed by the parties on the date first written above.

Witness:

____
[34]

____
[35]

*BY*_______________________
[36]

____
[37]

*BY*_______________________
[38]

INTRODUCTION TO CONTRACT CLAUSES TO BE USED WITH CONTRACT FOR SALE OF RESIDENCE

All of the following clauses may be incorporated into the preceding "Contract for Sale of Residence." They may be placed in any order the writer wishes and numbered accordingly. This section is intended to act as a check-list of common contract provisions. Reference to this section during negotiation for the sale of a house will help the Seller prepare a contract that contains all the necessary provisions.

CONTRACT CLAUSE— PURCHASE MONEY MORTGAGE (2-10)

This clause should be included in the Contract for Sale of Residence if any part of the purchase price is to be paid by a loan from the Seller to the Buyer that will be secured by a Mortgage (a Purchase Money Mortgage).

CONTRACT CLAUSE— PURCHASE MONEY MORTGAGE

[1] PURCHASE MONEY MORTGAGE - As a portion of the purchase price, Buyer, as Mortgagor, shall deliver at the closing to Seller, as Mortgagee, and Seller shall accept a Note secured by a Purchase Money Mortgage in the principal amount of ________[2]________ Dollars ($_______). The Note shall be payable in monthly installments of $_____[3]_____ with interest on the remaining principal balance due at the rate of ___[4]___ percent (___%) per annum. Buyer, as Mortgagor, shall pay to Seller, as Mortgagee, at the closing a payment of interest only at said interest rate calculated on the entire principal amount for the period from and including the date of the closing to and including the last day of the month in which the closing shall have occurred. Payments of principal and interest shall commence on the 1st day of the second full month after the date of the closing and shall continue monthly until the maturity date on which date all remaining unpaid principal and all accrued interest shall be due and payable. The term of the Note and Mortgage shall be ____[5]____ *[6][years.]* ***OR*** *[months.] [7][The Note shall permit the prepayment by the Buyer, as Mortgagor, at any time and without penalty.] [8][Additionally, the Note and Mortgage shall contain the following terms:*

____

____

____*.]*

________[9]________ shall prepare the Note and Mortgage which shall be in recordable form. Buyer agrees to reimburse Seller for the cost of Seller's reasonable attorneys' fees in preparing or reviewing such Note and Mortgage.

Seller shall have the right to obtain such credit, judgment and lien searches and reports as he shall see fit and Buyer agrees to pay all costs of obtaining any searches or reports. Buyer also agrees to sign and deliver to Seller or others that Seller may designate, such forms of consent or authorization as may be required. Buyer agrees at the closing to pay all mortgage and mortgage recording taxes, fees and charges *[10][and the cost of mortgagee title insurance]*.

1. The number of this clause when inserted into the Contract for Sale of Residence.
2. The principal amount, in words and numbers.
3. The amount, in numbers, of each monthly installment.
4. The rate of interest, in words and numbers.
5. The term of the loan in years or months, in words.
6. Choose one.
7. Delete if the Buyer will not be permitted to prepay the Note.
8. Insert any remaining terms. Otherwise delete.
9. Identify the party that will have the responsibility of preparing the Note and Mortgage, typically the Seller.
10. Delete if the Buyer will not pay for the title insurance.

CONTRACT CLAUSE— DEFERRED PAYMENTS SECURED BY RENTAL PAYMENTS (2-11)

This clause should be inserted into the Contract for Sale of Residence if any portion of the purchase price is to be paid by or secured by rental payments by the Buyer. This arrangement differs from a purchase money mortgage in which the Seller furnishes the mortgage to the Buyer. With a purchase money mortgage, the buyer receives title at the closing and becomes the legal owner of the property, making mortgage payments to the Seller. In the Deferred Payments situation, the Buyer takes possession, but not title, at the closing and the deed is held in escrow by the Seller (and not recorded) until the Buyer has paid in full.

Deferred Payments may appear attractive to a Seller if a Buyer does not want to close for some extended period of time or if the only interested Buyer appears unlikely to qualify for a mortgage. This arrangement has very different tax consequences from an outright sale for both the Buyer and the Seller. For this reason, it should be considered very carefully and each party should consult with a knowledgeable accountant or tax preparer.

Note that the last paragraph of this form provides that a Buyer who defaults loses not only any rental payments made but also his deposit or down-payment and all other money already paid. This is a harsh provision that the parties may want to modify. The parties are free to negotiate any default penalties they wish.

CONTRACT CLAUSE— DEFERRED PAYMENTS SECURED BY RENTAL PAYMENTS

1. The number of this clause when inserted into the Contract for Sale of Residence.

2. The portion of the purchase price, in words and numbers, being paid over time in the form of rental payments.

3. The number of months of rental payments, in words and numbers.

4. The monthly rental, in words and numbers.

[1] DEFERRED PAYMENT SECURED BY RENTAL PAYMENTS - The parties agree that the sum of ________[2]________ Dollars ($________) of the purchase price shall be paid monthly commencing on the 1st day of the month immediately following the closing and the 1st day of each and every month thereafter for ____[3]____ (__) months as rental payments in the amount of ________[4]________ Dollars ($________) per month. All such payments are to be made by check, subject to collection, directly to Seller at the address designated by him.

Seller agrees that until the sum of ________[2]________ Dollars ($________) has been paid in full, all such monthly rental payments shall be equal to one-twelfth (1/12) of the annual charge and shall be applied as follows and in the following order, it being the understanding of the parties that such payments are to be applied so as to keep Seller "current" with each such obligation:

(Document continued on next page)

5. Modify as appropriate. (For example, if the Seller's mortgage provides that a portion of the mortgage payments go towards taxes, no portion of the rent being paid by the Buyer should be allocated to taxes.)

6. The approximate amount of principal, in words and numbers, remaining due on the Seller's existing mortgage.

7. The name of the holder of the Seller's existing mortgage.

8. The monthly mortgage payment, in words and numbers, due on the Seller's existing mortgage.

Note: the information for Nos. 9 through 12 is typically found on the Seller's deed or the tax map of the property located in the office of the local tax authority.

9. The Tax Map date or other identifying feature.

10. The Tax Map Section in which the property is located.

11. The Tax Map Block in which the property is located.

12. The Lot(s) in which the property is located.

13. The present amount of the real estate taxes, in words and numbers.

14. The amount of insurance, in words and numbers.

[5] *(i) Seller's existing mortgage in the amount of ________[6]________ Dollars ($________) held by ________[7]________, and in accordance with which, Seller is required to pay the sum of ________[8]________ Dollars ($________) per month, it being understood that if this amount may by its terms be increased or decreased, the amount of rent due to Seller shall be adjusted accordingly on Seller's written notification to Buyer which shall include a copy of such notice of adjustment by the holder;*

(ii) all real estate or real property taxes, assessments, levies, and the like charged against the real property and improvements identified on the Tax Map of ____[9]____ as Section __[10]__, Block __[11]__, Lot(s) __[12]__, in the amount of ________[13]________ Dollars ($________) per year, it being understood that if this amount, whether by change in the tax rate or by change in assessment be increased or decreased, the amount of rent due to Seller shall be adjusted accordingly on Seller's written notification to Buyer which shall include a copy of such tax bill;

(iii) the payment of all premiums to keep and maintain all of the buildings, improvements on and to the property and including all fixtures, equipment and personal property included in this sale (the Premises), insured against loss, damage or destruction by fire, hazard, vandalism, liability or other insurable casualty in the amount of not less than ________[14]________ Dollars ($________) per year, it being understood that if this amount be increased or decreased, the amount of rent due to Seller shall be adjusted accordingly on Seller's written notification to Buyer which shall include a copy of such increase or decrease as provided by the insurance company; and it being further specifically UNDERSTOOD AND AGREED that Seller shall have no obligation to insure the person, liability or personal property of the Buyer.

It is also understood and agreed that Seller will not be responsible for, nor will any portion of the rent paid by Buyer be applied to or applicable to, the payment of any

(Document continued on next page)

15. The number of days, in words and numbers, during which the Buyer must fix any default of which the Seller has provided written notice (typically 10 or 15 days but may be longer or shorter as the parties might agree).

fuel, utility or telephone charges. Buyer agrees that he will contract separately and in his own name with the supplier(s) for fuel, utility or telephone, that he will pay all such costs when due and that he will not permit or take any act which may result in the creation of a lien against the Premises.

Buyer agrees not to remove or alter any portion of the real property, buildings or improvements, fixtures, equipment or personal property included in this sale (the Premises) without the express written consent of Seller and further agrees to neither commit nor permit any waste to the Premises. Buyer specifically agrees to maintain heat in and to the Premises so as to protect the Premises from the elements and agrees that Seller may use all or a portion of any amount previously paid for such purpose as Seller may deem necessary.

During the term of this agreement, and if Buyer is not in default of any of his obligations, Seller agrees that he will not further or in the future encumber or mortgage the Premises nor take any act which will result in an increase in the previously mentioned costs, nor will Seller undertake or perform any work on or to the Premises which may result in creation of a mechanic's lien against the Premises without the express written consent of Buyer. Buyer agrees that he will not further or in the future encumber or mortgage the Premises nor take any act which will result in an increase in the previously mentioned costs, nor will Buyer undertake or perform any work on or to the Premises which may result in creation of a mechanic's lien against the Premises without the express written consent of Seller.

Buyer shall be entitled to possession of the Premises upon Seller's signing of this agreement and may continue in possession while not in default of any of Buyer's obligations. If Buyer has not defaulted (or has after notice, timely cured any default) and has paid all sums required by this agreement, Seller shall deliver to Buyer the deed conveying title to the Premises.

IN THE EVENT OF DEFAULT BY BUYER WHICH SHALL REMAIN UNCURED FOR ___[15]___ (__) DAYS AFTER WRITTEN NOTICE TO BUYER, BUYER SHALL FORFEIT POSSESSION AND AS WELL SHALL FORFEIT ANY AND ALL MONIES PREVIOUSLY PAID ON ACCOUNT OF THIS AGREEMENT, WHETHER AS RENT OR AS A PORTION OF THE PURCHASE PRICE.

CONTRACT CLAUSE—
TITLE SUBJECT TO EXISTING MORTGAGE (2-12)

Most, but not all, mortgages contain a so-called "due on sale" provision requiring that the Mortgage must be paid off at the time the property is sold. This clause may be disregarded if the Seller's Mortgage contains such a provision.

This clause *should* be included in the Contract for Sale of Residence if the Seller's Mortgage is *not* to be satisfied and discharged (paid off) at or prior to the closing since a lien on the property will remain until the existing Mortgage is paid off.

CONTRACT CLAUSE—
TITLE SUBJECT TO EXISTING MORTGAGE

[1] EXISTING MORTGAGE - The Premises will be sold to Buyer subject to the lien of existing mortgage(s) as follows: a __[2]__ mortgage held by ________[3]_______ now in the unpaid principal amount of approximately $_____[4]_____ with interest at the rate of __[5]__ percent per year payable in monthly installments of $____[6]____, which include principal, interest and ________[7]_______, and with the balance of principal and interest due and payable on ________[8]________. If there is a mortgage escrow account held for the payment of taxes, insurance or other expenses, Seller agrees, if permitted by the holder, to assign same to Buyer, and Buyer agrees to pay the amount of the escrow account to the Seller at the closing.

The Seller agrees that: (a) only the payments required by the Existing Mortgage will be made; (b) no existing Mortgage contains any provision allowing the holder of the mortgage to require its immediate payment in full or to change any interest rate or other terms by reason of the transfer of title or closing, or Seller will pay, discharge and satisfy in full such existing mortgage at or before the closing; and (c) any existing mortgage will not be in default at the time of closing.

Mortgage Estoppel Certificate - Seller agrees to deliver to Buyer at closing, in such form as may be recorded, dated not more than 30 days before closing and signed by the holder of each existing mortgage, a certificate certifying the amount of the unpaid principal and interest, date of maturity, and rate of interest. Seller agrees to pay the fees for recording the certificate.

1. The number of this clause when inserted into the Contract for Sale of Residence.

2. Identify the Seller's existing Mortgage, for example: "First," "Second" or the like which will exist after the closing.

3. The name of the holder of the existing Mortgage.

4. The principal balance, in numbers, of the existing Mortgage remaining due at the closing.

5. The annual rate of interest, in numbers, of the existing Mortgage.

6. The amount of the monthly installments, in numbers, of the existing Mortgage.

7. Insert other components of the monthly installments such as real property taxes, water and sewer bills, insurance or the like.

8. The maturity date of the existing Mortgage.

CONTRACT CLAUSE—
BUYER TO ASSUME EXISTING MORTGAGE (2-13)

This clause should be included in the Contract for Sale of Residence if the Seller's existing Mortgage is to be assumed by the Buyer so that after the closing the Buyer will make all payments. The terms of the Seller's existing Mortgage must be reviewed to determine if an assignment by the Seller of the existing Mortgage will be permitted by the holder of the Seller's Mortgage. The Seller must also determine whether an assumption of his existing Mortgage actually relieves him of any further obligation, or whether it merely gives the holder of the Mortgage the right to go after the Seller *and* the Buyer in the event of non-payment. If the Seller were to remain obligated, he might decide not to permit his Mortgage to be assigned.

CONTRACT CLAUSE—
BUYER TO ASSUME EXISTING MORTGAGE

1. The number of this clause when inserted into the Contract for Sale of Residence.

2. Identify the Seller's existing Mortgage, for example: "First," "Second" or the like that will exist after the closing.

3. The name of the holder of the existing Mortgage.

4. The principal balance, in numbers, remaining due on the existing Mortgage at the time of the closing.

5. The annual rate of interest, in numbers, of the existing Mortgage.

6. The amount of the monthly installments, in numbers, of the existing Mortgage.

7. A description of other items, such as real property taxes, water and sewer bills, insurance or the like, which are included in the monthly bill.

8. The maturity date of the existing Mortgage.

[1] BUYER TO ASSUME EXISTING MORTGAGE - As a portion of the purchase price, Seller agrees to assign and Buyer agrees to assume and, commencing with the date of the closing, to pay as required and save Seller harmless from the existing mortgage(s) as follows: a ____[2]____ mortgage held by ________[3]________ now in the unpaid principal amount of approximately $_____[4]_____ with interest at the rate of __[5]__ percent per year payable in monthly installments of $_____[6]_____, which include principal, interest, and ____________[7]____________, and with the balance of principal and interest due and payable on ________[8]________. If there is a mortgage escrow account held for the payment of taxes, insurance or other expenses, Seller agrees, if permitted by the holder, to assign same to Buyer, and Buyer agrees to pay the amount of the escrow account to the Seller at the closing.

The parties acknowledge that the assignment by Seller and the assumption by Buyer of the existing mortgage is subject to the written consent to the assignment and assumption by the holder of the existing mortgage. Buyer and Seller agree to execute such documents, consents, authorizations and the like as may be required by the holder of the existing mortgage. Buyer agrees to pay all costs, charges and fees associated with any credit, judgment and lien searches as may be required by the holder and also agrees to pay all recording fees, mortgage taxes and the like.

CONTRACT CLAUSE—
BUYER TO OBTAIN MORTGAGE COMMITMENT
(MORTGAGE CONTINGENCY) (2-14)

This clause should be included in the Contract for Sale of Residence if any portion of the purchase price will be paid by a loan to the Buyer from a bank or other lending institution and the sale will be abandoned if the Buyer cannot obtain such a loan. Typically, the bank will issue a document called a "commitment" by which it is committing to make a loan at the closing. This clause provides that the Buyer has a fixed period of time to apply to a bank and that he has an additional fixed period of time to receive the commitment and further, that if he does not receive the commitment *and* advises the Seller in writing, the deal is off and the deposit is refunded to the Buyer. If the Buyer does not notify the Seller in writing that he has not been able to obtain the commitment, this "bail-out" is considered waived and the Buyer will be obligated to close. If the Buyer cannot close, he will forfeit his deposit.

CONTRACT CLAUSE—
BUYER TO OBTAIN MORTGAGE COMMITMENT
(MORTGAGE CONTINGENCY)

1. The number of this clause when inserted into the Contract for Sale of Residence.

2. The state in which the property is located.

3. The amount of the loan sought by the Buyer, in words and numbers.

4. The county in which the property is located.

5. The period of time in which the Buyer will have to apply for the loan (typically five business days).

[1] MORTGAGE CONTINGENCY - This sale and the obligations of the Buyer are subject to and conditioned upon the Buyer obtaining a commitment for a loan secured by a mortgage on the Premises pursuant to which any commercial or savings bank, savings and loan association, insurance company, financing company or other lender licensed to transact business in the state of _____[2]_____ shall agree to lend not less than ________[3]________ Dollars ($________) at not more than the prevailing interest rate for such loans offered by such lenders within the County of _____[4]_____ to non-depositors, for a term of not more than thirty (30) years, the proceeds of which loan are to be applied towards the purchase price. Such mortgage shall be obtained by Buyer at his sole cost and expense.

Buyer shall apply for such mortgage and shall furnish to the lending institution within _____[5]_____ after receipt of this agreement as signed by Seller such complete financial information as may be required by the lending institution and at the same time pay such fee as may be required. Buyer shall advise Seller of the name(s) and address(es) of such lending institution(s) to which application has been made and the date(s) of making of such applications.

Buyer shall accept any commitment complying with the terms of this paragraph and agrees to pay all application, appraisal, commitment, origination and other fees as

(Document continued on next page)

CONTRACT CLAUSE— BUYER TO OBTAIN MORTGAGE COMMITMENT (MORTGAGE CONTINGENCY) *continued*

6. The date by which the Buyer must have obtained the loan commitment (typically 30 to 45 days from the date of the Buyer's receipt of the signed contract from the Seller).

may be required and to promptly comply with the requirements of the commitment.

Provided that Buyer shall have fulfilled all of Buyer's obligations as contained in this paragraph, if such commitment is not obtained by ________[6]________, Buyer shall have the right to terminate this agreement on written notice given not more than five (5) days thereafter, and in such event, the deposit or down-payment paid by Buyer shall be refunded to Buyer without interest and this agreement shall terminate and neither party shall have any further obligation or liability to the other.

In the event, however, that Buyer shall fail to give such timely written notice of termination, this condition regarding the obtaining of a commitment shall be deemed waived.

CONTRACT CLAUSE— FIXTURES AND OTHER PERSONAL PROPERTY INCLUDED IN SALE (2-15)

This clause should be included in the Contract for Sale of Residence if there are any fixtures (such as equipment that may be an integral part of the operation of the residence or physically attached to the residence) or personal property, including furniture, that is made part of the sale. This clause should also be used to specifically *exclude* any fixtures or personal property that are *not* part of the sale. Experience has taught that this provision should list as much as possible (both included and excluded items) to avoid surprises at the closing.

CONTRACT CLAUSE— FIXTURES AND OTHER PERSONAL PROPERTY INCLUDED IN SALE

1. The number of this clause when inserted into the Contract for Sale of Residence.

2. Delete and add items as appropriate.

3. Delete and add items as appropriate.

[1] FIXTURES/PERSONAL PROPERTY - Included in this sale are all fixtures and articles of personal property attached to or used in connection with the Premises, unless specifically excluded. The Seller represents that the fixtures and personal property are paid for and owned by the Seller free and clear of any security interests or liens other than the existing mortgage(s).

Fixtures and personal property included in this sale are, but are not limited to: *[2]heating, air conditioning, plumbing, electrical and lighting fixtures, bathroom and kitchen fixtures and cabinets, storm windows and doors, screens, shades, venetian blinds, awnings, window boxes, mail boxes, wall-to-wall carpets, mantels, sump pumps, well pump, shrubbery, fences, exterior sheds, ranges, refrigerators, freezers, washing machines, clothes dryers, dishwashers, garbage disposal units, drapery and curtain hardware and rods,* ______________________________

____

____.

Not included in this sale are the following: [3]furniture, household furnishings, ______________________________

____

____.

CONTRACT CLAUSE—
SALE SUBJECT TO (STATEMENT OF PERMITTED ENCUMBRANCES) (2-16)

This clause sets forth the permitted exceptions to giving clear title. It should be included in the Contract for Sale of Residence so that the Seller cannot be held to sell something that he cannot sell because he does not have "ownership" or control of it. An example would be a stoop which may extend past the Seller's property line and "encroach" on the next door neighbor's property but to which the neighbor has never objected. The insertion of this clause will allow the sale to go through even though the Seller cannot "sell" that portion of the land underneath the stoop that is his neighbor's property (and also will allow the Seller to avoid the expense of removal of the stoop and construction of a "legal" stoop). The Seller does not want the Buyer to be able to back out of the sale because the Seller cannot give clear title.

CONTRACT CLAUSE—
SALE SUBJECT TO (STATEMENT OF PERMITTED ENCUMBRANCES)

1. The number of this clause when inserted into the Contract for Sale of Residence.

2. Insert such other matters that may "run with the land" and which the Seller must sell to the Buyer, such as utility or power company easements. These can be found in the Seller's deed. Otherwise delete this section and the preceding "; and."

[1] SALE SUBJECT TO/STATEMENT OF PERMITTED ENCUMBRANCES - The premises are sold and are to be transferred subject to:

(a) laws and government regulations that affect the use and maintenance of the Premises, provided that they are not violated by the building and improvements existing on the Premises or by their current use;

(b) the consent by the Seller or any former owner of the premises for the erection of any structure(s) on, under, or above any street or streets on which the Premises abuts;

(c) encroachments of stoops, areas, cellar steps, trim, and cornices, if any, upon any street or highway;

(d) any state of facts an accurate survey may show, provided same does not render title unmarketable; and

(e) covenants and restrictions of record, if any, provided the existing use of the property does not violate such covenants or restrictions*; and*

*[2] (f)*______________________________________

____

____

CONTRACT CLAUSE—
TITLE REPORT/MATTERS/OBJECTIONS (2-17)

This clause should be included in the Contract for Sale of Residence if the Buyer plans on obtaining a title inspection or report and title insurance. Even if the Buyer does not want title insurance, invariably the bank that is financing the purchase will insist on it (at least to the extent of the loan). This clause also gives the Seller an "out." If he chooses he may (but isn't required to) correct problems with the title, but may choose to terminate the contract instead.

CONTRACT CLAUSE—
TITLE REPORT/MATTERS/OBJECTIONS

1. The number of this clause when inserted into the Contract for Sale of Residence.

2. The county in which the property is located.

3. The party who will obtain the title report (typically the Buyer, since he will want to or be required to obtain title insurance).

4. The party who will be given a copy of the title report (typically the Seller).

5. The date by which the title report must be given to the party in No. 4.

[1] TITLE REPORT/MATTERS/OBJECTIONS - Seller will give and Buyer agrees to accept such title as any licensed title company with an office in the County of _____[2]_____ will be willing to approve and insure in accordance with the standard form of title policy issued by such company, subject only to those matters provided for in this agreement.

________[3]________ shall apply for and obtain and pay all costs and fees for and shall furnish to ________[4]________, on or before ________[5]_______, a complete abstract of title to the Premises current and up to date through the date of signing the contract and certified as correct by such title company that Seller has good and marketable title to the Premises free and clear of all encumbrances except those specifically stated in this contract. Both the Buyer and the Seller will be allowed a reasonable time for examination of any title report after the date of receipt by that party, the attorney of that party's selection, or a title company of that party's selection.

If Seller shall be unable to deliver to Buyer good and marketable title in accordance with this Contract but subject to those matters set forth in this Contract, Seller shall not be required to bring any action or proceeding or otherwise incur any expense to make title marketable. If Buyer shall refuse such title as Seller can deliver, Seller may rescind this contract and refund to Buyer the deposit, without interest, and if incurred by Buyer, the charges and fees for the examination of title to the Premises and this agreement shall terminate and neither party shall have any obligation or liability to the other.

CONTRACT CLAUSE— PROPERTY SOLD "AS IS" (2-18)

This clause should be included in the Contract for Sale of Residence as protection to the Seller since it puts the burden on the Buyer to inspect and evaluate the property, fixtures and personal property included in the sale. In effect, this provision tells the Buyer that "what you see is what you get" and nothing more.

Also, note that this clause contains the Seller's representation to the Buyer that the building and major systems are in working order. The Seller should resist giving such a representation but may have to if the Buyer refuses to sign the contract without it.

CONTRACT CLAUSE— PROPERTY SOLD "AS IS"

1. The number of this clause when inserted into the Contract for Sale of Residence.

2. Choose one.

3. Delete if not required by the Buyer.

[1] PROPERTY SOLD "AS IS" - Buyer acknowledges that he has *[2][inspected]* ***OR*** *[had full opportunity to inspect]* the buildings and improvements and all personal property included in this sale and is fully acquainted with their condition. Buyer agrees to purchase the Premises, the buildings and improvements and all personal property strictly "AS IS" and in their present condition subject only to reasonable use, wear and tear and natural deterioration between now and date of closing.

[3][Seller represents that the plumbing, heating/air conditioning and electrical systems and any appliances included in this sale will be in working order on the date of the closing.]

Buyer shall have the right, upon reasonable notice to Seller, to inspect the Premises, the buildings and improvements and all personal property during the twenty-four (24) hour period before closing.

CONTRACT CLAUSE—
PEST/ENGINEER'S INSPECTION (2-19)

This clause should be included in the Contract for Sale of Residence if the Buyer insists upon either a termite inspection or engineer's inspection of the property. In the event that the Buyer insists upon one but not the other, delete the appropriate sub-paragraph.

CONTRACT CLAUSE—
PEST/ENGINEER'S INSPECTION

1. The number of this clause when inserted into the Contract for Sale of Residence.

[1] PEST/ENGINEER'S INSPECTION - Buyer shall have ten (10) days from the date of receipt of this contract as signed by the Seller to obtain at Buyer's sole cost and expense:

(a) Termite/pest/infestation inspection. If the termite, pest and infestation inspection report indicates the presence of such infestation, Seller shall have the option of: (i) eliminating the infestation at Seller's sole cost and expense; or (ii) cancelling this contract by return of the down payment made by Buyer. Written notice of the Seller's intent to exercise either option shall be served upon Buyer within ten (10) days of receipt of such report.

(b) A physical inspection of the Premises, buildings and improvements and all fixtures and personal property included in this sale by a qualified engineer, architect or the like. If the engineer's report indicates structural or mechanical deficiencies, Seller shall have the option of: (i) correcting all or some deficiencies at Seller's sole cost and expense prior to the closing (and closing may be adjourned for this purpose at Seller's option); (ii) allowing a credit against the purchase price to be paid by Buyer in an amount equal to the reasonable estimate obtained by Buyer to correct all or some of the deficiencies; (iii) a combination of either of the foregoing; or (iv) cancelling this contract. Written notice of the Seller's intent to exercise any option shall be served upon Buyer within ten (10) days of receipt of such report.

If Seller shall elect to terminate this Contract, the deposit previously paid by Buyer upon signing this Contract shall be refunded and neither party shall have any further obligation or liability to the other.

CONTRACT CLAUSE—
DUTY TO APPORTION TAXES, FUEL OIL, ETC. (2-20)

This clause should be included in the Contract for Sale of Residence if there are any charges or costs for the property for which payments will have been made prior to the closing but which cover a period subsequent to the closing. The classic example of such a charge is real estate tax, typically paid annually or semi-annually. The closing, of course, rarely takes place on the first day of the new tax period. Since the Seller will have moved out in the middle of the tax period, he will be entitled to a credit for the real estate taxes already paid for the period from the closing until the end of the period that his tax payment covers. This payment will be apportioned.

CONTRACT CLAUSE—
DUTY TO APPORTION TAXES, FUEL OIL, ETC.

1. The number of this clause when inserted into the Contract for Sale of Residence.

2. Insert any other charges that are to be apportioned. If there are none, delete this section and the preceding "; and."

[1] APPORTIONMENTS - Items to be apportioned. The following are to be apportioned as of midnight of the day before closing:

(a) rents as and when collected;

(b) interest on existing mortgage(s);

(c) premiums on existing transferable insurance policies or renewals of those expiring prior to the closing;

(d) taxes, water charges, and sewer rents, if any, on the basis of the fiscal year for which assessed;

(e) fuel, if any*; and*

*[2] (f)*______________________________________
____
____.

If the closing shall occur before a new tax rate is fixed, the apportionment of taxes shall be upon the basis of the old tax rate for the preceding period applied to the latest assessed valuation.

Any errors or omissions in computing apportionments of any of the above items at closing shall be corrected, and this provision shall survive closing.

CONTRACT CLAUSE—
PROPERTY TO BE INSURED AGAINST LOSS (2-21)

This clause should be included in the Contract for Sale of Residence to provide for insurance to cover any loss, damage or destruction to the property between the signing of the contract and the closing. This clause provides that the Seller will pay the cost of the insurance.

CONTRACT CLAUSE—
PROPERTY TO BE INSURED AGAINST LOSS

[1] PROPERTY INSURED AGAINST LOSS - Until the closing of title as provided in this agreement, Seller shall pay all premiums and costs necessary and shall keep and maintain all of the buildings and improvements on and to the property and including all fixtures, equipment and personal property included in this sale (the Premises), insured against loss, damage, destruction by fire, hazard, vandalism, liability and other insurable casualty in an amount of not less than ________[2]________ Dollars ($________) . The policy(s) of insurance shall be maintained with a reputable insurance company licensed to transact business in the state of _____[3]_____ and shall provide that in the event of a claim, the loss-payee who shall receive benefits shall be either or both Seller and Buyer to the extent of their respective interests in the Premises.

1. The number of this clause when inserted into the Contract for Sale of Residence.

2. The amount of insurance coverage to be maintained, in words and numbers. This amount should be at least as much as the sale price of the property, but full replacement coverage is the more prudent approach.

3. The state in which the property is located.

CONTRACT CLAUSE— PROPERTY DAMAGED OR DESTROYED (2-22)

Neither a Seller nor a Buyer likes to think about what would happen if the property were damaged or destroyed between the signing of the contract and the closing. But both the Seller and the Buyer should. Many states have laws that provide for this situation. If a contract does not specifically deal with this potential problem, your state's law may. However, the parties to a contract are free to fashion their own remedies.

This clause sets forth one method for dealing with the problem of loss or damage to the property and should be included in the Contract for Sale of Residence if your state's law does not establish any method or if you wish to fashion your own.

CONTRACT CLAUSE— PROPERTY DAMAGED OR DESTROYED

1. The number of this clause when inserted into the Contract for Sale of Residence.

2. The number of days (typically five), in words and numbers, that the Seller will have for giving notice of the loss or destruction to the Buyer.

3. The number of days, in words and numbers, that the Seller will have to complete the repair or replacement. The parties may agree on a shorter or longer period depending on the Seller's estimate of the time such repair/replacement is likely to take. However, 60 days is the typical period since at the time of signing the contract the parties do not know what kind or degree of repair or replacement would be required.

[1] RISK OF LOSS OR DAMAGE - The risk of loss or damage to the Premises, or to the fixtures, equipment and personal property included in this sale, by fire or other cause, until the time of the closing, is assumed by Seller, but without any obligation on the part of Seller, except at Seller's option, to repair or replace any such loss or damage. Seller shall have the option to elect to make either repair or replacement. Seller shall notify Buyer of the loss or damage within ___[2]___ (__) days after the occurrence or by the date of closing, whichever occurs first. Seller's notice to Buyer will also advise Buyer whether or not Seller will repair or replace the loss or damage and if Seller elects to do so, that he will complete the repair or replacement within ___[3]___ (__) days and the closing will be adjourned for this purpose and without cost or penalty to either Seller or Buyer. If Seller elects to make repair/replacement, Seller's notice will also state the adjourned date for the closing.

If Seller does not elect to make repair/replacement, or if Seller elects to make repair/replacement but fails to complete same before the adjourned closing date, Buyer shall advise Seller of Buyer's option of either:

(i) declaring this agreement cancelled in which event the deposit or down-payment paid by Buyer shall be refunded to Buyer without interest and neither party shall have any further obligation or liability to the other; or

(ii) completing the purchase in accordance with this agreement without reduction in the purchase price except that if Seller's insurance covers the loss or damage, Seller shall turn over to Buyer at the closing the net proceeds (after legal and other expenses of collection) actually

(Document continued on next page)

4. The number of days, in words and numbers, that the Buyer will have to notify the Seller as to what the Buyer intends to do.

collected by Seller under the provisions of any insurance policies to the extent that they are attributable to the loss or damage to any property included in this sale and if Seller has not received such proceeds Seller shall assign (without recourse to Seller) Seller's insurance attributable to the loss or damage to any property included in this sale, less any sums expended by Seller.

Buyer's option, whether resulting from either: (i) Seller's election to not make repair/replacement, or (ii) Seller's failure, within the time provided, to make repair/replacement despite having elected to do so, shall be exercised within ___[4]___ (__) days of the earlier of: (i) Seller having advised Buyer of Seller's election to not make repair/replacement, or (ii) Seller's assignment of any insurance proceeds. Buyer's option resulting from Seller's failure to timely make repair/replacement shall be exercised within ___[4]___ (__) days of the adjourned closing date.

CONTRACT CLAUSE— DEPOSIT TO BE HELD IN ESCROW (2-23)

This clause should be included in the Contract for Sale of Residence if the deposit or down-payment paid by the Buyer when he signs the contract will not be given outright to the Seller until the closing but is to be held in escrow until then. Any third party selected by both the Seller and the Buyer can hold the funds (act as Escrow Agent), for example: an attorney (even the Seller's attorney, but not the Buyer's attorney), a title or abstract company, or even a bank if the parties open an account which requires both of their signatures for any withdrawals. Neither of the parties themselves should act as the Escrow Agent since, in the event of a default, neither party would want the defaulting party to be holding the deposit.

Note that the Escrow Agent must consent to being appointed as Escrow Agent. This consent is indicated by the Escrow Agent signing the contract under the words "I hereby agree to act as Escrow Agent," typically on the same page as the parties' signatures appear.

CONTRACT CLAUSE— DEPOSIT TO BE HELD IN ESCROW

1. The number of this clause when inserted into the Contract for Sale of Residence.

2. The amount, in words and numbers, of the deposit or down-payment that will be held in escrow. This amount should be the same as appears in the Contract for Sale of Residence (typically, but not necessarily, 10% of the purchase price).

3. Delete if the escrow funds will not be held in an interest bearing account. This is a negotiable term between the parties and must also be agreed to by the Escrow Agent. It is usually dependent on the sum of money involved and the length of time between contract signing and closing.

4. The name of the Escrow Agent.

5. The address of the Escrow Agent.

6. The state where the property is located.

7. Delete if the Escrow Agent is not the Seller's attorney.

[1] DEPOSIT TO BE HELD IN ESCROW - The sum of ________[2]________ Dollars ($________) (the "Escrow Fund") paid by Buyer as a deposit and on account of the purchase price shall be held in escrow in an *[3][interest bearing]* account maintained by ________[4]________, with office at __________[5]__________, (the "Escrow Agent"), until the closing or sooner termination of this agreement. In the event of a default by Buyer, the Escrow Fund shall be paid over to Seller as liquidated damages. In the event that this sale is not closed for any other reason, the Escrow Fund shall be refunded to Buyer. Interest, if any, earned by the Escrow Fund shall be paid to the party entitled to and who actually does receive the Escrow Fund. In the event that there shall be a dispute as to whether Seller or Buyer is entitled to all or part of the Escrow Funds, and the Escrow Agent shall have received written notice of the dispute, then the Escrow Agent may retain the Escrow Fund until the dispute is settled or may deposit the Escrow Fund into a court of competent jurisdiction in the state of ____[6]_____ (which court the parties agree shall have jurisdiction) and the Escrow Agent shall be released thereby from any and all obligations and liability for the Escrow Funds. In no event shall the Escrow Agent incur any liability of any kind hereunder for any act done or step taken or omitted by him or for any mistake of fact or law, except for the Escrow Agent's own willful misconduct or malfeasance. *[7][The Escrow Agent shall have the right to represent Seller in any dispute with respect to the Escrow Fund or otherwise.]*

CONTRACT CLAUSE— SELLER TO PAY BROKERAGE COMMISSION (2-24)

This clause should be included in the Contract for Sale of Residence even if there was no broker who brought about the sale since it protects both the Seller and the Buyer. Note that this clause provides that the Seller will pay the broker's commission since the law in most states is that the broker is the agent for the Seller and not the Buyer.

CONTRACT CLAUSE— SELLER TO PAY BROKERAGE COMMISSION

1. The number of this clause when inserted into the Contract for Sale of Residence.

2. Delete to the end of this paragraph if no broker brought about the sale.

3. The name of the broker.

4. The address of the broker.

[1] REAL ESTATE BROKER - Buyer represents to Seller that Buyer has not dealt with any real estate broker in connection with this purchase *[2][other than ________[3]________, located at _________[4]________ and Seller agrees to pay the commission as earned by said broker as more fully stated in a separate brokerage commission agreement. Buyer agrees to indemnify and hold Seller harmless from and against any and all liability, cost and expense (including reasonable attorneys' fees and disbursements) which may be incurred by Seller as a result of a claim for brokerage commission or other compensation made by any other broker who has dealt with Buyer in connection with this transaction. The provisions of this paragraph shall survive the closing or earlier termination of this agreement].*

CONTRACT CLAUSE—
OPTION TO CANCEL (2-25)

A Seller does not want to give a real estate Buyer an option to cancel. However, a Buyer may insist on such right or refuse to sign the contract. This clause should be included in the Contract for Sale of Residence if the Buyer insists on such an option.

CONTRACT CLAUSE—
OPTION TO CANCEL

[1] OPTION TO CANCEL - Within ___[2]___ (__) business days of the later of the signing of this contract or the date of actual receipt of this contract by Buyer as signed by Seller, Buyer may by written notice, cancel this agreement for any reason. Written notice, postmarked not later than the last day of the cancellation period, shall be sent to Seller by registered or certified mail, return receipt requested. Seller shall immediately refund to Buyer the deposit or down-payment paid on signing the contract and upon such refund this agreement shall terminate and neither party will have any further obligation or liability to the other.

1. The number of this clause when inserted into the Contract for Sale of Residence.

2. The number of business days, in words and numbers, that the Buyer will have to exercise his right to cancel (typically 3). Note: the law in most states is that legal holidays (either federal or state) do not count as business days.

MORTGAGE NOTE (Fixed Rate) (2-26)

A Note documents a loan from a Lender to a Borrower. A Mortgage Note is a special type of Note in which the Borrower gives to the Lender security (collateral) in the form of an interest in the Borrower's real property. This interest is known as a Mortgage. The property owner who is borrowing the money and giving this security interest is called the Mortgagor. The Lender is called the Mortgagee.

This form provides for a loan to be repaid at a fixed rate of interest over the entire term of the mortgage, with fixed payments. The loan contemplated by this Note is self-liquidating, meaning that the last payment will pay off the loan in full and without the need for a so-called "balloon" payment at the end.

This Mortgage Note also contains a "due on sale" provision. This provides that in the event of a sale of the property by the Mortgagor he must "satisfy" (pay off) his mortgage at or before the closing of the sale.

This form is presented with consumer protection laws and "plain language" laws in mind. It is similar to the one approved by both the Federal National Mortgage Administration (FNMA) and the Federal Home Loan Mortgage Corporation (FHLMC) and has been adopted by an increasing number of banks.

WARNING

A Note is the primary and only true evidence of a loan having been made. As with any Note, the Borrower should sign only one Mortgage Note, since multiple original Notes have the legal effect of multiple loans.

MORTGAGE NOTE (Fixed Rate)

U.S.$________[1]________ __________[2]__________

__________[3]__________

1. The principal amount of the loan, in numbers.

2. The city and state in which the loan is made.

3. The date of signing the loan.

(Document continued on next page)

4. The address of the property.

5. The city and state in which the property is located.

6. The county in which the property is located.

Note: the information for Nos. 7 through 9 is typically found on the Seller's deed or the tax map of the property located in the office of the local tax authority.

7. The Section in which the property is located.

8. The Block in which the property is located.

9. The Lot(s) in which the property is located.

10. The principal amount of the loan, in words and numbers.

11. The name of the Lender.

12. The address of the Lender.

13. The annual percentage rate, in numbers, of the loan.

14. The month and year during which the first full monthly payment of principal and interest is to be made. (Note: interest is paid only after it is earned—the first full monthly payment will be made starting with the *second* month after the closing, but will be for the prior 30-day period. For example, if the closing is on April 21st, at the closing a payment of interest only will be made for the period April 21 through April 30 and the first full payment of both principal and interest will be made on June 1, with the interest portion of the June 1 payment being for the period May 1 through May 31.)

Property Address:	Tax Map Designation:
__________[4]_________	Section:_______[7]______
__________[5]_________	Block: _______[8]______
County of _____[6]______	Lot(s) ________[9]______

1. BORROWER'S PROMISE TO PAY - In return for a loan that I have received, I promise to pay the sum of ________[10]________ U.S. Dollars ($________) , which is called "Principal," plus interest, to the order of the Lender. The Lender is ________[11]________, residing at __________[12]__________. I understand that the Lender may transfer this Note. The Lender or anyone who takes this Note by transfer and who is entitled to receive payments under this Note is called the "Note Holder."

2. INTEREST - Interest will be charged on unpaid principal until the full amount of principal has been paid. I will pay interest at a yearly rate of ___[13]___%.

The interest rate required by this Section 2 is the rate I will pay both before and after any default described in Section 6(B) of this Note.

3. PAYMENTS

(A) TIME AND PLACE OF PAYMENT - Except when this Note is dated the first (1st) day of the month, I will make a payment of interest only from the date of this Note to the first day of the following month. I will pay principal and interest by making payments every month. I will make my monthly payments on the first (1st) day of each month beginning with ________[14]________, 19__. I will make these payments every month until I have paid all of the principal and interest and any other charges described below that I may owe under this Note. My monthly payments will be applied to interest before princi-

(Document continued on next page)

15. The month and year during which the last full payment of interest and principal is to be made.

16. The address where the payments are to be made or mailed.

17. The dollar amount of each monthly payment, in numbers.

18. The number of days, in words and numbers, of the allowed "grace" period (typically 15 days).

19. Choose one and fill in the amount. A late charge may be expressed as either a fixed dollar amount or as a percentage of the payment due.

pal. If, on the first (1st) of ________[15]________, 19__, I still owe amounts under this Note, I will pay those amounts in full on that date, which is called the "Maturity Date."

I will make my monthly payments at __________[16]__________, or at a different place if required by the Note Holder.

(B) AMOUNT OF MONTHLY PAYMENTS - My monthly payments will be in the amount of U.S.$_____[17]_____.

4. BORROWER'S RIGHT TO PREPAY - I have the right to make payments of principal at any time before they are due. A payment of principal only is known as a "prepayment." When I make a prepayment, I will tell the Note Holder in writing that I am doing so. I may make a full prepayment or partial prepayments without paying a prepayment charge. The Note Holder will use all of my prepayments to reduce the amount of principal that I owe under this Note. If I make a partial prepayment, there will be no changes in the due date or in the amount of my monthly payments unless the Note Holder agrees in writing to those changes.

5. LOAN CHARGES - If a law, which applies to this loan and which sets maximum loan charges, is finally interpreted so that the interest or other loan charges collected or to be collected in connection with this loan exceed the permitted limits, then: (i) any such loan charge shall be reduced by the amount necessary to reduce the charge to the permitted limit; and (ii) any sums already collected from me which exceeded permitted limits will be refunded to me. The Note Holder may choose to make this refund by reducing the principal I owe under this Note or by making a direct payment to me. If a refund reduces principal, the reduction will be treated as a partial prepayment.

6. BORROWER'S FAILURE TO PAY AS REQUIRED

(A) LATE CHARGES FOR OVERDUE PAYMENTS - if the Note holder has not received the full amount of any monthly payment by the end of ___[18]___ (__) calendar days after the date it is due, I will pay a late charge to the Note Holder. The amount of the late charge will be *[19][$________]* ***OR*** *[__%]* of my overdue payment of principal and interest]. I will pay this late charge promptly but only once on each late payment.

(Document continued on next page)

(B) DEFAULT - If I do not pay the full amount of each monthly payment on the date it is due, I will be in default.

(C) NOTICE OF DEFAULT - If I am in default, the Note Holder may send me a written notice telling me that if I do not pay the overdue amount by a certain date, the Note Holder may require me to pay immediately the full amount of principal which has not been paid and all the interest that I owe on that amount. That date must be at least 30 days after the date on which the notice is delivered or mailed to me.

(D) NO WAIVER BY NOTE HOLDER - Even if, at a time when I am in default, the Note Holder does not require me to pay immediately in full as described above, the Note Holder will still have the right to do so if I am in default at a later time.

(E) PAYMENT OF NOTE HOLDER'S COSTS AND EXPENSES - If the Note Holder has required me to pay immediately in full as described above, the Note Holder will have the right to be paid back by me for all of its costs and expenses in enforcing this Note to the extent not prohibited by applicable law. Those expenses include, for example, reasonable attorneys' fees.

7. GIVING OF NOTICES - Unless applicable law requires a different method, any notice that must be given to me under this Note will be given by delivering it or by mailing it by first class mail to me at the Property Address above or at a different address if I give the Note Holder a notice of my different address. Any notice that must be given to the Note Holder under this Note will be given by mailing it first class mail to the Note Holder at the address stated in Section 3(A) above or at a different place if I am given notice of that different address.

8. OBLIGATIONS OF PERSONS UNDER THIS NOTE - If more than one person signs this Note, each person is fully and personally obligated to keep all of the promises made in this Note, including the promise to pay the full amount owed. Any person who is a guarantor, surety or endorser of this Note is also obligated to do these things. Any person who takes over these obligations, including the obligations of a guarantor, surety or endorser of this Note, is also obligated to keep all of the promises made in this

(Document continued on next page)

Note. The Note Holder may enforce its rights under this Note against each person individually or against all of us together. This means that any one of us may be required to pay all of the amounts owed under this Note.

9. WAIVERS - I and any other person who has obligations under this Note waive the rights of presentment and notice of dishonor. "Presentment" means the right to require the Note Holder to demand payment of amounts due. "Notice of Dishonor" means the right to require the Note Holder to give notice to other persons that amounts due have not been paid. Any guarantor, surety or endorser of this Note also waives these rights.

10. NOTE SECURED BY "SECURITY INSTRUMENT" - This Note is secured by a Mortgage, Deed of Trust or Security Deed (the "Security Instrument") dated the same day as this Note. In addition to the protections given to the Note Holder under this Note, the "Security Instrument" dated the same date as this Note protects the Note Holder from possible losses which might result if I do not keep the promises which I make in this Note.

That Security Instrument describes how and under what conditions I may be required to make immediate payment in full of all amounts I owe under this Note. Among those conditions are described as follows:

(Document continued on next page)

20. The name of the Witness to the signing of the Note printed below the line, with the Witness to sign above the line.

21. The name of the Borrower(s) printed below the line, with the Borrower(s) to sign above the line. Delete the second line if only one Borrower.

22. A Notary completes this section and affixes his stamp or seal.

TRANSFER OF THE PROPERTY OR BENEFICIAL INTEREST IN BORROWER - If all or any part of the Property or any interest in it is sold or transferred (or if a beneficial interest in Borrower is sold or transferred and Borrower is not a natural person) without Note Holder's prior written consent, Note Holder may, at its option, require immediate payment in full of all sums secured by the Security Instrument. However, this option shall not be exercised by the Note Holder if exercise is prohibited by federal law as of the date of the Security Instrument. If the Note Holder exercises this option, the Note Holder will give Borrower notice of acceleration. This notice shall provide a period of not less than 30 days from the date the notice is delivered or mailed within which Borrower must pay all sums secured by the Security Instrument. If Borrower fails to pay these sums prior to the expiration of this period, the Note Holder may invoke any of the remedies permitted by the Security Instrument without further notice or demand on Borrower.

Witness:

______________________ [20]

______________________ [21] Borrower

______________________ [21] Borrower

STATE OF _____[22]_____, COUNTY OF ________, ss.:

On _________[22]________, 19__, before me a _____[22]_____ personally came _________[22]________, to me known, and known to me to be the individual(s) described in and who executed the foregoing ___________[22]__________, and duly acknowledged to me that (he)(she)(they) executed the same.

______________________ Notary Public

MORTGAGE (2-27)

A Mortgage is an agreement to put up real estate as collateral to secure the repayment of a loan. The owner of the Property who is borrowing the money agrees that his real estate can be used as security for the repayment of the loan in the event of a default. He is called the "Mortgagor." The Lender who agrees to accept the real estate as security for repayment of the loan is called the "Mortgagee." At all times, legal title to the Property remains with the Mortgagor, the Borrower. The Mortgagee will record the Mortgage to alert the public that such collateral in the real estate exists.

This form is similar to the one approved by both the Federal National Mortgage Administration (FNMA) and the Federal Home Loan Mortgage Corporation (FHLMC) and has been adopted by an increasing number of banks. It is a "plain language" type of form.

WARNING

Since the Mortgage is only the security, and not evidence of the loan itself, the Mortgage must be used together with the preceding Mortgage Note.

1. The date of the Mortgage.
2. The name of the Borrower.
3. If the Borrower is a corporation, insert the state of incorporation. Otherwise delete.
4. The Borrower's address.
5. The name of the Lender.
6. If the Lender is a corporation, insert the state of incorporation. Otherwise delete.
7. The Lender's address.
8. The date of the Note. (Note: the date of the Note will most likely be the same as the date of the Mortgage, in No. 1 above, since the Note and the Mortgage are usually signed at the same time.)
9. The principal amount of the loan (the Note amount), in words.
10. The principal amount of the loan, in numbers.
11. The date on which the last payment on the loan is due (the maturity date).

MORTGAGE

WORDS USED IN THIS DOCUMENT

(A) "Security Instrument" and "Mortgage:" This document, which is dated ________[1]________, sometimes called either the "Security Agreement" or the "Mortgage."

(B) "Borrower:" __________[2]__________ *[3][, a corporation organized under the laws of _______,]* sometimes called either "Borrower," "I" or "me." Borrower's address is __________[4]__________.

(C) "Lender:" ________[5]__________ *[6][, a corporation organized under the laws of ________]* sometimes called "Lender." Lender's address is __________[7]__________.

(D) "Note:" The Note signed by the Borrower and dated ________[8]________ will be called the "Note." The Note shows that I owe Lender ________[9]________ U.S. Dollars ($_____[10]_____), plus interest.

I have promised to pay this debt in monthly payments and to pay the debt in full by ________[11]________.

(Document continued on next page)

12. The address of the Property being mortgaged.

13. The city in which the Property being mortgaged is located.

14. The county in which the Property being mortgaged is located.

15. The state in which the Property being mortgaged is located.

16. On a separate sheet, headed "Schedule A," set forth the so-called "metes and bounds" describing the Property being mortgaged by feet and compass direction—which is the best description of the Property. This description and the ones called for in Nos. 17 through 20 are typically found in the Property's original deed. The information should be copied from the Property's original deed EXACTLY.

17. The district number in which the Property is located.

18. The section number in which the Property is located.

19. The block number in which the Property is located.

20. The lot number(s) in which the Property is located.

(E) "Property:" The Property that is described below in the section titled "Description of the Property," will be called the "Property."

(F) "Sums secured:" The amounts described below in the section titled "Borrower's Transfer to Lender of Rights in Property" sometimes will be called the "sums secured."

BORROWER'S TRANSFER TO LENDER OF RIGHTS IN PROPERTY - I mortgage, grant and convey the Property to Lender subject to the terms of this Security Instrument. This means that, by signing this Security Instrument, I am giving Lender those rights that are stated in this Security Instrument and also those rights the law gives to lenders who hold mortgages on real property. I am giving Lender these rights to protect Lender from possible losses if I fail to:

(A) Pay all the amounts that I owe Lender as stated in the Note;

(B) Pay, with interest, any amounts that Lender spends under Paragraphs 2 and 7 of this Security Instrument to protect the value of the Property and Lender's rights in the Property; and

(C) Keep all of my other promises and agreements under this Security Instrument.

DESCRIPTION OF THE PROPERTY - I give Lender rights in the Property described in (A) through (J) below:

(A) The Property which is located at __________[12]__________, in the City of _______[13]_______, County of ______[14]____, State of ________[15]__________.

The Property has the legal description which is more fully stated on the attached [16] SCHEDULE A and as well has the following tax map designation:

District No.: ____[17]____
Section No. ____[18]____
Block No.: ____[19]____
Lot(s) No.: ____[20]____

(Document continued on next page)

21. If the state in which the Property being mortgaged taxes mortgages, the borrower initials the appropriate parentheses for the type of building on the Property. Or add a brief description of the type of building after the word "Other," for example: "Three story commercial property," or the like. Otherwise delete the section.

22. Delete if the mortgage is NOT used to enable the borrower to purchase the Property (if for example, this mortgage is a "refinance," equity loan, second mortgage or the like).

[21][FOR MORTGAGE TAX PURPOSES, Borrowers represent that the within Property is improved by:

( ) A legal one/two family residence
( ) A legal three/four family residence
( ) Other:____________________________

(HAVE BORROWERS INITIAL THE APPROPRIATE BOX)]

[22][BEING the same Property which was conveyed to the Borrower by deed delivered and intended to be recorded simultaneously with this Mortgage. This Mortgage is a purchase money mortgage given to secure a portion of the consideration expressed in said deed.]

(B) All buildings and other improvements that are located on the Property described in subparagraph (A) of this section;

(C) All rights in other property that I have as owner of the Property described in subparagraph (A) of this section. These rights are known as "easements, rights and appurtenances attached to the Property";

(D) All rents or royalties from the Property described in subparagraph (A) of this section;

(E) All mineral, oil, gas rights and profits, water rights and stock that are part of the Property described in subparagraph (A) of this section;

(F) All rights that I have in the land which lies in the streets or roads in front of, or next to, the Property as described in subparagraph (A) of this section;

(G) All fixtures that are now or in the future will be on this Property described in subparagraph (A) of this section;

(H) All of the rights and property described in subparagraphs (B) through (G) of this section that I acquire in the future;

(I) All replacements of or additions to the Property

(Document continued on next page)

described in subparagraphs (B) through (H) of this section; and

(J) All of the amounts that I pay to Lender under Paragraph 2 below.

BORROWER'S RIGHT TO MORTGAGE THE PROPERTY AND BORROWER'S OBLIGATION TO DEFEND OWNERSHIP OF THE PROPERTY - I promise that: (i) I lawfully own the Property; (ii) I have the right to mortgage, grant and convey the Property to Lender; and (iii) there are no outstanding claims or charges against the Property, except for those which are of public record.

I give a general warranty of title to Lender. This means that I will be fully responsible for any losses which Lender suffers because someone other than myself has some of the rights in the Property which I promise that I have. I promise that I will defend my ownership of the Property against any claim of such rights.

IN CONSIDERATION OF A LOAN MADE TO ME BY THE LENDER, I promise and I agree with Lender as follows:

1. BORROWER'S PROMISE TO PAY - I will pay to Lender on time principal and interest due under the Note and any prepayment and late charges due under the Note.

2. MONTHLY PAYMENTS FOR TAXES AND INSURANCE

(A) BORROWER'S OBLIGATIONS - I will pay to Lender all amounts necessary for taxes, assessments, leaseholds payments or ground rents (if any), and hazard insurance on the Property and mortgage insurance (if any). I will pay those amounts to Lender unless Lender tells me, in writing, that I do not have to do so, or unless the law requires otherwise. I will make those payments on the same day that my monthly payments of principal and interest are due under this Note.

Each of my payments under this Paragraph 2 will be the sum of the following: (i) One-twelfth of the estimated yearly taxes and assessments on the Property which under the law may be superior to this Security Instrument; plus (ii) One-twelfth of the estimated yearly leasehold payments

(Document continued on next page)

or ground rents on the Property, if any; plus (iii) One-twelfth of the estimated yearly premium for hazard insurance covering the Property; plus (iv) One-twelfth of the estimated yearly premium for mortgage insurance (if any).

Lender will estimate from time to time my yearly taxes, assessments, leasehold payments or ground rents and insurance premiums, which will be called "escrow items." Lender will use existing assessments and bills and reasonable estimates for future assessments and bills. The amounts that I pay to Lender for escrow items under this Paragraph 2 will be called the "Funds."

(B) LENDER'S OBLIGATIONS - Lender will keep the Funds in a savings or banking institution which has deposits or accounts insured by a federal or state agency. If Lender is such an institution, Lender may hold the Funds. Except as described in this Paragraph 2, Lender will use the Funds to pay the escrow items. Lender will give to me, without charge, an annual accounting of the Funds. That accounting must show all additions to and deductions from the funds and the reason for each deduction.

Lender may not charge me for holding or keeping the Funds, for using the Funds to pay escrow items, for analyzing my payment of Funds, or for receiving, verifying and totalling assessments and bills. However, Lender may charge me for these services if Lender pays me interest on the Funds and if the law permits Lender to make such a charge. Lender will not be required to pay me any interest or earnings of the Funds unless either (i) Lender and I agree in writing, at the time I sign this Security Instrument, that Lender will pay interest on the funds; or (ii) the law requires that the Lender pay interest on the Funds.

(C) ADJUSTMENT TO THE FUNDS - If Lender's estimates are too high or if taxes and insurance rates go down, the amounts that I must pay under this Paragraph 2 will be too large. If this happens at a time when I am keeping all of my promises and agreements made in this Security instrument, I will have the right to have the excess money promptly repaid to me as direct refund or credited to my future monthly payment of Funds. There will be excess amounts if, at any time, the sum of (i) the amount of Funds which Lender is holding or keeping, plus (ii) the amount of the monthly payments of Funds

(Document continued on next page)

which I must still pay between that time and the due dates of escrow items is greater than the amount necessary to pay the escrow items when they are due. If, when payments of escrow items are due, Lender has not received enough Funds to make those payments, I will pay to Lender whatever additional amount is necessary to pay the escrow items in full. I must pay that additional amount in one or more payments as Lender may require.

When I have paid all of the sums secured, Lender will promptly refund to me any Funds that are then being held by Lender. If, under Paragraph 20 below, Lender either acquires the Property or the Property is sold, then immediately before the acquisition or sale, Lender will use any Funds which Lender is holding at that time to reduce the sums secured.

3. APPLICATION OF BORROWER'S PAYMENTS - Unless the law requires otherwise, Lender will apply each of my payments under the Note and under Paragraphs 1 and 2 above in the following order and for the following purposes: first, to pay late charges due under the Note; next, to pay prepayment charges due under the Note; next, to pay the amounts due to Lender under Paragraph 2 above; next, to pay interest due; and last, to pay principal due.

4. BORROWER'S OBLIGATION TO PAY ALL CHARGES, ASSESSMENTS AND CLAIMS - I will pay all taxes, assessments and any other charges and fines that may be imposed on the Property and that may be superior to this Security Instrument. I will also make payments due under my lease if I am a tenant on the Property and I will pay ground rents (if any) due on the Property. I will do this either by making the payments to Lender that are described in Paragraph 2 above or, if I am not required to make payments under Paragraph 2, by making the payments on time to the person owed them. (In this Security Instrument, the word "person" means any person, organization, governmental authority or other party.) If I make direct payments, then promptly after making any of those payments I will give Lender a receipt which shows that I have done so. If I make payment to Lender under Paragraph 2, I will give Lender all notices or bills that I receive for the amounts due under this Paragraph 4.

Any claim, demand or charge that is made against property because an obligation has not been fulfilled is

(Document continued on next page)

known as a "lien." I will promptly pay or satisfy all liens against the Property that may be superior to this Security Instrument. However, this Security instrument does not require me to satisfy a superior lien if: (i) I agree in writing to pay the obligation which gave rise to the superior lien and Lender approves the way in which I agree to pay that obligation; or (ii) in good faith, I argue or defend against the superior lien in a lawsuit so that, during the lawsuit, the superior lien may not be enforced and no part of the Property must be given up; or (iii) I secure from the holder of that other lien an agreement, approved in writing by Lender, that the lien of this Security Instrument is superior to the lien held by that person. If Lender determines that any part of the Property is subject to a superior lien, Lender may give Borrower a notice identifying the superior lien. Borrower shall pay or satisfy the superior lien or take one or more of the actions set forth above within 10 days of the giving of the notice.

5. BORROWER'S OBLIGATION TO MAINTAIN HAZARD INSURANCE - I will obtain hazard insurance to cover all buildings and other improvements that now are or in the future will be located on the Property. This insurance must cover loss or damage caused by fire, hazards normally covered by "extended coverage" hazard insurance policies and other hazards for which Lender requires coverage. The insurance must be in the amounts and for periods of time required by the Lender. I may choose the insurance company, but my choice is subject to the Lender's approval. Lender may not refuse to approve my choice unless the refusal is reasonable.

All of the insurance policies and renewals of those policies must include what is known as a "standard mortgage clause" to protect Lender. The form of all policies and renewals must be acceptable to Lender. Lender will have the right to hold the policies and renewals. If Lender requires, I will promptly give Lender all receipts of paid premiums and renewal notices that I receive.

If there is a loss or damage to the Property, I will promptly notify the insurance company and Lender. If I do not promptly prove to the insurance company that the loss or damage occurred, then Lender may do so.

The amount paid by the insurance company is called "proceeds." The proceeds will be used to repair or to

(Document continued on next page)

restore the damaged Property unless: (i) it is not economically feasible to make the repairs or restoration; or (ii) the use of the proceeds for that purpose would lessen the protection to Lender by this Security Instrument; or (iii) Lender and I have agreed in writing not to use the proceeds for that purpose. If the repair or restoration is not economically feasible or if it would lessen Lender's protection under this Security Instrument, then the proceeds will be used to reduce the amount that I owe to Lender under the Note and under this Security Instrument. If any of the proceeds remain after the amount that I owe to Lender has been paid in full, the remaining proceeds will be paid to me.

If I abandon the Property, or if I do not answer, within 30 days, a notice from Lender stating that the insurance company has offered to settle a claim, Lender may collect the proceeds. Lender may use the proceeds to repair or restore the Property or to pay the sums secured. The 30-day period will begin when the notice is given.

If any proceeds are used to reduce the amount of principal which I owe to Lender under the Note, that use will not delay the due date or change the amount of any of my monthly payments under the Note and under Paragraphs 1 and 2 above. However, Lender and I may agree in writing to those delays or changes.

If Lender acquires the Property under Paragraph 19 below, all of my rights in the insurance policies will belong to Lender. Also, all of my rights in any proceeds which are paid because of damage that occurred before the Property is acquired by Lender or sold will belong to Lender. However, Lender's rights in those proceeds will not be greater than the sums secured immediately before the Property is acquired by Lender or sold.

6. BORROWER'S OBLIGATION TO MAINTAIN THE PROPERTY AND TO FULFILL ANY LEASE OBLIGATIONS - I will keep the Property in good repair. I will not destroy, damage or substantially change the Property, and I will not allow the Property to deteriorate. If I do not own but am a tenant on the Property, I will fulfill my obligations under my lease. I also agree that, if I acquire the fee title to the Property, my lease interest and the fee title will not merge unless Lender agrees to the merger in writing.

(Document continued on next page)

7. LENDER'S RIGHT TO PROTECT ITS RIGHTS IN THE PROPERTY (MORTGAGE INSURANCE) - If either: (i) I do not keep my promises and agreements made in this Security Instrument, or (ii) someone, including me, begins a legal proceeding that may significantly affect Lender's rights in the Property (such as a legal proceeding in bankruptcy, in probate, for condemnation or to enforce laws or regulations), Lender may do and pay for whatever is necessary to protect the value of the Property and Lender's rights in the Property. Lender's actions may include appearing in court, paying reasonable attorneys' fees and entering on the Property to make repairs. Lender must give me notice before Lender may take any of these actions. Although Lender may take action under this Paragraph 7, Lender does not have to do so.

I will pay to Lender any amounts, with interest, which Lender spends under this Paragraph 7. I will pay those amounts to Lender when Lender sends me a notice requesting that I do so. I will also pay interest on those amounts at the Note rate. Interest on each amount will begin on the date that the amount is spent by Lender. However, Lender and I may agree in writing to terms of payment that are different from those in this paragraph. This Security Instrument will protect Lender in case I do not keep this promise to pay those amounts with interest.

If Lender has required mortgage insurance as a condition of making the loan that I promise to pay under the Note, I will pay the premiums for that mortgage insurance. I will pay the premiums until the requirement for mortgage insurance ends according to my written agreement with Lender or according to law. Lender may require me to pay the premiums in the manner described in Paragraph 2 above.

8. LENDER'S RIGHT TO INSPECT THE PROPERTY - Lender, and others authorized by Lender, may enter on and inspect the Property. They must do so in a reasonable manner and at reasonable times. Before or at the time an inspection is made, Lender must give me notice stating a reasonable purpose for the inspection.

9. AGREEMENTS ABOUT CONDEMNATION OF THE PROPERTY - A taking of property by any governmental authority by eminent domain is known as "condemnation." I give to Lender my right: (i) to proceeds of

(Document continued on next page)

all awards or claims for damages resulting from condemnation or other governmental taking of the Property; and (ii) to proceeds from a sale of the Property that is made to avoid condemnation. All of those proceeds will be paid to Lender.

If all of the Property is taken, the proceeds will be used to reduce the sums secured. If any of the proceeds remain after the amount that I owe to Lender has been paid in full, the remaining proceeds will be paid to me. Unless Lender and I agree otherwise in writing, if only a part of the Property is taken, the amount I owe to Lender will be reduced only by the amount of proceeds multiplied by the following fraction: the total amount of the sums secured immediately before the taking, divided by the fair market value of the Property immediately before the taking. The remainder of the proceeds will be paid to me.

If I abandon the Property, or I do not answer, within 30 days, a notice from Lender stating that a governmental authority has offered to make a payment or to settle a claim for damages, Lender has the authority to collect the proceeds. Lender may then use the proceeds to repair or restore the Property or to reduce the sums secured. The 30-day period will begin when the notice is given.

If any proceeds are used to reduce the amount of principal which I owe to Lender under the Note, that use will not delay the due date or change the amount of monthly payments under the Note and under Paragraph 1 and 2 above. However, Lender and I may agree in writing to those delays or changes.

10. CONTINUATION OF BORROWER'S OBLIGATIONS AND OF LENDER'S RIGHTS

(A) BORROWER'S OBLIGATIONS - Lender may allow a person who takes over my rights and obligations to delay or to change the amount of the monthly payments of principal and interest due under the Note or under this Security Instrument. Even if Lender does this, however, that person and I will both still be fully obligated under the Note and under this Security Instrument.

Lender may allow those delays or changes for a person who takes over my rights and obligations, even if Lender is requested not to do so. Lender will not be re-

(Document continued on next page)

quired to bring a lawsuit against such a person for not fulfilling obligations under the Note or under this Security Instrument, even if Lender is requested to do so.

(B) LENDER'S RIGHTS - Even if Lender does not exercise or enforce any right of Lender under this Security Instrument or under the law, Lender will still have all of those rights and may exercise or enforce them in the future. Even if Lender obtains insurance, pays taxes, or pays other claims, charges or liens against the Property, Lender will have the right under Paragraph 19 below to demand that I make immediate payment in full of the amount that I owe to the Lender under the Note and under this Security Instrument.

11. OBLIGATIONS OF BORROWER AND OF PERSONS TAKING OVER BORROWER'S RIGHTS OR OBLIGATIONS - Any person who takes over my rights or obligations under this Security Instrument will have all of my rights and will be obligated to keep all of my promises and agreements made in this Security Instrument. Similarly, any person who takes over Lender's rights of obligations under this Security Instrument will have all of Lender's rights and will be obligated to keep all of Lender's agreements made in this Security Instrument.

If more than one person signs this Security Instrument as Borrower, each of us is fully obligated to keep all of Borrower's promises and obligations contained in this Security Instrument. Lender may enforce Lender's rights under this Security Instrument against each of us individually or against all of us together. This means that any one of us may be required to pay all of the sums secured. However, if one of us does not sign the Note: (i) that person is signing this Security Instrument only to give that person's rights in the Property to Lender under the terms of this Security Instrument; and (ii) that person is not personally obligated to pay the sums secured; and (iii) that person agrees that Lender may agree with the other Borrowers to delay enforcing any of the Lender's rights or to modify or make any accommodations with regard to the terms of this security Instrument or the Note without that person's consent.

12. LOAN CHARGES - If the loan secured by this Security Instrument is subject to a law which sets maximum loan charges, and that law is finally interpreted so that

(Document continued on next page)

the interest or other loan charges collected or to be collected in connection with the loan exceed permitted limits: (i) any such loan charge shall be reduced by the amount necessary to reduce the charge to the permitted limit; and (ii) any sums already collected from the Borrower which exceeded permitted limits will be refunded to Borrower. Lender may choose to make this refund by reducing the principal owed under the Note or by making a direct payment to Borrower. If a refund reduces principal, the reduction will be treated as a partial prepayment without any prepayment charge under the Note.

13. LEGISLATION AFFECTING LENDER'S RIGHTS - If a change in applicable law would make any provision of the Note or Security Instrument unenforceable, Lender may require immediate payment in full of all sums secured by this Security Instrument as that phrase is defined in Paragraph 19 below. If Lender requires immediate payment in full under this Paragraph 13, Lender will take the steps and may act as specified in the last paragraph of Paragraph 17 below.

14. NOTICES REQUIRED UNDER THIS SECURITY INSTRUMENT - Any notice that must be given to me under this Security Instrument will be given by delivering it or mailing it by first class mail unless applicable law requires the use of another method. The notice will be addressed to me at the address stated in the section above titled "Description of Property." A notice will be given to me at a different address if I give the Lender a notice of a different address. Any notice must be given to Lender under this Security Instrument will be given by mailing it to Lender's address stated in paragraph (C) of the section above "Words Used in This Document." A notice will be mailed to Lender at a different address if Lender gives me notice of the address. A notice required by this Security Instrument is given when it is mailed or when it is delivered according to the requirements of this Paragraph 14 or of applicable law.

15. LAW THAT GOVERNS THIS SECURITY INSTRUMENT - This Security Instrument is governed by federal law and the law that applies in the place where the Property is located. If any term of this Security Instrument or of the Note conflicts with the law, all other terms of this Security Instrument and of the Note will still remain in effect if they can be given effect without the conflicting

(Document continued on next page)

23. Delete these two paragraphs if the Lender will NOT require immediate payment in full of the loan on a sale or transfer of the Property.

24. Delete these three paragraphs if the Lender will NOT permit an assumption of the Note and Mortgage by another.

term. This means that any terms of this Security Instrument and of the Note which conflict with the law can be separated from the remaining terms, and the remaining terms will still be enforced.

16. BORROWER'S COPY - I will be given one conformed copy of the Note and of this Security Instrument.

17. AGREEMENTS ABOUT LENDER'S RIGHTS IF THE PROPERTY IS SOLD OR TRANSFERRED OR ANY RIGHTS IN THE PROPERTY ARE SOLD OR TRANSFERRED

[23][(A) "DUE ON SALE" - Lender may require immediate payment in full, as this term is described in this Mortgage, of all sums secured by this Security Instrument if all or any part of the Property, or if any right in the Property, is sold or transferred without Lender's prior written permission. Lender also may require immediate payment in full if a beneficial interest in Borrower is sold or transferred and Borrower is not a natural person. However, Lender shall not require immediate payment in full if this is prohibited by federal law on the date of this Security Instrument.

If Lender requires immediate payment in full under this Paragraph 17, Lender will give me a notice which states this requirement. The notice will give me at least 30 days to make the required payment. The 30-day period will begin on the date the notice is mailed or delivered. If I do not make the required payment during that period, Lender may act to enforce its rights under this Security Instrument without giving me further notice or demand for payment.]

[24][(B) ASSUMPTION OF MORTGAGE - If I sell or transfer all or any part of the Property or sell or transfer any rights in the Property, any person to whom I sell or transfer the Property or any rights to the Property may take over all of my obligations and rights under the Mortgage. This is called an "assumption of the Mortgage." The Lender may, but need not, give its consent. The Lender may charge a different rate of interest that will be paid on the remaining principal balance due, either higher or lower. An assumption of the Mortgage will be permitted if: (i) I give the Lender notice of the sale or transfer and (ii) if Lender agrees that the credit of the person that I wish to sell or transfer to is satisfactory; and (iii) that person

(Document continued on next page)

25. Delete this paragraph if the Lender will NOT permit any second, junior, subordinate, or inferior mortgage on the Property.

Note: change the paragraph letters (A, B and C) if you have deleted any of the paragraphs described in Nos. 24 through 26.

agrees, in writing: (a) to pay all amounts due to Lender under the Note and Mortgage at whatever rate of interest the Lender shall then require and (b) the person signs an agreement of assumption of the Mortgage in the form acceptable to the Lender and which states that that person agrees to assume the Mortgage and agrees to be obligated to fulfill all of the Borrower's obligations as stated in the Note and Mortgage. If all of these conditions are met and the Lender agrees to permit an assumption of the Mortgage, the Lender will also agree to release me from all of my obligations under the Note and this Mortgage.

If I sell or transfer all or any part of the Property or my rights and the above conditions (i) through (iii)(b) of this paragraph 17(B) are not met, I will still be obligated under the Note and this Mortgage and the Lender may require immediate payment in full as that term is defined in this Mortgage.

The Lender will not have the right to require Immediate Payment in Full in the event of either of the following transfers: (i) rights in household appliances (but only to a person who provides me with money to buy those appliances and in order to protect that person against loss); (ii) to surviving co-owners, following the death of a co-owner, when such transfer is automatic according to law; or (iii) a lease of the Property for a term of less than three (3) years and in the event that such lease does not give to tenant an option to buy the Property.]

[25][(C) OTHER LIENS, MORTGAGES OR ENCUMBRANCES - Other than the lien created by this Mortgage, I will not create nor allow the creation of any liens, mortgages or encumbrances, including any that may be junior, second or subordinate or inferior to the lien created by this Mortgage, without the written consent of the Lender on such terms as the Lender may require.]

18. BORROWER'S RIGHT TO HAVE LENDER'S ENFORCEMENT OF THIS SECURITY INSTRUMENT DISCONTINUED - Even if Lender has required immediate payment in full, I may have the right to have enforcement of this Security Instrument discontinued. I will have this right at any time before sale of the Property under any power of sale granted by this Security Instrument or at any time before a judgment has been entered enforcing this Security Instrument if I meet the following conditions:

(Document continued on next page)

(A) I pay to Lender the full amount that would have been due under this Security Instrument and the Note if Lender had not required immediate payment in full; and

(B) I correct my failure to keep any of my other promises or agreements made in this Security Instrument; and

(C) I pay all of Lender's reasonable expenses in enforcing this Security Instrument including, for example, reasonable attorneys' fees; and

(D) I do whatever Lender reasonably requires to assure that Lender's rights in the Property, Lender's rights under this Security Instrument, and my obligations under the Note and this Security Instrument continue unchanged.

If I fulfill all of the conditions in this Paragraph 18, then the note and this Security Instrument will remain in full effect as if immediate payment in full had never been required. However, I will not have the right to have Lender's enforcement of this Security Instrument discontinued if Lender has required immediate payment in full under Paragraph 13 or 17 above.

19. LENDER'S RIGHTS IF BORROWER FAILS TO KEEP PROMISES - Except as provided in Paragraphs 13 and 17 above, if all of the conditions stated in subparagraphs (A), (B) and (C) of this Paragraph 19 are met, Lender may require that I pay immediately the entire amount then remaining unpaid under this Note and under this Security Instrument. Lender may do this without making any further demand for payment. This requirement is called "immediate payment in full."

If Lender requires immediate payment in full, Lender may bring a lawsuit to take away all of my remaining rights to the Property and have the Property sold. At this sale Lender or another person may acquire the Property. This is known as "foreclosure and sale." In any lawsuit for foreclosure or sale, Lender will have the right to collect all costs allowed by law.

Lender may require immediate payment in full under this Paragraph 19 only if the following conditions are met:

(Document continued on next page)

(A) I fail to keep any promise or agreement made in this Security Instrument, including the promise to pay when due all sums secured.

(B) Lender sends to me, in the manner described in Paragraph 14 above, a notice that states: (i) the promise of agreement that I failed to keep; (ii) the action that I must take to correct the default; (iii) a date by which I must correct the default (and the date must be at least 30 days from the date on which the notice is given); (iv) that if I do not correct the default by the date stated in the notice, Lender may require immediate payment in full, and as well Lender or another person may acquire the Property by means of foreclosure and sale; (v) that if I meet the conditions stated in Paragraph 18 above, I will have the right to have Lender's enforcement of this Security Instrument discontinued and to have the Note and this Security Instrument remain fully effective as if immediate payment in full had never been required; and (vi) that I have the right in any lawsuit for foreclosure and sale to argue that I did keep my promises and agreements under the Note and under this Security Instrument, and to present any other defenses that I may have.

(C) I do not correct the default stated in the notice from Lender by the date stated in that notice.

20. LENDER'S RIGHTS TO RENTAL PAYMENTS AND TO TAKE POSSESSION OF THE PROPERTY - If Lender requires immediate payment in full, or if I abandon the Property, then Lender, persons authorized by Lender, or a receiver appointed by a court at Lender's request may: (i) collect the rental payments, including overdue rental payments, directly from tenants; (ii) enter on and take possession of the Property; (iii) manage the Property; and (iv) sign, cancel and change leases. If Lender notifies the tenants that Lender has the right to collect rental payments directly from them under this Paragraph 20, I agree that the tenants may make those rental payments to Lender without having to ask whether I have failed to keep my promises and agreements under this Security Instrument.

If there is a judgment for Lender in a lawsuit for

(Document continued on next page)

foreclosure and sale, I will pay to Lender reasonable rent from the date the judgment is entered for as long as I occupy the Property. However, this does not give me the right to occupy the Property.

All rental payments collected by Lender or by a receiver, other than the rent paid by me under this Paragraph 20, will be used first to pay the costs of collecting rental payments and or managing the Property. If any part of the rental payment remains after those costs have been paid in full the remaining part will be used to reduce the sums secured. The cost of managing the Property may include the receiver's fees, reasonable attorneys' fees and the cost of any necessary bonds.

21. BORROWER'S USE OF PROPERTY, COMPLIANCE WITH LAW AND ALTERATIONS

(A) USE OF PROPERTY, COMPLIANCE WITH LAW - Borrower agrees to use and maintain the Property so as to be in compliance with all laws, ordinances, regulations and requirements of any governmental body applicable to the Property. Borrower agrees that the Property shall be used only as permitted by law or zoning classification on the date of signing of this Security Instrument and agrees not to use or to seek, agree to or make or permit any change in the use of the Property without the written consent of the Lender.

(B) ALTERATIONS - Borrower agrees not to remove, demolish, destroy or materially alter or permit any other person to remove, demolish, destroy or alter the Property or any buildings or improvements located on the Property without the written consent of the Lender.

22. LENDER'S OBLIGATION TO DISCHARGE THIS SECURITY INSTRUMENT - When Lender has been paid all amount due under the Note and under this Security Instrument, Lender will discharge this Security Instrument by delivering a certificate stating that this Security Instrument has been satisfied. I will not be required to pay Lender for this discharge, but I will pay all costs of recording the discharge in the proper official records.

(Document continued on next page)

26. The name of the the Borrower if a corporation. Otherwise delete the line.

27. The name of the Witness to the signing of the Note printed directly below the line, with the Witness to sign above the line.

28. If the Borrower is an individual, delete "BY" and print the Borrower's name directly below the line, with the Borrower to sign above the line. If the Borrower is a corporation, print the name and title of the individual acting for the corporation directly below the line, with that person to sign above the line.

29. Insert the Notary Statement for an Individual or Notary Statement for a Corporation, found elsewhere in this book, depending upon whether the Borrower is an individual or a corporation. The Notary will complete the Notary Statement.

BY SIGNING THIS MORTGAGE AND ACCEPTING THE LOAN FROM LENDER, Borrower accepts and agrees to the promises and agreements contained in this Security Instrument and in any rider(s) executed by Borrower and recorded with this Security Instrument.

Witness:

__________*[26]*__________

______________________ *BY*______________________

[27] [28] Borrower

[29] [Notary Statement for Borrower]

ASSIGNMENT OF MORTGAGE (2-28)

This form is used when the Seller of real estate does not want to pay off his existing Mortgage but rather would like to assign his existing mortgage to the Buyer. Note: the Seller must very carefully review the terms of his Note and Mortgage to determine whether an assignment is permitted and if so, whether the Lender has the right to impose new repayment terms.

1. The name of the Buyer of the Property, the person who will take over (assume) the existing mortgage (the Assignee).

2. If the Buyer is a corporation, insert the state of incorporation. Otherwise delete.

3. The Buyer's address.

4. The name of the Seller of the Property (the Assignor).

5. If the Seller is a corporation, insert the state of incorporation. Otherwise delete.

6. The Seller's address.

7. The address of the Property.

8. The city in which the Property is located.

9. The county in which the Property is located.

10. The state in which the Property is located.

11. On a separate sheet, headed "Schedule A," set forth the so-called "metes and bounds" that describe the property being mortgaged by feet and compass direction—which is the best description of the property. This description and the ones called for in Nos. 12 through 19 are typically found on the Property's original deed. The information should be copied from that deed EXACTLY.

ASSIGNMENT OF MORTGAGE

1. WORDS USED IN THIS DOCUMENT

(A) "BUYER:" ________[1]________, *[2][a corporation organized under the laws of ________,]* whose address is __________[3]__________, sometimes called either "Buyer" or "Assignee."

(B) "SELLER:" ________[4]________, *[5][a corporation organized under the laws of ________,]* whose address is __________[6]__________, sometimes called either "Seller" or "Assignor."

(C) "PROPERTY:" located at ____________[7]____________, in the City of _____[8]_____, County of _____[9]_____, State of _____[10]_____, and which has the legal description which is more fully stated on the attached SCHEDULE A [11] and as well has the following

(Document continued on next page)

12. The district number in which the Property is located.

13. The section number in which the Property is located.

14. The block number in which the Property is located.

15. The lot number(s) in which the Property is located.

16. The title of the city, county, district or state office responsible for recording deeds.

17. Choose one.

18. The number of the "Liber" (book) or "Reel" (microfilm) where the Seller's deed was recorded.

19. The Page Number of the Liber or Reel where the Seller's deed was recorded.

20. The name of the Lender.

21. Choose one. (Note: the Note and the Mortgage will state whether the Lender, typically a bank, is chartered under the laws of the United States or under state law.)

22. The state of incorporation of the Lender.

23. The address of the Lender.

24. The date of the Seller's Note.

25. The principal amount, in numbers, of the Seller's Note.

26. The annual interest rate, in numbers, due on the Seller's Note.

27. The amount, in numbers, of monthly payments due on the Seller's Note.

28. The date of the first payment due on the Seller's Note.

tax map designation: District No.: __[12]__, Section No. __[13]__, Block No.: __[14]__, Lot(s) No.: _____[15]_____, and together with all buildings and improvements and the fixtures, equipment and personal property located on the Property, and intended to be the Property sold and transferred to Seller by deed recorded in the Office of ________[16]________ at *[17][Liber]* ***OR*** *[Reel]* __[18]__, Page __[19]__, sometimes called the "Property."

(D) "LENDER:" __________[20]__________, *[21][an association formed and which exists under the laws of the United States of America.]* ***OR*** *[a corporation organized under the laws of ____[22]_____.]* Lender's address is __________[23]__________.

2. SELLER'S REPRESENTATIONS

(A) SELLER'S LOAN - As evidenced by Note dated ________[24]________, Seller borrowed the principal sum of $_____[25]_____ from Lender and that this principal amount was to be repaid with interest at the rate of __[26]__% per year with monthly payments in the amount of $_____[27]_____ commencing __________[28]__________ with a maturity date of

(Document continued on next page)

29. The maturity date of the Seller's Note.

30. A brief description of any prepayment terms that are contained in the Seller's Note, such as penalties or accelerated payments.

31. Choose one.

32. Choose one.

33. The title of the city, county, district or state office responsible for recording Mortgages.

34. Choose one.

35. The number of the "Liber" (book) or "Reel" (microfilm) where the Seller's Mortgage and Note were recorded. This and No. 36 are found in the Seller's Mortgage and Note.

36. The Page Number of the Liber or Reel where the Seller's Mortgage and Note were recorded.

37. Delete if the Note and/or Mortgage do not require the maintenance of any escrow funds for real estate taxes or the like, and skip to No. 39.

38. Insert any other escrow funds required by the Note and/or Mortgage.

39. The principal amount, in numbers, remaining due on Seller's Note.

__________[29]__________ . The Note provided that prepayment could be made __________[30]__________ *[31][with]* ***OR*** *[without]* penalty. The Note also provided that the Seller's promise to repay the loan could be assigned by the Seller and assumed by another *[32][with]* ***OR*** *[without]* the consent of the Lender.

(B) SELLER'S MORTGAGE - In order to secure the repayment of Seller's Loan, Seller, as Mortgagor, gave and Lender, as Mortgagee, accepted a Mortgage of the Property which was recorded in the Office of ________[33]________ at *[34][Liber]* ***OR*** *[Reel]* ___[35]___, Page __[36]__.

(C) SELLER'S PAYMENTS - Seller has timely made all payments of principal and interest *[37][and all required payments to any escrow funds for real estate taxes, insurance and _____[38]____]* required by the Note and the Mortgage and there remains due the principal amount of $_____[39]_____.

(D) SELLER'S TRANSFER OF THE PROPERTY - By written contract, the Seller has agreed to sell and Buyer has agreed to purchase the Property for valuable consideration but contingent upon the Lender's consent to this assignment and release of the Seller from the obligations stated in the Note and Mortgage. Upon the consent of the Lender, Buyer agrees to pay any additional money due towards the purchase price of the Property and to assume the Note and Mortgage. Seller agrees to deliver a deed to the Property in recordable form to Buyer.

3. SELLER'S ASSIGNMENT OF NOTE AND MORTGAGE - Upon the consent of the Lender on such terms as the Lender may require to this assignment and Lender's release of the Seller, for value received, Seller hereby assigns to Buyer the Note and Mortgage and all of Seller's obligations as stated in the Note and Mortgage.

4. BUYER'S ASSUMPTION OF THE NOTE AND MORTGAGE - For value received, Buyer assumes the

(Document continued on next page)

40. Delete if there are no additional terms or conditions, and skip to No. 42.

41. Insert any other terms or conditions that are imposed by the Lender in order to give its consent.

42. The name of the Seller if a corporation. Otherwise delete the line.

Note and Mortgage in place and instead of Seller, and Buyer agrees to assume all of Seller's obligations stated in the Note and Mortgage. Buyer further agrees to be bound by all of the terms and conditions of the Note and Mortgage and any additional or different terms and conditions that the Lender may have required in exchange for giving its consent to this assignment by Seller and assumption by Buyer.

5. LENDER'S CONSENT - By this agreement, Lender consents to: (i) the assignment of the Note and Mortgage to Buyer; (ii) the release of the Seller from any further obligation or liability under either the Note or the Mortgage; (iii) Buyer's assumption of the Note and Mortgage and all of the obligations and liabilities under both the Note and the Mortgage *[40][; and (iv) Buyer's additional promise to ___________[41]___________].*

Seller, Buyer and Lender agree to all of the above terms.

_________*[42]*_________

(*Document continued on next page*)

43. If the Seller is an individual, delete "BY" and print the Seller's name directly below the line, with the Seller to sign above the line. If the Seller is a corporation, print the name and title of the individual acting for the corporation directly below the line, with that person to sign above the line.

44. The name of the Buyer if a corporation. Otherwise delete the line.

45. If the Buyer is an individual, delete "BY" and print the Buyer's name directly below the line, with the Buyer to sign above the line. If the Buyer is a corporation, print the name and title of the individual acting for the corporation directly below the line, with that person to sign above the line.

46. The name of the Lender if a corporation. Otherwise delete the line.

47. If the Lender is an individual, delete "BY" and print the Lender's name directly below the line with, the Lender to sign above the line. If the Lender is a corporation, print the name and title of the individual acting for the corporation directly below the line, with that person to sign above the line.

48. Insert a Notary Statement, found elsewhere in this book, for the Seller, either an Individual or Corporate form as appropriate.

49. Insert a Notary Statement, found elsewhere in this book, for the Buyer, either an Individual or Corporate form as appropriate.

50. Insert a Notary Statement, found elsewhere in this book, for the Lender, either an Individual or Corporate form as appropriate.

*BY*________________________
[43] (Seller)

__________*[44]*__________

*BY*________________________
[45] (Buyer)

__________*[46]*__________

*BY*________________________
[47] (Lender)

[48] [Notary Statement for Seller]

[49] [Notary Statement for Buyer]

[50] [Notary Statement for Lender]

SATISFACTION OF MORTGAGE (2-29)

This form is used to acknowledge that a Note and Mortgage have been paid in full ("satisfied"). It is signed by the Lender and given to the Borrower. The Borrower will want this document recorded with the government office which recorded his Mortgage since it is necessary to "clear the record." Note: a recorded document is never removed from the files or records; rather it is cleared by the recording of a subsequent document with the same office.

1. The name of the Lender.

2. Choose one depending on whether the Lender is a corporation.

3. The Lender's address, if the Lender is an individual.

4. The state in which the Lender is incorporated, if the Lender is a corporation.

5. The Lender's address.

6. Choose one depending on whether the Mortgage has been assigned and the assignment recorded.

7. The name of the Borrower.

8. The date of the Mortgage.

9. The principal amount of the loan, in numbers.

10. The title of the city, county, district or state office responsible for recording mortgages.

11. Choose one. (See No. 12 for an explanation.)

12. The number of the "Liber" (book) or "Reel" (microfilm) where the Mortgage was recorded. This information and for Nos. 13 through 21 are found in the property's Mortgage.

13. The page number of the Liber or Reel where the mortgage was recorded.

SATISFACTION OF MORTGAGE

KNOW ALL MEN BY THESE PRESENTS:

________[1]________, *[2][residing at ________[3]__________,]* ***OR*** *[a corporation organized under the laws of _____[4]_____ with its principal office at __________[5]__________,]* as owner and holder does acknowledge and certify that the following Note and Mortgage, which *[6][has]* ***OR*** *[has not]* been assigned of record, is fully satisfied, paid and discharged and does direct the Clerk to cancel of record the mortgage given by ________[7]________ to ________[1]________ dated ________[8]________ in the principal sum of $_____[9]_____ recorded in the office of ________[10]________ at *[11][Liber]* ***OR*** *[Reel]* __[12]__, Page __[13]__ and securing certain promises and obligations upon property located at

(Document continued on next page)

14. The address of the property.

15. The city in which the property is located.

16. The county in which the property is located.

17. The state in which the property is located.

18. The district number in which the property is located.

19. The section number in which the property is located.

20. The block number in which the property is located.

21. The lot number(s) in which the property is located.

22. The name of the Lender if a corporation. Otherwise delete the line.

23. If the Lender is an individual, delete "BY" and print the Lender's name directly below the line, with the Lender to sign above the line. If the Lender is a corporation, print the name and title of the individual acting for the corporation directly below the line, with that person to sign above the line.

24. Insert a Notary Statement, found elsewhere in this book, for the Lender, either for an Individual or a Corporation as appropriate.

__________[14]__________, in the City of _____[15]_____, County of _____[16]_____, State of _____[17]_____ and which is designated on the tax map as: District No. __[18]__, Section No. __[19]__, Block No. __[20]__, Lot(s) No. ____[21]____.

__________*[22]*__________

*BY*____________________
[23]

[24] [Notary Statement for Lender]

GRANT OF EASEMENT OF RIGHT OF WAY (2-30)

Ownership of property is considered to continue underneath the land to the center of the Earth (mineral rights, etc.), and above the land to the end of the universe (air rights). An owner may not want to sell his rights either above or below his land but may agree to sell the right to enter on or walk over or string cables over a portion of the land. For example, suppose someone owns lakefront property. He may wish to grant to his neighbor the right to cross his land (to trespass) to gain access to the lake. Or suppose the power company wants to run its cables over a portion of the land. The landowner grants to his neighbor or to the power company the right, in effect, to trespass, which is called an Easement.

WARNING

An Easement is a grant of a right or interest in land. The Grantee (the one receiving the right) is strongly urged to record the Easement just as he would any deed.

GRANT OF EASEMENT OF RIGHT OF WAY

INDENTURE, made as of _____[1]_____, 19__, by and between ________[2]________ *[3][, a ________ corporation]* ("Owner" or "Grantor"), and ________[4]________ *[5][, a ________ corporation]* ("Grantee").

1. GRANTOR'S REPRESENTATION - Grantor is the owner of the real property *[6][including all buildings and improvements on and to said property]* located in the City of _____[7]_____, County of _____[8]_____, State of

(Document continued on next page)

1. The date of signing the agreement.

2. The name of the owner of the property, the party who is granting the Easement (the Grantor).

3. If the Grantor is a corporation, insert the state of incorporation. Otherwise delete.

4. The name of the party who is being granted the Easement (the Grantee).

5. If the Grantee is a corporation, insert the state of incorporation. Otherwise delete.

6. Delete if the property owned is land only and does not have any improvements on it such as buildings.

7. The city in which the property is located.

8. The county in which the property is located.

9. The state in which the property is located.

Note: the information for Nos. 10 through 20 is typically found on the Seller's deed or the tax map of the property located in the office of the local tax authority.

10. Delete through No. 15 if your locality does not use a "block and lot" system of identifying property.

11. The name of the town, county or district where the tax map referred to is filed.

12. Identify the specific tax map by the date of its filing.

13. The Section in which the property is located.

14. The Block in which the property is located.

15. The Lot(s) in which the property is located.

16. The address of the property.

17. The title of the city, county, district or state office responsible for recording deeds.

18. Choose one (see the explanation in No. 19 below).

19. The number of the "Liber" (book) or "Reel" (microfilm) where the Grantor's deed was actually recorded.

20. The Page Number of the Liber or Reel where the Grantor's deed was actually recorded.

_____[9]_____, *[10][identified on the Tax Map of _____[11]_____, dated ________[12]________ as Section ___[13]___, Block ___[14]___, Lot(s) ___[15]___],* known by the street address ________[16]________ and intended to be the same property conveyed to Seller by Deed recorded in the Office of ______[17]______ at *[18][Liber]* ***OR*** *[Reel]* __[19]__, Page __[20]__ (the "Premises").

(Document continued on next page)

21. Choose one. Some states require that all deeds to be recorded state the full amount (the consideration) actually paid for the Easement (for the state's use in computing any real estate transfer or sales taxes). If your state does require this, choose the second alternative.

22. The amount, in words and numbers, paid for the Easement.

23. Choose one depending on whether the Easement being granted is exclusive to the Grantee or granted to others as well.

24. Choose one and either on a separate sheet headed "Schedule A" attach a copy of the survey showing the exact location of the Easement, or insert the legal description (the so-called "metes and bounds") of the Easement.

25. The purpose of the Easement. For example: "For the sole purpose of obtaining access to Lake _____" or "For the purpose of constructing, erecting and maintaining electrical power lines" or "For the sole purpose of installing and maintaining water pipes," or the like.

26. Delete if not appropriate and also delete "; and" from the end of the previous paragraph.

2. AGREEMENT - In consideration of the sum of *[21][Ten Dollars ($10.00), lawful money of the United States and other valuable consideration]* ***OR*** *[_______[22]__________ Dollars ($__________) lawful money of the United States]* paid by Grantee, the receipt of which is acknowledged, Owner as Grantor does by this Indenture grant, release and forever quit-claim to Grantee, and Grantee's heirs, successors, assigns and grantees and their grantees, *[23][a non-exclusive]* ***OR*** *[an exclusive]* EASEMENT OF RIGHT OF WAY to pass and repass over that portion of Grantor's land as more particularly described *[24][on Schedule A annexed to and made part of this Grant of Easement of Right of Way.]* ***OR*** *[as follows: beginning at a point ____.]*

3. PURPOSE OF PERMITTED EASEMENT - ______________________[25]_______________________ ____ ____.

4. COVENANT TO RUN WITH THE LAND - This Easement and the rights granted shall run with the land and any sub-division(s) of the land and pass to Grantee's heirs, successors, assigns and grantees and their grantees. This Easement and the rights granted are IRREVOCABLE and shall be granted and construed to be granted and incorporated by reference by this Indenture into each and every respective deed, indenture and conveyance affecting the Premises, subject only and always to the following conditions:

(i) any and all present and future local, state and/or federal regulations, ordinances or laws affecting the use of the Premises as may be promulgated by competent authority having jurisdiction*; and*

[26] (ii) any temporary disruption or suspension of the use of said access because of construction or related activities.

5. INDEMNITY - By accepting this Easement of Right of Way, Grantee, Grantee's heirs, successors, assigns and grantees and their grantees agree to indemnify and hold harmless Grantor and Grantor's heirs, successors and assigns from any and all claim for damages or liability of

(Document continued on next page)

any kind on the part of any person by reason of Grantee's acts.

IN WITNESS WHEREOF, this contract has been duly executed by the parties on the date first written above.

____________*[27]*____________

*BY*________________________
[28]

Grantor's Taxpayer
Identification No.:______[29]______

Witness:

________________ ____________*[31]*____________
[30]

*BY*________________________
[32]

Grantee's Taxpayer
Identification No.:______[33]_____

[34][Notary Statement for Grantor]

[35][Notary Statement for Grantee]

27. The name of the Grantor if a corporation. Otherwise delete the line.

28. If the Grantor is an individual, delete "BY" and print the Grantor's name directly below the line, with the Grantor to sign above the line. If the Grantor is a corporation, print the name and title of the individual acting for the corporation directly below the line, with the Grantor to sign above the line.

29. The Grantor's Taxpayer Identification Number (which for an individual is his Social Security Number).

30. The name of the Witness to the signing of the contract printed below the line, with the Witness to sign above the line.

31. The name of the Grantee if a corporation. Otherwise delete the line.

32. If the Grantee is an individual, delete "BY" and print the Grantee's name directly below the line, with the Grantee to sign above the line. If the Grantee is a corporation, print the name and title of the individual acting for the corporation directly below the line, with the Grantee to sign above the line.

33. Grantee's Taxpayer Identification number.

34. Insert a Notary Statement for the Grantor—either for an Individual or for a Corporation as appropriate. The Notary Statements are found elsewhere in this book. The Notary completes this part of the form.

35. Insert a Notary Statement for the Grantee—either for an Individual or for a Corporation as appropriate. The Notary completes this part of the form.

APPLICATION FOR RESIDENTIAL LEASE (2-31)

This form is used to obtain information about a potential tenant for a Residential Lease. It should be given to any potential tenant before agreeing to lease to that tenant.

The form is self-explanatory; add or delete as appropriate or necessary for your rental.

APPLICATION FOR RESIDENTIAL LEASE

Name ____

Present Address ____________________________________
____

Telephone # ________________________

Social Security # ____________________

Driver's Lic. # and State________________

Employer _____________ Telephone # ______________

Address _______________ Length of Employment ____
____

Position ______________ Annual Income ____________

Amount and Source of Any Additional Income:
____
____

Banks:
Checking A/C #________ Bank ____________________
____

Savings A/C #__________ Bank ____________________
____

Credit Cards:
(List Card Issuer and Account No.)
____
____

Business Reference ______________ Telephone # ______
____

Business Reference ______________ Telephone # ______
____

Business Reference ______________ Telephone # ______
____

(Document continued on next page)

Pets (kind and number) ______________________________

Number of People Who Will Occupy This Dwelling: _____

Reason(s) for Moving ________________________________

Number of Months/Years at Present Address __________

Has Applicant Ever Been Evicted?___________________

Applicant(s) and references must be satisfactory to the Landlord. Landlord will not be bound and possession will not be given until lease is signed by Landlord and delivered to Applicant. Landlord assumes no responsibility to the applicant for delay or failure to give possession due to failure of present occupant to vacate or any other reason.

Applicant acknowledges that Landlord is relying on the statements made above. Applicant warrants that any and all information and statements made on this application are true.

Applicant(s) signature _________________ Date________

Applicant(s) signature _________________ Date________

RESIDENTIAL LEASE (2-32)

A Residential Lease is the document by which the owner of real estate (the Landlord) gives the right of possession and occupancy for its use as a residence or dwelling to someone else (the Tenant) in exchange for payment (Rent). The Landlord gives this right for a stated length of time (the Term) and for a specific amount of rent, but usually (except in the case of seasonal or short-term Leases) permits the Tenant to pay that amount in monthly installments.

WARNING

Most states (and cities) have laws for the protection of Tenants that restrict the rights of Landlords. Therefore, because laws vary widely from state to state and, in some cases, even from city to city within the same state, every Landlord should consult his local housing authority or an attorney who is familiar with local laws.

1. The date of signing the Lease.

2. The name of the Landlord.

3. Choose one depending on whether the Landlord is a corporation.

4. The address of the Landlord.

5. The state of incorporation of the Landlord.

6. The address of the Landlord corporation's principal office.

7. The name of the Tenant.

8. Choose one depending on whether the Tenant is a corporation.

9. The address of the Tenant.

10. The state of incorporation of the Tenant.

11. The address of the Tenant corporation's principal office.

12. Choose one.

RESIDENTIAL LEASE

LEASE, made the __[1]__ day of _______, 19__ between ________[2]________, *[3][residing at _________[4]_________]* ***OR*** *[a _____[5]_____ corporation with its principal office at _________[6]_________]*, as "Landlord" and ________[7]________, *[8][residing at _________[9]_________]* ***OR*** *[a _____[10]_____ corporation with its principal office at _________[11]_________]*, as "Tenant."

1. PREMISES/TERM/USE - Landlord agrees to lease to Tenant the *[12][house located at]* ***OR*** *[apartment known*

(Document continued on next page)

13. The apartment number, condominium unit or cooperative apartment number being rented.

14. The address of the house or the building in which the apartment, condominium unit or cooperative apartment is located.

15. The number of years or months of the Lease, in words.

16. Choose one.

17. The starting date of the Lease.

18. The ending date of the Lease.

19. The party or parties that may use the premises, such as "Tenant and Tenant's immediate family."

20. Choose one. If this is to be a typical Lease (where the rent will be paid monthly), choose the first alternative. If the Lease is for a seasonal rental (such as the summer beach season or the winter skiing season) where the custom is for the entire rent to be paid in advance in full, choose the second alternative and skip to No. 23.

21. The total rent due, in numbers.

22. The monthly rent, in numbers.

23. The total rent due, in numbers.

24. The amount, in numbers, of any deposit advanced by Tenant.

25. The balance of total rent due, in numbers.

as _____[13]_____ in the building located at] OR [condominium unit known as _____[13]_____ in the building located at] ***OR*** *[cooperative apartment _____[13]_____ in the building located at]* __________[14]__________ (the "Premises") for a term of __[15]__ *[16][years]* ***OR*** *[months]* beginning on ________[17]________ and ending on ________[18]________ for use and occupancy by ________[19]________ as a strictly residential dwelling.

2. RENT - *[20][The rent for the term is $_____[21]_____ payable in advance without demand or notice, in equal monthly installments of $_____[22]_____ on the first day of each and every month during the term.]* ***OR*** *[The rent for term is $_____[23]_____ payable by the Tenant to the Landlord upon the signing of this Agreement. The parties acknowledge that $_____[24]_____ has been paid in advance, leaving a balance of $_____[25]_____ due upon execution.]*

(Document continued on next page)

26. Delete this paragraph if this is NOT to be a typical Lease where the purpose of the security deposit is primarily to guaranty payment of the rent.

27. The amount, in numbers, of the security deposit (typically, an amount equal to one month's rent for each year of the Lease term).

28. Choose one, depending on whether state or local housing laws require the payment of interest on rent security deposits.

29. Choose one, depending on whether state or local housing laws require deposit in a bank and depending on whether such laws require that separate accounts be maintained.

30. The name and address of the bank to which the Tenant's security deposit has been deposited.

31. The number of days, in numbers, in which the Landlord will return the Tenant's security deposit.

32. Delete this paragraph if the Lease is NOT for a seasonal rental where the purpose of the security deposit is primarily for repairs.

33. The amount, in numbers, of the seasonal security deposit.

[26][3. SECURITY - Landlord acknowledges receipt from Tenant of the sum of $_____[27]_____ as security deposit, which [28][shall] ***OR*** *[shall not] bear interest, [29][need not be kept separate from other monies belonging to Landlord]* ***OR*** *[shall be deposited to ________[30]________ and shall not be commingled with other monies belonging to Landlord], and shall be returned to Tenant within __[31]__ days of the peaceful termination of the full term of this lease and surrender of possession, less the cost of any repairs which shall have been made necessary by acts of the Tenant.]*

[32][3. SECURITY - Tenant has deposited with the Landlord the sum of $_____[33]_____ upon signing of this lease, said sum to be held by the Landlord for a period of thirty (30) days after termination of this Lease, said deposit money to be used by the Landlord in the event of damage or loss resulting to either the real or personal property contained in said demised Premises not properly repaired or replaced by Tenant within twenty (20) days of termination, said sum of money to be used to clean, repair or replace same, said sum of money also to be used to pay for any unpaid utilities, services, fuels and supplies, to the extent that there are any, for which the Tenant is responsible; however, said deposit does not release Tenant from the obligation to pay for same when bills are presented, and the balance, if any, shall be returned to the Tenant within thirty (30) day of the termination of this Lease. The Tenant hereby authorizes the Landlord to pay out of the aforesaid deposit such charges and expenses herein set forth.]

4. OCCUPANCY AND USE - The Premises shall be used solely as a private dwelling for Tenant and his immediate family and for no others except with written permission of Landlord. Tenant agrees not to use or permit the use of the Premises for unlawful or immoral purposes. Tenant shall keep the grounds in neat order, to remove ashes, waste and refuse from the Premises and to dispose of same only in accordance with all local laws, rules and regulations. Tenant agrees to keep Premises clean, sanitary and in good order, and agrees not to hamper, disturb or interfere with other tenants in the building, nor to create or suffer any nuisances in the Premises affecting the rights of others, and agrees to comply with all laws, ordinances, rules, regulations and directions of governmental authorities and the Board of Fire Underwriters. Upon termination of this lease, Tenant agrees to surrender possession in as

(Document continued on next page)

34. Delete if NOT a condominium unit.

35. The name of the condominium.

36. Delete if NOT a cooperative apartment.

37. The name of the Cooperative Apartment Corporation.

38. Add or delete items as appropriate.

39. Add or delete items as appropriate.

good condition and repair as when received, ordinary wear and tear excepted.

[34] [(A) It is specifically understood by the parties that this Lease is made in connection with a Condominium Unit and is presented in this form for convenience only. This lease and the rights of Landlord, as owner of the Condominium Unit, and Tenant are subject and subordinate to all covenants and restrictions contained in the Master or Unit Owner's Deed to the ________[35]________ and the by-laws and "house rules" of the Condominium Association as they may exist from time to time.]

[36] [(A) Tenant understands and acknowledges that the Building in which the Apartment is located is a cooperative apartment building and that the Owner is the owner of shares of stock of ________[37]__________ (the Apartment Corporation) appurtenant to the Apartment and entitled to occupancy of the Apartment pursuant to a proprietary lease for the Apartment. Accordingly, it is agreed that this instrument is a sub-lease and that it is subject to and subordinate to Owner's Proprietary Lease, and "house rules" and the by-laws of the Apartment Corporation, as they may exist from time to time.]

(i) The parties acknowledge and agree that this sublease and the occupancy of the Apartment by the Tenant named herein is subject to the consent of the Board of Directors of the cooperative apartment corporation.

(ii) Tenant agrees to abide by the terms and conditions of the Proprietary Lease, the "house rules" and the by-laws of the Apartment Corporation and further agrees that a violation of any of the terms and conditions of the Proprietary Lease, the "house rules" and the by-laws as they apply to Tenant shall be deemed a material violation of this sublease.]

5. EQUIPMENT/APPLIANCES - The Premises is furnished by the Landlord with a *[38][range, refrigerator, disposal, dishwasher]* among other mechanical installations and *[39][furniture, furnishings, bedding supplies, including blankets, bed-linens, towels, kitchen supplies, including utensils]*. Tenant agrees to use and maintain all such equipment, and plumbing fixtures and all other equipment, furniture, furnishings and supplies with which Premises is

(Document continued on next page)

40. Add or delete items as appropriate.

furnished, in accordance with manufacturers' specifications and the regulations of the Landlord now or hereafter provided, and to be responsible for all repairs and any damages to the Premises brought about by misuse or neglect of such equipment by the Tenant. All repairs to equipment furnished by Landlord shall be made by licensed persons approved by Landlord. Should Tenant fail or refuse to make repairs after reasonable notice from Landlord, Landlord may cause same to be done and the cost thereof shall be additional rent immediately due from Tenant to Landlord.

6. ALTERATIONS/ADDITIONS/IMPROVEMENTS - Tenant agrees not to make any alterations, additions, improvements or changes in the Premises, interior or exterior, or to the equipment and fixtures provided by Landlord or to install any major appliances in the Premises without written consent of the Landlord.

7. SERVICES/UTILITIES - Tenant acknowledges that Owner has no obligation to provide *[40][electrical service, heating/cooking fuel/oil, telephone service]* and that no part of the rent is for such service or services. Tenant shall make such separate arrangement with the local utility providing such service as may be required, shall have accounts with said suppliers in Tenant's name, shall timely pay all bills therefore and will not suffer or permit any charges for such services to become a lien against the Premises or separate account of the Landlord.

(A) Interruption of Service - Interruption or failure of any service maintained for the Premises, if due to causes beyond Landlord's control, shall not entitle Tenant to any claim against Landlord or to any reduction in rent, and shall not constitute constructive eviction unless Landlord shall fail to take such measures as may be reasonable in the circumstances to restore the service without undue delay.

8. ASSIGNMENT - No assignment or sub-lease of the Premises shall be binding upon the Landlord or confer any rights on the proposed assignee or sub-lessee without the written consent of Landlord. No assignment or sub-lease shall release Tenant from the obligations of this lease.

9. POSSESSION/DELAY IN TENDER OF POSSESSION - Taking of possession of the Premises by Tenant

(Document continued on next page)

41. Choose one.

42. Identify, by kind and number, any permitted pets.

43. The time period in days, in numbers, during which the Landlord can show the leased space to prospective Tenants.

shall be conclusive evidence against Tenant that he received the Premises in good condition. If Landlord is unable to give possession on the commencement date, rent shall abate until possession is given, and Tenant shall pay a fractional part from the date of possession up to the first day of the next month following date of possession. Tenant waives all damages by reason of Landlord's failure to give possession on the commencement date. Delay in tendering possession shall not extend the termination date of this lease.

10. RELEASE OF LIABILITY - The Tenant assumes all risk of any damage to person or property that may occur by reason of water or the bursting or leaking of any pipes or waste about said Premises or from any act of negligence of any co-tenants or occupants of the building or of any other person, or fire or hurricane or other act of God or from any cause whatsoever, provided that Landlord shall make necessary repairs to prevent further damage upon reasonable diligence after notice given to it, and the Tenant agrees to give the Landlord prompt written notice of any accident to or defect in the water pipes, electricity or of any plumbing, heating or cooling apparatus or device.

11. PETS - It is the specific understanding of Landlord and Tenant that *[41][no pets]* ***OR*** *[the ______[42]______ presently owned by the Tenants shall be allowed in the Premises, but no other animals or pets]* shall be permitted.

12. TENANT'S PROPERTY - If, upon the termination of this lease or abandonment of the Premises by Tenant, Tenant abandons or leaves any property in the Premises, Landlord shall have the right, without notice to Tenant, to store or otherwise dispose of the property at Tenant's cost and expense, without being liable in any respect to the Tenant.

13. PARKING - Tenant shall use only that parking space designated for his use by the Landlord, and the Tenant shall see to it that Tenant's guests use only the parking space provided for guest parking.

14. RIGHT OF ENTRY - Landlord shall have the right to enter the Premises at all times which are necessary to make needed repairs, and this right shall exist whether or not Tenant or other occupant shall be on the Premises at such time. During the last __[43]__ days of the term of the

(Document continued on next page)

44. The amount of fire/theft insurance coverage, in numbers, required to be maintained by the Tenant.

45. The amount of liability insurance coverage, in numbers, required to be maintained by the Tenant.

46. The amount, expressed as a percentage of the monthly rental, in numbers, of any late charge to be assessed by the Landlord (typically five percent of the rent).

47. The number of days' notice, in words and numbers, which the Landlord will give for the Tenant to cure any default (typically ten or more, but not more than thirty).

48. The number of days' notice, in words and numbers, which the Landlord will give for termination of the Lease based upon failure to cure a default after notice (typically ten days).

lease, Landlord shall have the right to enter the Premises at reasonable hours to show the same to prospective tenants.

15. FIRE AND CASUALTY - If the Premises is damaged by fire or other casualty, Landlord may cause the damage to be repaired and the rent will be abated from such period of time as Premises remain untenantable, but if the Premises is destroyed or so damaged that Landlord shall decide that it is inadvisable to repair same, this lease shall cease and terminate, and rental shall be adjusted to the date when such fire or casualty occurred. Tenant agrees to release Landlord from any and all claims for loss, damage or inconvenience arising from such fire or casualty.

16. INSURANCE - Tenant shall obtain and maintain a homeowner's insurance policy with a qualified insurance company with respect to the Premises and Tenant's personal property therein with minimum coverage for fire and theft in the amount of no less than $_____[44]_____ and personal liability claims in an amount of no less than $_____[45]_____.

17. LATE CHARGE - Tenant understands that timely payment of rent is of the essence of this agreement. Tenant agrees to pay as additional rent a late charge equal to __[46]__ percent of any rent payment received by Owner more than ten (10) days after it is due.

18. DEFAULT - If Tenant shall fail to pay the rent or any other charge required to be paid by Tenant, or if Tenant shall breach any of the terms of this lease or the rules attached hereto, if any, or enacted from time to time, then as to every default or breach, except non-payment of rent, Landlord may give Tenant ____[47]____ (__) days' written notice thereof, and if such default has not been cured within such period, then Landlord may give Tenant ____[48]____ (__) days' notice of the termination of this lease, and this lease shall expire accordingly and Tenant shall surrender possession to Landlord, but Tenant shall remain liable as hereinafter provided. If the Premises becomes vacant or abandoned, this lease shall expire and terminate and Landlord may re-enter and may take possession of the Premises in the manner provided by law. In case Landlord shall recover possession of the Premises, Landlord may, but shall not be required to remove the property of Tenant and store the same at Tenant's expense, or he may dispose of said property, and Tenant agrees that in no respect shall Land-

(Document continued on next page)

49. Delete if there are no "House Rules" governing the use of the Premises. Then renumber paragraph 20 as paragraph 19 and delete No. 54. (Note: if the Premises being rented is a condominium unit or cooperative apartment, it is likely that the owner, the Landlord, will himself be subject to so-called "House Rules," in which event these same rules should be made part of any Lease so that the Tenant will be bound by them as well.

lord be responsible in damages for any action in entering said Premises or removing and disposing of Tenant's property, with or without process of law. Notwithstanding anything stated herein, Tenant agrees that whether possession is taken or this lease is cancelled by Landlord, the entire unpaid balance of rent shall accelerate and immediately become due and payable and Tenant shall be responsible for all costs, including attorneys' fees incurred by Landlord in enforcing this and any other provision of this lease.

In the event of a default by Tenant, Landlord shall not be required to return any part or portion of the security deposit but may retain all or any part or portion of the security deposit as liquidated damages or apply all or any part or portion of the security deposit against actual damages sustained by reason of Tenant's default. The retention of the security deposit shall not be the only remedy to which Landlord is entitled but Landlord shall have all recourse against Tenant provided by this lease and by law, and all remedies shall be cumulative and non-exclusive. Tenant agrees to pay Landlord's reasonable attorneys' fees and expenses incurred in and about enforcing any of the terms of this lease, in collecting past due rent, and in and about recovering possession from Tenant, should the services of an attorney be retained by Landlord in so doing.

19. [49][RULES AND REGULATIONS - There are attached hereto certain Rules and Regulations which are made a part of this lease. Tenant agrees to comply with all current rules and regulations, together with any subsequent reasonable rules and regulations which may be adopted by the Landlord for the general benefit of all tenants in the building. Any violation of these rules or any one of them shall be cause for termination of this lease at the option of the Landlord.]

20. QUIET ENJOYMENT - In the event that Tenant pays the rent as provided for herein and otherwise performs all of the covenants and conditions to be performed by the Tenant and abides by all of the rules and regulation as set forth herein and referred to, Tenant shall have peaceful and

(Document continued on next page)

50. The name of the Landlord if a corporation. Otherwise delete the line.

51. If the Landlord is an individual, delete "BY" and print the Landlord's name directly below the line, with the Landlord to sign above the line. If the Landlord is a corporation, print the name and title of the individual acting for the corporation directly below the line, with that person to sign above the line.

52. The name of the Tenant if a corporation. Otherwise delete the line.

53. If the Tenant is an individual, delete "BY" and print the Tenant's name directly below the line, with the Tenant to sign above the line. If the Tenant is a corporation, print the name and title of the individual acting for the corporation directly below the line, with that person to sign above the line.

Note: if the Tenant is a corporation, the Landlord may want to consider requiring that the Tenant corporation's Lease obligations (particularly the payment of rent) be personally guaranteed by an officer of the corporation. A Personal Guaranty form is found elsewhere in this book.

54. A typical set of "House Rules" is set forth. Rules can be added, deleted or modified to fit a particular situation. For example, if the Premises does not have an elevator, delete those rules which refer to an elevator. It is also suggested that a copy of any "House Rules" be attached to the Lease and initialed by the Tenant (to prove his receipt). Delete if paragraph 19 was deleted. (See instruction No. 49.)

quiet enjoyment of all the demised Premises for the term of this lease.

IN WITNESS WHEREOF, the Landlord and Tenant have executed this lease the day and year first above written.

__________*[50]*__________

*BY*______________________
[51] (Landlord)

__________*[52]*__________

*BY*______________________
[53] (Tenant)

[54]RULES AND REGULATIONS

1. *Public halls and stairways shall not be obstructed or used for any purpose other than for ingress to, and egress from, the apartments.*

2. *Passenger and service elevators shall be operated only by employees of the Landlord, without any interference whatsoever by the Tenants, members of their families, or their agents, servants or visitors.*

3. *No Tenant shall make or permit any disturbing noises in the building by himself, his family, agents, servants or visitors; nor do, nor permit any of such persons to do, anything that will interfere with the rights, comforts or convenience of other Tenants. No Tenant shall play upon, or suffer to be played upon or operated, any musical instrument, phonograph, radio or other like device in the demised premises between the hours of eleven o'clock P.M. and the following eight o'clock A.M., if the same shall disturb or annoy other occupants of the building.*

4. *Tenants, their families, agents, servants and visitors*

(Document continued on next page)

shall not throw anything whatever out of the windows or doors, or in the halls of the building.

5. *Supplies, goods and packages of every kind shall be delivered to Tenants at the entrance provided for deliveries, through service elevators; and the Landlord shall not be responsible for loss of, or damage to, any such property, notwithstanding such loss or damage may occur through the carelessness or negligence of employees of the Landlord. Landlord shall not be responsible for any article left with any employee.*

6. *All garbage and refuse must be sent to the basement from the apartments and kitchens, at such times as may be directed, and in accordance with the Landlord's superintendent.*

7. *No baby carriages, tricycles, or bicycles will be allowed in passenger elevators, or in the halls, passageways, areas or courts of the building.*

8. *Baggage must be taken in and out through the service entrance.*

9. *Each Tenant shall keep the premises leased in a good state of preservation and cleanliness and shall not sweep or throw or permit to be swept or thrown from the premises leased, any dirt or other substance into any of the corridors, halls, elevators or stairways of the building, or into any of the light shafts or ventilators of it.*

10. *No garbage can, kitchen supplies, or other article, shall be placed in the halls or on the staircase landings, nor shall anything be hung from the windows or balconies, or placed upon any window sill or ledge. Nor shall any article be shaken or hung from any of the windows or doors.*

11. *The obstruction of the fire escapes is prohibited by the Fire Department as well as by the Landlord.*

12. *The water-closets and other water apparatus shall not be used for any purposes other than those for which they were constructed. Any resulting damage*

(Document continued on next page)

from misuse shall be borne by the Tenant by whom, or upon whose premises, it shall have been caused.

13. *Children shall not play in the public halls, stairways or elevators, nor be permitted in the service elevators.*

14. *No sign, signal, advertisement or illumination shall be inscribed or exposed on or at any window, or other part of the building, except such as first shall have been approved in writing by the Landlord, nor shall anything be projected out of any window without such written consent.*

15. *No shades, awnings or window guards shall be used except such as shall have been first approved in writing by the Landlord.*

16. *No dogs or other animals shall be kept or harbored in the leased premises.*

17. *The Landlord reserves the right to make such other rules and regulations, from time to time, as may be deemed needful for the safety, care and cleanliness of the premises and for securing the comfort and convenience of all Tenants.*

18. *Each Tenant, without charge, shall have the use of a reasonable portion of the storeroom space to be designated by the Landlord, provided that the Landlord shall not be liable for any loss or damage to property left, placed or stored in such storeroom.*

EXTENSION/RENEWAL OF RESIDENTIAL LEASE (2-33)

A Residential Lease Extension/Renewal is typically less complex than one for commercial property. This form is to be used when the only change in the Residential Lease is a new rent (and payment of additional security based on the higher rental).

This form also provides for the Tenant, or for one of the Tenants in the case of Joint Tenants, to indicate his desire not to extend or renew his lease.

WARNING

Many states regulate residential housing by law. It is recommended that you consult your local housing authority to determine any local requirements such as the length of an extension or renewal that **must** be offered to a Tenant not in default as well as the maximum permitted rent increase.

1. The name of each Tenant as it appears on the Lease.

2. The date of the Lease being extended.

3. Identify the leased premises by apartment number, street address, etc.

4. The expiration date of the existing Lease or Extension.

5. The commencement date of this Extension.

6. The annual rent, in numbers, to be charged during the Extension period.

7. The monthly rent, in numbers, to be charged during the Extension period.

8. The length of the Extension period in years or months, in words, for example "two years."

9. The ending date of the Extension period.

10. The amount, in numbers, of additional security required.

11. The total security that will be held upon payment of the additional security.

EXTENSION/RENEWAL
OF RESIDENTIAL LEASE

Tenant(s): _______[1]_______ Re: Lease
_______[1]_______ Dated: ____[2]____, 19__
Premises: _______[3]_______ Expires:___[4]____, 19__
____

Dear Tenant(s):

The Lease referred to above expires shortly. If you wish to extend this Lease, the annual rent for the Premises commencing on ______[5]______, 19__, will be $_____[6]_____ payable $___[7]___ monthly in advance, for an extended term of ______[8]______ ending on ______[9]______, 19__.

If you elect to extend your Lease, additional security will be required in the amount of $___[10]___, making the total security $___[11]___.

All other terms, covenants and conditions of the Lease shall remain in full force and effect for the duration of the extended term. HOWEVER, IF PRIOR TO THE COMMENCEMENT OF THE EXTENDED TERM YOU DEFAULT IN ANY OF THE TERMS, COVENANTS AND CONDITIONS OF THIS LEASE, THIS AGREEMENT OF EXTENSION SHALL, AT THE OPTION OF THE LANDLORD, BE NULL AND VOID.

Each Tenant named on the original Lease who wishes to extend the term of the original Lease must sign this agreement where indicated (X) and return two (2) copies to the Landlord together with a check in the amount

(Document continued on next page)

12. The number of days, in numbers, prior to the expiration date by which the Tenant must sign and return the Extension.

13. The name of the Tenant wishing to extend and renew his Lease printed directly below the line, with the Tenant to sign above the line.

14. The name of the Landlord if a corporation. Otherwise delete the line.

15. If the Landlord is an individual, delete "BY" and print the Landlord's name directly below the line, with the Landlord to sign above the line. If the Landlord is a corporation, print the name and title of the individual acting for the corporation directly below the line, with that person to sign above the line.

16. The name of the Tenant wishing to vacate (and NOT extend and renew his lease) printed directly below the line, with the Tenant to sign above the line.

of the additional security not less than __[12]__ days BEFORE the expiration date noted above. If any Tenant named on the original Lease intends to vacate the Premises, each such Tenant should sign his name under the words "Tenant(s) will vacate the Premises at the end of the present term" and return a copy to the Landlord.

(Sign here to extend Lease)
Tenant(s):

This EXTENSION AGREEMENT does not become binding until the return to you of a copy signed by Landlord.

X____________________
[13] (Tenant)

________*[14]*________

X____________________
[13] (Tenant)

*BY*____________________
[15] (Landlord)

Tenant(s) will vacate the Premises at the end of the term:

X____________________
[16] (Tenant)

X____________________
[16] (Tenant)

APPLICATION FOR COMMERCIAL LEASE (2-34)

This form is used to obtain information about a potential tenant for a Commercial Lease. It should be given to any potential tenant before agreeing to lease space to that tenant.

The form is self-explanatory; add or delete as appropriate or necessary.

APPLICATION FOR COMMERCIAL LEASE

Name of Business ______________________
Contact Person ______________________

Present Address ______________ Telephone # _______
____

Federal Taxpayer ID No. ______________________

Date Business Established ____________

Type of Business: ______________________

No. of Employees to Be at This Location ____________

Special Operating Permits Required ____________
____

Banks:
Checking A/C #_________ Bank ______________
____

Checking A/C #_________ Bank ______________
____

Bank Reference ______________ Telephone # _______
____
Bank Reference ______________ Telephone # _______
____

Personal Reference ____________ Telephone # _______
____
Personal Reference ____________ Telephone # _______
____

No. of Parking Spaces Required and
Other Special Requirements
____

Reason(s) for Moving ______________________
____

Number of Months/Years at Present Address ____________

(Document continued on next page)

Has Applicant Ever Been Evicted?____________________

Applicant(s) and references must be satisfactory to the Landlord. Landlord will not be bound and possession will not be given until lease is signed by Landlord and delivered to Applicant. Landlord assumes no responsibility to the applicant for delay or failure to give possession due to failure of present occupant to vacate or any other reason.

Applicant acknowledges that Landlord is relying on the statements made above. Applicant warrants that any and all information and statements made on this application are true.

Applicant(s) signature ________________ Date________

Applicant(s) signature ________________ Date________

COMMERCIAL LEASE (2-35)

At its simplest level, a Lease is an agreement by an owner of property (the Landlord) to allow another (the Tenant) to use, occupy and possess (but not own) that property for a particular period of time (the Term) and for the Tenant to pay for that use (Rent). Note that the contract between the Landlord and the Tenant is essentially one in which the rent charge is permitted to be paid over time (that is, over the term of the Lease). But in reality the entire, total rent is what the Landlord is entitled to as the consideration for permitting the use and occupancy by the Tenant. Thus, if the Tenant defaults at some time during the term of the Lease, he is still obligated for the total rent less whatever he paid prior to the default.

The extent to which a "modern" Lease deals with matters other than the bare-bones use, rent and term issues is a reflection of the fact that a Landlord wants to pass through to the Tenant any increase in operating costs during the term of the Lease or expenses that may be caused by the Tenant's use of the property. This is particularly so for Commercial Leases which typically are not subject to regulation (unlike Residential Leases which are regulated in most states) based on the theory that a businessman probably needs less protection from the Landlord than does an individual renting a home.

Note that while the current real estate tax is reflected in the rent, this Lease provides that any increase will be paid by the Tenant. A Landlord should always be aware of costs that are likely to increase over the term of a Lease and should provide in the Lease for passing these on to the Tenant. Additionally, a Landlord should consider any other financial exposure, based on the type of business that will be conducted by the Tenant, and protect himself accordingly in the Lease.

COMMERCIAL LEASE

LEASE, between ________[1]________, *[2][residing at _________[3]__________]* ***OR*** *[a _____[4]_____ corporation with its principal office at __________[5]__________]*, as "Landlord" and ________[6]________, *[7][residing at __________[8]__________]* ***OR*** *[a ____[9]____ corpo-*

(Document continued on next page)

1. The name of the Landlord.
2. Choose one depending on whether the Landlord is a corporation.
3. The address of the Landlord.
4. The state of incorporation of the Landlord.
5. The address of the Landlord corporation's principal office.
6. The name of the Tenant.
7. Choose one depending on whether the Tenant is a corporation.
8. The address of the Tenant.
9. The state of incorporation of the Tenant.

ration with its principal office at ________[10]__________], as "Tenant."

1. PREMISES, TERM AND USE - Landlord agrees to lease to Tenant _____[11]_____ known as _____[12]_____ *[13][and more particularly described on the plan annexed to and made part of this Lease]* in the building located at __________[14]__________ in the City of _____[15]_____, County of _____[16]_____, State of _____[17]_____ (the "Premises"), for a term of ___[18]___ *[19][years]* ***OR*** *[months]* beginning on __________[20]__________ and ending on __________[21]__________ for use and occupancy as ________________[22]________________.

10. The address of the Tenant corporation's principal office.

11. A description of the leased space, for example "a suite," "a room," "a floor," etc.

12. Identify the specific space being leased, such as the suite number, room number or floor number.

13. If only a portion of a building is being leased (such as part of one floor), it is recommended that plans be made a part of the Lease (annexed) to identify exactly which space is being leased. Otherwise delete.

14. The address of the building.

15. The city in which the space being leased is located.

16. The county in which the space being leased is located.

17. The state in which the space being leased is located.

18. The number of years or months, in words, of the term of the Lease.

19. Choose one.

20. The first day of the term of the Lease (the "commencement date").

21. The last day of the term of the Lease.

22. The use of the space which is permitted by the Landlord.

(Document continued on next page)

23. The annual rent being charged, in words and numbers.

24. If the rent will automatically increase during the term of the Lease, insert the increased amounts along with the starting and ending dates of each increase. Otherwise delete.

25. The day of the month on which rent must be paid (typically the 1st).

26. The amount of the security deposit, in numbers. (In some areas, the custom is for the security to equal one or two month's rent, in other areas the custom is an amount equal to one month's rent for each year of the Lease.)

27. Choose one. (Note: some states require the payment of interest on rent security deposits while others do not. In addition, some states prohibit combining security deposits with the Landlord's own monies.)

2. RENT - Tenant shall pay the annual rental of _____[23]_____ Dollars ($______)
[24][____
____]
paid in equal monthly installments in advance on the __[25]__ day of each and every month during the term of this Lease.

3. SECURITY - Tenant has deposited with Landlord $_____[26]_____ as security for the faithful performance by Tenant of all the terms, covenants and conditions of this Lease on Tenant's part to be performed. Provided Tenant has fully and faithfully carried out all of said terms, covenants and conditions on Tenant's part to be performed, this security deposit shall be returned to Tenant after the expiration of this Lease *[27][with]* ***OR*** *[without]* interest.

(A) In the event of a bona fide sale, subject to this Lease, Landlord shall have the right to transfer the security to the buyer for the benefit of Tenant. Landlord, upon notice to Tenant of such sale and assignment of the security deposit to the buyer, shall be released from all liability for the return of such security. Tenant agrees to look solely to the new Landlord for the return of the said security, and it is agreed that this shall apply to subsequent transfer or assignment of the security to any new Landlord.

(B) The security deposited under this Lease shall not be mortgaged, assigned or encumbered by the Tenant without the written consent of the Landlord.

4. CARE OF PREMISES, ALTERATIONS, ETC. - Tenant shall take good care of the Premises and any fixtures which are and shall remain the property of the Landlord which may be located or situated on, in or made a part of the Premises and shall, at Tenant's own cost and expense make all repairs to the Premises and fixtures other than structural repairs. At the end of the term of this Lease, Tenant shall deliver the Premises in good order and condition, damages by the elements excepted.

(A) The Tenant shall promptly execute and comply with all statutes, ordinances, rules, orders, regulations and requirements of any governmental or quasi-governmental authority, including departments, bureaus and the like, having jurisdiction applicable to the Premises, for the correction, prevention, and abatement of violations,

(Document continued on next page)

nuisances or other grievances, in, upon, or connected with the Premises during the term of this Lease, at the Tenant's own cost and expense.

(B) Tenant's, Tenant's successors, heirs, executors or administrators shall not make any alterations to the Premises without the Landlord's consent in writing; or occupy, or permit or suffer the same to be occupied for any business or purpose deemed disreputable or extra-hazardous on account of fire, under the penalty of damages and forfeiture, and in the event of a breach thereof, the term herein shall immediately cease and terminate at the option of the Landlord as if it were the expiration of the original term.

(C) Tenant will not do anything in or to the Premises, or bring anything into the Premises, or permit anything to be done or brought into or kept in the Premises, which will in any way increase the rate of fire insurance on said Premises, nor use the Premises or any part thereof, nor allow or permit its use for any business or purpose which would cause an increase in the rate of fire insurance on said building, and the Tenant agrees to pay as additional rent the cost of any increase in fire insurance on demand by Landlord.

(D) Tenant shall not encumber or obstruct the sidewalk in front of, entrance to, or halls and stairs of said Premises, nor allow the same to be obstructed or encumbered in any manner.

(E) Landlord is exempt from any and all liability for any damage or injury to person or property caused by or resulting from steam, electricity, gas, water, rain, ice or snow, or any leak or flow from or into any part of said building or from any damage or injury caused by or due to the negligence of the Landlord.

5. SERVICES PROVIDED BY LANDLORD - As long as Tenant is not in default of any of the terms and conditions of this Lease, Landlord agrees to provide the following services:

[28] [(A) Heat, when and as required by law and except for holidays, Monday through Friday from _____ A.M. to _____ P.M. and Saturdays from _____ A.M. to _____ P.M.

28. Add or delete as appropriate depending on exactly what services the Landlord is providing. (For example, a two story building is unlikely to have an elevator, in which case the reference to elevator service should be deleted. On the other hand, if the building does have an elevator which is not self–service the Landlord should specify what time the elevator will be attended to avoid a Tenant's claim of a so-called constructive eviction if he should be working late at night and the elevator is not in operation.)

(Document continued on next page)

(B) Air conditioning/cooling/ventilation, except for holidays from May 15th through September 30th from _____ A.M. to _____ P.M. and Saturdays _____ A.M. to _____ P.M.

(C) Elevator except for holidays, Monday through Friday from _____ A.M. to _____ P.M. and Saturdays from _____ A.M. to _____ P.M.

(D) Water for ordinary lavatory purposes, except that if, in the sole determination of Landlord, Tenant shall use or consume water for any other purpose or in unusual quantities, Tenant shall pay to Landlord the rent or charge which may, during the term of this Lease, be assessed or imposed for the water used or consumed in or on the said Premises, whether determined by meter or otherwise, as soon as and when the same may be assessed or imposed and will also pay the expenses for the installation, setting and maintenance of a water meter in the said Premises should a meter be required by Landlord. Tenant shall pay Tenant's proportionate part of the sewer rent or charge imposed upon the building. All such rents or charges or expenses shall be paid as additional rent when billed by Landlord.

(E) Electrical service at all times except that if the Premises shall not be separately metered, Tenant agrees to pay as additional rent ___% of the electric bill as Landlord may determine based upon a survey of the consumption and equipment used by Tenant (or such additional percentage as may be determined by Landlord based upon changes in consumption by Tenant) and if the Premises shall be separately metered, Tenant agrees to make its own arrangements with the utility company providing electricity and to pay all bills in its own name.

(F) Cleaning services on business days provided that the Premises are kept in order by Tenant. Tenant shall pay as additional rent the cost of removal of Tenant's rubbish or refuse. Window cleaning shall be at Landlord's sole cost and expense and at such times as Landlord may determine, it being understood and agreed that Tenant is strictly forbidden and prohibited from cleaning any window from the outside.]

6. NO ABATEMENT OF RENT OR ADDITIONAL RENT - Landlord shall not be liable for failure to give

(Document continued on next page)

possession of the Premises upon commencement date by reason of the fact that the Premises are not ready for occupancy or because a prior tenant or any other person is wrongfully holding over or is in wrongful possession, or for any other reason. The rent shall not commence until possession is given or is available, but the term herein shall not be extended.

(A) This lease and the obligation of Tenant to pay rent hereunder and perform all of the other covenants and agreements hereunder on part of Tenant to be performed shall in no way be affected, impaired or excused because Landlord is unable to supply or is delayed in supplying any service expressly or impliedly to be supplied or is unable to make, or is delayed in making any repairs, additions, alterations or decorations or is unable to supply or is delayed in supplying any equipment or fixtures if Landlord is prevented or delayed from so doing by reasons of government preemption in connection with a National Emergency or in connection with any rule, order or regulation of any department or subdivision thereof of any governmental agency or by reason of the conditions of supply and demand which have been or are affected by war or other emergency.

(B) No diminution or abatement of rent, or other compensation, shall be claimed or allowed for inconvenience or discomfort arising form the making of repairs or improvements to the building or to its appliances, nor for any space taken to comply with any law, ordinance or order of a government authority. In respect to the various "services" if any, herein expressly or impliedly agreed to be furnished by Landlord to Tenant, it is agreed that there shall be no diminution or abatement of the rent, or any other compensation, for interruption or curtailment of such "service" when such interruption or curtailment shall be due to accident, alteration or repairs desirable or necessary to be made or to inability or difficulty in securing supplies or labor for the maintenance of such "service" or to some other cause, nor gross negligence on the part of Landlord. No such interruption or curtailment of any such "service" shall be deemed a constructive eviction. Landlord shall not be required to furnish, and Tenant shall not be entitled to receive any "services" during any period when Tenant shall be in default in respect to the payment of rent. Neither shall there be any abatement or diminution of rent because of making of repairs, improvements or decorations to the

(Document continued on next page)

29. If the Tenant is leasing part of the building, insert the percentage leased (usually based on square footage). Otherwise delete.

Premises after the date above fixed for the commencement of the term, it being understood that rent shall, in any event, commence to run at such date so above fixed.

7. REAL ESTATE TAXES - *[29][Tenant acknowledges that the Premises comprise approximately ____% of the building and which shall be defined as "Tenant's share."]* In the event that real estate taxes due and owing by Landlord for the building shall be increased above those charges during the base year (which is defined as the tax or fiscal year used by the governmental authority assessing such taxes in effect on the commencement date of this Lease), Tenant agrees to pay as additional rent within thirty (30) days of receipt of notice from Landlord, an amount equal to such additional real estate taxes or Tenant's share of additional real estate taxes.

8. DAMAGE TO THE PREMISES - Tenant must give Landlord prompt notice of fire, accident, casualty, damage or dangerous or defective condition. If the Premises can not be used because of fire or other casualty, Tenant is not required to pay rent for the time the Premises are unusable. If part of the Premises can not be used, Tenant must pay rent for the usable part. Landlord shall have the right to decide which part of the Premises is usable. Landlord need only repair the damaged structural parts of the Premises. Landlord is not required to repair or replace any equipment, fixtures, furnishings or decorations unless originally installed by Landlord. Landlord is not responsible for delays due to settling insurance claims, obtaining estimates, labor and supply problems or any other cause not fully under Landlord's control.

(A) If the fire or other casualty is caused by an act or neglect of Tenant, Tenant's employees or persons on the Premises with permission of Tenant, or at the time of the fire or casualty Tenant is in default in any term of this Lease, then all repairs will be made at Tenant's expense and Tenant must pay the full rent with no adjustment. The cost of the repairs will be added to the rent.

(B) Landlord has the right to demolish or rebuild the building if there is substantial damage by fire or other casualty. Landlord may cancel this Lease within 30 days after the substantial fire or casualty by giving Tenant notice of Landlord's intention to demolish or rebuild. The Lease will end 30 days after Landlord's cancellation notice to Tenant. Tenant must deliver the Premises to Landlord on

(Document continued on next page)

or before the cancellation date in the notice and pay all rent due to the date of the fire or casualty. If the lease is cancelled, Landlord is not required to repair the Premises or building. The cancellation does not release Tenant of liability in connection with the fire or casualty.

9. INSPECTION AND ENTRY BY LANDLORD - Tenant agrees that Landlord and Landlord's agents and other representatives shall have the right to enter into and upon the Premises, or any part hereof, at all reasonable hours for the purpose of examining the same, or making such repairs or alterations therein as may be necessary for the safety and preservation of the Premises.

(A) Tenant also agrees to permit Landlord or the Landlord's agents to show the Premises to persons wishing to lease or purchase the Premises. Tenant further agrees that on and after the sixth month preceding the expiration of the term of this Lease, Landlord or Landlord's agents shall have the right to place notices on the front of said Premises, or any part thereof, offering the Premises "To Let" or "For Sale" and the Tenant agrees to permit the same to remain thereof without hindrance or molestation.

(B) If the Premises, or any part thereof shall be deserted or become vacant during the term of this Lease, or if Tenant shall default in the payment of rent or any part thereof or shall default in the performance of any of the covenants herein contained, Landlord or its representatives may re-enter the Premises by force, summary proceeding or otherwise, and remove all persons therefrom, without being liable to prosecution therefor, and Tenant hereby expressly waives the service of any notice in writing of intention to re-enter, and Tenant shall pay at the same time as the rent becomes payable under the terms hereof a sum equivalent to the rent herein, and the Landlord may rent the Premises on behalf of the Tenant, reserving the right to rent the Premises for a longer period of time than fixed in the original lease without releasing the original Tenant from any liability, applying any moneys collected, first to the expense of resuming or obtaining possession, second to restoring the Premises to a rentable condition, and then to the payment of the rent and all other charges due and to become due to the Landlord, any surplus to be paid to the Tenant, who shall remain liable for any deficiency.

10. GLASS - Landlord may replace, at the expense of Tenant, any and all broken glass in and about the Premises.

(Document continued on next page)

30. The limits of insurance the Tenant must maintain. It is recommended that the Landlord discuss this with his insurance agent.

Landlord may insure, and keep insured, all plate glass in the Premises for and in the name of Landlord. Bills for the premiums therefor shall be rendered by Landlord to Tenant at such times as Landlord may elect, and shall be due from and payable by Tenant when rendered, and the amount thereof shall be deemed additional rental. Damage and injury to the said Premises, caused by the carelessness, negligence or improper conduct on the part of Tenant or Tenant's agents or employees shall be repaired as speedily as possible by Tenant at Tenant's own cost and expense.

11. SIGNS - Tenant shall neither place, nor cause nor allow to be placed, any sign or signs of any kind whatsoever at, in or about the entrance to said Premises or any part of same, except in or at such place or places as may be indicated by the Landlord and upon written consent by Landlord. In the event Landlord or Landlord's representatives shall deem it necessary to remove any such sign in order to paint the Premises or the building wherein same is situated or make any repairs, alterations, improvements in or upon the Premises or the building or any part of the Premises or the building, Landlord shall have the right to do so, providing any sign be removed and replaced at Landlord's expense whenever the said repairs, alterations or improvements shall be completed.

12. INSURANCE - Tenant agrees to maintain in full force and effect during the entire term of this Lease, liability insurance insuring Landlord against any loss or damage sustained or to which Landlord may be subject by reason of Tenant's occupancy and use of the Premises, which policy shall have the following limits of liability: __________[30]__________. Tenant agrees to furnish to Landlord, prior to the effective date of this Lease, a binder or other such certificate evidencing such insurance coverage.

(A) Tenant agrees that it will, at its own cost and expense, keep its furniture, fixtures, equipment, records, and personal property insured against loss or damage by fire or other peril normally covered by "extended coverage" endorsements, and shall deliver to Landlord prior to the effective date of this Lease, a binder or other such certificate of such insurance coverage.

13. SUBLETTING OR ASSIGNMENT - Neither the Premises nor any portion of the Premises may be sublet,

(Document continued on next page)

31. The number of days, in words and numbers, that the Tenant would have to cure his Lease violation.

32. The number of days, in words and numbers, after which the Lease would automatically expire and the Tenant could legally be evicted.

nor may this Lease be assigned without the express written consent of Landlord upon such terms and conditions as Landlord may require.

14. DEFAULT - If Tenant defaults in fulfilling any of the terms and conditions of this Lease other than the payment of rent or additional rent; or if the Premises becomes vacant or deserted; or if any execution or attachment shall be issued against Tenant or any of Tenant's property located or situated at or on the Premises whereby the Premises shall be taken or occupied by someone other than Tenant; or if this Lease shall be rejected under any applicable provision of the bankruptcy laws; or if Tenant shall fail to take possession within fifteen (15) days of the commencement of this Lease; and upon Landlord serving written notice to Tenant specifying the nature of the default, Tenant shall have ___[31]____ (__) days from the date of receipt of such notice to cure the default (or if such default cannot be cured within such period, Tenant must diligently and in good faith proceed to cure the default). If Tenant shall have failed to cure or proceed to cure the default within such period, Landlord may serve a ____[32]____ (__) day notice of cancellation of this Lease upon Tenant and upon the expiration of the cancellation period this Lease shall terminate and expire and Tenant shall quit and surrender the Premises to Landlord but Tenant shall remain liable as provided in this Lease.

(A) If after default in payment of rent or violation of any other provision of this Lease, or upon the expiration of this Lease, Tenant moves out or is dispossessed and fails to remove any trade fixtures or other property prior to such said default, removal, expiration of Lease, or prior to the issuance of the final order or execution of the warrant, then and in that event, the said fixtures and property shall be deemed abandoned by the said Tenant and shall become the property of Landlord.

15. NO WAIVER BY LANDLORD - The failure of Landlord to insist upon a strict performance of any of the terms, conditions and covenants herein shall not be deemed a waiver of any rights or remedies that Landlord may have, and shall not be deemed a waiver of any subsequent breach or default in the terms, conditions and covenants herein contained. This instrument may not be changed, modified, discharged or terminated orally.

(Document continued on next page)

33. The date of signing the Lease.

34. The name of the Landlord if a corporation. Otherwise delete the line.

35. If the Landlord is an individual, delete "BY" and print the Landlord's name directly below the line, with the Landlord to sign above the line. If the Landlord is a corporation, print the name and title of the individual acting for the corporation directly below the line, with that person to sign above the line.

36. The name of the Tenant if a corporation. Otherwise delete the line.

37. If the Tenant is an individual, delete "BY" and print the Tenant's name directly below the line, with the Tenant to sign above the line. If the Tenant is a corporation, print the name and title of the individual acting for the corporation directly below the line, with that person to sign above the line.

Note: if the Tenant is a corporation, the Landlord may want to consider requiring that the Tenant corporation's Lease obligations (particularly the payment of rent) be personally guaranteed by an officer of the corporation. A Personal Guaranty form is found elsewhere in this book.

16. LEASE NOT A LIEN - This Lease shall not be a lien against the Premises in respect to any mortgage that may now or in the future be placed against said Premises, and that the recording of such mortgage or mortgages shall have preference and precedence and be superior and prior in lien of this Lease, irrespective of the date of recording, and the Tenant agrees to execute without cost any such instrument which may be deemed necessary or desirable to further effect the subordination of this Lease to any such mortgages, and a refusal to execute such instrument shall entitle the Landlord, or the Landlord's assigns and legal representative to the option of cancelling this Lease without incurring any expenses or damages and the term hereby granted is expressly limited accordingly.

17. QUIET POSSESSION - Landlord covenants that Tenant, on paying the rent and additional rent, and faithfully performing the covenants required or imposed upon Tenant, shall and may peacefully and quietly have, hold and enjoy the Premises for the term of this Lease, provided however, that this covenant shall be conditioned upon the retention of title to the Premises by the Landlord.

18. BINDING EFFECT - It is mutually understood and agreed that the covenants and agreements contained in this Lease shall be binding upon the parties hereto and upon their respective successors, heirs, executors and administrators.

IN WITNESS WHEREOF, the parties have set their hand and seal this __[33]__ day of _________, 19__.

__________*[34]*__________

*BY*______________________
[35] (Landlord)

__________*[36]*__________

*BY*______________________
[37] (Tenant)

EXTENSION/RENEWAL OF COMMERCIAL LEASE (2-36)

This form may be used when a Landlord or Tenant wishes to extend or renew an existing Commercial Lease with only minor changes (such as a new expiration date, a new rent or the like) without the necessity of preparing a new Lease. Both the Landlord and the Tenant must be careful however, since this form carries forward all terms and conditions of the original Lease except those specifically changed. On the other hand, with an Extension/Renewal both parties are protected from the problems that might arise by having mistakenly forgotten to carry forward certain terms from the original Lease into a new Lease.

EXTENSION/RENEWAL
OF COMMERCIAL LEASE

EXTENSION/RENEWAL AGREEMENT, made on ________[1]________, 19__, between ________[2]________, *[3][residing at __________[4]__________]* ***OR*** *[a _____[5]_____ corporation with its principal office at __________[6]__________]*, as "Landlord" and ________[7]________, *[8][residing at __________[9]__________]* ***OR*** *[a _____[10]_____ corporation with its principal office at __________[11]__________]*, as "Tenant."

1. The date of signing the Agreement.

2. The name of the Landlord.

3. Choose one depending on whether the Landlord is a corporation.

4. The address of the Landlord.

5. The state of incorporation of the Landlord.

6. The address of the Landlord corporation's principal office.

7. The name of the Tenant.

8. Choose one depending on whether the Tenant is a corporation.

9. The address of the Tenant.

10. The state of incorporation of the Tenant.

11. The address of the Tenant corporation's principal office.

(Document continued on next page)

1. LEASE - Landlord and Tenant acknowledge that they have previously entered into a lease for a _____[12]_____ known as _____[13]_____ *[14][and more particularly described on the plan annexed to and made part of this Lease]* in the building located at __________[15]__________ in the City of _____[16]_____, County of _____[17]_____, State of _____[18]_____ (the "Premises"), for a term of ___[19]___ *[20][years]* ***OR*** *[months]* ending on _______[21]______ (the "Lease").

(A) Landlord and Tenant acknowledge that neither party is now in default of any of the obligations imposed upon the other under the terms and conditions of the Lease *[22][except ______________________________ ______________________________]*.

2. EXTENSION/RENEWAL OF LEASE - In consideration of the payment of $_____[23]_____ by Tenant, the receipt of which is acknowledged, Landlord and Tenant agree to extend and renew the Lease as follows:

(A) Term - ___________[24]______________ ______________________________.

(Document continued on next page)

12. A description of the leased space, for example "a suite," "a room," "a floor," etc.

13. Identify the specific space being leased, such as the suite number, room number or floor number.

14. If only a portion of a building is being leased (such as part of one floor), it is recommended that plans be made a part of the Lease (annexed) to identify exactly which space is being leased. Otherwise delete.

15. The address of the building.

16. The city in which the space being leased is located.

17. The county in which the space being leased is located.

18. The state in which the space being leased is located.

19. The number of years or months, in words, of the term of the Lease.

20. Choose one.

21. The last day of the term of the Lease.

22. The nature of any default by either party. Otherwise delete.

23. The amount, in numbers, charged by the Landlord for consenting to the extension/renewal. If none, insert "0."

24. The length of the extension in years and months and the last date of the extended period, for example "for two additional years ending December 31, 1994."

EXTENSION/RENEWAL OF COMMERCIAL LEASE *continued*

25. The amount, in numbers, of rent to be charged during each year of the extension/renewal period, including any automatic increases and when such increases will begin.

26. The amount, in numbers, of the present security deposit.

27. The amount, in numbers, of any additional security deposit required. Otherwise delete. (Note: since the rental during the extension/renewal period is most likely greater than during the initial period, the Landlord should consider requesting such additional security as may be necessary to keep the total security deposit held equal to the same monthly rent multiple as originally charged.)

28. The "base year" to be used for calculation of escalation provisions during the extension/renewal period.

29. Any changes, modifications, alterations, additions or deletions to the terms of the original Lease. If none, delete.

(B) Rent - ___________[25]_____________
____.

(C) Security - The parties acknowledge that Landlord is presently holding the sum of $_____[26]_____ as a security deposit for the faithful performance of the obligations of Tenant under the Lease and Landlord will continue to hold this sum as security during the period of this extension/renewal. *[Tenant agrees to deposit with Landlord as additional security $_____[27]____.]*

(D) "Base Year for Escalations" - The base year for the calculation of all escalations shall be ___[28]___.

[29] [(E) ______________________________________
____
____.]

3. RATIFICATION OF LEASE - In all other respects, Landlord and Tenant ratify, extend and renew the Lease and agree that the Lease shall be deemed a part of this extension/renewal and incorporated by reference into this extension and renewal with the same force and effect as if set forth in its entirety in this agreement of extension and renewal.

(Document continued on next page)

IN WITNESS WHEREOF, the parties have set their hand and seal this __[1]__ day of __________, 19__.

__________*[30]*__________

*BY*________________________
[31] (Landlord)

__________*[32]*__________

*BY*________________________
[33] (Tenant)

30. The name of the Landlord if a corporation. Otherwise delete the line.

31. If the Landlord is an individual, delete "BY" and print the Landlord's name directly below the line, with the Landlord to sign above the line. If the Landlord is a corporation, print the name and title of the individual acting for the corporation directly below the line, with that person to sign above the line.

32. The name of the Tenant if a corporation. Otherwise delete the line.

33. If the Tenant is an individual, delete "BY" and print the Tenant's name directly below the line, with the Tenant to sign above the line. If the Tenant is a corporation, print the name and title of the individual acting for the corporation directly below the line, with that person to sign above the line.

Note: if the Tenant's obligations under the original Lease were personally guaranteed, the Landlord should require a new, personal guaranty of the Extension/renewal Agreement since the law in most states is that a change in the terms of the agreement being guaranteed releases the person giving the guarantee. A Personal Guaranty form is found elsewhere in this book.

ASSIGNMENT AND ASSUMPTION OF COMMERCIAL LEASE (2-37)

This form is used when an existing Commercial Lease is to be assigned by the Tenant (the Assignor) to another party (the Assignee) who agrees to assume all of the obligations of the Lease. This form assumes a typical situation in which payment is made to the Landlord for obtaining his approval for assigning the Lease.

The Lease to be assigned must be reviewed carefully to determine the rights of the Tenant to assign the Lease and the rights of the Landlord in the event of a request to assign the Lease.

ASSIGNMENT AND ASSUMPTION OF COMMERCIAL LEASE

AGREEMENT OF ASSIGNMENT AND ASSUMPTION OF LEASE made on _______[1]_______, 19__, between ________[2]________, *[3][residing at __________[4]__________]* ***OR*** *[a _____[5]_____ corporation with its principal office at __________[6]__________]*, as "Assignor" and ________[7]________, *[8][residing at __________[9]__________]* ***OR*** *[a _____[10]_____ corporation with its principal office at __________[11]__________]*, as "Assignee."

1. LEASE - Assignor acknowledges that *[12][he]* ***OR*** *[it]* has previously entered into a lease for a ____[13]_____ known as _____[14]_____ in the building located at

1. The date of signing the Assignment.

2. The name of the Landlord.

3. Choose one depending on whether the Landlord is a corporation.

4. The address of the Landlord.

5. The state of incorporation of the Landlord.

6. The address of the Landlord corporation's principal office.

7. The name of the Tenant.

8. Choose one depending on whether the Tenant is a corporation.

9. The address of the Tenant.

10. The state of incorporation of the Tenant.

11. The address of the Tenant corporation's principal office.

12. Choose one.

13. A description of the leased space, for example "a suite," "a room," "a floor," etc.

14. Identify the specific space being leased, such as the suite number, room number or floor number.

(Document continued on next page)

15. The address of the building.

16. The city in which the space being leased is located.

17. The county in which the space being leased is located.

18. The state in which the space being leased is located.

19. The number of years or months, in words, of the term of the Lease.

20. Choose one.

21. The last day of the term of the Lease.

22. Delete if the lease is not available. However, it is strongly recommended that a copy be attached to preclude the Assignee from later claiming that he was unfamiliar with all of its terms.

23. The nature of any default by the Assignor. If none, delete.

24. The amount, in words and numbers, paid by the Assignee to the Assignor for the Assignment.

25. The date the Assignment is to begin.

__________[15]__________ in the City of _____[16]_____, County of _____[17]_____, State of _____[18]_____ (the "Premises"), for a term of ___[19]___ *[20][years]* ***OR*** *[months]* ending on __________[21]__________ *[22][, a true and complete copy of which is attached to and made a part of this Agreement]* (the "Lease").

(A) Assignor represents to Assignee and Landlord:

(i) that Assignor is not in default of any of the obligations imposed upon Assignor under the terms and conditions of the Lease *[23][except ____];*

(ii) that Assignor has not done or suffered anything to be done which might impose any liability upon Landlord or Assignee; and

(iii) that there are no claims, security interests or liens against the Premises, the Lease or any equipment, fixtures or personal property installed by Assignor in or attached to the Premises.

(B) Assignee represents to Assignor and Landlord that Assignee has examined the attached Lease and is familiar with all of its terms and conditions.

(C) Assignor and Assignee represent to each other and to Landlord that Landlord's consent to this Assignment and assumption is necessary and may be conditioned upon such additional terms and conditions as Landlord may require. In the event that Landlord shall have failed or refused to give its consent, this agreement shall be null and void and neither party shall have any further obligation to the other.

2. ASSIGNMENT BY ASSIGNOR - Assignor, in consideration of the sum of _____[24]_____ Dollars ($_____) to be paid by Assignee upon receipt by Assignee of a copy of this Assignment consented to by the Landlord, does hereby assign to Assignee the Lease from and after ________[25]________, 19__, (the "Effective Date") for all the rest and remainder of the term of the Lease and any renewals or extensions of the Lease subject only to the

(Document continued on next page)

26. The amount, in numbers, of the previously paid security deposit.

27. Choose one depending on whether the security deposit is to be returned to the Assignor.

28. Choose one.

29. The amount, in numbers, of the new security to be paid by the Assignee.

30. The payment, in numbers, required by the Landlord for giving his consent to the Assignment.

31. The party paying money to the Landlord for giving his consent to the Assignment, typically the Assignee or Assignor.

32. A description of any additional conditions imposed by the Landlord. If none, delete.

33. The name of the Assignor if a corporation. Otherwise delete the line.

34. If the Assignor is an individual, delete "BY" and print the Assignor's name directly below the line, with the Assignor to sign above the line. If the Assignor is a corporation, print the name and title of the individual acting for the corporation directly below the line, with that person to sign above the line.

covenants, conditions and limitations contained in the Lease.

(A) Assignor agrees that the security deposit of $_____[26]_____ previously paid by Assignor, together with interest earned but unpaid, if any, shall be *[27][similarly assigned to Assignee and Assignor waives any claim or interest in the security deposit.]* ***OR*** *[refunded and returned to Assignor.]*

3. ASSUMPTION BY ASSIGNEE - Assignee assumes the Lease and all the terms, covenants and conditions imposed by the Lease upon the Tenant and agrees to perform and comply with all of the terms, covenants, and conditions imposed upon Tenant by the Lease on or after the Effective Date as if Assignee had originally executed the Lease.

(A) Assignee acknowledges that the security deposit in the sum of $_____[26]_____ *[28][previously paid by Assignor shall be assigned to the account of and for the benefit of Assignee.]* ***OR*** *[shall be returned and refunded to Assignor in which event Assignee shall pay to Landlord the sum of $_____[29]_____ as and for security for the faithful performance of the term, covenants and conditions of the Lease by Assignee.]*

4. CONSENT BY LANDLORD - In consideration of the payment of $___[30]___ by ______[31]________, the receipt of which is hereby acknowledged, and upon Assignee's assumption of all of the terms, covenants and conditions imposed upon Tenant in the Lease, Landlord consents to the Assignment of the Lease *[32][upon the following additional conditions: ____________________ ____].*

IN WITNESS WHEREOF, the parties have set their hand and seal on the date written above.

__________*[33]*__________

*BY*______________________

[34] (Assignor)

(Document continued on next page)

35. The name of the Assignee if a corporation. Otherwise delete the line.

36. If the Assignee is an individual, delete "BY" and print the Assignee's name directly below the line, with the Assignee to sign above the line. If the Assignee is a corporation, print the name and title of the individual acting for the corporation directly below the line, with that person to sign above the line.

Note: if the Assignee is a new corporation or one without a tested credit history, the Landlord should consider requiring a personal guaranty of the Lease terms being assumed by the Assignee. A Personal Guaranty is found elsewhere in this book.

37. The date through which all rent, additional rent and other charges imposed by the Lease have been paid.

38. The date of signing the consent by the Landlord.

39. The name of the Landlord if a corporation. Otherwise delete the line.

40. If the Landlord is an individual, delete "BY" and print the Landlord's name directly below the line, with the Landlord to sign above the line. If the Landlord is a corporation, print the name and title of the individual acting for the corporation directly below the line, with that person to sign above the line.

__________*[35]*__________

*BY*________________________
[36] (Assignee)

CERTIFICATION AND CONSENT BY LANDLORD

Landlord certifies that: (i) all rent, additional rent and other sundry charges under the Lease are paid through _____[37]_____, 19__; (ii) that the Lease is in full force and effect and that Landlord has not been notified of any lien, pledge or encumbrance upon or against the Lease; and (iii) that there is no known existing default of any of the terms, covenants or conditions imposed upon Assignor as Tenant under the Lease.

Upon the foregoing, Landlord hereby consents to the Assignment of the Lease by Assignor and the Assumption of the Lease by Assignee as of the Effective Date.

Dated: ______[38]______, 19___

__________*[39]*__________

*BY*________________________
[40] (Landlord)

SUBLEASE AGREEMENT (2-38)

A Sublease Agreement is used when a Tenant wants to Lease all or a portion of his space to another party while retaining his interest (either in the rest of the space or in the entire space if the Tenant expects to return). The Tenant is called the "Over–Tenant" and the Tenant's Lease with the Landlord is called the "Over-Lease." The party subleasing the space is called the "Under-Tenant." This Sublease provides for obtaining the consent of the Landlord. A copy of the original Lease is to be attached (annexed) to the Sublease Agreement.

This Sublease can be used for both Commercial and Residential Leases. Note that in most states, the Landlord's consent is usually not required in a Commercial Lease but is most likely required in a Residential Lease. Also, state and local laws will likely govern subleasing and you are therefore urged to consult your local housing authority.

SUBLEASE AGREEMENT

1. The name of the Over-Tenant (the original Tenant).
2. The address of the Over-Tenant.
3. The name of the Under-Tenant (the party subleasing the space).
4. The address of the Under-Tenant.
5. The name of the Landlord.
6. The address of the Landlord.
7. The date of signing the Over-Lease (the original Lease).
8. The commencement date of the Over-Lease.
9. The ending date of the Over-Lease.

The parties agree as follows:

Parties to this Sublease:

A. Over-Tenant: ________[1]________

Address: ________[2]________

____

B. Under-Tenant: ________[3]________

Address: ________[4]________

____

Information From Over-Lease, a complete copy of which is annexed to and made a part of this Sublease:

A. Landlord: ________[5]________

Address: ________[6]________

____

B. Over-Tenant: ________[1]________

Address: ________[2]________

____

C. Date, Term of Over-Lease: ____[7]____, 19__, commencing on _____[8]___, 19__ and ending on _____[9]___, 19__.

1. SUBLEASE - Over-Tenant agrees to sublet to

(Document continued on next page)

Under-Tenant and Under-Tenant agrees to sublet _______[10]________ known as ____[11]_____ in the building located at __________[12]__________ in the City of _____[13]_____, County of _____[14]_____, State of _____[15]_____ (the "Premises"), for a term of ___[16]___ *[17][years]* ***OR*** *[months]* commencing on __________[18]__________, 19__ and ending on __________[19]__________, 19__ on the following terms:

(A) Use of the Premises - ________________________[20]________________________.

(B) Monthly Rent - $_____[21]_____ payable in advance on the first day of each month.

(C) Security - Under-Tenant shall pay to Over-Tenant the sum of $_____[22]_____ as security for the faithful performance of Under-Tenant's obligations which *[23] [will]* ***OR*** *[will not]* be deposited to an interest bearing account.

[24] [(D) Additional Rent -
____
____.]

2. OVER-TENANT'S DUTIES - The Over-Lease sets forth the duties of the Landlord. Over-Tenant is not obligated to perform the duties of Landlord. If Landlord fails or refuses to perform its duties, Under-Tenant must advise Over-Tenant and upon receipt of such notice, Over-Tenant will promptly request Landlord to perform Landlord's duties under the Over-Lease. Over-Tenant's duties in this regard are limited to promptly requesting that Landlord perform its duties. The parties acknowledge that Under–Tenant may not pay rent directly to Landlord and has no authority to contact or make any agreement with Landlord.

10. A description of the leased space, such as a "suite," "apartment," "room," "floor," etc.

11. Identify the specific space being leased, such as the suite number, apartment number, room number or floor number.

12. The address of the building in which the space being subleased is located.

13. The city in which the space being subleased is located.

14. The county in which the space being subleased is located.

15. The state in which the space being subleased is located.

16. The number of years or months, in words, of the Sublease.

17. Choose one.

18. The commencement date of the Sublease.

19. The ending date of the Sublease.

20. The use of the space which is permitted by the Landlord.

21. The amount, in numbers, of monthly rent to be paid.

22. The amount, in numbers, of the security deposit to be paid by the Under-Tenant.

23. Choose one.

24. A description detailing rent escalation charges that are being passed through to the Under-Tenant. Include references to the specific paragraph numbers of the Over-Lease. If none, delete.

(Document continued on next page)

25. A description of any other duties of the Over-Tenant. If none, delete this paragraph and renumber the remaining paragraphs.

26. Insert the appliances to be furnished. If none, delete.

27. A description of any other duties of the Under-Tenant. If none, delete.

[25] [(A) Over-Tenant's Additional Duties -

____

____.]

(B) Under-Tenant acknowledges that Over-Tenant has no obligation to supply or provide heat, hot water, electricity or telephone service and that no part of the rent is for such service. Under-Tenant shall make such separate arrangements with the utility company customarily providing any such service as may be required, shall have accounts with any such supplier in his own name, shall timely pay all bills and will not suffer or permit any charges for such service to become a lien against the Premises or any separate account(s) of Over-Tenant.

[26] [(C) Under-Tenant acknowledges that the Premises is equipped and furnished with

____,
collectively called "the Appliances," that Under-Tenant has inspected the Appliances and that they are in working order. Under-Tenant agrees to take good care of the Appliances and return them at the end of this Sublease in the same or similar condition, ordinary wear and tear excepted. Under-Tenant agrees to pay to Over-Tenant the replacement or repair cost of any Appliance lost or damaged through Under-Tenant's negligence or failure to act.]

3. UNDER-TENANT'S DUTIES - Under-Tenant agrees to pay directly to Over-Tenant rent, additional rent and other charges as required by this Sublease and to do everything required of Under-Tenant by this Sublease. The parties acknowledge that Under-Tenant may not pay rent directly to Landlord and has no authority to contact or make any agreement with Landlord.

[27] [(A) Under-Tenant's Additional Duties -

____

____.]

4. SUBJECT TO OVER-LEASE - This Sublease is subject to the Over-Lease and to any agreement to which the Over-Tenant is subject. The provisions of the Over-Lease are made a part of this Sublease and all provisions binding on the Over-Tenant are binding on the Under-Tenant who has read the Over-Lease and agrees not to violate it in any way. Over-Tenant shall have all the rights and remedies against Under-Tenant that Landlord has

(Document continued on next page)

28. The number of days, in numbers, by which the Landlord's consent must be received.

29. The date of signing the Sublease Agreement.

30. The name of the Over-Tenant if a corporation. Otherwise delete the line.

31. If the Over-Tenant is an individual, delete "BY" and print the Over-Tenant's name directly below the line, with the Over-Tenant to sign above the line. If the Over-Tenant is a corporation, print the name and title of the individual acting for the corporation directly below the line, with that person to sign above the line.

32. The name of the Under-Tenant if a corporation. Otherwise delete the line.

33. If the Under-Tenant is an individual, delete "BY" and print the Under-Tenant's name directly below the line, with that individual to sign above the line. If the Under-Tenant is a corporation, print the name and title of the individual acting for the corporation directly below the line, with that person to sign above the line.

Note: if the Under-Tenant is a new corporation or one without a tested credit history, the Over-Tenant should consider requiring a Personal Guaranty of the Sublease by the Under-Tenant, found elsewhere in this book.

against Over-Tenant for breach of the Over-Lease or a default by Over-Tenant. If Over-Tenant is found to have breached its obligation to the Landlord as a result of any breach of Under–Tenant's obligation to Over-Tenant, or if such breach by Over-Tenant was caused by Under-Tenant then Under-Tenant shall fully indemnify Over-Tenant for any and all losses, including but not limited to legal and other professional fees, disbursements and costs suffered or incurred as a result of Under-Tenant's breach.

5. CONSENT OF LANDLORD - If Landlord's consent to this Sublease is required, this consent must be received within __[28]__ days from the date of this Sublease. If Landlord's consent is not received within such time, this Sublease shall be null and void; any payments made by Under-Tenant shall be refunded and each party shall be released from any further liability or obligation to the other.

6. ASSIGNMENT OR FURTHER SUBLETTING - Under-Tenant shall not be permitted to assign this Sublease or further sublet the Premises without the express written consent of the Over-Tenant and Landlord (if Landlord's consent for this Sublease was required) on such other or additional terms as either Over-Tenant or Landlord may require.

IN WITNESS WHEREOF, the parties have set their hand and seal this __[29]__ day of ________, 19__.

__________*[30]*__________

*BY*______________________
[31] (Over-Tenant)

__________*[32]*__________

*BY*______________________
[33] (Under-Tenant)

(Document continued on next page)

34. Delete the remainder of the form if the Landlord's consent is NOT required for the Sublet.

35. The date of signing the consent by the Landlord.

36. The name of the Landlord if a corporation. Otherwise delete the line.

37. If the Landlord is an individual, delete "BY" and print the Landlord's name directly below the line, with the Landlord to sign above the line. If the Landlord is a corporation, print the name and title of the individual acting for the corporation directly below the line, with that person to sign above the line.

[34] [CONSENT BY LANDLORD

Landlord hereby consents to the Sublease.

Dated: ________[35]________, 19___

__________[36]__________

BY______________________
[37] (Landlord)]

Buying and Selling Goods 3

Whether purchasing something tangible, like an automobile, or intangible, like a license to sell someone else's product, buying and selling are the lifeblood of commerce. The common thread that runs through the agreements in this chapter is the requirement to accurately and completely describe what is being bought and sold.

Selling Personal Property Personal property is any property other than real estate. This section provides forms that can be used by individuals to sell property. The forms also may be used by businesses for the sale of items that are not sold in the ordinary course of that business. For example, if a business is selling a computer because it is no longer needed, the Bill of Sale—Personal Property form in this section is applicable. However, if the business sells computers as its regular business, it should use a form in the next section.

Selling and Leasing—Business It is important to decide exactly what is to be bought or sold and how it is to be paid for before deciding which of the contracts for sale of goods to use. For example, if a seller wishes to limit his merchandise warranties, the Contract for Sale of Goods—Warranties should be considered. An Equipment Lease is also provided, since many businesses lease rather than purchase.

Assignments and Licenses An Assignment is used by one party to transfer his rights to another. Several Assignment forms are found in this section, including those for assigning trademarks, copyrights and literary works. Often a sale does not involve the transfer of a product, but rather the right to manufacture or sell that product, which is a license. This section offers licensing forms for both trademarks and general use.

BILL OF SALE—AUTOMOBILE (3-01)

This Bill of Sale establishes a change of ownership of an automobile (or truck), and of any added accessories such as an audio system, from the current owner (the Seller) to a new owner (the Buyer). Additionally, this form satisfies federal law requiring certain statements by sellers of used cars regarding odometer readings (mileage) and odometer alterations.

BILL OF SALE—AUTOMOBILE

________[1]________, residing at __________[2]__________ ("Seller"), in consideration of the sum of ________[3]_______ Dollars ($_____[4]_____) received from ________[5]________, residing at __________[6]__________ ("Buyer"), receipt of which is acknowledged, hereby sells, transfers and conveys the following automobile:

Model Year: __[7]__, Manufacturer/Make: _____[8]_____, ("V.I.N.") Vehicle Identification No.: _______[9]_______, *[10][Engine Serial No.: _______________]*, Model: _____[11]_____, Body Type: ____[12]____, Color: ___[13]___, *[14][together with the following accessories: ____,]* (the "Automobile").

Seller warrants to Buyer the following: (i) Seller is the owner of the Automobile; (ii) Seller has the legal right to sell the Automobile; (iii) the Automobile is free and

(Document continued on next page)

1. The name of the Seller.

2. The address of the Seller.

3. The selling price, in words.

4. The selling price, in numbers.

5. The name of the Buyer.

6. The address of the Buyer.

7. The model year of the automobile, for example "1981."

8. The manufacturer of the automobile, for example "Alfa Romeo."

9. The "V.I.N." (Vehicle Identification Number), for example "ZARAA6695B121." (Note: on most automobiles, the V.I.N. can be found stamped on a metal plate visible from the outside of the car in the corner of the windshield on the driver's side.)

10. The engine serial number if it is not the original engine. Otherwise delete.

11. The model name or type, for example "GTV-6/2.5."

12. The body type, for example "two door sedan."

13. The color.

14. Insert descriptions and serial numbers, if available, for all accessories added after the original purchase that will be included in the sale, for example "Alpine radio, serial no. ____." If none, delete.

15. Insert the name of any lender, such as a bank, for which there may be an outstanding loan and the amount owed. If none, delete.

16. If the odometer reading was reset to "0000" or it is a replacement unit, insert the previous mileage, in numbers.

17. The odometer reading, in numbers.

18. Choose one.

19. The date of signing the Bill of Sale by the Seller.

20. The name of the Seller printed directly below the line, with the Seller to sign above the line.

clear of all liens and encumbrances *[15][except: ________________];* and (iv) Seller will defend title of the Automobile against any claim or demand except any lienholder disclosed in this Bill of Sale.

BUYER HAS EXAMINED OR HAS HAD AN OPPORTUNITY TO EXAMINE THE AUTOMOBILE. THE AUTOMOBILE IS SOLD AND DELIVERED IN A STRICTLY "AS IS" CONDITION AND SELLER EXPRESSLY DISCLAIMS ALL WARRANTIES, EXPRESS OR IMPLIED, OF MERCHANTABILITY OR FITNESS FOR A PARTICULAR PURPOSE.

Seller certifies that while the Automobile was in Seller's possession, the odometer was (check one box ONLY):

( ) not altered or disconnected;

( ) altered for repair/replacement and that the mileage registered is the same as before the repair/replacement;

( ) reset to 0000 miles/kilometers and that the registered mileage before such repair/replacement was ____[16]___.

Seller certifies that the odometer reading is ____[17]____ *[18][miles]* ***OR*** *[kilometers]* and that to the best of Seller's knowledge the foregoing odometer reading (check one box ONLY):

( ) reflects the actual mileage.

( ) reflects the actual mileage in excess of 99,999 miles/kilometers.

( ) is NOT the actual mileage.

Dated: ______[19]______ ______________________

[20] (Seller)

(Document continued on next page)

21. The Notary Public completes this part of the form, and signs and seals it by affixing his stamp or seal.

STATE OF _____[21]_____, COUNTY OF _____[21]_____, ss.:

On ________[21]________, 19__, before me ________[21]________ personally came ________[21]________, to me known, and known to me to be the individual(s) described in and who executed the foregoing ____________[21]____________, and duly acknowledged to me that (he)(she)(they) executed the same.

____
Notary Public

BILL OF SALE—PERSONAL PROPERTY (3-02)

This Bill of Sale is used to establish a change in ownership of personal property, as distinguished from real property (land and buildings) for which there are different requirements (see the real estate forms elsewhere in this book). Care should be taken to identify each item of property as completely as possible to distinguish the property being bought from other, similar items.

BILL OF SALE—PERSONAL PROPERTY

________[1]________, *[2][residing at __________[3]__________]* ***OR*** *[a _____[4]_____ corporation with its principal office at __________[5]__________* ("Seller"), in consideration of the sum of ________[6]________ Dollars ($_____[7]_____) received from ________[8]________, *[9][residing at __________[10]__________]* ***OR*** *[a _____[11]_____ corporation with its principal office at __________[12]__________* ("Buyer"), receipt of which is acknowledged, hereby sells, transfers and conveys the *[13][personal property listed on the attached Schedule A]* ***OR*** *personal property: ____________[14]____________]* ("Property").

Seller warrants to Buyer the following: (i) Seller is the owner of the Property and each item of property listed; (ii) Seller has the legal right to sell the Property and each item of property listed; (iii) the Property and each item of property is/are free and clear of all liens and encumbrances

(Document continued on next page)

1. The name of the Seller.
2. Choose one depending on whether the Seller is a corporation.
3. The address of the Seller.
4. The state of incorporation of the Seller.
5. The address of the Seller corporation's principal office.
6. The selling price, in words.
7. The selling price, in numbers.
8. The name of the Buyer.
9. Choose one depending on whether the Buyer is a corporation.
10. The address of the Buyer.
11. The state of incorporation of the Buyer.
12. The address of the Buyer corporation's principal office.
13. Choose one. If the use of a "Schedule A" is chosen, on a separate sheet of paper headed "Schedule A" list the names of the items to be sold and their serial numbers, if any.
14. A description of each item of property and its serial number, if any.

15. On a separate sheet headed "Schedule A", or on Schedule A if it was already created in No. 13 above, insert the names of any parties who have liens against the property being sold and the amount owed to each.

16. The date of signing the Bill of Sale.

17. The name of the Seller if a corporation. Otherwise delete the line.

18. If the Seller is an individual, delete "BY" and print the name of the Seller directly below the line, with the Seller to sign above the line. If the Seller is a corporation, print the name and title of the person acting for the corporation directly below the line, with that person to sign above the line.

19. Insert a Notary Statement, found elsewhere in this book, for the Seller, either an Individual or Corporate form, as appropriate. The Notary will complete the form.

except as shown on the attached Schedule A[15]; and (iv) Seller will defend title of the Property and of each item of property against any claim or demand except any lienholder disclosed in this Bill of Sale.

BUYER HAS EXAMINED OR HAS HAD AN OPPORTUNITY TO EXAMINE THE PROPERTY AND EACH ITEM OF PROPERTY SOLD. THE PROPERTY AND EACH ITEM OF PROPERTY IS SOLD AND DELIVERED IN A STRICTLY "AS IS" CONDITION AND SELLER EXPRESSLY DISCLAIMS ALL WARRANTIES, EXPRESS OR IMPLIED, OF MERCHANTABILITY OR FITNESS FOR PARTICULAR PURPOSE.

Dated: ______[16]______ __________*[17]*_________

*BY*____________________
[18] (Seller)

[19] [Notary Statement]

CONTRACT FOR SALE OF GOODS—GENERAL (3-03)

As a general rule, a Contract relating to the Sale of Goods whose value is more than $500 cannot be enforced unless the agreement is in writing and signed by both the Buyer and Seller. Therefore, this Contract should be used when buying or selling goods whose value is in excess of that amount.

A Contract for the Sale of Goods may contain any terms to which the parties agree but should, at the very least, include a description of exactly what is being sold and the price and delivery terms. Additional contract clauses are found elsewhere in this book and may be inserted as necessary.

A cautionary note: nobody likes to consider what would happen in the event that one of the parties defaulted. The guiding principal should be to "hope for the best, but plan for the worst." This Contract deals with that issue.

CONTRACT FOR SALE OF GOODS—
GENERAL

AGREEMENT made this __[1]__ day of ______, 19__ by and between ________[2]________ *[3][, a ________ corporation,]* with its office at __________[4]__________ ("Seller") and ________[5]________ *[6][, a ________ corporation,]* with its office at __________[7]__________ ("Buyer").

1. SALE - Seller has agreed to sell and Buyer has agreed to purchase ______________[8]______________ in accordance with the plans and specifications set forth on the attached Schedule A.[9]

2. PRICE - The total price for the goods is $_____[10]_____ at __________[11]__________, it being

(Document continued on next page)

1. The date of signing the Contract.

2. The name of the Seller.

3. If the Seller is a corporation, insert the state of incorporation. Otherwise delete.

4. The address of the Seller.

5. The name of the Buyer.

6. If the Buyer is a corporation, insert the state of incorporation. Otherwise delete.

7. The address of the Buyer.

8. A detailed description of the goods being purchased, for example "5,000 cases of widgets, 12 per case, on pallets of 100 cases each."

9. On a separate sheet of paper headed "Schedule A" list the specifications (size, weight, etc.) of the goods being purchased.

10. The price, in numbers, of the goods being purchased.

11. The location at which title (ownership) to the goods passes to the Buyer, for example: "Seller's loading dock" or "Buyer's loading dock."

understood that the price *[12][does not include freight, shipping and delivery and insurance costs, which shall be the sole responsibility of Buyer.]* ***OR*** *[includes freight, shipping and delivery and insurance costs.]*

(A) Payment shall be made as follows: *[13][the entire amount due shall be paid in full not later than __[14]__ days after receipt by Buyer of the items purchased.]* ***OR*** *[$___[15]____ upon signing of this Agreement, $___[16]___ upon receipt of each shipment and the balance of $__[17]___ upon receipt of the shipment containing the balance of the items purchased.]* ***OR*** *___________________[18]___________________.]*

3. DELIVERY/SHIPPING/ACCEPTANCE -

(A) Delivery of the goods purchased shall be *[19][as set forth in the attached Schedule B.]* ***OR***

(Document continued on next page)

12. Choose one, depending on whether the price includes freight and insurance.

13. Choose one depending on the desired payment schedule. If the third alternative is chosen, skip to instruction No. 18. (Note: the choices shown are examples only. The method and timing of payment can be upon whatever terms the parties agree.)

14. The number of days, in numbers, after receipt of the items by which payment must be made. Then skip to instruction No. 19.

15. The amount, in numbers, of any deposit or down-payment made by the Buyer.

16. The amount, in numbers, due upon the Buyer's receipt of each shipment.

17. The amount, in numbers, of any unpaid balance remaining due.

18. Any other payment terms agreed upon by the parties.

19. Choose one, and if the use of a "Schedule B" is chosen, on a separate sheet of paper headed "Schedule B" list the the delivery schedule and skip to instruction No. 27. If the third alternative is chosen, skip to instruction No. 26. (As with the terms of payment, so too the delivery schedule can contain any terms to which the parties agree.)

CONTRACT FOR SALE OF GOODS—GENERAL *continued*

20. The quantity of the first shipment.

21. The date by which the first shipment must be received.

22. The quantity of the second shipment.

23. The date by which the second shipment must be received.

24. The quantity of the final shipment.

25. The date by which the final shipment must be received.

26. Any other delivery schedule agreed upon by the parties.

27. The specific shipping terms agreed upon, including the method (such as via the Seller's trucks, independent motor carrier, rail, air or a combination) and who will pay the costs of shipping and insurance. Be sure to be consistent with your choice in No. 12 above.

28. The number of days, in numbers, after receipt by which the Buyer must notify the Seller of rejection of any item.

29. The party who will pay the costs of shipping rejected items back to the Seller.

30. The number of days, in numbers, by which rejected items must be returned to the Seller.

[___[20]___ on or before _______[21]______, ___[22]___ on or before _______[23]______ and the balance of ___[24]___ not later than ______[25]______.]
OR *[____________________[26]____________________.]*

(B) Shipment of the goods purchased shall be ____________________[27]____________________.

(C) Buyer shall examine each shipment promptly upon receipt and will advise Seller in writing of the number or quantity accepted and rejected and the reason(s) for rejection within __[28]__ days of receipt of each shipment. All items not accepted shall be returned to Seller at _____[29]_____ expense and any item not returned within __[30]__ days of notification to Seller shall be deemed accepted.

(Document continued on next page)

31. A description of the Seller's obligations to continue to perform the terms of the contract (essentially to continue to manufacture and ship the goods) and Seller's remedies in the event of a default by the Buyer. For example, the Seller may not wish to continue to produce or deliver goods if the Buyer has defaulted in making a payment. To protect himself, the Seller may wish to provide that "Seller is not obligated to deliver goods if any payment is not received within 10 days after the date due."

32. A description of the Buyer's obligations to continue to perform the terms of the contract (essentially to continue to pay) and the Buyer's remedies in the event of a default by the Seller. For example, where a Buyer is relying on the delivery of a continuous "stream" of goods from the Seller, to protect himself the Buyer may wish to provide for a monetary damage penalty. Note: in many cases, such damages may not be easy to calculate. Therefore, the parties may agree on a specific dollar amount to be included in the contract (called "liquidated damages," the language for which is found in the Contract for Sale of Goods— "Custom Made" with Liquidated Damages found elsewhere in this chapter).

33. It is suggested that the Seller very carefully consider what, if any, warranties will be given to the Buyer. This paragraph states that there is no warranty. If a warranty is to be given, replace this paragraph with one stating the terms of the warranty.

4. BUYER'S DEFAULT - ________[31]__________
____.

5. SELLER'S DEFAULT - _________[32]_________
____.

[33][6. SELLER'S WARRANTIES - It is understood and agreed by the parties that Seller does not warrant the Buyer's use of the items purchased and does not warrant to Buyer or any other that the items are merchantable or fit for any particular purpose.]

(Document continued on next page)

34. The name of the Seller if a corporation. Otherwise delete the line.

35. If the Seller is an individual, delete "BY" and print the Seller's name directly below the line, with the Seller to sign above the line. If the Seller is a corporation, print the name and title of the person acting for the corporation directly below the line, with that person to sign above the line.

36. The name of the Buyer if a corporation. Otherwise delete the line.

37. If the Buyer is an individual, delete "BY" and print the Buyer's name directly below the line, with the Buyer to sign above the line. If the Buyer is a corporation, print the name and title of the person acting for the corporation directly below the line, with that person to sign above the line.

IN WITNESS WHEREOF, the parties have signed this Agreement on the date first written above.

__________*[34]*__________

*BY*________________________
[35] (Seller)

__________*[36]*__________

*BY*________________________
[37] (Buyer)

CONTRACT FOR SALE OF GOODS— "BUYER'S REQUIREMENTS" (3-04)

A "Buyer's Requirements" contract is one in which the Seller agrees to supply all of the Buyer's Requirements, usually for a stated period of time. This differs from a General Contract of Sale in which the parties agree to a specific number of units at a fixed price to be delivered on a fixed date or dates. A "Buyer's Requirements" contract typically, but not always, gives the Seller the right to adjust the unit price based on factors that are not within the Seller's control such as changes in materials costs or the like. The Buyer would like the contract to permit no price modifications but may be forced to agree to such a provision in order to secure a source of supply. With such a contract, the Buyer knows that the Seller cannot raise his price to increase his profit.

A "Buyer's Requirements" contract may contain any terms to which the parties agree but should, at the very least, include a description of exactly what is being sold and the price and delivery terms. Additional contract clauses are found elsewhere in this book and may be inserted as necessary.

A cautionary note: nobody likes to consider what would happen in the event that one of the parties defaulted. The guiding principal should be to "hope for the best but plan for the worst." This Contract deals with that issue.

CONTRACT OF SALE OF GOODS— "BUYER'S REQUIREMENTS"

AGREEMENT made this __[1]__ day of _______, 19__ by and between ________[2]________ *[3][, a ________ corporation,]* with its office at __________[4]__________ ("Seller") and ________[5]________ *[6][, a ________ corporation,]* with its office at __________[7]__________ ("Buyer").

1. SALE - Seller has agreed to sell and Buyer has agreed to purchase from Seller Buyer's entire requirement of ____________________[8]____________________ which Buyer requires for actual use in Buyer's business from _______[9]_______, 19__ to _______[10]_______, 19__ (the "Term" of this agreement) in accordance with the

(Document continued on next page)

1. The date of signing the Contract.
2. The name of the Seller.
3. If the Seller is a corporation, insert the state of incorporation. Otherwise delete.
4. The address of the Seller.
5. The name of the Buyer.
6. If the Buyer is a corporation, insert the state of incorporation. Otherwise delete.
7. The address of the Buyer.
8. A thorough description of the goods being purchased, for example "5,000 cases of widgets, 12 per case, on pallets of 100 cases each."
9. The starting date of the Seller's shipments of the goods.
10. The ending date of the Seller's shipments of the goods.

11. On a separate sheet of paper headed "Schedule A" list the specifications (size, weight, etc.) of the goods being purchased.

12. Choose one. Enter the price for each item either in the Contract or on a separate sheet of paper headed "Schedule B."

13. The price, in numbers, for each item supplied.

14. Choose one depending on whether the price includes freight and insurance.

15. A description of the circumstances under which the Seller may raise its price, such as an increase in the Seller's materials costs. The event that "triggers" any such increase should be some factor that is both outside of the Seller's control and independently verifiable by the Buyer.

16. Choose one depending on the desired payment schedule. If the third alternative is chosen, skip to instruction No. 21. (Note: the choices shown are examples only. The method and timing of payment can be upon whatever terms the parties agree.)

17. The number of days, in numbers, after receipt of the items by which payment must be made. Then skip to instruction No. 22.

18. The amount, in numbers, of any deposit or down-payment made by the Buyer.

19. The amount, in numbers, due upon the Buyer's receipt of each shipment.

20. The amount, in numbers, of any unpaid balance remaining due.

plans and specifications and quantities set forth on the attached Schedule A.[11]

2. PRICE - During the Term of this agreement, the price for each item shall be *[12][$___[13]___]* ***OR*** *[as set forth on the attached Schedule B]*, it being understood that the price *[14][does not include freight, shipping and delivery and insurance costs which shall be the sole responsibility of Buyer.]* ***OR*** *[includes freight, shipping and delivery and insurance costs.]*

(A) Adjustment in Price - The price may, at the option of Seller, be adjusted in accordance with ____________________[15]____________________.

(B) Payment shall be made as follows: *[16][the entire amount due shall be paid in full not later than __[17]__ days after receipt by Buyer of the items purchased.]* ***OR*** *[$_____[18]_____ upon signing of this Agreement, $_____[19]_____ upon receipt of each shipment and the balance of $_____[20]_____ upon receipt of*

(Document continued on next page)

the shipment containing the balance of the items purchased.] ***OR*** *[____________[21]______________.]*

3. DELIVERY/SHIPPING/ACCEPTANCE -

(A) Delivery of the goods purchased shall be *[22][as set forth in the attached Schedule C.]* ***OR*** *[____[23]_____ on or before ________[24]________, _____[25]_____ on or before ________[26]________ and the balance of _____[27]_____ not later than ________[28]________.]* ***OR*** *[_________[29]__________ ____.]*

(B) Shipment of the goods purchased shall be ________________________[30]____________________.

(C) Buyer shall examine each shipment promptly upon receipt and will advise Seller in writing of the number or quantity accepted and rejected and the reason(s) for rejection within __[31]__ days of receipt of each shipment. All items not accepted shall be returned to Seller at ________[32]________ expense and any item not

(Document continued on next page)

21. Any other payment terms agreed upon by the parties.

22. Choose one depending on the delivery schedule desired. If the first alternative is chosen, on a separate sheet of paper headed "Schedule C" (or headed "Schedule B" if there is no previous "Schedule B" from No. 12) list the delivery schedule and then skip to instruction No. 30. If the third alternative is chosen, skip to instruction No. 29.

23. The quantity of the first shipment.

24. The date by which the first shipment must be received.

25. The quantity of the second shipment.

26. The date by which the second shipment must be received.

27. The quantity of the final shipment.

28. The date by which the final shipment must be made.

29. Any other delivery schedule agreed upon by the parties.

30. The specific shipping terms agreed upon, including method (such as Seller's trucks, independent motor carrier, rail, air or combination) and who will pay the costs of shipping, insurance and the like. Be sure to be consistent with the choice in No. 14.

31. The number of days, in numbers, after receipt by which the Buyer must notify the Seller of rejection of any item received.

32. The party who will pay the costs of shipping any rejected items back to the Seller.

returned within __[33]__ days of notification to Seller shall be deemed accepted.

4. BUYER'S DEFAULT - ________[34]________
____.

5. SELLER'S DEFAULT - ________[35]________
____.

[36][6. SELLER'S WARRANTIES - It is understood and agreed by the parties that Seller does not warrant the Buyer's use of the items purchased and does not warrant to Buyer or any other that the items are merchantable or fit for any particular purpose.]

(Document continued on next page)

33. The number of days, in numbers, by which rejected items must be returned to the Seller.

34. A description of the Seller's obligations to continue to perform the terms of the contract (essentially to continue to manufacture and ship the goods) and the Seller's remedies in the event of a default by the Buyer. For example, the Seller may not wish to continue to produce or deliver goods if the Buyer has defaulted in making a payment. To protect itself, the Seller may wish to provide that "Seller is not obligated to deliver goods if any payment is not received within 10 days after the date due."

35. A description of the Buyer's obligations to continue to perform the terms of the contract (essentially to continue to pay) and the Buyer's remedies in the event of a default by the Seller. For example, where a Buyer is relying on the delivery of a continuous "stream" of goods from the Seller, to protect itself the Buyer may wish to provide for a monetary damage penalty. Note: in many cases, such damages may not be easily calculated. Therefore, the parties may agree on a specific dollar amount to be included in the contract (called "liquidated damages," the language for which is found in the Contract for Sale of Goods—"Custom Made" with Liquidated Damages elsewhere in this chapter).

36. It is suggested that the Seller very carefully consider what, if any, warranties will be given to the Buyer. This paragraph states that there is no warranty. If a warranty is to be given, replace this paragraph with one stating the terms of the warranty.

37. The name of the Seller if a corporation. Otherwise delete the line.

38. If the Seller is an individual, delete "BY" and print the Seller's name directly below the line, with the Seller to sign above the line. If the Seller is a corporation, print the name and title of the person acting for the corporation directly below the line, with that person to sign above the line.

39. The name of the Buyer if a corporation. Otherwise delete the line.

40. If the Buyer is an individual, delete "BY" and print the Buyer's name directly below the line, with the Buyer to sign above the line. If the Buyer is a corporation, print the name and title of the person acting for the corporation directly below the line, with that person to sign above the line.

IN WITNESS WHEREOF, the parties have signed this Agreement on the date first written above.

_________*[37]*_________

*BY*____________________
[38] (Seller)

_________*[39]*_________

*BY*____________________
[40] (Buyer)

CONTRACT FOR SALE OF GOODS—WARRANTIES (3-05)

Generally, a business can give Warranties for its own products as it wants or feels it must to remain competitive, or it can chose to give no Warranties at all. However, if the Seller is a merchant, that is, he deals in goods of a particular kind, holds himself out as having knowledge or skill related to goods of a particular kind, or if he employs a broker or agent who has such knowledge or skills, the law will consider the Seller to give certain implied Warranties unless specifically disclaimed in writing.

This Contract gives an example of a Seller's Warranty limited to his own materials and workmanship (areas that a Seller who is also the manufacturer can control) and also gives examples of disclaimers of Warranties.

CONTRACT FOR SALE OF GOODS—WARRANTIES

1. The date of signing the Contract.
2. The name of the Seller.
3. If the Seller is a corporation, insert the state of incorporation. Otherwise delete.
4. The address of the Seller.
5. The name of Buyer.
6. If the Buyer is a corporation, insert the state of incorporation. Otherwise delete.
7. The address of the Buyer.
8. A detailed description of the goods being purchased, for example "5,000 cases of widgets, 12 per case, on pallets of 100 cases each."
9. On a separate sheet of paper headed "Schedule A" list the specifications (size, weight, etc.) of the goods being purchased.
10. The price, in numbers, of the goods being purchased.
11. The location at which title (ownership) to the goods passes to the Buyer, for example: "Seller's loading dock" or "Buyer's loading dock."

AGREEMENT made this __[1]__ day of ______, 19__ by and between ________[2]________ *[3][, a ________ corporation,]* with its office at __________[4]__________ ("Seller") and ________[5]________ *[6][, a ________ corporation,]* with its office at __________[7]__________ ("Buyer").

1. SALE - Seller has agreed to sell and Buyer has agreed to purchase ______________[8]______________ in accordance with the plans and specifications set forth on the attached Schedule A.[9]

2. PRICE - The total price for the goods is $_____[10]_____ at __________[11]__________, it being

(Document continued on next page)

understood that the price *[12][does not include freight, shipping and delivery and insurance costs, which shall be the sole responsibility of Buyer.]* **OR** *[includes freight, shipping and delivery and insurance costs.]*

(A) Payment shall be made as follows: *[13][the entire amount due shall be paid in full not later than __[14]__ days after receipt by Buyer of the items purchased.]* **OR** *[$___[15]____ upon signing of this Agreement, $___[16]___ upon receipt of each shipment and the balance of $__[17]___ upon receipt of the shipment containing the balance of the items purchased.]* **OR** *[____________________[18]____________________.]*

3. DELIVERY/SHIPPING/ACCEPTANCE

(A) Delivery of the goods purchased shall be *[19][as set forth in the attached Schedule B.]* **OR** *[___[20]___ on or before _______[21]______,*

(Document continued on next page)

12. Choose one, depending on whether the price includes freight and insurance.

13. Choose one depending on the desired payment schedule. If the third alternative is chosen, skip to instruction No. 18. (Note: the choices shown are examples only. The method and timing of payment can be upon whatever terms the parties agree.)

14. The number of days, in numbers, after receipt of the items by which payment must be made. Then skip to instruction No. 19.

15. The amount, in numbers, of any deposit or down-payment made by the Buyer.

16. The amount, in numbers, due upon the Buyer's receipt of each shipment.

17. The amount, in numbers, of any unpaid balance remaining due.

18. Any other payment terms agreed upon by the parties.

19. Choose one, and if the use of a "Schedule B" is chosen, on a separate sheet of paper headed "Schedule B" list the the delivery schedule and then skip to instruction No. 27. If the third alternative is chosen, skip to instruction No. 26. (As with the terms of payment, so too the delivery schedule can contain any terms to which the parties agree.)

20. The quantity of the first shipment.

21. The date by which the first shipment must be received.

22. The quantity of the second shipment.

23. The date by which the second shipment must be received.

24. The quantity of the final shipment.

25. The date by which the final shipment must be received.

26. Any other delivery schedule agreed upon by the parties.

27. The specific shipping terms agreed upon, including the method (such as via the Seller's trucks, independent motor carrier, rail, air or a combination) and who will pay the costs of shipping and insurance. Be sure to be consistent with your choice in No. 12 above.

28. The number of days after receipt by which the Buyer must notify the Seller of rejection of any item.

29. The party at whose expense it will be to ship rejected items back to the Seller, for example "Seller's."

30. The number of days by which rejected items must be returned to the Seller.

31. If the agreement of the parties is that the goods are being sold in a so-called "as is" condition and without any Warranties, use this paragraph and delete paragraphs 32 and 33.

32. If the Seller is generally disclaiming all Warranties, use this paragraph and delete paragraphs 31 and 33.

___[22]___ on or before _______[23]______ and the balance of ___[24]___ not later than ______[25]______.]
OR *[______________________[26]______________________.]*

(B) Shipment of the goods purchased shall be ___________________________[27]______________________.

(C) Buyer shall examine each shipment promptly upon receipt and will advise Seller in writing of the number or quantity accepted and rejected and the reason(s) for rejection within __[28]__ days of receipt of each shipment. All items not accepted shall be returned to Seller at _____[29]_____ expense and any item not returned within __[30]__ days of notification to Seller shall be deemed accepted.

4. SELLER'S WARRANTIES

[31] [Buyer acknowledges that Buyer has or has had the opportunity to make a full and complete inspection of the goods. IT IS UNDERSTOOD AND AGREED THAT THE GOODS SOLD TO BUYER ARE SOLD STRICTLY "AS IS" AND "WITH ALL FAULTS" AND BUYER ACKNOWLEDGES THAT THERE ARE NO WARRANTIES, EITHER EXPRESS OR IMPLIED OF EITHER MERCHANTABILITY OR FITNESS FOR ANY PARTICULAR PURPOSE.]

[32] [IT IS UNDERSTOOD AND AGREED THAT SELLER NEITHER GIVES NOR MAKES ANY WARRANTIES, EITHER EXPRESS OR IMPLIED, AS TO DESCRIPTION OF GOODS, QUALITY OF GOODS, MERCHANTABILITY OR FITNESS FOR ANY PARTICULAR PURPOSE OR ANY OTHER MATTER. BUYER ACKNOWLEDGES THAT SELLER SHALL IN NO WAY BE RESPONSIBLE OR LIABLE TO BUYER OR ANY OTHER PARTY FOR ANY USE OR PROPER USE OF THE GOODS. BUYER ACKNOWLEDGES THAT BUYER HAS NOT AND DOES NOT RELY ON SELLER'S SKILL OR JUDGMENT WITH REGARD TO THE SELECTION OF THE GOODS AS FIT OR SUITABLE FOR ANY PARTICULAR PURPOSE. NOTWITHSTANDING ANYTHING CONTAINED IN THIS AGREEMENT, BUYER WAIVES ALL RIGHT OF REFUSAL OR RIGHT TO RETURN THE GOODS OR ANY ITEM THEREOF.]

(Document continued on next page)

33. If the Seller warrants the parts and workmanship to be free from defect but makes no other Warranties, use this paragraph and delete paragraphs 31 and 32.

34. If the goods sold are for a particular use or environment, describe the use, for example "home, non-commercial" or "office, non-industrial use."

35. The duration of the Warranties, in words and numbers, for example "Thirty (30) days," "Ninety (90) days," "one (1) year."

36. A description of the Seller's obligations to continue to perform the terms of the contract (essentially to continue to manufacture and ship the goods) and the Seller's remedies in the event of a default by the Buyer. For example, the Seller may not wish to continue to produce or deliver goods if the Buyer has defaulted in making a payment. To protect himself, the Seller may wish to provide that "Seller is not obligated to deliver goods if any payment is not received within 10 days after the date due."

[33] [Seller warrants to Buyer, or if Buyer is a dealer only, to the original purchaser, the goods manufactured by Seller to be free from defects in material and workmanship under normal ________[34]________ for a period of _____[35]_____ from the date of sale to the Buyer or from the date of installation by the original purchaser. In the event of such defect in material or workmanship, Seller's obligations under this warranty shall be limited to repair or replacement, at the sole option of Seller, of any defective part(s). THE FOREGOING WARRANTY IS EXPRESSLY MADE IN LIEU AND IN PLACE AND STEAD OF ALL OTHER WARRANTIES EXPRESS OR IMPLIED INCLUDING ANY WARRANTY OF MERCHANTABILITY OR FITNESS FOR ANY PURPOSE AND OF ANY OTHER LIABILITY OR OBLIGATION. THE FOREGOING WARRANTY SHALL NOT APPLY TO ANY GOODS OR PARTS WHICH HAVE BEEN SUBJECT TO IMPROPER INSTALLATION, ACCIDENT, NEGLIGENCE, ALTERATION, ABUSE OR MISUSE. BUYER ACKNOWLEDGES THAT BUYER HAS NOT AND DOES NOT RELY ON SELLER'S SKILL OR JUDGMENT WITH REGARD TO THE SELECTION OF THE GOODS AS FIT OR SUITABLE FOR ANY PARTICULAR PURPOSE.]

5. BUYER'S DEFAULT - ________[36]________
____.

(Document continued on next page)

6. SELLER'S DEFAULT - ________[37]________
____.

IN WITNESS WHEREOF, the parties have signed this Agreement on the date first written above.

________*[38]*________

*BY*____________________
[39] (Seller)

________*[40]*________

*BY*____________________
[41] (Buyer)

37. A description of the Buyer's obligations to continue to perform the terms of the contract (essentially to continue to pay) and the Buyer's remedies in the event of a default by Seller. For example, where a Buyer is relying on the delivery of a continuous "stream" of goods from the Seller, to protect himself the Buyer may wish to provide for a monetary damage penalty. Note: in many cases, such damages may not be easy to calculate. Therefore, the parties may agree on a specific dollar amount to be included in the contract (called "liquidated damages," the language for which is found in the Contract for Sale of Goods—"Custom Made" with Liquidated Damages found elsewhere in this chapter).

38. The name of the Seller if a corporation. Otherwise delete the line.

39. If the Seller is an individual, delete "BY" and type the Seller's name below the signature line with that individual to sign above the line. If the Seller is a corporation, type the name and title of the person acting for the corporation below the line with that person to sign above the line.

40. The name of the Buyer if a corporation. Otherwise delete the line.

41. If the Buyer is an individual, delete "BY" and type the Buyer's name below the signature line with that individual to sign above the line. If the Buyer is a corporation, type the name and title of the person acting for the corporation below the line with that person to sign above the line.

CONTRACT FOR SALE OF GOODS— "CUSTOM MADE" WITH LIQUIDATED DAMAGES CLAUSE (3-06)

In the normal course of business, if a Buyer defaults (for example, fails to pay the Seller), the Seller can usually recoup a portion, if not all, of his damages (his losses) by sale of the goods to another party, since one Buyer is usually as good as another. However, goods that have been produced to the unique plans and specifications of a particular Buyer present special problems for the Seller since he cannot sell these goods to another Buyer. Where goods have been "custom made" it is typical for the parties to agree to an amount of damages (called "Liquidated Damages") so that the injured Seller does not have to establish the exact amount of his damages in any subsequent law suit. The parties should be careful to establish a reasonable amount as the Liquidated Damages.

CONTRACT FOR SALE OF GOODS— "CUSTOM MADE" WITH LIQUIDATED DAMAGES CLAUSE

AGREEMENT made this __[1]__ day of ______, 19__ by and between ________[2]________ *[3][, a ________ corporation,]* with its office at __________[4]__________ ("Seller") and ________*[5]*________ *[6][, a ________ corporation,]* with its office at __________[7]__________ ("Buyer").

1. SALE - Seller has agreed to sell and Buyer has agreed to purchase ______________[8]______________ in accordance with the plans and specifications set forth on the attached Schedule A.[9]

2. PRICE - The total price for the goods is $_____[10]_____ at __________[11]__________, it being

(Document continued on next page)

1. The date of signing the Contract.

2. The name of the Seller.

3. If the Seller is a corporation, insert the state of incorporation. Otherwise delete.

4. The address of the Seller.

5. The name of the Buyer.

6. If the Buyer is a corporation, insert the state of incorporation. Otherwise delete.

7. The address of the Buyer.

8. A detailed description of the goods being purchased, for example "5,000 cases of widgets, 12 per case, on pallets of 100 cases each."

9. On a separate sheet of paper headed "Schedule A" list the specifications (size, weight, etc.) of the goods being purchased.

10. The price, in numbers, of the goods being purchased.

11. The location at which title (ownership) to the goods passes to the Buyer, for example: "Seller's loading dock" or "Buyer's loading dock."

12. Choose one, depending on whether the price includes freight and insurance.

13. Choose one depending on the desired payment schedule. If the third alternative is chosen, skip to instruction No. 18. Note: the choices shown are examples only. The method and timing of payment can be upon whatever terms the parties agree.

14. The number of days, in numbers, after receipt of the items by which payment must be made. Then skip to instruction No. 19.

15. The amount, in numbers, of any deposit or down-payment made by the Buyer.

16. The amount, in numbers, due upon the Buyer's receipt of each shipment.

17. The amount, in numbers, of any unpaid balance remaining due.

18. Any other payment terms agreed upon by the parties.

19. Choose one depending on whether damages will be a fixed amount or a percentage of the sale.

20. The dollar amount, in numbers, of the damages as agreed to by the parties (Liquidated Damages).

21. The percentage, in numbers, of the damages agreed to by the parties (Liquidated Damages) as calculated on the total sale price of the goods.

understood that the price *[12][does not include freight, shipping and delivery and insurance costs, which shall be the sole responsibility of Buyer.]* ***OR*** *[includes freight, shipping and delivery and insurance costs.]*

(A) Payment shall be made as follows: *[13][the entire amount due shall be paid in full not later than __[14]__ days after receipt by Buyer of the items purchased.]* ***OR*** *[$___[15]____ upon signing of this Agreement; $___[16]___ upon receipt of each shipment and the balance of $__[17]___ upon receipt of the shipment containing the balance of the items purchased.]* ***OR*** *____________________[18]____________________.]*

3. CUSTOM MADE GOODS - The parties acknowledge that the goods are to be produced at the specific request, insistence and behest of Buyer and only in accordance with plans, specifications and standards prepared by Buyer and furnished to Seller by Buyer and set forth on the attached Schedule A. Buyer acknowledges that it has freely selected Seller only for the purpose of manufacturing the goods and that it has not relied on any representations of Seller, Seller's agents or employees or any other party. Buyer acknowledges that the goods are unique and are "custom made" for Buyer and only for Buyer and that other than Buyer, there is no market or other potential purchaser for the goods.

(A) Based upon the foregoing, the parties acknowledge that it will be difficult if not impossible to adequately ascertain damages to Seller in the event of default by Buyer. It is expressly understood and agreed that in the event that Buyer shall fail or refuse to comply with any of the terms and conditions contained in this Agreement imposed on Buyer, Buyer shall pay to Seller *[19][the sum of $_____[20]_____]* ***OR*** *[an amount equal to __[21]__% of the total sale price set forth above]* as liquidated and agreed damages. In addition, Buyer acknowledges that Seller may elect to enforce any other remedies which Seller may have at law or equity.

(Document continued on next page)

CONTRACT FOR SALE OF GOODS— "CUSTOM MADE" WITH LIQUIDATED DAMAGES CLAUSE *continued*

22. Choose one, and if the use of a "Schedule B" is chosen, on a separate sheet of paper headed "Schedule B" list the the delivery schedule and then skip to instruction No. 30. If the third alternative is chosen, skip to instruction No. 29. As with the terms of payment, so too the delivery schedule can contain any terms to which the parties agree.

23. The quantity of the first shipment.

24. The date by which the first shipment must be received.

25. The quantity of the second shipment.

26. The date by which the second shipment must be received.

27. The quantity of the final shipment.

28. The date by which the final shipment must be received.

29. Any other delivery schedule agreed upon by the parties.

30. The specific shipping terms agreed upon, including the method (such as via the Seller's trucks, independent motor carrier, rail, air or a combination) and who will pay the costs of shipping and insurance. Be sure to be consistent with your choice in No. 12 above.

31. The number of days, in numbers, after receipt by which the Buyer must notify the Seller of rejection of any item.

32. The party at whose expense it will be to ship rejected items back to the Seller, for example "Seller's."

4. DELIVERY/SHIPPING/ACCEPTANCE

(A) Delivery of the goods purchased shall be *[22][as set forth in the attached Schedule B.]* ***OR*** *[___[23]___ on or before _______[24]______, ___[25]___ on or before _______[26]______ and the balance of ___[27]___ not later than ______[28]______.]* ***OR*** *[__________________[29]__________________.]*

(B) Shipment of the goods purchased shall be ____________________[30]__________________.

(C) Buyer shall examine each shipment promptly upon receipt and will advise Seller in writing of the number or quantity accepted and rejected and the reason(s) for rejection within __[31]__ days of receipt of each shipment. All items not accepted shall be returned to Seller at _____[32]_____ expense and any item not re-

(Document continued on next page)

turned within __[33]__ days of notification to Seller shall be deemed accepted.

[34][5. SELLER'S WARRANTIES - It is understood and agreed by the parties that Seller does not warrant the Buyer's use of the items purchased and does not warrant to Buyer or any other that the items are merchantable or fit for any particular purpose.]

IN WITNESS WHEREOF, that parties have signed this Agreement on the date first written above.

__________*[35]*__________

*BY*________________________
[36] (Seller)

__________*[37]*__________

*BY*________________________
[38] (Buyer)

33. The number of days, in numbers, by which rejected items must be returned to the Seller.

34. It is suggested that the Seller very carefully consider what, if any, warranties will be given to the Buyer. This paragraph states that there is no warranty. If a warranty is to be given, replace this paragraph with one stating the terms of the warranty.

35. The name of the Seller if a corporation. Otherwise delete the line.

36. If the Seller is an individual, delete "BY" and print the Seller's name directly below the line, with the Seller to sign above the line. If the Seller is a corporation, print the name and title of the person acting for the corporation directly below the line, with that person to sign above the line.

37. The name of the Buyer if a corporation. Otherwise delete the line.

38. If the Buyer is an individual, delete "BY" and print the Buyer's name directly below the line, with the Buyer to sign above the line. If the Buyer is a corporation, print the name and title of the person acting for the corporation directly below the line, with that person to sign above the line.

CONSIGNMENT SALES AGREEMENT (3-07)

A Consignment Sale is defined as the act of shipping, transferring or depositing goods with a merchant, agent or factor for sale by the merchant, agent or factor. Products are deposited with a merchant (the CONSIGNEE) for sale to others but for the account of the seller (the CONSIGNOR). In consignment sales, the merchant does not take ownership of the products; the merchant makes a commission when he makes the sale of the CONSIGNOR's products. Since the merchant is the agent of the seller (rather than the owner of the products himself), the merchant, as CONSIGNEE, is placed in a position of trust with respect to the products and must account to the seller.

CONSIGNMENT SALES AGREEMENT

1. The date of the Agreement.

2. The name of the seller of the goods or products (the CONSIGNOR).

3. If the CONSIGNOR is a corporation, insert the state of incorporation. Otherwise delete.

4. The address of the CONSIGNOR.

5. The name of the merchant, agent or factor (the CONSIGNEE).

6. If the CONSIGNEE is a corporation, insert the state of incorporation. Otherwise delete.

7. The address of the CONSIGNEE.

8. A description of the products placed with the CONSIGNEE for sale.

AGREEMENT made as of ______[1]______ 19__, between _________[2]_________, *[3][a __________ corporation,]* with a place of business at ___________[4]___________ ("CONSIGNOR") and ___________[5]___________, *[6][a __________ corporation,]* with a place of business at ___________[7]___________ ("CONSIGNEE").

1. Consignment of Products: CONSIGNOR shall, subject to causes beyond its control, ship to CONSIGNEE, on consignment, _______________[8]_______________ ("Products") in such quantity as CONSIGNOR may determine. CONSIGNEE shall accept the Products and shall store them either at CONSIGNEE's place of business or at such other locations specified in writing. Shipments shall be F.O.B. place of manufacture or CONSIGNOR's place of business. The Products shall be held by CONSIGNEE for sale to others. CONSIGNEE shall perform all acts required by law to protect the rights of CONSIGNOR to the consigned Products, including but not limited to segregation of the Products from other goods of CONSIGNEE and identification of the Products as consigned goods of CONSIGNOR, wherever and whenever possible. CONSIGNEE, after receipt of the Products, shall pay all expenses incident to the Products, including all expenses of storage, insurance, selling and delivering to customers, and all taxes and other charges which may be assessed or levied on the Products while in CONSIGNEE's possession.

2. Title to Products: The consigned Products shall remain the property of CONSIGNOR until sold by CONSIGNEE, and title to the proceeds of the sales of Products shall vest in and belong to CONSIGNOR until accounted for and paid over to CONSIGNOR.

(Document continued on next page)

9. The date of the month by which the CONSIGNEE must prepare its report (accounting) to the CONSIGNOR.

10. The date of the expiration of the Agreement.

3. Loss or Damage to Products: CONSIGNEE shall be responsible to and shall reimburse CONSIGNOR for all loss and expense to CONSIGNOR resulting from theft of, damage to or destruction of the consigned Products, or from levy or attachment by any process or lien thereon while in CONSIGNEE's possession and until such time as title passes by reason of the sale of the Products and the proceeds of the sale have been accounted for and remitted to CONSIGNOR. CONSIGNEE shall keep the consigned Products fully insured, at CONSIGNEE's expense, for the benefit of CONSIGNOR and shall provide CONSIGNOR with a Certificate of Insurance naming CONSIGNOR as an additional insured with a loss payable to CONSIGNOR provision.

4. Report of Sales and Payment: On the ___ [9]___ day of each month, CONSIGNEE shall report to the CONSIGNOR sales of Products made by CONSIGNEE since the last report. CONSIGNEE shall make payment to CONSIGNOR for all sales at the time of the report. Every six (6) months a physical inventory of consigned Products shall be taken by CONSIGNEE. CONSIGNOR reserves the right to have a representative present and report the inventory to CONSIGNOR. If consigned Products are found missing CONSIGNEE shall immediately pay CONSIGNOR for missing Products.

5. Term: This Agreement shall terminate on _______[10]______, at which time all sold Products shall be accounted and paid for. At CONSIGNOR's sole option unsold Products may be returned, freight prepaid, or paid for by CONSIGNEE. Notwithstanding the foregoing, CONSIGNOR may terminate this Agreement without prior notice if CONSIGNEE violates any term of this Agreement or in the event that CONSIGNOR, in its sole determination, becomes dissatisfied with the financial stability of CONSIGNEE.

6. Authority to Act for CONSIGNOR: CONSIGNEE shall conduct the entire business of selling CONSIGNOR's Products in CONSIGNEE's name and at CONSIGNEE's cost and expense. Nothing in this Agreement shall authorize or empower CONSIGNEE to assume or create any obligation or responsibility whatsoever, express or implied, on behalf of or in the name of CONSIGNOR, or to bind CONSIGNOR in any manner, or make any representation, warranty, or commitment on behalf of

(Document continued on next page)

11. The state whose laws will govern the Agreement, typically the state in which the CONSIGNOR is located.

12. The city in which arbitration will take place.

13. The state in which arbitration will take place, typically the state in which the CONSIGNOR is located.

CONSIGNOR, this Agreement being limited solely to the consignment of Products.

7. Indemnity: CONSIGNEE shall indemnify and hold CONSIGNOR harmless against any loss or damage caused by acts of the CONSIGNEE not authorized by this Agreement.

8. Financing Statement: CONSIGNEE agrees to sign and deliver to CONSIGNOR such financing statements, security agreements or continuation statements, in a form satisfactory to CONSIGNOR, as CONSIGNOR may from time to time reasonably request. CONSIGNOR may, at its expense, file the statements with the appropriate government agency.

9. Benefit: This Agreement shall be binding upon and inure to the benefit of the parties hereto, and their respective successors and assigns. This Agreement may not be assigned by CONSIGNEE without the express written consent of the CONSIGNOR.

10. Controlling Law: This Agreement shall be governed by and construed under the laws of the State of _____[11]_____.

11. Arbitration: Any controversy or claim arising out of or relating to this Agreement, or the breach thereof, shall be settled by arbitration, in the City of ___[12]____, State of ____[13]____, in accordance with the Commercial Arbitration Rules of the American Arbitration Association, and judgment upon the award rendered by the arbitrator(s) may be entered in any court having jurisdiction thereof.

(Document continued on next page)

14. The name of the CONSIGNOR if a corporation. Otherwise delete the line.

15. If the CONSIGNOR is an individual, delete "BY" and print the CONSIGNOR's name directly below the line, with the CONSIGNOR to sign above the line. If the CONSIGNOR is a corporation, print the name and title of the individual acting for the corporation directly below the line, with that person to sign above the line.

16. The name of the CONSIGNEE if a corporation. Otherwise delete the line.

17. If the CONSIGNEE is an individual, delete "BY" and print the CONSIGNEE's name directly below the line, with the CONSIGNEE to sign above the line. If the CONSIGNEE is a corporation, print the name and title of the individual acting for the corporation directly below the line, with that person to sign above the line.

12. Notice: All notices shall be sent by certified mail, return receipt requested, to the party to be notified, at the addresses stated above, or at such other address as either party shall designate in writing.

IN WITNESS WHEREOF, the parties have executed this Agreement.

__________*[14]*__________

*BY*________________________
[15]

__________*[16]*__________

*BY*________________________
[17]

EQUIPMENT LEASE (3-08)

Businesses increasingly rely on equipment and machinery ranging from computers to photocopiers to package handling equipment to lathes and milling machines. The outright purchase of such equipment diverts capital from other uses such as payroll (for people to operate the equipment and machinery) or raw materials (necessary to produce whatever the business sells). One solution to this problem is to lease equipment so that the supplier or dealer of the equipment retains title (ownership) but allows the customer to use the equipment during a stated time period. The owner of the equipment is the Lessor, the user is the Lessee, the stated time period is referred to as the Term of the Lease and the "rental" payment for use of the equipment is the monthly Lease payment.

1. The name, address and telephone number of the Lessor (the owner of the equipment who is leasing it to another).

2. The name, address and telephone number of the Lessee (the party leasing the equipment from the owner of the equipment).

3. The quantity of each piece of equipment.

4. The name of the manufacturer or supplier and a description (model, type or the like) of each piece of equipment.

5. The serial number of each piece of equipment.

6. The location where each piece of equipment will be installed and kept. Or list on a separate sheet headed "Schedule of Equipment."

7. The initial term of the Lease in months, in numbers.

8. The dollar amount, in numbers, of each monthly Lease payment.

9. The dollar amount, in numbers, of the advance payment.

EQUIPMENT LEASE

LESSOR: ______[1]______ LESSEE: ______[2]______
______________________ ______________________
______________________ ______________________
Tel. ______________________ Tel. ______________________

QTY.	DESCRIPTION OF EQUIP.	SERIAL NO.
__[3]__	__________[4]__________	____[5]____
__[3]__	__________[4]__________	____[5]____
__[3]__	__________[4]__________	____[5]____
__[3]__	__________[4]__________	____[5]____
__[3]__	__________[4]__________	____[5]____

EQUIPMENT LOCATION:
______________________[6]______________________
____

INITIAL TERM	MONTHLY PAYMENT	ADVANCE PAYMENT
__[7]__ Months	$______[8]_____	$_____[9]_____

THIS LEASE CANNOT BE CANCELLED EXCEPT AS EXPRESSLY PROVIDED. THIS LEASE SHALL BECOME EFFECTIVE UPON SIGNING BY LESSOR AND LESSEE.

1. TERMS AND CONDITIONS - Lessor agrees to lease and Lessee leases from Lessor the equipment described above and on any attached Schedule (the "Equipment") in accordance with the terms and conditions stated in this Lease Agreement. Lessee authorizes Lessor to insert in this Equipment Lease Agreement (the "Lease") serial numbers and other identification information when deter-

(Document continued on next page)

10. The number of days, in numbers, permitted for the Lessee to give notice that the leased equipment does not perform as promised.

mined by Lessor. This Lease constitutes the full and entire agreement between the Lessor and Lessee in connection with the Equipment and merges any and all other understandings. Neither party relies on any other statement or representation made by the other or any third party. This Lease can neither be cancelled nor modified except by written agreement signed by both Lessor and Lessee. Lessee's acceptance of the Equipment shall be irrevocable unless Lessor and Vendor each receive Lessee's written notice of substantial non-conformance of the Equipment within __[10]__ days after acceptance of the Equipment.

2. PAYMENT - Lessee agrees to make all monthly Lease payments in advance on the 1st day of each and every month commencing with the first full month after delivery of the Leased Equipment, and to pay such other charges as provided in this Agreement. Lease payments shall be increased by any cost or expense Lessor incurs to preserve the Equipment or to pay any taxes, assessments, fees, penalties, liens or encumbrances. Each payment received will be applied to the oldest charge due under this Lease. Lessee agrees to make payments regardless of any problems Lessee might or may have with the Equipment including its operations, capability, installation or repair and regardless of any claim, set-off, counterclaim or defense Lessee might or may have against the Vendor or Manufacturer (the "Supplier"), Salesperson or other Third Party. Without Lessor's prior written consent, any payment to Lessor of a smaller sum than due at any time under this Agreement shall not constitute release or an accord or satisfaction for any greater sum due or to become due regardless of any restrictive endorsement. An advance payment shall be held by Lessor as a security deposit for the faithful performance of this Lease.

3. TAXES/ASSESSMENTS/FEES - Lessee agrees: to pay all licensing, filing and registration fees reasonably required; to keep the Equipment free of all liens and encumbrances; to show the Equipment as "Leased Equipment" on Lessee's tax returns; to pay Lessor for all personal property taxes assessed against the Equipment; to pay all other taxes, assessments, fees and penalties which may be levied or assessed with respect to the Equipment, its use or any interest thereon or any lease payments, including but not limited to all federal, state and local taxes however designated, levied or assessed whether upon Lessee or Lessor of the Equipment or upon any sale, ownership, use or op-

(Document continued on next page)

11. The percentage, in numbers, of the monthly Lease payment that the Lessor will charge as an escrow for taxes.

12. The amount, in numbers, to be charged by the Lessor for the preparation and filing of any Financing Statements permitted by the Uniform Commercial Code ("U.C.C."), credit searches and the like.

eration excepting any income taxes levied on the lease payments to Lessor. Lessor may, at its option, collect from Lessee an escrow fee of up to __[11]__ percent of the Equipment cost per month for a tax escrow fund. Lessor will pay on Lessee's behalf such taxes and other amounts and file applicable returns. In addition, Lessee authorizes Lessor to file at Lessor's option informational financing statements without Lessee's signature and if a signature is required by law, Lessee appoints Lessor as Lessee's attorney-in-fact to execute such financing statements. Lessee agrees to pay Lessor a fee of $_____[12]_____ to reimburse Lessor's expenses of preparing such financing statements and of making credit checks and analysis of Lessee's and guarantor's financial status and of Lessor's other administrative costs. Lessee and any guarantor agree to reimburse Lessor for reasonable costs incurred in collecting taxes, assessments or fees for which Lessee is liable and any collection charges attributable thereto including reasonable attorneys' fees. Lessee agrees that Lessor is entitled to all tax benefits resulting from ownership of the Equipment including any investment tax credit and depreciation. Lessee agrees that should any of such tax benefits be disallowed, Lessee shall indemnify Lessor for such loss by paying Lessor an amount equal to the value of the lost benefits as stipulated and liquidated herein.

4. LESSEE'S AND GUARANTOR'S WARRANTIES TO LESSOR - Lessee and any guarantor expressly warrant to Lessor and Lessor relies on the fact that Lessee and any guarantor: (a) have read and understood this Lease before it was signed; (b) have selected and are fully satisfied with both the Equipment and the Supplier who sold the Equipment to Lessor for the purposes set forth in this Lease; (c) will authorize Lessor to pay for the Equipment only after Lessee has received and accepted the Equipment as fully operable for Lessee's purposes; (d) have freely chosen to lease, not buy, from Lessor only after having considered other means of obtaining the use of the Equipment; (e) freely acknowledge that neither the manufacturer nor the supplier of the Equipment nor any of its salespersons are, or have acted as, Lessor's agents or employees; (f) have provided accurate and correct financial information and other statements and same will be updated upon Lessor's request during the term of the Lease; (g) are currently meeting all debts as such come due; (h) will use the Equipment exclusively for Lessee's business purposes and not for personal, family or household purposes; (i) have

(Document continued on next page)

unrestricted power to enter into this Lease, have duly authorized the person executing it and certify that all signatures are authentic; and (j) will pay all costs connected with the Equipment including taxes, insurance, repairs, shipping, collection costs and other expenses normally paid in a net lease.

5. LESSEE'S WAIVER OF DAMAGES AND WARRANTIES FROM LESSOR - Lessee acknowledges that it has selected the Equipment and each piece of the Equipment and that in doing so Lessee has not relied upon any statements of Lessor, Lessor's salespeople, agents or employees. Lessee further acknowledges that: (a) Lessee leases the Equipment from Lessor in a strictly "AS IS" condition; Lessor makes absolutely no warranties express or implied, including any warranty of merchantability for fitness for a particular purpose; (b) if the Equipment is not properly installed, does not operate as represented or warranted by the manufacturer or supplier, or is unsatisfactory for any reasons whatsoever, Lessee shall make any claim on account thereof solely against the manufacturer or supplier and Lessee hereby waives any such claim against Lessor (all warranties from the Supplier to Lessor are hereby assigned to Lessee for the term of the Lease for Lessee's exercise at Lessee's expense); (c) Lessee shall hold Lessor harmless and shall be responsible for any loss, damage or injury to persons or property caused by the Equipment; (d) no representation or warranty by the manufacturer, supplier or salesperson is binding on Lessor nor shall breach of such warranty relieve Lessee of Lessee's obligations to Lessor; and (e) in no case shall Lessor be liable to Lessee for special, indirect or consequential damages.

6. OWNERSHIP AND TITLE - Lessor is the sole owner of the Equipment, has sole title to the Equipment, has the right to inspect the Equipment and has the right to affix and display notice of Lessor's ownership thereon. The Equipment shall remain Lessor's personal property whether or not affixed to realty and shall not be part of any real property on which it is placed. All additions, attachments and accessories placed on the Equipment become part of the Equipment and Lessor's property. Lessee agrees to maintain the Equipment so that it may be removed from the property or building where located without damage.

(Document continued on next page)

7. OPERATION AND TERMINATION - Lessee shall be solely responsible for the installation, operation, and maintenance of the Equipment, shall keep it in good condition and running order and shall use and operate the Equipment in compliance with applicable law. Lessee agrees to keep and use the Equipment only at the business address specified above ("Equipment Location"), to never abandon or move the Equipment from that address, nor relinquish possession of the Equipment except to Lessor's agent. At the end of the Lease Term, Lessee must contact Lessor who will designate the return location within the continental United States, and Lessee shall at Lessee's expense, immediately crate, insure and return the Equipment to the designated location in as good a condition as when Lessee received it, excepting only reasonable wear and tear. Until Lessor actually receives the Equipment at the return location, the Lease renews automatically from month to month and Lessee agrees to continue to make lease payments at the last effective rate under the Lease.

8. RISK OF LOSS AND INSURANCE - Until Lessee has returned the Equipment to the designated location, Lessee bears the entire risk of loss or damage to the Equipment regardless how arising. Lessee shall immediately notify Lessor of the occurrence of any loss or other occurrence affecting Lessor's interests and shall make repairs or corrections at Lessee's expense. In such event, Lessee agrees to continue to meet all payment and other obligations under the Lease. Lessee agrees to keep the Equipment insured at Lessee's expense against risk of loss or damage from any cause whatsoever. Lessee agrees that such insurance shall be not less than the greater of the unpaid balance of the rentals due or the then-current fair market value of the Equipment. Lessee also agrees that the insurance shall be in such additional amount as is reasonable to cover Lessor for public liability and property damage arising from the Equipment or Lessee's use of it. Lessee agrees to name Lessor as the loss payee. Each policy shall provide that the insurance cannot be cancelled without thirty (30) days prior written notice to Lessor. Upon request by Lessor, Lessee agrees to furnish proof of each insurance policy including a certificate of insurance and a copy of the policy. The proceeds of such insurance shall be applied at Lessor's sole election toward the replacement or repair of the Equipment or payment towards Lessee's obligations. Lessee appoints Lessor as attorney-in-fact to make any claim for, receive payment of, or execute or endorse all

(Document continued on next page)

documents, checks or drafts for loss or damage or return of premium under such insurance. Because of increased credit risks to Lessor when not insured by Lessee, Lessee agrees to pay to Lessor each month a risk charge stipulated and liquidated at 25% of Lessor's original equipment cost until Lessee provides proof of compliance with insurance requirements. In spite of such risk charge, Lessee has no right to any insurance benefits from Lessor. Lessee is still liable for all losses and such risk charge is not in lieu of the insurance requirements of this Lease.

9. INDEMNITY - Lessee agrees to indemnify and hold Lessor harmless from and against any and all losses, damages, injuries, demands and expense (a "Claim"), including any and all attorneys' fees and legal expenses, arising from or caused directly or indirectly by any actual or alleged use, possession, maintenance, condition (whether or not latent or discoverable), operation, location, delivery or transportation of any item of Equipment. Should Lessee be entitled under applicable law to revoke its acceptance of the Equipment, Lessee agrees to pay and indemnify Lessor for any payment by Lessor to the manufacturer or supplier of the Equipment.

10. COLLECTION CHARGES AND ATTORNEYS' FEES - If any part of any sum due to Lessor is not received by Lessor within ten (10) days of the due date or if any sum paid by check shall be dishonored or returned to Lessor on account of uncollected funds or for insufficient funds, Lessee agrees to pay Lessor: (a) a one-time late charge to compensate Lessor for collecting and processing the late sum, equal to the greater of 15% of any delayed sum or $25.00, plus (b) an interest charge for every month after the first month in which the sum is late to compensate Lessor for the inability to reinvest the sum, such interest charge stipulated and liquidated at 1 1/2% per month or the maximum allowed by applicable law, whichever is less.

11. LESSEE AND ANY GUARANTOR AGREE TO PAY LESSOR'S REASONABLE ATTORNEYS' FEES AS DAMAGES AND NOT COSTS - In all proceedings arising under this lease, such proceedings including any arbitration, bankruptcy proceeding, civil action, mediation or counterclaim on which Lessor prevails seeking relief from stay in bankruptcy or post-judgment action or appeal with respect to any of the foregoing, reasonable attorneys' fees

(Document continued on next page)

are stipulated and liquidated at not less than the greater of $500.00 or 25% of Lessor's total amount in collection.

12. DEFAULT - Lessee shall be in default of this Lease on any of the following events: (a) Lessee fails to pay any month's rent within ten (10) days after it first becomes due; (b) Lessee assigns, moves, pledges, subleases, sells or relinquishes possession of the Equipment or attempts to do so, without Lessor's prior written authorization; (c) Lessee breaches any of its warranties or other obligations under this Lease or any other agreement with Lessor and fails to cure such breach within ten (10) days after Lessor sends Lessee a notice of the existence of such breach; (d) any execution or writ of process is issued in any action or proceeding to seize or detain the Equipment; (e) Lessee or any guarantor gives Lessor reasonable cause to be insecure about Lessee's willingness or ability to perform obligations under the Lease or any other agreement with Lessor; (f) Lessee or any guarantor dies, becomes insolvent or unable to pay debts when due, stops doing business as a going concern, consolidates, merges, transfers all or substantially all of its assets, makes an assignment for the benefit of creditors, appoints a trustee or receiver or undergoes a substantial deterioration of financial health; or (g) Lessor or any guarantor fails to reaffirm this lease obligation within thirty (30) days of the filing of any petition for protection under the United States Bankruptcy Code.

13. REMEDIES - Should Lessee default, Lessor has the right to exercise any or all of the following: Lessor may without notice accelerate all sums under the Lease and require Lessee to immediately pay Lessor all sums that are already due and the discounted value of those that will become due and (i) require the immediate return of the Equipment to Lessor or (ii) if Lessee agrees after Lessee pays all other sums under the Lease, sell the Equipment to Lessee at the estimated lease-end fair market Equipment value discounted to the date of sale. Such estimated lease-end fair market Equipment value is stipulated and liquidated as the Lessor's cost of the Equipment less 2% per month during the first 12 months of the Lease and less 1% per month thereafter up until the date of acceleration. Lessor has the right to immediately retake possession of the Equipment without any court or other process of law and for such purpose may enter upon any premises where the Equipment may be and remove the same. Lessor has the right to exercise any remedy at law or equity, notice thereof

(Document continued on next page)

13. The city and state in which any arbitration hearing is to be held, typically the state in which the Lessor is located.

14. The state whose laws will govern the contract, typically the state in which the Lessor is located.

being expressly waived by Lessee and any guarantor; Lessor's action or failure to act on any one remedy constitutes neither an election to be limited thereon nor a waiver of any other remedy nor a release of Lessee from the liability to return the Equipment or for any Loss or Claim with respect thereto. The provisions of this Lease are severable and shall not be affected or impaired if any one provision is held unenforceable, invalid or illegal. Any provision held in conflict with any statute or rule of law shall be deemed inoperative only to the extent of such conflict and shall be modified to conform with such statute or rule.

14. ARBITRATION - Lessor may, at its option, submit any matter arising out of this Lease Agreement, including any claim, counterclaim, setoff or defense to binding arbitration by the American Arbitration Association in the City of _____[13]_____, State of _____[13]_____ irrespective of the fact that neither the Lessee, any guarantor or the Equipment may be located in that City now or then. The decision and award of the arbitrator(s) shall be final and binding and may be entered as rendered in any court having jurisdiction thereof.

15. CONSENT TO JURISDICTION, VENUE AND NON-JURY TRIAL - Lessee and any guarantor consent, agree and stipulate that: (a) this Lease shall be deemed fully executed and performed in the State of _____[14]_____ and shall be governed by and construed in accordance with the laws thereof; and (b) in any action, proceeding, or appeal on any matter related to or arising out of this lease, Lessor, Lessee and any guarantor: (i) shall be subject to the personal jurisdiction of the State of _____[14]_____ including any state or federal court sitting therein and all court rules thereof; (ii) shall accept venue in any federal or state court in _____[14]_____; and (iii) expressly waive any right to a trial by jury so that trial shall be by and only to the court. Nothing contained herein is intended to preclude Lessor from commencing any action hereunder in any court having jurisdiction thereof.

16. CONSENT TO SERVICE OF PROCESS - Lessee and any guarantor agree that any process served for any action or proceeding shall be valid if mailed by Certified Mail, return receipt requested, with delivery restricted to

(Document continued on next page)

15. The date of signing the Lease by the Lessee.

16. The name of the Lessee if a corporation. Otherwise delete the line.

17. If the Lessee is an individual, delete "BY" and print the Lessee's name directly below the line, with the Lessee to sign above the line. If the Lessee is a corporation, print the name and title of the person acting for the corporation directly below the line, with that person to sign above the line.

18. The date of signing the Lease by the Lessor.

19. The name of the Lessor if a corporation. Otherwise delete the line.

20. If the Lessor is an individual, delete "BY" and print the Lessor's name directly below the line, with the Lessor to sign above the line. If the Lessor is a corporation, print the name and title of the person acting for the corporation below the line, with that person to sign above the line.

21. The date of signing the Statement of Acceptance by the Lessee.

22. The name of the Lessee if a corporation. Otherwise delete the line.

23. If the Lessee is an individual, delete "BY" and print the Lessee's name directly below the line, with the Lessee to sign above the line. If the Lessee is a corporation, print the name and title of the person acting for the corporation directly below the line, with that person to sign above the line.

either the addressee, its registered agent or any agent appointed in writing to accept such process.

Dated: ________[15]________

__________*[16]*__________

*BY*________________________
[17] (Lessee)

ACCEPTED:
Date of Acceptance: ________[18]________

__________*[19]*__________

*BY*________________________
[20] (Lessor)

==

LESSEE'S STATEMENT OF ACCEPTANCE
OF LEASE EQUIPMENT

Lessee acknowledges that all of the items set forth above (the "Leased Equipment") have been received by Lessee; that all required installation, preparation, set-up and other work has been performed; and that in all respects, the Lease Equipment is satisfactory and is hereby accepted by Lessee.

Dated: ____[21]_____

__________*[22]*__________

*BY*________________________
[23] (Lessee)

RECEIPT (3-09)

At its simplest, a receipt is nothing more than an acknowledgement of having received something. As our society has grown more complex, and more people pay for items upon delivery (as opposed to at the time of the sale) and pay by credit card, more information is required to facilitate delivery. This Receipt contains the necessary information for such deliveries.

1. The name of the seller or party making the delivery.

2. The date of the delivery.

3. The home telephone number of the party receiving the delivery.

4. The business telephone number of the party receiving the delivery.

5. The name and address to which the delivery is being made.

6. The number of pieces being delivered.

7. A description, model number or the like of each item being delivered.

8. The amount of payment made by cash or certified check.

9. The account number of the credit card being used for payment.

10. The expiration date of the credit card used for payment.

11. The dollar amount, in numbers, being charged.

12. The credit card charge authorization number received.

RECEIPT
FROM

_______________[1]_______________

DEL. DATE: _______________[2]_______________

HOME PHONE #: _______________[3]_______________

BUSINESS PHONE #: ___________[4]_______________

DELIVER TO: ___________[5]___________ Apt.#____
____
____

DESCRIPTION

No.	Item
__[6]__	_______________[7]_______________
__[6]__	_______________[7]_______________
__[6]__	_______________[7]_______________
__[6]__	_______________[7]_______________

PAYMENT

C.O.D. _______________[8]_______________
cash or certified check

CREDIT CARD
( ) VISA ( ) MC ( ) AMEX ( ) DINERS

CARD #_______________[9]_______________

EXP. DATE:____[10]_____

AMOUNT OF CHARGE (TOTAL) $______[11]______

AUTH.#_______________[12]_______________

(Document continued on next page)

13. The billing address of the credit card being used for payment.

14. The name of the person receiving (signing for) the goods printed directly below the line, with that person to sign above the line. (If a credit card is used, the name and signature of the credit card holder.)

15. Insert any directions as to the place of delivery, special handling, delivery or pick-up instructions.

BILLING
ADDRESS________________[13]________________
____
____

CARDHOLDER NAME ____________________________

YOUR SIGNATURE CONSTITUTES ACCEPTANCE OF ALL MERCHANDISE AND INDICATES 100% SATISFACTION AS PER ORDER. ALL SALES ARE FINAL.

X ____
[14]

FOR CREDIT CARDS ONLY: The issuer of the card identified on this item is authorized to pay the amount shown as TOTAL upon proper presentation. I promise to pay such TOTAL (together with any other charges due thereon) subject to and in accordance with the Agreement governing the use of such card.

DIRECTIONS/OTHER DELIVERY OR PICK-UP INSTRUCTIONS:
____________________[15]____________________
____
____

DOOR-TO-DOOR SALES/ 3-DAY CANCELLATION NOTICE (3-10)

The Federal Trade Commission and most states require that the buyer of a product sold in the home be offered the opportunity to cancel the purchase within 3 business days after the date of the sale ("the cooling-off period"). In addition to leaving two copies of the written Notice with the buyer, the seller must orally inform the buyer of his right to cancel.

The Federal Trade Commission defines a Door-to-Door Sale as:

> A sale, lease or rental of consumer goods or services with a purchase price of $25 or more, whether under single or multiple contracts, in which the seller or the seller's representative personally solicits the sale, including those in response to or following an invitation by the buyer, and the buyer's agreement or offer to purchase is made at a place other than the place of business of the seller.

Some states have a slight variation in language for the Notice (Iowa, for example) and if business is conducted in only one state, that state's language should be followed. Some states include Saturday as a business day and some exclude it. As a general rule Saturday, Sunday and legal holidays should not be counted as business days.

DOOR-TO-DOOR SALES 3-DAY CANCELLATION NOTICE

1. This statement must be printed in 10 point bold type on the face of the contract of sale.

2. The entire Notice of Right to Cancel must be printed in 10 point bold type. The Notice may be part of the contract of sale or a separate sheet attached to the contract of sale.

3. The date of the sale.

[1] You, the buyer, may cancel this transaction at any time prior to midnight of the third business day after the date of this transaction. See the attached notice of cancellation form for an explanation of this right.

[2] NOTICE OF RIGHT TO CANCEL

Date of Transaction _____[3]_____

You may cancel this transaction, without any penalty or obligation, within 3 business days from the above date.

If you cancel, any property traded in, any payments made by you under the contract of sale, and any negotiable instrument executed by you will be returned within 10 business days following receipt by the seller of your cancellation notice, and any security interest arising out of the transaction will be cancelled.

If you cancel, you must make available to the seller at your residence, in substantially as good condition as when received, any goods delivered to you under

(Document continued on next page)

DOOR-TO-DOOR SALES/ 3-DAY CANCELLATION NOTICE *continued*

4. The name of the company making the sale.

5. The address of the company.

6. The date by which the Notice must be sent.

7. The date the Notice is sent by the buyer.

8. The buyer's name printed directly below the line, with the buyer to sign above the line.

this contract of sale; or you may, if you wish, comply with the instructions of the seller regarding the return shipment of the goods at the seller's expense and risk.

If you do make the goods available to the seller and the seller does not pick them up within 20 days of the date of your notice of cancellation, you may retain or dispose of the goods without any further obligation. If you fail to make the goods available to the seller, or if you agree to return the goods to the seller and fail to do so, then you remain liable for performance of all obligations under the contract.

To cancel this transaction, mail or deliver a signed and dated copy of this cancellation notice or any other written notice or send a telegram to _______[4]_______ at _________[5]_________ not later than midnight of _______[6]_______.

I hereby cancel this transaction.

Date: ______[7]_____

____
[8] (Buyer)

ASSIGNMENT AND ASSUMPTION OF LIMITED PARTNERSHIP INTEREST (3-11)

Virtually anything, tangible or intangible, can be sold or transferred for value to someone else. An interest in an existing Limited Partnership is no different except that one does not sell such an interest but rather assigns his interest. The limited partner is the "Assignor" and he assigns his interest to the "Assignee." As part of the transaction (usually required to obtain the consent of the Limited Partnership), the Assignee also agrees to assume all of the risks and obligations of the Assignor. An Assignee is said to "stand in the shoes of the Assignor." This form is the Assignment by the Assignor to the Assignee and the Assignee's Agreement to assume the obligations of the Assignor.

WARNING

This form should be used only after a thorough review of the Limited Partnership Agreement and relevant financial information concerning the partnership. The Limited Partnership Agreement must be examined to ascertain whether or not this particular Limited Partnership permits one of its partners to assign his interest and, if so, under what circumstances and conditions.

1. The amount paid for the Assignment, in words and numbers.

2. The name of the Limited Partner making the Assignment (the Assignor).

3. The legal name of the Limited Partnership.

4. The name of the person or entity paying the money and receiving the Assignment of interest (the Assignee).

5. The percentage interest of the Limited Partnership being purchased, in words and numbers.

6. The specific title of the Limited Partnership Agreement being assigned.

ASSIGNMENT AND ASSUMPTION
OF LIMITED PARTNERSHIP INTEREST

In consideration of the sum of _______[1]________ Dollars ($____[1]____), receipt of which is hereby acknowledged, ________[2]________ ("Assignor") as a Limited Partner in ________[3]________ LIMITED PARTNERSHIP (the "Company"), hereby assigns to ________[4]________ ("Assignee") Assignor's interest as a Limited Partner in the Company to the extent of ____[5]____ Percent (____%) of One Hundred Percent (100%) of Net Profits in the Company as defined in the __________________[6]_________________, a copy of which Assignee acknowledges having received and read.

Said assignment is solely out of the share of Net Profits owned by the Assignor as a Limited Partner in the Company.

Subject to the acceptance of this assignment and assumption by the Company, Assignee shall become: (i) a substitute Limited Partner in the Company to the extent of the assignment; (ii) entitled to receive from the Company (at the time, in the manner, and upon the conditions set forth in the Partnership Agreement) repayment as a contribution to the Company of the aforesaid sum paid to Assignor; and (iii) entitled to receive payment of an amount equal to ____[5]____ Percent (____%) of the Net Profits of the Company.

(Document continued on next page)

ASSIGNMENT AND ASSUMPTION OF LIMITED PARTNERSHIP INTEREST *continued*

7. The date of the Assignment.

8. The name of the Assignor printed below the line, with the Assignor to sign above the line.

9. The name of the Assignee printed below the line, with the Assignee to sign above the line.

10. The address of the Assignee.

11. The Social Security number or Federal Taxpayer Identification Number of the Assignee.

The Assignee, by execution hereof, agrees to assume Assignor's proportionate share of the obligations of the Assignor as a Limited Partner of the Company under the Partnership Agreement, to the same extent as if the Assignee had been an original Limited Partner and agrees to pay all of the liabilities and obligations imposed upon a Limited Partner of the Company under the Partnership Agreement, including the obligation to repay, in the manner set forth in the Partnership Agreement and any contributions returned or Net Profits distributed to any Limited Partner of the Company.

IN WITNESS WHEREOF, the parties have executed this agreement as of the __[7]__ day of ______[7]______, 19__.

BY________________ [8]

BY________________ [9]

Address of Assignee
___________[10]___________
____

Federal I.D. Number of Assignee
(or S.S. No.) _______[11]_______

(Document continued on next page)

12. The name of the General Partner (or other person authorized by the Limited Partnership Agreement to bind and sign for the Limited Partnership) printed below the line, with that person to sign above the line.

13. The Notary Public will complete these sections acknowledging the signatures of the Assignor and Assignee, and sign his name and affix his stamp or seal.

ACCEPTED AND AGREED:

__________[3]__________

BY______________________
[12]

On the __[13]__ day of ________, 19__, before me personally came ________[2]________, to me known and known to me to be the individual described in and who executed the foregoing instrument and he acknowledged to me that he executed the same.

__________[13]__________
Notary Public

On the __[13]__ day of ________, 19__, before me personally came ________[4]________, to me known and known to me to be the individual described in and who executed the foregoing instrument and he acknowledged to me that he executed the same.

_________[13]_________
Notary Public

ASSIGNMENT OF TRADEMARK (3-12)

A Trademark is an asset which may be sold in the same manner as any other asset. To formalize the transfer, an assignment must be filed with the U.S. Patent & Trademark Office so that the new owner becomes the registered owner of record. This Assignment of Trademark form is acceptable to the U.S. Patent & Trademark Office.

The Trademark Office address is: U.S. Department of Commerce, Patent and Trademark Office, Washington, D.C. 20231.

1. The name of the registered owner of the Trademark (the Assignor).
2. If the registered owner is a corporation, insert the state of incorporation. Otherwise delete.
3. The address of the registered owner.
4. The registered Trademark.
5. The registration number assigned by the U.S. Trademark & Patent Office.
6. The name of the buyer (the Assignee).
7. If the buyer is a corporation, insert the state of incorporation. Otherwise delete.
8. The address of the buyer.
9. The amount, in numbers, being paid.

ASSIGNMENT OF TRADEMARK

WHEREAS ________[1]________, *[2][a _______ corporation,]* having a principal place of business at __________[3]__________, has adopted and used the mark "__________[4]__________" which mark is registered in the United States Patent & Trademark Office under the Registration No. ______[5]______; and

WHEREAS ________[6]________, *[7][a _______ corporation,]* having a principal place of business at __________[8]__________, is desirous of acquiring the mark "__________[4]__________," the registration and the goodwill associated with the mark;

NOW, THEREFORE, in consideration of the payment of $____[9]____, the receipt of which is hereby acknowledged, ________[1]________ does hereby assign unto ________[6]________, all right, title and interest in and to the mark "__________[4]__________," Registration No.______[5]______, together with the goodwill of the

(Document continued on next page)

business symbolized by the mark and the registration.

__________*[10]*__________

*BY*________________________
[11]

[12] [Notary Statement]

10. The name of the registered owner if a corporation. Otherwise delete the line.

11. If the registered owner is an individual, delete "BY" and print the registered owner's name directly below the line, with that individual to sign above the line. If the registered owner is a corporation, print the name and title of the person acting for the corporation directly below the line, with that person to sign above the line.

12. Insert a Notary Statement, found elsewhere in this book, for the registered owner, either an Individual or Corporate form as appropriate. The Notary will complete the form.

ASSIGNMENT OF COPYRIGHT (3-13)

Copyright is a protection provided to the authors of "original works of authorship" including literary, dramatic, musical, artistic and certain other intellectual works, for example, advertisements. Copyright protection exists from the time the work is created. Notice and registration is not needed to gain protection but if registered with the Copyright Office within 3 months of creation, additional significant advantages are gained.

For complete information and forms contact: Copyright Office, Library of Congress, Washington, D.C. 20559.

Mere sale or possession of a copyrighted work does not give the physical owner Copyright ownership. That ownership remains with the creator of the work unless formally transferred. This Assignment meets the requirements of a transfer of Copyright and should, if the Copyright has been registered, be recorded with the Copyright Office.

ASSIGNMENT OF COPYRIGHT

WHEREAS ________[1]________, *[2][a _______ corporation,]* having a principal place of business at __________[3]__________, is the copyright owner of ____________[4]____________, an original work *[5][registered with the Copyright Office bearing Certificate No. _____[6]_____]* ***OR*** *[created in ________[7]_______ and bearing the copyright notice _______[8]_______]*; and

1. The name of the owner of the Copyright.

2. If the owner is a corporation, insert the state of incorporation. Otherwise delete.

3. The address of the owner.

4. A description of the work, for example "a book entitled 'Divorce Made Easy'."

5. Choose one. If the work has been registered with the Copyright Office use the first alternative; otherwise use the second alternative.

6. The number of The Registration Certificate issued by The Copyright Office.

7. The year of first publication of the work.

8. The Copyright notice. A Copyright notice takes the form: Copyright © 1991 Round Lake Publishing Company. The year is the year of first publication of the work (the same as in No. 7 above). The name is the owner of the copyright (the same as in No. 1 above). The word "Copyright" and the © symbol must precede the year to insure both U.S. and foreign (Universal) copyright protection.

(Document continued on next page)

9. The name of the buyer.

10. If the buyer is a corporation, insert the State of incorporation. Otherwise delete.

11. The address of the buyer.

12. The amount, in numbers, being paid.

13. The number of the Registration Certificate. Delete if not registered.

14. The date of the Assignment.

15. The name of the owner if a corporation. Otherwise delete the line.

16. If the owner is an individual, delete "BY" and print the owner's name directly below the line, with the owner to sign above the line. If the owner is a corporation, print the name and title of the person acting for the corporation directly below the line, with that person to sign above the line.

17. Insert a Notary Statement, found elsewhere in this book, for the owner, either an Individual or Corporate form, as appropriate. The Notary will complete the form.

WHEREAS ________[9]________, *[10][a ______ corporation,]* having a principal place of business at __________[11]__________, is desirous of acquiring the copyright ownership of ____________[4]____________, the registration therefor, and all other incidence thereof;

NOW, THEREFORE, in consideration of the payment of $_____[12]_____, the receipt of which is hereby acknowledged, ________[1]________ does hereby assign unto ________[9]________ all rights, title and interest in and to the copyright for ________[4]________ *[, Certificate No. _____[13]_____].*

Dated: ________[14]________

__________*[15]*__________

BY ______________________
[16]

[17] [Notary Statement]

ASSIGNMENT OF LITERARY WORK (3-14)

An Assignment of Literary Work is used when an Author sells a book that is already written to a publisher or other promoter of literary properties. The Agreement requires an advance payment against future royalties and a flat percentage of sales as a royalty. Royalties are usually negotiated. Rights are typically assigned by type of usage such as paperback rights, television rights, movie rights, stage dramatization, etc.

1. The date the Agreement is signed.

2 The name of the Author of the Work.

3. The name of the Company receiving the assignment.

4. If the Company receiving the assignment is a corporation, insert the state of incorporation. Otherwise delete.

5. The title of the Literary Work.

6. This form is found elsewhere in this chapter.

ASSIGNMENT OF LITERARY WORK

Agreement made this __[1]__ day of ______, 19__, by and between ________[2]________ ("Author") and ________[3]________ *[4][, a _____ corporation]* ("Company").

Author is the owner of an original work (the "Work") entitled "____________[5]____________"; and

Company is desirous of obtaining all rights of the Author to the Work.

In consideration of the mutual terms, conditions and covenants hereinafter set forth, Author and Company agree as follows:

1. Author sells, assigns, grants, transfers, sets over, and delivers to the Company, its successor and assigns, all right, title and interest to the Work.

2. Author shall, simultaneously with the execution of this Agreement execute an Assignment of Copyright [6] in the form as annexed hereto as Exhibit A and such other documents as are reasonably requested by Company to transfer the ownership in and to all rights to the Work.

3. Author warrants that the Work does not violate any copyright law, nor unlawfully infringes or interferes in any way with any literary property of another, nor contains any libelous matter, and in such event agrees that Author will forever warrant and defend the Company at Author's own expense against any alleged infringement of copyright or property rights based upon publication of the Work and against all claims, demands, suits, losses, costs, damages and expenses the Company may sustain or incur by reason of any libelous matter contained or alleged to be contained in the Work.

(Document continued on next page)

7. The amount of the advance, in numbers.

8. The royalty percentage, in numbers.

4. Company shall pay to Author a royalty for the Work as follows:

(a) Author shall receive, upon the execution of this Agreement, a non-refundable advance, to be applied against earned royalties, in the amount of $_____[7]_____.

(b) Company shall pay to Author a royalty representing __[8]__% of Company's net sales of the Work. Payments shall be based upon actual cash received. "Net Sales" shall be defined as gross sales less commissions, discounts, rebates, freight, postage and handling, returns, refunds and reshipments. Net sales shall not include sales of subsidiary rights; e.g. movie or television dramatizations of the Work, which shall be negotiated separately. "Actual cash Received" shall be defined as payment received for net sales.

(c) Payments shall be made to Author without any deductions for federal, state or local income tax or social security.

5. Company shall prepare royalty reports covering quarterly periods in the following manner.

(a) The quarterly royalty periods shall end on March 31, June 30, September 30 and December 31 of each year. The first royalty period shall be from the date of publication of the Work to the end of the next quarterly royalty period. Reports thereafter will cover each succeeding period of three (3) months.

(b) Each royalty report shall disclose the net sales of the Work, if any, during the reporting period and the amount of royalties calculated upon those net sales. The report shall also show the amount and general nature of all charges debited against the Author's account during the reporting period. The amount due the Author under the royalty report shall be the difference between its earned royalties and the charges debited against it as shown on the report. A deficit balance on any royalty report shall be carried forward as a debit on succeeding reports until fully offset by future royalties.

(c) Such royalty reports may, from time to time, contain negative sales figures. Such negative sales figures

(Document continued on next page)

9. The address of the Company.

10. The address of the Author.

will reflect sales which were credited to the Author's account during a preceding reporting period and returns of the Work in the current reporting period. Where such returns exceed the sales during the current reporting periods, a negative figure will result which will be charged against the Author's royalties for that period.

(d) Company shall provide Author with the royalty report within thirty (30) days of the end of each quarterly period and shall enclose therewith payment of any amounts due thereunder.

6. Author, or its representative, shall have the right to inspect, at the Company or such other location as the Company may designate, the books, records, reports and accounts of the Company with respect to the sales of the Work, upon forty-eight (48) hours' written notice to the Company, during normal business hours.

7. Author consents to the use of Author's name, signature, likeness, and biographical material concerning Author, on and with published copies, and in publicity, promotional material and advertising concerning the Work and the Company.

8. All notices required or permitted to be given hereunder shall be in writing and may be delivered personally or by Certified Mail - Return Receipt Requested, postage prepaid. Notice shall be addressed:

To Company: __________ [9] __________

____

To Author: __________ [10] __________

____

(Document continued on next page)

11. The state whose laws will govern the Agreement, typically the state in which the Company is located.

12. The name of the Company if a corporation. Otherwise delete the line.

13. If the Company is not a corporation, delete "BY" and print the individual's name directly below the line, with that person to sign above the line. If the Company is a corporation, print the name and title of the person acting for the corporation directly below the line, with that person to sign above the line.

14. The name of the Author printed directly below the line, with the Author to sign above the line.

9. Any controversy or claim arising out of or relating to this Agreement, or the breach thereof, shall be settled by arbitration in accordance with the Commercial Arbitration Rules of the American Arbitration Association, and judgment upon the award rendered by the arbitrator(s) may be entered in any court having jurisdiction thereof.

10. This Agreement shall be construed in accordance with and governed by the laws of the State of _____[11]_____, irrespective of the fact that a party hereto may not be a resident of that State.

11. It is agreed between the parties hereto that there are no other agreements or understandings between them relating to the subject matter of this Agreement. This Agreement supersedes all prior agreements, oral or written, between the parties and is intended as a complete and exclusive statement of the agreement between the parties. No change or modification of this Agreement shall be valid unless the same be in writing and signed by the parties.

INTENDING TO BE LEGALLY BOUND, the parties have executed this Agreement as of the date first above written.

_________*[12]*_________

*BY*________________________
[13] (Company)

____
[14] (Author)

TRADEMARK LICENSING AGREEMENT (3-15)

A Trademark may be licensed to another party. For example, Coca-Cola® licenses its Trademark for the manufacture of memorabilia. A license allows the owner of a Trademark to maintain control over the manner in which the Trademark is used by permitting the owner of the Trademark to monitor the quality of the manufactured products bearing the Trademark.

TRADEMARK LICENSING AGREEMENT

1. The date the Agreement is signed.
2. The name of the owner of the Trademark (the Licensor).
3. If the Licensor is a corporation, insert the state of incorporation. Otherwise delete.
4. The address of the Licensor.
5. The name of the party receiving the license (the Licensee).
6. If the Licensee is a corporation, insert the state of incorporation. Otherwise delete.
7. The address of the Licensee.
8. The Trademark.
9. Choose one.
10. A description of the territory in which the Licensee may use the Trademark, for example "North America."
11. A description of the products for which the license is granted, such as "tee shirts," "golfing equipment" or "plush toys."
12. The term of the License, in words and numbers, for example "three (3) years."

Agreement made this __[1]__ day of _______, 19__ by and between ________[2]________, *[3][a ________ corporation,]* having a principal place of business at __________[4]__________ ("Licensor") and ________[5]________, *[6][a ______ corporation,]* having a principal place of business at __________[7]__________ ("Licensee").

Licensor is the registered owner of the mark "________[8]________" together with the goodwill associated with the mark; and

Licensor desires to permit Licensee to use the mark; and

In consideration of the mutual terms, conditions and covenants hereinafter set forth, the parties agree as follows:

1. Licensor grants to Licensee *[9][exclusive]* ***OR*** *[non–exclusive]* license to use the mark "________[8]________" in __________[10]__________ in connection with the manufacture and sale of __________[11]__________.

2. The term of the license shall be _______[12]______ unless sooner terminated.

(Document continued on next page)

13. A description of the license fee, which can take many forms such as a single payment: "$25,000," a payment per unit: "$.05 per unit," or payment based upon sales: "5% of gross sales of Licensee."

14. When payments are to be made, for example "on the 15th day of the month for sales made in the prior month."

15. The number of days, in words and numbers, upon which the Agreement can be cancelled.

16. The name of the Licensor if a corporation. Otherwise delete the line.

17. If the Licensor is an individual, delete "BY" and print the Licensor's name directly below the line, with the Licensor to sign above the line. If the Licensor is a corporation, print the name and title of the person acting for the corporation directly below the line, with that person to sign above the line.

18. The name of the Licensee if a corporation. Otherwise delete the line.

19. If the Licensee is an individual, delete "BY" and print the Licensee's name directly below the line, with the Licensee to sign above the line. If the Licensee is a corporation, print the name and title of the person acting for the corporation directly below the line, with that person to sign above the line.

3. Licensee shall pay to Licensor a license fee of ________[13]________ payable ________[14]________.

4. Licensee agrees that Licensor shall have full control over the manner in which Licensee uses the licensed mark. Licensee agrees that it will not use the mark in connection with the sale or advertising of any goods or in a manner which has not been approved by Licensor in writing.

5. Licensee agrees to permit representatives of Licensor to inspect the facilities of Licensee, during normal business hours but without advance notice, to insure that the requirements of paragraph 4 are fulfilled. If Licensor determines that the requirements have been violated, it may, at its sole option, declare this Agreement to be terminated.

6. Licensee shall have the right to terminate this Agreement upon _____[15]_____ (__) days' notice to Licensor sent via U.S. Mail, Postage Prepaid, Certified Mail, Return Receipt Requested.

7. If the Agreement is terminated for any reason, Licensee will immediately cease and desist from further use of the licensed mark and will deliver to Licensor all unused material containing the licensed mark, or will make a showing, to the satisfaction of Licensor, that such items have been destroyed.

INTENDING TO BE LEGALLY BOUND, the parties have signed this License Agreement as of the date first above written.

__________*[16]*__________

*BY*________________________
[17] (Licensor)

__________*[18]*__________

*BY*________________________
[19] (Licensee)

LICENSING AGREEMENT—GENERAL (3-16)

A Licensing Agreement is used when one party receives a license from another party to manufacture or market a product. The Agreement requires the party receiving the license to market the Product in a specified territory and to purchase or manufacture a minimum quantity of the Product. A Licensing Agreement differs from a franchise in that with a Licensing Agreement there are no fees to be paid to the Licensor other than for Product purchased or manufactured.

LICENSING AGREEMENT—GENERAL

1. The date the Agreement is signed.

2. The name of the party giving the license (the Licensor).

3. If the Licensor is a corporation, insert the state in which incorporated. Otherwise delete.

4. The name of the party receiving the license (the Licensee).

5. If the Licensee is a corporation, insert the state in which incorporated. Otherwise delete.

6. Insert either "manufacture" or "market."

7. A description of the Product being licensed.

8. Insert either "manufacture" or "market."

9. Insert either "exclusive" or "non-exclusive."

10. Insert either "manufacturer" or "market."

11. A description of the territory for which the license is granted, for example "North America."

12. The date the license is to begin.

13. The number of years, in numbers, of the license.

14. The number of years, in numbers, for renewal of the license.

Agreement made this __[1]__ day of _______, 19__ by and between _______[2]________ *[3][, a _______ corporation]* ("Licensor") and ________[4]________ *[5][, a _____ corporation]* ("Licensee").

Licensor has the exclusive rights to _____[6]_____ the ________[7]________ ("Product"); and

Licensee is desirous of obtaining a license to _____[8]_____ the product; therefore

In consideration of the mutual terms, conditions and covenants hereinafter set forth, Licensor and Licensee agree as follows:

1. (a) Licensor grants to Licensee the ____[9]____ and non–transferable right to _____[10]_____ the product in ________[11]________ for a period commencing on ________[12]________ (the "Effective Date") and ending __[13]__ years from the Effective Date (the "Initial Term") unless sooner terminated pursuant to the provisions of this Agreement.

(b) It is mutually agreed that either party may terminate this Agreement at the end of the Initial Term by giving the other party written notice thereof at least six (6) months prior to the end of the Initial Term. Should either party fail to give such notice, this Agreement shall continue upon the same terms and conditions in force immediately prior to the expiration of the Initial Term, for an additional period of __[14]__ years. After the Initial Term, either party may terminate the renewal of the Agreement by giving six months' written notice of its intention to terminate at any time prior to the expiration of the then current term.

(Document continued on next page)

15. Insert either "manufacture" or "market."

16. Choose one.

17. Insert either "manufacture" or "market."

18. Insert the number of units of the Product the Licensee must manufacture or sell each year.

19. Insert either "manufactured" or "sold."

20. If the Licensee is to manufacture the Product, delete this paragraph.

2. (a) Licensee hereby accepts the right to _____[15]_____ the Product and agrees to do so in accordance with this Agreement.

(b) Licensee shall *[16][purchase all of the Licensee's requirements for Product only from Licensor, and not directly or indirectly from any other person, firm or corporation.]* ***OR*** *[manufacture the Product in strict conformity with the specifications and standards provided to Licensee by Licensor. Licensor reserves the right to amend the specifications and standards from time to time.]*

3. Licensee is an independent contractor and nothing contained in this Agreement shall be deemed or interpreted to constitute Licensee to be the agent or legal representative of Licensor for any purpose whatsoever. Licensee is not granted any right or authority to assume or create any obligation or responsibility, express or implied, on behalf of or in the name of Licensor, or to bind Licensor in any manner or fashion whatsoever.

4. Commencing with the Effective Date, Licensee shall _____[17]_____ ____[18]____ units of Product per twelve month period. Licensee may consider the total units of Product _____[19]_____ in any twelve month period over and above the specified volume as cumulative, to be carried forward to the succeeding twelve month periods.

[20][Licensor shall fill all orders from Licensee with reasonable promptness, except that in case of fire, riots, strikes or accidents or other conditions, whether or not similar in character to those specifically named, which unavoidably stop the making of deliveries contracted for, orders may be cancelled or partially cancelled, as the case may require, upon written notice or telegraph notice to Licensee. Such interruption of deliveries, however, shall not invalidate the remainder of this Agreement, but upon removal of the cause of the interruption, delivery shall continue as before. During the period of interruption, the Licensee's obligations to purchase the minimum units shall abate and, if required to meet Licensee's obligations, Licensee may obtain inventory and goods from such other source as required to mitigate any damages Licensee might sustain by virtue of the interruption.]

(Document continued on next page)

5. Licensee shall pay to Licensor *[21][a royalty for each unit of Product manufactured as follows: __________[22]__________.]* ***OR*** *[upon the usual trade terms of Licensor, the wholesale price of Product plus freight. Licensor shall not charge Licensee a higher price than any other Licensee purchasing equal quantities and making payment on the same terms.]*

6. The provisions of Paragraph 1(a) and 1(b) notwithstanding, in the event that Licensee shall default in the performance of the terms and conditions of this Agreement on Licensee's part to be kept, performed and observed, including without limiting the generality of the foregoing, prompt payment __________[23]__________ and other obligations incurred under the terms of this Agreement, this Agreement shall be subject to cancellation by Licensor upon fourteen (14) days' written notice by Certified Mail, Return Receipt Requested, to Licensee, during which period of fourteen (14) days Licensee shall have the right to remedy such default. Upon the remedying of such default, the cancellation notice shall have no further force or effect.

7. Licensee agrees that it will obtain and maintain during the term of this Agreement and any renewal thereof product liability insurance in the amount of $____[24]____.

8. In the event of the termination of this Agreement, whether voluntary or involuntary, Licensee agrees that Licensee will not, for a period of __[25]__ years from the effective date of termination, engage in the manufacture, sale or distribution of product similar to Product in the ________[26]________.

9. It is agreed between the parties hereto that there are no oral or other agreements or understandings between them relating to the selling or servicing of Product. This Agreement supersedes all prior agreements between the parties, and is intended as a complete and exclusive statement of the full agreement between the parties.

10. In the event of any dispute between Licensor and Licensee arising under or pursuant to the terms of this Agreement, the same shall be settled only by Arbitration in the State of _____[27]_____, under the then pertaining rules and regulations of the American Arbitration Association. The determination of the arbitrators shall be final and

(Document continued on next page)

21. Choose one depending on whether the Licensee is to buy or manufacture the Product.

22. Insert the agreed upon royalty rate expressed as a percentage, in numbers, typically of the wholesale price of the Product, and when royalties are to be paid, such as "calendar quarterly" or "semi-annually."

23. Insert either "of all royalties" or "for all Product purchased from Licensor," depending on whether the Product is to be manufactured or purchased from the Licensor.

24. The amount of product liability insurance, in numbers, to be carried.

25. The period of non-competition, in numbers. It is advisable not to exceed three years. (Note: in some states, for example California, non-competition restrictions are prohibited by law. Check your state's law before including this provision.)

26. A description of the territory in which the Licensee may not compete, such as "the states of New York and New Jersey."

27. The state in which any arbitration will take place, typically the state in which the Licensor is located.

28. The state whose laws will govern the Agreement, typically the state in which the Licensor is located.

29. The name of the Licensor if a corporation. Otherwise delete the line.

30. If the Licensor is an individual, delete "BY" and print the Licensor's name directly below the line, with the Licensor to sign above the line. If the Licensor is a corporation, print the name and title of the person acting for the corporation directly below the line, with that person to sign above the line.

31. The name of the Licensee if a corporation. Otherwise delete the line.

32. If the Licensee is an individual, delete "BY" and print the Licensee's name directly below the line, with the Licensee to sign above the line. If the Licensee is a corporation, print the name and title of the person acting for the corporation directly below the line, with that person to sign above the line.

binding upon the parties and may be enforced in any court of appropriate jurisdiction.

11. This Agreement shall be construed in accordance with and governed by the Laws of _____[28]_____.

INTENDING TO BE LEGALLY BOUND, the parties hereto have caused the License Agreement to be executed as of the date first above written.

__________*[29]*__________

*BY*________________________
[30] (Licensor)

__________*[31]*__________

*BY*________________________
[32] (Licensee)

Borrowing and Lending Money 4

The flow of capital, money, is the grease that lubricates the wheels of commerce. Over the years, important rights and protections have been developed to ensure that this flow is continuous and uninterrupted.

Promissory Notes Promissory Notes are essentially promises to repay borrowed money. The times, rates and numbers of payments can be varied, depending on the particular form chosen.

Loan Agreements and Letters of Credit These forms provide different options to deal with what will happen if a loan is not repaid. The section also contains an application for a Letter of Credit.

Guarantees These forms set up various ways of providing for another person to repay a debt if the borrower cannot—or for another person to put up collateral if the borrower is unable to.

Demands This series of forms provides the necessary first legal steps to getting payment from a borrower who has not paid his loan, or from the party that guaranteed the loan.

Financing Forms for two ways of raising money for a business are provided in this section.

PROMISSORY NOTE—FIXED INTEREST WITH INSTALLMENT PAYMENTS (4-01)

This type of Promissory Note is used when payment is to be made in equal amounts. Interest is computed on the remaining balance due as of the date of payment.

PROMISSORY NOTE—FIXED INTEREST WITH INSTALLMENT PAYMENTS

$ ________[1]________ __[2]__% Interest Per Annum

________[3]________, 19___

In installments, as set forth, for value received, the undersigned, ________[4]________ *[5][, a ________ corporation]* promises to pay to ________[6]________ *[7][, a ________ corporation]* or order at ____________[8]____________, the sum of ________[9]________ Dollars ($_____[10]_____), together with interest from the date above on the unpaid principal balance due at the rate of ___[11]___ percent (__[12]__%) per annum. Principal shall be payable monthly in installments of _____[13]_____ Dollars ($___[14]___) on the first day of _____[15]_____, 19___ and on the first day of each month thereafter [16] until the sum of ________[9]________ Dollars ($_____[10]_____) is paid in full, and interest accrued to the date of payment shall be payable on such dates.

Should interest not be paid when due it shall thereafter bear interest at the same rate as the principal, but such unpaid interest so compounded shall not exceed an amount equal to the maximum rate of interest permitted by law computed on the unpaid principal balance. All payments shall be payable in lawful currency of the United States of America. The undersigned agrees to pay all costs of collection including reasonable attorneys' fees.

(Document continued on next page)

1. The dollar amount of the loan, in numbers.
2. The yearly interest rate, in numbers.
3. The date the loan is given and the Note is signed.
4. The name of the borrower.
5. If the borrower is a corporation, insert the state of incorporation. Otherwise delete.
6. The name of the lender.
7. If the lender is a corporation, insert the state of incorporation. Otherwise delete.
8. The address where payment is to be made.
9. The amount of the loan, in words.
10. The amount of the loan, in numbers.
11. The yearly rate of interest, in words.
12. The yearly rate of interest, in numbers.
13. The amount of each payment, in words.
14. The amount of each payment, in numbers.
15. The date the first payment is due.
16. If the last payment is unequal add "and a final payment of ________ Dollars ($________)", in words and numbers.

PROMISSORY NOTE—FIXED INTEREST WITH INSTALLMENT PAYMENTS *continued*

17. If the Note cannot be prepaid, delete this paragraph.

18. If the Note is part of another agreement, identify the parties to that agreement and the date of that agreement. Otherwise delete.

19. If the Note is part of a Security Agreement, identify the parties to the Security Agreement and the date of the Security Agreement. Otherwise delete.

20. The name of the borrower if a corporation. Otherwise delete the line.

21. If the borrower is an individual, delete "BY" and print the borrower's name directly below the line, with the borrower to sign above the line. If the borrower is a corporation, print the name and title of the individual acting for the corporation directly below the line, with that person to sign above the line.

[17][This Note may be prepaid at any time or from time to time in whole or in part without penalty, premium or permission. Any partial payment under this Section shall be applied to the installments of the Note in the inverse order of their maturities.]

[18][This Note is the Note referred to in a certain Agreement between _______________ and _________________ dated the ____ day of ________, 19___ and is subject to all of the terms and provisions of the Agreement.] [19][This Note is secured pursuant to and as more specifically set forth in a certain Security Agreement between ________________ and _________________ dated the ____ day of ________, 19___ and is subject to all of the terms and provisions of the Security Agreement.]

________*[20]*________

BY ________________
[21]

PROMISSORY NOTE—DEMAND (4-02)

This type of Promissory Note is used when payment is to be made upon demand in a single payment. The form can be modified so that it becomes a Note due on a specific date or on demand, whichever the lender chooses. To make this change, for the opening phrase "On Demand" substitute "On ____(date)____ or upon Demand."

PROMISSORY NOTE—DEMAND

1. The dollar amount of the loan, in numbers.

2. The annual interest rate, in numbers.

3. The date the loan is given and the Note is signed.

4. The name of the borrower.

5. If the borrower is a corporation, insert the state of incorporation. Otherwise delete.

6. The name of the lender.

7. If the lender is a corporation, insert the state of incorporation. Otherwise delete.

8. The address where payment is to be made.

9. The amount of the loan, in words.

10. The amount of the loan, in numbers.

11. The annual interest rate, in words.

12. The annual interest rate, in numbers.

13. If the Note cannot be prepaid, delete this paragraph.

14. If the Note is part of another agreement, identify the parties to that agreement and the date of that agreement. Otherwise delete.

15. If the Note is part of a Security Agreement, identify the parties to the Security Agreement and the date of the Security Agreement. Otherwise delete.

$ ______[1]______ ___[2]___% Interest Per Annum

_________[3]_________, 19__

On Demand, the undersigned, _______[4]_______ *[5][, a ________ corporation]* promises to pay to ________[6]________ *[7][, a ________ corporation]* or order at ____________[8]____________, the sum of ________[9]________ Dollars ($_____[10]_____), together with interest thereon at the rate of ___[11]___ percent (__[12]__%) per annum from the date above.

All payments shall be payable in lawful currency of the United States of America. The undersigned agrees to pay all costs of collection, including reasonable attorneys' fees.

[13][This Note may be prepaid at any time or from time to time in whole or in part without penalty, premium or permission. Any partial payment under this Section shall be applied to the installments of the Note in the inverse order of their maturities.]

[14][This Note is the Note referred to in a certain Agreement between ______________ and ______________ dated the ____ day of ________, 19__ and is subject to all of the terms and provisions of the Agreement.] [15][This Note is secured pursuant to and as more specifically set forth in a certain Security Agreement between ________________ and ________________ dated the

(*Document continued on next page*)

16. The name of the borrower if a corporation. Otherwise delete the line.

17. If the borrower is an individual, delete "BY" and print the borrower's name directly below the line, with the borrower to sign above the line. If the borrower is a corporation, print the name and title of the individual acting for the corporation directly below the line, with that person to sign above the line.

____ day of ________, 19__ and is subject to all of the terms and provisions of the Security Agreement.]

_________*[16]*_______

BY ________________
[17]

PROMISSORY NOTE—SERIES (4-03)

This type of Promissory Note is to be used when a debt is to be repaid in installments that are not equal in amount or payable at uniform time intervals.

1. The dollar amount of the loan, in numbers.

2. The annual rate of interest, in numbers.

3. The date the loan is given and the Note is signed.

4. The number of days in which payment is due, i.e.: thirty, forty-five. Or an actual date may be substituted by using "on or before (date), the undersigned..."

5. The name of the borrower.

6. If the borrower is a corporation, insert the state of incorporation. Otherwise delete.

7. The name of the lender.

8. If the lender is a corporation, insert the state of incorporation. Otherwise delete.

9. The address where payment is to be made.

10. The amount of this Note, in words.

11. The amount of this Note, in numbers.

12. The annual rate of interest, in words.

13. The annual rate of interest, in numbers.

14. The number of this particular Note (one, two, twelve, etc.).

15. The total number of Notes in this series (twelve, twenty, etc.).

PROMISSORY NOTE—SERIES

$ _____[1]_____ __[2]__% Interest Per Annum

________[3]________, 19__

___[4]___ days after date, the undersigned ________[5]________ *[6][, a ________ corporation]* promises to pay to ________[7]_________ *[8][, a ________ corporation]* or order at _________[9]________, the sum of _______[10]_______ Dollars ($____[11]____), together with interest at the rate of _____[12]_____ percent (___[13]___%) from the date above.

Payment shall be payable in lawful currency of the United States of America.

The undersigned agrees to pay all costs of collection, including reasonable attorneys' fees.

This Note is No. __[14]__ of a series of __[15]__

(Document continued on next page)

16. The total dollar amount of the entire series of Notes, in words.

17. The total dollar amount of the entire series of Notes, in numbers.

18. The name of the borrower if a corporation. Otherwise delete the line.

19. If the borrower is an individual, delete "BY" and print the borrower's name directly below the line, with the borrower to sign above the line. If the borrower is a corporation, print the name and title of the individual acting for the corporation directly below the line, with that person to sign above the line.

Notes due on successive dates and totalling _______[16]_______ Dollars ($___[17]___). Upon default in the payment of any Note in this series, the remaining Notes and outstanding balance shall immediately become due and payable, without notice to the undersigned.

__________*[18]*_________

*BY*____________________
[19]

PROMISSORY NOTE—BALLOON PAYMENT (4-04)

This type of Promissory Note is used when payment is to be made in equal payments of principal and interest but the total amount does not fully pay off the loan. The remaining unpaid balance is due in one final payment (the "balloon").

PROMISSORY NOTE—BALLOON PAYMENT

$______[1]______ __[2]__% Interest Per Annum

______[3]______, 19__

In installments, as set forth, for value received, the undersigned, ________[4]________ *[5][, a ________ corporation]* promises to pay to _________[6]_________ *[7][, a __________ corporation]* or order at ____________[8]____________, the sum of _________[9]_________ Dollars ($_____[10]_____), together with interest from the date above on the unpaid principal balance due at the rate of ____[11]____ percent (___[12]___%) per annum. Payment shall be made in consecutive monthly installments of ________[13]________ Dollars ($______[14]_____) on the first day of ______[15]______, 19__ and on the first day of each month thereafter except that the final installment shall be in the amount of the balance of the principal and accrued interest then remaining unpaid on this Note.

All payments shall be payable in lawful currency of the United States of America.

The undersigned agrees to pay all costs of collection, including reasonable attorneys' fees.

[16][This Note may be prepaid at any time or from time to time in whole or in part without penalty, premium or permission. Any partial payment under this Section shall be applied to the installments of the Note in the inverse order of their maturities.]

[17][This Note is the Note referred to in a certain Agreement between ______________ and ______________

(Document continued on next page)

1. The dollar amount of the loan, in numbers.
2. The yearly interest rate, in numbers.
3. The date the loan is given and the Note is signed.
4. The name of the borrower.
5. If the borrower is a corporation, insert the state of incorporation. Otherwise delete.
6. The name of the lender.
7. If the lender is a corporation, insert the state of incorporation. Otherwise delete.
8. The address where payment is to be made.
9. The amount of the loan, in words.
10. The amount of the loan, in numbers.
11. The yearly interest rate, in words.
12. The yearly interest rate, in numbers.
13. The amount of each payment, in words.
14. The amount of each payment, in numbers.
15. The month the first payment is due.
16. If the Note cannot be prepaid, delete this paragraph.
17. If the Note is part of another agreement, identify the parties to that agreement and the date of that agreement. Otherwise delete.

18. If the Note is part of a Security Agreement, identify the parties to the Security Agreement and the date of the Security Agreement. Otherwise delete.

19. The name of the borrower if a corporation. Otherwise delete the line.

20. If the borrower is an individual, delete "BY" and print the borrower's name directly below the line, with the borrower to sign above the line. If the borrower is a corporation, print the name and title of the individual acting for the corporation directly below the line, with that person to sign above the line.

dated the ____ day of ________, 19__ and is subject to all of the terms and provisions of the Agreement.] [18][This Note is secured pursuant to and as more specifically set forth in a certain Security Agreement between ________________ and ________________ dated the ____ day of _________, 19__ and is subject to all of the terms and provisions of the Security Agreement.]

_________*[19]*_________

BY ____________________
[20]

LOAN AGREEMENT (4-05)

When the terms of a Loan are more complex than can be contained in a simple Promissory Note, a Loan Agreement is useful. If the Loan is to be guaranteed by a third party, add a Guaranty (either Personal or Corporate, as appropriate, found elsewhere in this chapter) to the end of this form—after the signatures of the Borrower and Lender. Forms for Exhibits A and B, referenced in this Agreement, are to be found as separate documents in this chapter.

LOAN AGREEMENT

1. The date the Loan Agreement is signed.

2. The name of the Borrower. If the Borrower is a corporation, add ", a ______ corporation" inserting the state in which incorporated.

3. The name of the Lender. If the Lender is a corporation, add ", a ______ corporation" inserting the state in which incorporated.

4. The date the money is to be loaned.

5. The amount of the loan, in words.

6. The amount of the loan, in numbers.

7. The yearly interest rate, in words.

8. The yearly interest rate, in numbers.

9. A multiple in which partial payment is to be made, i.e. $100, $1,000.

10. The minimum payment, in numbers, the Lender will accept.

11. Insert either "360" or "365." Note: most banks still typically use a 360-day year to compute interest.

Loan Agreement made this __[1]__ day of __________, 19__, by and between ________[2]________ ("Borrower") and ________[3]________ ("Lender").

In consideration of the mutual terms, conditions and covenants hereinafter set forth Borrower and Lender agree as follows:

1. LOAN: Subject to and in accordance with this Agreement, its terms, conditions and covenants Lender agrees to lend to Borrower on __________[4]__________ (the "Closing" date) the principal sum of ________[5]________ Dollars ($_____[6]_____).

2. NOTE: The Loan shall be evidenced by a Note in the form attached hereto as Exhibit A (the "Note") executed by the Borrower and delivered to Lender on Closing.

3. INTEREST: The Loan shall bear interest on the unpaid principal at an annual rate of ______[7]______ percent (__[8]__%). In the event of a default in payment the aforesaid interest rate shall apply to the total of principal and interest due at the time of default.

4. PAYMENT: Payment shall be in accordance with the terms contained in the Note. The Note may, at any time and from time to time, be paid or prepaid in whole or in part without premium or penalty, except that any partial prepayment shall be (a) in multiples of $______[9]______, (b) a minimum of $______[10]______, applied to any installments due under the Note in the inverse order of their maturity. Upon the payment of the outstanding principal in full or all of the installments, if any, the interest on the Loan shall be computed and a final adjustment and payment of interest shall be made within five (5) days of the receipt of notice. Interest shall be calculated on the basis of a year of __[11]__ days and the actual number of days elapsed.

(Document continued on next page)

12. The grace period for making payment, in words.

13. The grace period, in numbers.

5. SECURITY: Borrower agrees to secure the repayment of the Loan by executing those security documents attached hereto as Exhibit B and shall deliver said security documents on Closing. From time to time Lender may demand, and Borrower shall execute, additional loan documents which are reasonably necessary to perfect Lender's security interests.

6. REPRESENTATIONS AND WARRANTIES: Borrower represents and warrants: (i) that the execution, delivery and performance of this Agreement, and the Note and Security Documents have been duly authorized and are proper; (ii) that the financial statement submitted to Lender fairly presents the financial condition of the Borrower as of the date of this Agreement knowing that the Lender has relied thereon in granting the Loan; (iii) that the Borrower has no contingent obligations not disclosed or reserved against in said financial statement, and at the present time there are no material, unrealized or anticipated losses from any present commitment of Borrower; (iv) that there will be no material adverse changes in the financial condition of the Borrower at the time of Closing; (v) that Borrower will advise of material adverse changes which occur at any time prior to Closing and thereafter to the date of final payment; and (vi) that Borrower has good and valid title to all of the property given as Security hereunder. Borrower represents and warrants that such representations and warranties shall be deemed to be continuing representations and warranties during the entire life of this Agreement.

7. DEFAULT: Borrower shall be in default: (i) if any payment due hereunder is not made within ____[12]____ (_[13]_) days of the date due; (ii) in the event of assignment by Borrower for the benefit of creditors; (iii) upon the filing of any voluntary or involuntary petition in bankruptcy by or against Borrower; or (iv) if Borrower has breached any representation or warranty specified in this Agreement.

8. GOVERNING LAW: This Agreement, Note(s) and Security Documents shall be governed by, construed and

(Document continued on next page)

14. The state whose laws will govern the Agreement, typically the state in which the Lender is located.

15. The name of the Borrower if a corporation. Otherwise delete the line.

16. If the Borrower is an individual, delete "BY" and print the Borrower's name directly below the line, with the Borrower to sign above the line. If the Borrower is a corporation, print the name and title of the individual acting for the corporation directly below the line, with that person to sign above the line.

17. The name of the Lender if a corporation. Otherwise delete the line.

18. If the Lender is an individual, delete "BY" and print the Lender's name directly below the line, with the Lender to sign above the line. If the Lender is a corporation, print the name and title of the individual acting for the corporation directly below the line, with that person to sign above the line.

enforced in accordance with the laws of the State of _____[14]_____.

INTENDING TO BE LEGALLY BOUND, the parties hereto have caused this Loan Agreement to be executed as of the date first above written.

__________*[15]*__________

*BY*________________________
[16]

__________*[17]*__________

*BY*________________________
[18]

EXHIBIT A

Attach a copy of the Note.

EXHIBIT B

Attach a copy of a Security Agreement or Pledge Agreement.

PLEDGE OF PERSONAL PROPERTY (4-06)

A Pledge Agreement is used in conjunction with a Loan Agreement where the Borrower pledges tangible personal property (i.e. stocks, bonds, certificates of deposit, jewelry, etc.) that can be delivered to the Lender to hold as security for the Loan. A Pledge Agreement may also be used, with modification, to secure a past due debt. In such a case, references to the Loan Agreement would be eliminated and the Loan would be termed the "Debt." This differs from the following Security Agreement in that in a Pledge of Personal Property, the Lender actually holds the property or security.

1. The date the Pledge Agreement is signed.

2. The name of the Borrower. If the Borrower is a corporation, add ", a _____ corporation" inserting the state in which incorporated.

3. The name of the Lender. If the Lender is a corporation, add ", a _____ corporation" inserting the state in which incorporated.

4. The date of the Loan Agreement.

5. The amount of the Loan, in numbers.

PLEDGE OF PERSONAL PROPERTY

Pledge Agreement made this __[1]__ day of ________, 19__, by and between ________[2]________ ("Borrower") and ________[3]________ ("Lender"), and is made with reference to the following facts:

A. Borrower and Lender have entered into a Loan Agreement dated ________[4]________ for a Loan in the amount of $_____[5]_____.

B. Pursuant to the Loan Agreement Borrower is to pledge certain personal property as collateral to secure repayment of the Loan which personal property is listed on Schedule A attached hereto (the "Collateral").

C. Lender would not have extended credit to Borrower pursuant to the Loan Assignment and Note but for the Borrower's execution of this Pledge Agreement.

THEREFORE, in order to induce Lender to loan to Borrower, Borrower agrees:

1. SECURITY INTEREST: As security for the Loan, Borrower hereby pledges, assigns, transfers and grants to Lender a security interest in and to the personal property described in Schedule A attached hereto.

2. DELIVERY TO AND DUTIES OF LENDER: In furtherance of the pledge, assignment, transfer and grant Borrower shall deliver to Lender the personal property described in Schedule A attached hereto together with such assignments or powers necessary at the time of Closing. Borrower agrees that Lender shall have no liability of any kind or nature whatsoever with respect to the Collateral, other than to hold, release or dispose of the same in accordance with the terms and provisions of this Pledge Agreement.

(Document continued on next page)

6. The name of the Borrower if a corporation. Otherwise delete the line.

7. If the Borrower is an individual, delete "BY" and print the Borrower's name directly below the line, with the Borrower to sign above the line. If the Borrower is a corporation, print the name and title of the individual acting for the corporation directly below the line, with that person to sign above the line.

8. The name of the Lender if a corporation. Otherwise delete the line.

9. If the Lender is an individual, delete "BY" and print the Lender's name directly below the line, with the Lender to sign above the line. If the Lender is a corporation, print the name and title of the individual acting for the corporation directly below the line, with that person to sign above the line.

3. COSTS: Borrower shall pay or reimburse Lender for all costs and expenses advanced or incurred by Lender in connection with the perfection and protection of the security interest granted herein or the preservation or disposition of the Collateral, or any part thereof.

4. TITLE: Lender is the legal and beneficial owner of all the Collateral, has and will have good and marketable title to the Collateral free and clear of any security interest, lien, pledge, option, claim, lease or other encumbrance unless otherwise indicated on Schedule A attached hereto.

5. INSURANCE and RISK OF LOSS: Borrower shall keep the Collateral insured for its full value at all times and retains the risk of loss of such Collateral.

6. NOTIFICATION: The parties shall promptly notify each other in writing of any event which affects the value of the Collateral.

INTENDING TO BE LEGALLY BOUND, the parties hereto have caused this Pledge Agreement to be executed as of the date first above written.

__________*[6]*__________

*BY*____________________
[7]

__________*[8]*__________

*BY*____________________
[9]

SCHEDULE A

Quantity	Description of Property	Liens or Encumbrances (if any)

SECURITY AGREEMENT (4-07)

A Security Agreement is used in conjunction with a Loan Agreement or a Note representing a debt. In a Security Agreement, the Lender is given a secured interest in the form of personal property. The Uniform Commercial Code requires the filing of a "Financing Statement" (Form U.C.C.-1) as notice to the world that the Lender has the secured interest. These forms are available at all stationery and office supply stores. Unless the forms are filed with the state in which the Borrower does business, the security interest is not "perfected" and could be lost.

SECURITY AGREEMENT

1. The date the Security Agreement is signed.

2. The name of the Borrower. If the Borrower is a corporation, add ", a _____ corporation" inserting the state in which incorporated.

3. The name of the Lender. If the Lender is a corporation, add ", a _____ corporation" inserting the state in which incorporated.

4. Delete those categories of personal property in which a security interest is not being granted and renumber the sections.

5. The date of the Loan Agreement.

6. The amount of the Loan, in numbers.

Security Agreement made this __[1]__ day of ________ ,19__, by and between ________[2]_______ ("Borrower") and ___________[3]___________ ("Lender").

In consideration of the mutual terms, conditions and covenants hereinafter set forth, Borrower and Lender agree as follows:

1. SECURITY: The Borrower hereby assigns and grants to Lender a security interest in the following described personal property (the "Collateral").

[4][1.1 Accounts. All present and future accounts, chattel paper, debts of any kind and collateral therefore, documents, notes, drafts, or other forms of obligations to Borrower.

1.2 Inventory. All present and hereafter acquired inventory wherever located, including, but not limited to, raw materials, works in progress and finished goods.

1.3 Intangibles. All general intangibles, including but not limited to, trade-names, service marks, goodwill, trademarks, copyrights, patents, patent applications, inventions, royalties or commissions.

1.4 Equipment. All present and hereafter acquired equipment wherever located.]

1.5 Proceeds. This security interest shall apply to the above described Collateral and to the proceeds thereof.

2. DEBTS: The Security Interest herein granted shall secure the Loan granted to the Borrower by Lender pursuant to a Loan Agreement or Note between the parties dated _____[5]_____ for the Loan in the amount of $____[6]_____.

(Document continued on next page)

7. The state whose laws will govern the Security Agreement, typically the state in which the Lender is located.

8. The name of the Borrower if a corporation. Otherwise delete the line.

9. If the Borrower is an individual, delete "BY" and print the Borrower's name directly below the line, with the Borrower to sign above the line. If the Borrower is a corporation, print the name and title of the individual acting for the corporation directly below the line, with that person to sign above the line.

10. The name of the Lender if a corporation. Otherwise delete the line.

11. If the Lender is an individual, delete "BY" and print the Lender's name directly below the line, with the Lender to sign above the line. If the Lender is a corporation, print the name and title of the individual acting for the corporation directly below the line, with that person to sign above the line.

3. DUTIES OF BORROWER: Borrower will maintain and care for the Collateral, defend the Collateral against all claims and demands, insure the Collateral for its full value against all hazards and will keep the Collateral free and clear of all liens, claims, security interest and encumbrances.

4. SALE OF COLLATERAL: Borrower will not sell or otherwise dispose of any of the of the Collateral except in the ordinary course of Borrower's business.

5. WAIVER: Any waiver, express or implied, of any provision of this Agreement or Loan Agreement or any failure or delay to enforce any provision shall not be deemed a continuing waiver of that or any other provision.

6. ADDITIONAL DOCUMENTS: Lender may request and Borrower shall execute such other agreements, documents or interests in connection with this Security Agreement in a form and substance satisfactory to Lender as Lender may reasonably deem necessary.

7. U.C.C.: All terms not defined in this Security Agreement shall be governed by, construed and enforced in accordance with the Uniform Commercial Code of the State of _____[7]_____.

8. COSTS: Borrower agrees to promptly pay all costs and expenses, together with reasonable attorneys' fees, incurred by Lender to enforce this Security Agreement, protect Lender's security interest or to protect or preserve the Collateral.

INTENDING TO BE LEGALLY BOUND, the parties hereto have caused this Security Agreement to be executed as of the date above first written.

_________*[8]*_________

*BY*__________________
[9]

_________*[10]*_________

*BY*__________________
[11]

INSTALLMENT AGREEMENT TO PAY DEBT (4-08)

An Installment Agreement is used when there is an existing debt that is past due and the Debtor is unable to make payment. This form creates an Installment loan for the outstanding balance of the loan.

1. The date the Agreement is signed.

2. The name of the Debtor. If the Debtor is a corporation, add ", a _____ corporation" inserting the state in which incorporated.

3. The name of the Creditor. If the Creditor is a corporation, add ", a _____ corporation" inserting the state in which incorporated.

4. The amount of the debt, in numbers.

5. The annual rate of interest, in numbers, to be applied to the debt.

6. The amount of each installment payment, in numbers.

7. The date the first payment is due.

8. The day of the month that each subsequent payment is due.

9. The amount of the debt with interest, in numbers.

INSTALLMENT AGREEMENT TO PAY DEBT

Agreement made this __[1]__ day of ________, 19__, by and between ________[2]________ ("Debtor") and ________[3]________ ("Creditor").

Debtor is presently indebted to Creditor in the principal sum of $_____[4]_____, which debt is now due and payable. In consideration of Creditor not pursuing legal action to seek payment, Creditor agrees to the payment of the debt as follows:

In installments, together with interest from the date above on the unpaid principal balance due at the rate of __[5]__% per annum. Payment shall be made in consecutive monthly payments of $_____[6]_____ on the __[7]__ day of ________, 19___ and on the __[8]__ day of each month thereafter until the sum of $_____[9]_____ is paid in full, and interest accrued to the date of payment shall be payable on such dates.

Should interest not be paid when due it shall thereafter bear interest at the same rate as the principal, but such unpaid interest so compounded shall not exceed an amount equal to the maximum rate of interest permitted by law computed on the unpaid principal balance. All payments shall be payable in lawful currency of the United States of America. The undersigned agrees to pay all costs of collection including reasonable attorneys' fees.

This Note may be prepaid at any time or from time to time in whole or in part without penalty, premium or permission. Any partial prepayment under this Section shall be applied to the installments of the Note in the inverse order of their maturities.

Should Debtor default in the payment of any installment or interest due hereunder, the amount of principal and any accrued but unpaid interest then remaining unpaid may be declared immediately due and

(Document continued on next page)

10. The annual rate of interest, in numbers, to be applied after default.

payable and shall bear interest at the rate of __[10]__% per annum until paid.

11. The name of the Debtor, if a corporation. Otherwise delete the line.

_________*[11]*_________

12. If the Debtor is an individual, delete "BY" and print the Debtor's name directly below the line, with the Debtor to sign above the line. If the Debtor is a corporation, print the name and title of the individual acting for the corporation directly below the line, with that person to sign above the line.

*BY*____________________
[12]

13. The name of the Creditor, if a corporation. Otherwise delete the line.

_________*[13]*_________

14. If the Creditor is an individual, delete "BY" and print the Creditor's name directly below the line, with the Creditor to sign above the line. If the Creditor is a corporation, print the name and title of the individual acting for the corporation directly below the line, with that person to sign above the line.

*BY*____________________
[14]

APPLICATION FOR LETTER OF CREDIT (4-09)

A Letter of Credit is a promise by a bank or other financial institution to pay a specific amount of money at the request of, and in accordance with, the instructions of its customer, to a third party (supplier or manufacturer) for merchandise to be shipped—provided that the required documentation is presented. A Letter of Credit is commonly used when merchandise is shipped to the United States from a foreign destination. Banks and other financial institutions use their own forms for Letters of Credit. This form is an Application submitted for the issuance of a Letter of Credit.

A "Notation Letter of Credit," for which this form is an Application, has the running (declining) balance recorded ("notated") on the back of each draft of the Letter of Credit. Each draft, or a writing attached to the draft, must indicate that the notation has been made on the Letter of Credit. The notation must be attached to the last draft when the amount of the Letter of Credit has been used up. The draft would be endorsed on the back: "Noted to Letter of Credit dated _______." The Letter of Credit would be endorsed: "Draft dated _______ in the amount of $_________."

APPLICATION FOR LETTER OF CREDIT

1. The name and address of the bank or other financial institution issuing the Letter of Credit.

2. The name and address of the party requesting the Letter of Credit.

3. The name and address of the party to whom the Letter of Credit will be delivered (the supplier or manufacturer of the merchandise).

4. The number of days, in numbers, after the presentation that the draft against the Letter of Credit is to be honored. Note: this is to be negotiated with the bank but will usually be determined by the bank.

5. The expiration date of the Letter of Credit.

6. The total amount of the Letter of Credit, in numbers.

TO: ________[1]________
____
____

FROM: ________[2]________
____
____

You are herewith requested to issue a Letter of Credit as follows:

1. The Credit is to be irrevocable and nontransferable.

2. The Credit is to be a Notation Credit.

3. The beneficiary is to be ________________[3]________________.

4. Drafts against the Credit are to be drawn at ___[4]___ days sight and presented for payment before the expiration of the Credit on ________[5]________.

5. The total of all drafts drawn against the Credit shall not exceed $ ______[6]______.

(Document continued on next page)

6. To cover the full cost of merchandise described in the accompanying invoices as ________[7]________ which are to be delivered from __________[8]__________ to ___________[9]___________ on or before ________[10]________, which merchandise is to be insured by the buyer.

7. The following documents are required: invoice in duplicate, insurance policies or certificates covering not less than full invoice cost, bills of lading made to the issuer's order.

8. The Credit shall be governed by, construed and enforced in accordance with the Uniform Commercial Code of the State of _____[11]_____.

__________*[12]*__________

*BY*_______________________
[13]

7. A description of the merchandise being purchased, i.e. Dresses.

8. The name and address of the supplier or manufacturer.

9. The name and address of the recipient of the merchandise.

10. The last date on which the merchandise can be shipped.

11. The state whose laws shall govern the Letter of Credit.

12. The name of the party requesting the Letter of Credit if a corporation. Otherwise delete the line.

13. If the party requesting the Letter of Credit is an individual, delete "BY" and print the party's name directly below the line, with that party to sign above the line. If the party requesting the Letter of Credit is a corporation, print the name and title of the individual acting for the corporation directly below the line, with that person to sign above the line.

PERSONAL GUARANTY OF PAYMENT OF THE DEBTS OF ANOTHER (4-10)

A Lender may not feel secure with the collateral it is holding and may have greater requirements if it is to make a loan. The Lender may suggest that another person (the Guarantor) be liable for payment if the Borrower defaults. The Guarantor agrees with the Lender to make the payments of the Borrower if the Borrower is in default and cannot meet the loan payments. The Lender must first seek payment from the Borrower before he turns to the Guarantor for payment.

PERSONAL GUARANTY OF PAYMENT OF THE DEBTS OF ANOTHER

1. The name of the Lender.

2. The name of the Borrower.

3. The name of the Guarantor.

4. The name of the Witness printed directly below the line, with the Witness to sign above the line.

5. The name of the Guarantor printed directly below the line, with the Guarantor to sign above the line.

In consideration of and as an inducement to ________[1]________ ("Lender") to extend credit to ________[2]________ ("Borrower"), and in further consideration of the sum of One Dollar ($1.00) paid to the undersigned, the receipt and sufficiency of which are hereby acknowledged,

I, ________[3]________ ("Guarantor") hereby guaranty to Lender, the prompt payment, when due, of each and every claim which Lender may have against Borrower. This continuing guaranty shall remain in force until revoked by the undersigned by written notice to Lender but any such revocation shall be effective only as to any claims which may arise out of transactions entered into after receipt of notice of revocation. This guaranty shall be effective as to the renewal of any claims guaranteed hereby or extensions of time of payment, and shall not be affected by the surrender or release by Lender of any other or additional security Lender may hold for any claim hereby guaranteed. The Lender shall be under no obligation to give the undersigned notice of renewals or extensions of existing loans.

In the event of default by Borrower in the making of any payment when due, the undersigned hereby agrees to pay on demand all sums then due and all losses or expenses which may be incurred by Lender, including but not limited to reasonable attorneys' fees, without Lender having first or prior thereto proceeded against Borrower.

Witness:

________________ ________________

[4] [5]

CORPORATE GUARANTY OF PAYMENT OF THE DEBTS OF ANOTHER (4-11)

A Lender may not feel secure with the collateral it is holding and may have greater requirments if it is to make a loan. The Lender may suggest that a corporation (the Guarantor) be liable for payment if the Borrower defaults. The Guarantor agrees with the Lender to make the payments of the Borrower if the Borrower is in default and cannot meet the loan payments. The Lender must first seek payment from the Borrower before he turns to the Guarantor for payment.

1. The name of the Lender.

2. The name of the Borrower.

3. The name of the corporation (the Guarantor).

4. The state of incorporation of the corporation.

5. The date of the resolution of the corporation's Board of Directors authorizing the giving of the Guaranty.

CORPORATE GUARANTY OF PAYMENT OF THE DEBTS OF ANOTHER

In consideration of and as an inducement to ________[1]________ ("Lender") to extend credit to ________[2]________ ("Borrower"), and in further consideration of the sum of One Dollar ($1.00) paid to the undersigned, the receipt and sufficiency of which are hereby acknowledged,

________[3]________, a ________[4]________ corporation ("Guarantor"), hereby guarantees to Lender, the prompt payment, when due, of each and every claim which Lender may have against Borrower. This continuing guaranty shall remain in force until revoked by the undersigned by written notice to Lender but any such revocation shall be effective only as to any claims which may arise out of transactions entered into after receipt of notice of revocation. This guaranty shall be effective as to the renewal of any claims guaranteed hereby or extensions of time of payment, and shall not be affected by the surrender or release by Lender of any other or additional security Lender may hold for any claim hereby guaranteed. The Lender shall be under no obligation to give undersigned notice of renewals or extensions of existing loans.

In the event of default by Borrower in the making of any payment when due, the undersigned hereby agrees to pay on demand all sums then due and all losses or expenses which may be incurred by Lender, including but not limited to reasonable attorneys' fees, without Lender having first or prior thereto proceeded against Borrower.

The guaranty was duly authorized by resolution of the Board of Directors of ________[3]________, dated ________[5]________ whereby the undersigned as

(Document continued on next page)

CORPORATE GUARANTY OF PAYMENT OF THE DEBTS OF ANOTHER *continued*

6. The title of the officer of the corporation authorized to sign the Guaranty.

______[6]______ was authorized and directed to execute this guaranty and to affix the corporate seal hereto.

7. The Secretary of the corporation to sign above the line.

Attest: __________[3]__________

8. The name and title of No. 6 above printed directly below the line, with that person to sign above the line.

__________[7]__________
Secretary

BY____________________
[8]

CONTINUING GUARANTY AGREEMENT (4-12)

A Continuing Guaranty Agreement is used when a corporation or individual (the Customer) wishes to buy merchandise from the Seller but has neither the cash nor the credit to do so. A credit-worthy corporation or individual will guarantee the payment for the merchandise. The Guaranty is not restricted to a specific dollar amount or time period. Termination of the Guaranty requires notification and covers purchases made only after the receipt of the notice.

Note that in a Continuing Guaranty, the Guarantor is liable for the Customer's default of all obligations, including present or future obligations, until the Guarantor notifies the creditor (the Seller) of his revocation of the Guaranty as to future obligations.

CONTINUING GUARANTY AGREEMENT

To induce ________[1]__________ (the "Seller") having ________[2]_______ at __________[3]__________ to extend credit in such sum and upon such terms as Seller may deem best to ________[4]________ (the "Customer") having ________[5]_______ at _________[6]_________, the undersigned ________[7]________ (the "Guarantor") having ________[8]________ at _________[9]_________, guarantees prompt performance and payment by the Customer when due, or at any time thereafter with interest at __[10]__% per annum, of all obligations heretofore or hereafter incurred by the Customer if not performed or paid promptly by the Customer when due.

This guaranty is an absolute, unconditional, present and continuing guarantee of payment and not of collectability and is in no manner conditional or contingent upon any attempt to collect from the Customer or upon any other condition or contingency.

If the Customer shall fail to perform or pay promptly any of its obligation to Seller or shall file a petition in bankruptcy, reorganization or arrangement or shall consent to a petition in bankruptcy filed against it or not obtain a dismissal of any such petition within twenty (20) days after it has been filed, or shall make an arrangement for the benefit of creditors, or shall take advantage of any insolvency act, Seller may accelerate the performance or payment of Customer's obligations.

Guarantor waives: (i) notice of the acceptance by Seller of the Guaranty Agreement; (ii) notice of all transactions with Customer; (iii) notice of the conversion of any indebtedness to promissory notes and any requirements

1. The name of the Seller. If a corporation, add ", a ______ corporation" inserting the state of incorporation of the Seller.

2. If the Seller is an individual, insert "a residence." If a corporation, insert "a place of business."

3. The address of the Seller.

4. The name of the Customer. If a corporation, add ", a ______ corporation" inserting the state of incorporation of the Customer.

5. If the Customer is an individual, insert "a residence." If a corporation, insert "a place of business."

6. The address of the Customer.

7. The name of the party guaranteeing the debt (the Guarantor). If a corporation, add ", a _______ corporation" inserting the state of incorporation of the Guarantor.

8. If the Guarantor is an individual, insert "a residence." If a corporation, insert "a place of business."

9. The address of the Guarantor.

10. The interest rate, in numbers, to be applied to past due amounts.

(Document continued on next page)

11. The state whose laws will govern the Agreement, usually the state where the Seller is located.

12. The date of signing the Guaranty Agreement.

13. The name of the Guarantor if a corporation. Otherwise delete the line.

14. If the Guarantor is an individual, delete "BY" and print the Guarantor's name directly below the line, with the Guarantor to sign above the line. If the Guarantor is a corporation, print the name and title of the individual acting for the corporation directly below the line, with that person to sign above the line.

15. Insert the Notary Statement, found elsewhere in this book, for an Individual or for a Corporation, as appropriate, for the Guarantor. The Notary will complete the Notary Statement.

for presentment, protest and notice of protest and non-payment.

This Guaranty Agreement may be terminated by Guarantor only by written notice given to Seller by personal service or Certified Mail, Return Receipt Requested and shall be effective only as to credit given to or obligations incurred by Customer subsequent to receipt of the written notice to Seller.

Guarantor will pay all costs and expenses, including but not limited to reasonable attorneys' fees, incurred by Seller in enforcing the obligations of the Customer and Guarantor.

Seller may, if it assigns the underlying debt or any portion thereof of Customer to Seller, assign the rights granted hereunder as they apply to the assigned debt or portion thereof.

This Guaranty Agreement shall be governed by and construed in accordance with the laws of the State of _______[11]_______.

Dated: ________[12]________

__________*[13]*__________

*BY*______________________
[14]

[15] [Notary Statement]

LIMITED GUARANTY AGREEMENT (4-13)

In contrast to the preceding Continuing Guaranty Agreement, a Limited Guaranty Agrement is restricted to a specific dollar amount and to obligations that arise within a specified period of time.

LIMITED GUARANTY AGREEMENT

Guaranty given by ________[1]________ (the "Guarantor") having ________[2]________ at __________[3]__________ to ________[4]________ ("the Lender") having ________[5]________ at __________[6]__________ to induce Lender to extend credit to ________[7]________ (the "Borrower") having ________[8]________ at __________[9]__________.

In consideration of the foregoing, the Guarantor hereby guarantees to the Lender, its successors and assigns the prompt payment by the Borrower to the Lender at maturity of any order for the payment of money, claim or indebtedness in connection with which the Borrower is or shall become liable to the Lender from this date to ________[10]________. The liability of the Guarantor shall not during the lifetime of this Guaranty exceed the sum of $_____[11]_____ with interest thereon, plus all attorneys' fees, costs and expenses of collection incurred by the Lender in connection with this Guaranty.

Upon default by the Borrower in any payment due to Lender, Guarantor agrees to pay such amounts on

(Document continued on next page)

1. The name of the party guarantying the debt (the Guarantor). If the Guarantor is a corporation, add ", a ______ corporation" inserting the state of incorporation of the Guarantor.

2. If the Guarantor is an individual, insert ", a residence." If a corporation, insert " a place of business."

3. The address of the Guarantor.

4. The name of the party giving the credit (the Lender). If the Lender is a corporation, add ", a ______ corporation" inserting the state of incorporation of the Lender.

5. If an individual insert ", a residence." If a corporation, insert ", a place of business."

6. The address of the Lender.

7. The name of the party receiving the credit (the Borrower). If a corporation, add ", a ______ corporation" inserting the state of incorporation of the Borrower.

8. If an individual, insert ", a residence." If a corporation, insert "a place of business."

9. The address of the Borrower.

10. The date the Guaranty will expire.

11. The dollar limit, in numbers, of the Guaranty.

12. The date of signing the Guaranty Agreement.

13. The name of the Guarantor if a corporation. Otherwise delete the line.

14. If the Guarantor is an individual, delete "BY" and print the Guarantor's name directly below the line, with the Guarantor to sign above the line. If the Guarantor is a corporation, print the name and title of the individual acting for the corporation directly below the line, with that person to sign above the line.

15. Insert the Notary Statement, found elsewhere in this book, for an Individual or a Corporation, as appropriate, for the Guarantor. The Notary will complete the Notary Statement.

demand, subject to the above limitations as to time and amount. Guarantor hereby waives notice of all transactions subject to this Guaranty, protest and non-payment.

Dated: ________[12]________

__________*[13]*__________

*BY*______________________
[14]

[15] [Notary Statement]

REVOCATION OF GUARANTY AGREEMENT (4-14)

Because a Guaranty Agreement guarantees the debts of another, the Revocation or termination of that Guaranty should be documented. Whether or not the Guaranty Agreement requires notification by Certified Mail—Return Receipt Requested, it should be sent that way to provide proof of receipt. A copy must also be sent to the party whose debt is being guaranteed.

1. The date of signing the Revocation.

2. The name and address of the party who granted the credit (the Lender).

3. The date of the Guaranty Agreement.

4. The name of the party whose debt was guaranteed (the Borrower).

5. The name of the Guarantor if a corporation. Otherwise delete the line.

6. If the Guarantor is an individual, delete "BY" and print the Guarantor's name directly below the line, with the Guarantor to sign above the line. If the Guarantor is a corporation, print the name and title of the individual acting for the corporation directly below the line, with that person to sign above the line.

7. The name and address of the Borrower.

REVOCATION OF GUARANTY AGREEMENT

________[1]________

TO: ________[2]________

____

____

Gentlemen:

On ________[3]________ I executed a Guaranty Agreement guaranteeing certain of the debts of ________[4]________. Pursuant to the terms of the Guaranty Agreement, the Guaranty is herewith terminated as to all credit or obligations incurred by ________[4]________ as of this date.

By a copy of this revocation I have notified ________[4]________ that the Guaranty has been terminated.

Very truly yours,

__________*[5]*__________

*BY*____________________
[6]

cc: [7]____________________

____

DEMAND FOR SECURITY COLLATERAL (4-15)

Upon the default in the payment of a debt which has been secured by collateral (any property used as security), a formal Demand for the delivery of the collateral should be made by the Lender. If either the Security Agreement or the underlying Loan Agreement provides for a method of giving Notice, that procedure must be followed. In any event, it is good practice to use a means that provides the Lender with a receipt signed by the Borrower, such as sending the Notice via Certified Mail—Return Receipt Requested.

1. The date of the Notice.

2. The name and address of the holder of the collateral (the Borrower).

3. The date of the Security Agreement.

4. The name and address where the collateral is to be delivered.

5. The date the collateral is to be delivered.

6. The time of day when the collateral is to be delivered.

7. A detailed list of the collateral so that it may be identified without the possibility of confusion.

8. The name of the party making the Demand (the Lender) if a corporation. Otherwise delete the line.

9. If the Lender is an individual, delete "BY" and print the Lender's name directly below the line, with the Lender to sign above the line. If the Lender is a corporation, print the name and title of the individual acting for the corporation directly below the line, with that person to sign above the line.

DEMAND FOR SECURITY/COLLATERAL

__________[1]__________

TO: ________[2]________

____

____

Gentlemen:

On __________[3]__________ you executed a Security Agreement wherein you granted a security interest in the following collateral to secure an indebtedness. The debt having become due and payable and your having defaulted in the payment, demand is herewith made that the collateral be delivered to ____________[4]____________ on ___________[5]__________ at _____[6]_____.

[7] <u>Collateral:</u>

Very truly yours,

__________*[8]*__________

*BY*____________________
[9]

DEMAND FOR PAYMENT (4-16)

A Demand for Payment is used when a debt has become due and the Borrower has failed to make payment. Many states require that a Demand for Payment be made before instituting legal action to collect. If a document pertaining to the Loan provides for a method of making demand for payment, that procedure must be followed. In any event, it is good practice to use a means that provides the Lender with a receipt signed by the Borrower, such as sending the Notice via Certified Mail—Return Receipt Requested.

1. The date of the Notice.

2. The name and address of the Borrower.

3. The date of the Note.

4. The amount of the Note, in numbers.

5. If partial payments have been made, include this language. Otherwise delete.

6. The balance now due on the Note, in numbers.

7. The date the Note was payable.

8. The amount now due, in numbers. Note: this amount may include late payment penalties or accelerated future payments, depending on the terms of the original loan agreement or Note.

9. The interest rate on the Note, in numbers.

DEMAND FOR PAYMENT

__________[1]__________

TO: ________[2]________

____

____

Gentlemen:

On __________[3]__________ you executed a Note in the amount of $________[4]________ *[5][of which $ ____[6]____ is outstanding]*. The Note was payable on __________[7]__________. Payment has not been received and you are now in default.

Payment in the amount of $ ________[8]________ together with interest thereon at __[9]__% per annum in the

(Document continued on next page)

10. The amount of interest due, in numbers.

11. The name and address of the party who is to receive payment.

12. The date when payment is to be made.

13. The name of the party making the Demand (the Lender) if a corporation. Otherwise delete the line.

14. If the Lender is an individual, delete "BY" and print the Lender's name directly below the line, with the Lender to sign above the line. If the Lender is a corporation, print the name and title of the individual acting for the corporation directly below the line, with that person to sign above the line.

amount of $________[10]________ is herewith demanded. Payment should be delivered to _________[11]________ on or before _____[12]_____ by cash or bank check.

Very truly yours,

__________*[13]*__________

*BY*________________________
[14]

DEMAND UPON GUARANTOR (4-17)

This form is used when a Borrower defaults in the payment of a loan or fails to make payments on a credit purchase, either of which has been guaranteed by another party. If the Note or Guaranty Agreement provides for a method of making the Demand upon the Guarantor, that procedure must be followed. In any event, it is good practice to use a means that provides a receipt for the Demand, such as sending the Demand via Certified Mail—Return Receipt Requested.

1. The date of the Demand.
2. The name and address of the party who guaranteed the payment (the Guarantor).
3. The date of the Guaranty.
4. The name of the party (the Borrower) whose payment or performance was guaranteed.
5. The name or description of the document which contained the guaranty, i.e. "Promissory Note," "Guaranty Agreement," etc.
6. The name of the Borrower.
7. The unpaid balance, in numbers.
8. The name of the party to whom payment was to be made.
9. The date payment was due.
10. The amount of principal, in numbers, now due.
11. The interest rate, in numbers, if any, to be applied to the amount now due. If none, delete.

DEMAND UPON GUARANTOR

__________[1]__________

TO: ________[2]________

____

____

Gentlemen:

On __________[3]__________ you guaranteed the performance and payment by ________[4]________ pursuant to a __________[5]__________.

Although performance and payment were duly demanded, ________[6]________ has failed to pay the indebtedness of $_____[7]_____ to ________[8]________ on __________[9]__________.

Pursuant to the __________[5]__________, demand is herewith made for payment in the amount of $_____[10]_____, *together with interest at __[11]__% per annum on the unpaid balance of $____[7]____*. Payment

(Document continued on next page)

12. The total amount, in numbers, now due including principal and interest.

13. The date that payment is to be made.

14. The name and address of the party to whom payment is to be made.

15. The name of the party making the Demand, if a corporation. Otherwise delete the line.

16. If the party making the Demand is an individual, delete "BY" and print the the party's name directly below the line, with the party to sign above the line. If the party is a corporation, print the name and title of the individual acting for the corporation directly below the line, with that person to sign above the line.

of $_____[12]_____ is to be made on or before ________[13]________ to __________[14]____________.

Very truly yours,

_________*[15]*_________

*BY*____________________
[16]

NOTICE OF DEFAULT (4-18)

Agreements may contain provisions for a Default which would trigger a termination of the agreement. If there is a Default, the defaulting party must receive Notice of the Default in order for the payment to be due, for the agreement to be terminated, or for whatever consequences are provided for in the contract's Default provisions to take effect. If the agreement provides for a method of giving Notice, that procedure must be followed. In any event, it is good practice to use a means that provides a receipt for the Notice, such as sending the Notice via Certified Mail—Return Receipt Requested.

1. The date of the Notice.

2. The name and address of the party who defaulted and who is receiving Notice.

3. The date of the agreement containing the provision(s) which has been violated.

4. The name of the other party to the agreement, typically the party sending the Notice.

5. The exact language from the agreement that sets forth the terms of Default.

6. The number of days, in words and numbers, in which a cure of the Default may be made.

7. A detailed description of how the Default may be cured.

NOTICE OF DEFAULT

__________[1]__________

TO: ________[2]________

____

____

Gentlemen:

On __________[3]__________ you entered into an Agreement with ________[4]________ which provided that you would be in default if _________ [5] ___________
____
____.

You are now in default.

You have __[6]__ (__) days to cure the default by _____________________[7]_____________________
____
____.

(Document continued on next page)

8. A description of the consequences of the termination, i.e. "payment of $_____ will be due and payable," "the obligation of ABC Corporation to manufacture widgets will be terminated," etc.

9. The name of the party giving the Notice, if a corporation. Otherwise delete the line.

10. If the party giving the Notice is an individual, delete "BY" and print the the party's name directly below the line, with the party to sign above the line. If the party is a corporation, print the name and title of the individual acting for the corporation directly below the line, with that person to sign above the line.

If you fail to cure this default, the Agreement between us will terminate and __________[8]__________
____.

Very truly yours,

__________*[9]*__________

*BY*____________________
[10]

ASSIGNMENT OF PROMISSORY NOTE (4-19)

This form is used to transfer a Lender's interest in a Promissory Note to another.

1. The date of the Assignment.

2. The name of the party assigning the Promissory Note (the Assignor). If the Assignor is a corporation, add ", a _____ corporation" inserting the state in which incorporated.

3. The name of the party accepting the assignment (the Assignee). If the Assignee is a corporation, add ", a ______ corporation" inserting the state in which incorporated.

4. The name of the party (the Borrower) who signed the Promissory Note.

5. The name of the Assignor.

6. The date of the Promissory Note.

7. The amount of the Promissory Note, in numbers.

8. The annual rate of interest, in numbers, of the Promissory Note.

9. A description of how the Promissory Note is payable, i.e. "On Demand," "in installments of $_____ commencing ____," etc.

ASSIGNMENT OF PROMISSORY NOTE

Assignment made this __[1]__ day of ________. 19__ by ________[2]________ ("Assignor") to ________[3]________ ("Assignee").

For valuable consideration, the receipt of which is hereby acknowledged, Assignor hereby assigns to Assignee the entire interest of Assignor in a Promissory Note from ________[4]________ to ________[5]________, dated ________[6]________, for the payment of $_____[7]_____ with interest at the annual rate of __[8]__% per annum which Promissory Note is payable ________[9]________.

Assignor warrants and represents that the Promissory Note arose out of a loan by ________[2]________ to ________[4]________, that the Promissory Note has not matured and has not been paid in part or in full, that Assignor will do nothing to discharge

(Document continued on next page)

10. The name of the Assignor if a corporation. Otherwise delete the line.

11. If the Assignor is an individual, delete "BY" and print the the Assignor's name directly below the line, with the Assignor to sign above the line. If the Assignor is a corporation, print the name and title of the individual acting for the corporation directly below the line, with that person to sign above the line.

12. Insert the Notary Statement, found elsewhere in this book, for an Individual or Corporation, as appropriate for the Assignor. The Notary will complete the Notary Statement.

the Promissory Note or hinder its collection, and that there are no offsets or defenses to the underlying debt.

In Witness Whereof the Assignor has executed this Agreement.

________*[10]*__________

*BY*____________________
[11]

[12] [Notary Statement]

ASSIGNMENT OF ACCOUNTS RECEIVABLE (4-20)

This Assignment is used when a business assigns all or a portion of its Accounts Receivable either for cash or in payment of a debt owed to a third party. The Assignment may be for the full face value of the accounts or may be discounted. This type of Assignment is different from "factoring" in that it is a one-time assignment rather than a continuing relationship.

Note: on a separate sheet of paper, headed "Schedule A", list all of the accounts being assigned and the value ("face amount") of each.

ASSIGNMENT OF ACCOUNTS RECEIVABLE

1. The date of the Assignment.

2. The name of the party assigning the accounts (the Assignor). If the Assignor is a corporation, add ", a ______ corporation" inserting the state in which incorporated.

3. The name of the party accepting the assignment (the Assignee). If the Assignee is a corporation, add ",a ______ corporation" inserting the state in which incorporated.

4. The total face amount of the accounts being assigned. If the accounts are being transferred for less than full face value, add either " ____ % of face value," i.e 80%; or "$_______," the actual discounted payment being made.

Assignment made this __[1]__ day of ____________ ,19__ by ________[2]________ ("Assignor") to ________[3]________ ("Assignee").

For valuable consideration, the receipt of which is hereby acknowledged, Assignor hereby assigns to Assignee the accounts set forth in Schedule A attached hereto, having an aggregate value of ________[4]________, together with: all amounts due or to become due upon the accounts; title to the goods represented by the accounts whether or not received, rejected, returned or reconsigned; and title to any new account, including amounts to become due, created by a subsequent resale and not received, rejected, returned or reconsigned.

Concurrent with the execution of this Assignment, Assignor delivers to Assignee, receipt of which is hereby acknowledged, all invoices and shipping documents representing the goods and accounts receivable herein assigned. Assignor agrees to deliver and execute such other documents as are reasonably requested by Assignee with respect to this Assignment.

Assignor herewith warrants and represents to Assignee:

1. Schedule A attached hereto is a true and accurate statement of open accounts now owing to Assignor, that all sales are bona fide sales and that said goods have been shipped as ordered, received and accepted.

2. Schedule A attached hereto reflects the true

(Document continued on next page)

5. This paragraph is a "recourse" clause. If the accounts are being transferred "without recourse" (the Assignor is not required to buy back the account if the Assignee is not paid by the buyer of the goods) then substitute the following for this paragraph: "The assignment and transfer of accounts receivable herein is without recourse to the Assignor."

6. The name of the Assignor if a corporation. Otherwise delete the line.

7. If the Assignor is an individual, delete "BY" and print the Assignor's name directly below the line, with the Assignor to sign above the line. If the Assignor is a corporation, print the name and title of the individual acting for the corporation directly below the line, with that person to sign above the line.

8. Insert the Notary Statement, found elsewhere in this book, for an Individual or Corporation as appropriate for the Assignor. The Notary will complete the Notary Statement.

net balances and payment history of each account and the date payment of each account is due.

3. All accounts are free of any lien, security interest or any encumbrance and payment is not subject to any contingency not yet performed by any party.

4. Assignor had at the time of the delivery of the goods free and clear title to the goods and Assignor has the full legal right to make this assignment.

5. Any payments received by the Assignor for the accounts herein transferred shall be received by the Assignor on behalf of and as the property of the Assignee and shall be immediately transferred to the Assignee, subject to collection, or properly endorsed.

[5][In the event of default in the payment of any account herein transferred and upon demand by Assignee the Assignor shall repurchase the defaulted account at the value paid for that account.]

Assignor acknowledges that Assignee has relied on Assignor's warranties and representations in taking this Assignment.

In Witness Whereof the Assignor has executed this Assignment.

_________*[6]*_________

*BY*______________________
[7]

[8] [Notary Statement]

FINDER'S AGREEMENT (4-21)

At some point a business may look for an outside source of capital by finding an investor. This Agreement sets forth the basic understanding between a business and a "middle-man" or FINDER who locates that source of capital. Of critical importance in such an Agreement is a determination as to the moment in time when the FINDER's fee is earned and becomes payable.

FINDER'S AGREEMENT

1. The date of signing the Agreement.
2. The name of the business seeking capital.
3. The name of the FINDER of the capital.
4. If the business seeking capital is a corporation, insert the state of incorporation. Otherwise delete.
5. The address of the business seeking capital.
6. If the FINDER of the capital is a corporation, insert the state of incorporation. Otherwise delete.
7. The address of the FINDER.

AGREEMENT made on _____[1]_____, 19__, by and between ______[2]_______ and _______[3]________.

1. THE PARTIES

1.1 ________[2]_______, *[4][a corporation organized under the laws of the State of _________]* with its principal office at __________[5]_______________.

1.1.1 The person executing this Agreement on behalf of _________[2]________ represents to _________[3]_________ that he has full and complete authority to do so and has been designated to do so by the directors and/or owners of ________[2]________.

1.2 ________[3]_________, *[6][a corporation organized under the laws of the State of ________]* with its principal office at ___________[7]_____________ ("FINDER").

2. THE AGREEMENT

2.1 ________[2]_________ seeks a purchaser of all or part of its stock and/or assets and/or trade name and goodwill and/or an investor to invest cash, credits or other tangible or intangible assets in or on behalf of _________[2]________. Such purchase and/or investment may take the form, without limitation, of a purchase of assets, or of stock of _______[2]_______, for cash or a combination of cash, notes and stock, but in any event on terms and conditions satisfactory to ________[2]________, as a result of any introduction made through FINDER and as a result of negotiations with any such purchaser and/or investor. FINDER will not, and is not required to, take part in any of such negotiations.

2.2 _______[2]________ shall be under no obligation to pay any fee or other monies whatsoever to FINDER on account of this Agreement until any purchase

(Document continued on next page)

8. Note: the fee schedule shown in this Finder's Agreement is only an example to indicate where the agreed upon fee should appear. The example shown is a sliding fee based upon the total amount of the ultimate investment.

of and/or investment in ________[2]________ contemplated by this Agreement has closed with any purchaser and/or investor and has resulted exclusively from the introduction by FINDER to _______[2]________ of the purchaser and/or investor. FINDER shall not be entitled to any fee or other monies until _______[2]________ has entered into a binding arrangement with the purchaser and/or investor. For purposes of this Agreement, the total amount of the fee due FINDER shall be due and payable on the date of the closing or, in the event that any such purchase and/or investment shall be of payments over time, on the date of the first payment made by such purchaser and/or investor.

2.3 Nothing contained in this Agreement shall be construed to give FINDER any exclusive rights, it being understood and agreed that FINDER shall be entitled to a fee only in connection with the entry by _______[2]______ into a binding agreement with a purchaser and/or investor introduced by FINDER.

3. THE FEE

3.1 The fee for introduction by FINDER to _______[2]_______ of any such purchaser and/or investor, to be paid to FINDER by _______[2]________ pursuant to this Agreement, shall be a sum computed on the total purchase and/or investment price as follows:

[8]less than $1,000,000.00	*5%*
$1,000,000.00 but less than $2,000,000.00	*4%*
$2,000,000.00 but less than $3,000,000.00	*3%*
$3,000,000.00 but less than $4,000,000.00	*2%*
$4,000,000.00 or more	*1%*

3.2 FINDER shall not be entitled to any fee or other monies until _______[2]________ has entered into a binding arrangement with any purchaser and/or investor.

4. OTHER

4.1 Any arrangements made by FINDER with any broker or other persons with whom FINDER is or may be involved are the total responsibility of FINDER. Upon payment made by ________[2]_________ to FINDER of the finder's fee, FINDER will hold ________[2]_______ free and harmless from any and all claims, liabilities, com-

(Document continued on next page)

9. The city in which arbitration will take place.

10. The state in which arbitration will take place.

11. The state whose laws will govern the Agreement.

missions, fees or expenses in connection with the transaction from any party who alleges a relationship with or through FINDER and the purchaser and/or investor.

4.2 It is specifically understood and agreed that the dominant purpose of this Agreement is the entry by ________[2]________ into a contract of purchase of and/or investment in _______[2]________ and a transfer of any interest in or to real estate is merely incidental to this dominant purpose. It is further understood that this dominant purpose shall not be defeated or diminished by the inclusion in any such purchase and/or investment in ________[2]________ by the transfer of any interest in real estate from _______[2]________ and related companies to any such purchaser and/or investor. Despite the foregoing it is understood that the value (or present value) of any interest in real estate shall be included in determining the amount upon which the fee is computed.

4.3 In the event of any dispute between ________[2]_______ and FINDER arising under or pursuant to the terms of this Agreement, or any matters arising under the terms of this Agreement, the same shall be settled only by arbitration in the City of ____[9]_____, State of _____[10]_____, in accordance with the rules and regulations of the American Arbitration Association. The determination of the arbitrators shall be final and binding upon _______[2]_______ and FINDER and may be enforced in any court of appropriate jurisdiction.

4.4 This Agreement shall be construed by and governed under the laws of the State of ____[11]______.

4.5 This Agreement contains the entire agreement between FINDER and ______[2]_______ concerning the introduction of a purchaser and/or investor to _______[2]_______ and correctly sets forth the rights

(Document continued on next page)

and duties of each of the parties to each other concerning that matter as of this date. Any agreement or representation concerning the subject matter of this Agreement or the duties of FINDER to ______[2]______ in relation thereto, not set forth in this Agreement, is null and void.

IN WITNESS WHEREOF, the parties have signed this Agreement on the date first written above.

___________*[12]*___________

BY___________________________
[13]

___________*[14]*___________

BY___________________________
[15]

12. The name of the business if a corporation. Otherwise delete the line.

13. If the business is not a corporation, delete "BY" and print the owner's name directly below the line, with the owner to sign above the line. If it is a corporation, print the name and title of the individual acting for the corporation directly below the line, with that person to sign above the line.

14. The name of the FINDER if a corporation. Otherwise delete the line.

15. If the FINDER is an individual, delete "BY" and print the FINDER's name directly below the line, with the FINDER to sign above the line. If the FINDER is a corporation, print the name and title of the individual acting for the corporation directly below the line, with that person to sign above the line.

INVESTMENT OF CAPITAL FROM AN OUTSIDE SOURCE (4-22)

This agreement is typically used when a company needs additional capital and normal lending channels are not open to it. The agreement is written for the protection of the Investor.

1. The date the Investment agreement is signed.

2. The name of the Investor.

3. If the Investor is a corporation, insert the state in which incorporated. Otherwise delete.

4. The name of the Company in which the investment is made.

5. If the Company is a corporation, insert the state in which incorporated. Otherwise delete.

6. A general description of the business's activities, i.e. "manufacturing," "retailing," etc.

7. The amount, in numbers, being invested.

8. The date the money is to be given to the Company.

9. A description of the purposes for which the investment is to be used, such as "general," "raw materials," "inventory," "advertising."

10. The date the Investment is to be repaid. It may be a specific date or "upon demand" or "___ days after demand."

INVESTMENT OF CAPITAL FROM AN OUTSIDE SOURCE

AGREEMENT made this __[1]__ day of _________ 19__, by and between ________[2]________ *[3][, a ________ corporation]* ("Investor") and ________[4]________ *[5][, a ________ corporation]* ("Company").

Company is in the business of _______[6]_______ and requires the investment of capital in the Company; and

Investor desires to invest capital in the Company and to participate in the profits of the Company.

In consideration of the mutual terms, conditions and covenants hereinafter set forth the parties agree as follows:

1. Investor shall advance to the Company the sum of $_____[7]_____ on ________[8]________, which Investment shall be used for _____[9]_____ purposes only, which sum shall be repayable by the Company to Investor on ________[10]________.

2. The Company shall have no right of repayment of the Investment without the written consent of the Investor, which consent shall be at the sole discretion of the Investor.

3. During the period of the Investment the Company shall not: increase the compensation of any officer, director or employee; pledge, assign or encumber any asset, tangible or intangible, of the Company; borrow any funds; sell or transfer any asset of the Company other than in the normal course of business; or otherwise conduct the business that preceded this Agreement without the prior written consent of the Investor.

(Document continued on next page)

11. The name(s) of the shareholders or principals (owners) of the Company. Add or delete spaces as required to accommodate the actual number of names.

12. Insert "Shareholders" if the Company is a corporation or "Principals" if not a corporation.

13. The date the Investor will receive the first financial statement.

14. The interval at which financial statements will be issued; i.e. month, quarter.

15. Insert either "Shareholders" or "Principals." (See No. 12.)

16. A description of the property in which a security interest is given, such as "accounts receivable," "inventory."

17. The frequency with which the Investor is to receive the share of profits, i.e. monthly, quarterly.

18. The percentage, in numbers, of profits to be paid to the Investor.

19. A number of days that is reasonable, in words and numbers, such as three (3).

4. ________[11]________, ________[11]________ and ________[11]________, being all of the _____[12]_____ of the Company hereby subrogate any and all loans heretofore made to the Company and any and all claims for past due compensation to the advance made pursuant to this Agreement and such loans and claims shall not be paid without the prior written consent of the Investor.

5. The Company shall, commencing ________[13]________ and every ___[14]___ thereafter, submit to Investor a financial statement indicating the profit/loss for the preceding period and year to date.

6. The books, records, reports and accounts of the Company shall be kept at all times so as to accurately reflect the business and financial condition of the Company. Investor shall, at all times during normal business hours, have access to and may inspect said books, records, reports and accounts.

7. The Company and the _____[15]_____ guarantee the repayment of the Investment to the Investor and shall grant to the Investor a security interest in _____[16]_____, shall execute a Guaranty in favor of the Investor in a form as attached to this Agreement and shall execute all documents reasonably required and necessary to perfect the security interest.

8. No less often than ____[17]____ during the period of the Investment, the Company shall pay to Investor __[18]__% of the net profit, as determined by standard accounting practices, for that period. Losses shall be carried forward to the next period and shall not under any circumstances be applied retroactively to prior periods.

9. All notices required or permitted to be given hereunder shall be in writing and may be delivered personally or by U.S. Mail, Certified Mail - Return Receipt Requested, postage prepaid. Receipt of notice shall be deemed to have been given upon receipt if personally delivered or within ___[19]___ (__) days after being deposited in the U.S. Mails. Notice shall be addressed:

(Document continued on next page)

20. The name and address of the person to receive notices on behalf of the Company.

21. The name and address of the person to receive notices on behalf of the Investor.

22. The name of the state whose laws will govern the agreement.

If to Company: __________[20]__________

____

____

If to Investor: __________[21]__________

____

____

10. Any controversy or claim arising out of or relating to this contract, or the breach thereof, shall be settled by arbitration in accordance with the Commercial Arbitration Rules of the American Arbitration Association, and judgment upon the award rendered by the arbitrator(s) may be entered in any court having jurisdiction thereof.

11. This Agreement shall be construed in accordance with and governed by the laws of the State of _____[22]_____, irrespective of the fact that a party hereto may not be a resident and/or maintain an office in that state.

(Document continued on next page)

23. The name of the Company if a corporation. Otherwise delete the line.

24. If the Company is not a corporation, delete "BY" and print the individual's name directly below the line, with the individual to sign above the line. If the Company is a corporation, print the name and title of the person acting for the corporation directly below the line, with that person to sign above the line.

25. The name of the Investor if a corporation. Otherwise delete the line.

26. If the Investor is an individual, delete "BY" and print the Investor's name directly below the line, with the Investor to sign above the line. If the Investor is a corporation, print the name and title of the person acting for the corporation directly below the line, with that person to sign above the line.

27. Insert either "Shareholders" or "Principals." (See No. 12.)

28. The name of each shareholder or principal printed directly below the line, with that person to sign above the line. Add or delete lines as required to accommodate the actual number of names.

29. Insert a Personal or Corporate Guaranty, as appropriate, for the Company. The Guaranties are found elsewhere in this book.

INTENDING TO BE LEGALLY BOUND, the parties hereto have caused this Agreement to be executed as of the date first above written.

________*[23]*________

*BY*____________________
[24] (Company)

________*[25]*________

*BY*____________________
[26] (Investor)

The undersigned, being all of the _____[27]_____ of the Company hereby agree to the foregoing.

____
[28]

____
[28]

____
[28]

[29] [Guaranty]

Starting a Business 5

New businesses, like new babies, fill us with hope and promise. As the "newborn" emerges, the proud "parents" make long range plans. The first step in realizing long range goals is to build a strong foundation. The forms in this chapter will put a new business on a solid foundation, whether it is a partnership, joint venture or corporation.

Partnerships and Joint Ventures When two or more individuals or companies go into business on a continuing basis as co–owners, equally sharing profits and losses, it is called a partnership. When two or more individuals or companies go into business for a specific situation or for a fixed period of time it is called a joint venture. Forms for both types of associations are found in this section.

Corporations One or more individuals may decide to enjoy the benefits of ownership with the added protection of limiting loss to the amount of each participant's investment. A corporation presents this type of protection. Pre-incorporation, stock subscription, shareholders agreements and organizational meeting forms are presented in this section to set a corporation on the right path.

PARTNERSHIP AGREEMENT (5-01)

A Partnership exists when two or more parties conduct business on a continuing basis. It is not the Partnership Agreement that creates the Partnership relationship, but the parties' voluntary and continued intention to conduct business as co-owners. A written Agreement is advisable, however, because it permits the parties to define the rights and obligations of the Partnership in conformance with their wishes. In the absence of such an agreement, the Uniform Partnership Act will apply. That legislation may not, however, reflect the parties' desires.

A Partnership differs from a Joint Venture, which is usually a relationship covering a single business situation. This Partnership Agreement purposely has been kept general, with the specifics of the operation of the Partnership to be determined by the action of the Partners at a Partnership meeting.

PARTNERSHIP AGREEMENT

1. The date the Partnership Agreement is signed.

2. The name of each Partner (add or delete spaces as necessary).

3. The purpose of the Partnership, for example "real estate investment" or "the practice of accounting."

4. The name of the Partnership.

5. The location where the Partnership initially will conduct business.

6. The county and state where the Partnership initially will conduct business.

Partnership Agreement made this __[1]__ day of ________,19__ by and between ________[2]________, ________[2]________ and ________[2]________, (individually the "Partner" and collectively the "Partners").

In consideration of the mutual terms, conditions and covenants hereinafter set forth, the Partners agree as follows:

I. GENERAL

1.1 The purpose of the Partnership shall be ___________[3]___________.

1.2 The name of the Partnership shall be ________[4]________, (the "Partnership").

1.3 The initial address of the Partnership shall be __________[5]__________, which address may be changed from time to time by the Partners.

1.4 The Partners shall execute the necessary documents to register the Partnership name and existence with the proper governmental offices in the County of _____[6]_____, State of _____[6]_____.

1.5 The Partnership shall continue until, and dissolve upon, the first happening of:

a) The death of one Partner; or

b) The withdrawal, by written notice, of one Partner; or

(Document continued on next page)

7. The dollar amount, in numbers, of each Partner's initial capital (cash) contribution.

8. The Partnership interest of each Partner expressed as a percentage, in numbers. (Note: unless there are extenuating circumstances, i.e. the Partnership business is the unique concept of one Partner for which that Partner is to receive a disproportionate share, the Partnership interest typically will be the percentage of a Partner's capital contribution to the total capital of the Partnership.)

c) The affirmative vote of a majority in interest of the Partners.

II. CAPITALIZATION

2.1 The Partners shall contribute to the Partnership in the following amounts which shall reflect their Partnership interest:

________[2]________ $____[7]____ __[8]__%

________[2]________ $____[7]____ __[8]__%

________[2]________ $____[7]____ __[8]__%

2.2 No Partner shall receive interest on his capital contribution.

2.3 A separate "Capital Account" shall be maintained for each Partner.

a) A Capital Account shall be increased by (i) the contribution to the capital of the Partnership, including the initial contribution (Paragraph 2.1. above) and (ii) the distributive share of the Net Profits of the Partnership; and decreased by (i) distributions, (ii) the distributive share of Net Losses of the Partnership and (iii) the distributive share of expenditures of the Partnership not deductible in computing Net Profits/Losses and not properly treated as capital expenditures.

b) Distributions in kind shall be valued at fair market value less any liability which the Partner assumes on the distribution or to which the asset distributed is subject.

2.4 If in the opinion of the majority in interest of the Partnership additional capital is needed for the proper conduct of the business of the Partnership, each Partner shall contribute pro rata in accordance with his interest.

2.5 Each Partner shall be indemnified by the other Partners as to excess over the Partner's interest in the Partnership in the event a Partner is compelled to pay and does pay any Creditor of the Partnership in satisfaction of

(Document continued on next page)

9. The percentage of the Partnership, in numbers, necessary to call a meeting.

10. The date of the first Partnership meeting.

11. The location of the first Partnership meeting.

12. The time of the first Partnership meeting, such as 5:00 PM.

13. The fiscal year of the Partnership, for example "calendar year," or "July 1 to June 30."

an obligation of the Partnership. It is the intent and purpose of this provision that all of the Partners shall pay their pro rata share of the Partnership debts, regardless of whether a creditor of the Partnership recovers payment from some but not all of the Partners.

III. MANAGEMENT

3.1 All matters to be determined by the Partners shall be determined by affirmative vote of a majority in interest of the Partners at a meeting. All matters determined by the Partners shall be recorded in a Minute Book reflecting the date, matter discussed and the action taken.

3.2 The Partners shall meet at least once each year. Additional meetings may be held at the request of __[9]__% of the Partnership by interest. All meetings shall be by written notice reasonably in advance so that each Partner may be present either in person or by written proxy authorization.

3.3 At the first meeting of the Partnership to be held on ________[10]________, at __________[11]__________, at __[12]__ __M, the Partnership shall determine:

a) the manner in which the business of the Partnership shall be managed;

b) the hiring of employees;

c) salaries to be paid to employees and the Partner(s) who participate in the day-to-day management of the business of the Partnership;

d) banking procedures; and

e) any other matters which may properly come before the Partnership.

3.4 The fiscal year of the Partnership shall be ________[13]________.

3.5 Each Partner shall have the right to inspect the books, records, reports and accounts of the Partnership during normal business hours, which books, records, reports and accounts shall be kept at the Partnership's place

(Document continued on next page)

of business or at such other place as determined from time to time by the Partnership.

IV. PROHIBITIONS

4.1 No Partner shall sell, assign, mortgage, hypothecate or encumber his interest in the Partnership without the express written permission of all the remaining Partners, without regard to interest.

4.2. All Partners shall meet their personal obligations and debts as they become due and each agrees to save and hold the remaining Partners and the Partnership harmless from all costs, claims and demands with respect to such obligations and debts.

4.3. No Partner shall, except upon the approval of the Partnership by affirmative vote:

a) lend any Partnership funds;

b) incur any obligation in the name of or on the credit of the Partnership;

c) lend any of the Partner's funds to the Partnership, with or without interest;

d) sell, assign, mortgage, hypothecate or encumber any asset of the Partnership;

e) make an assignment of the assets of the Partnership for the benefit of creditors of the Partnership;

f) execute any guarantee on behalf of the Partnership;

g) release, assign or transfer a Partnership claim or any asset of the Partnership;

h) borrow in the name of the Partnership;

i) submit any Partnership claim or liability to arbitration;

(Document continued on next page)

14. The state in which the Partnership is located.

15. The city and state where arbitration is to take place, typically the state in which the Partnership is located.

j) initiate, conduct or settle litigation in the name of or pertaining to the Partnership; or

k) invest Partnership funds or other assets.

4.4 Any Partner who commits a prohibited act shall be individually liable to the remaining Partners, pro rata to their Partnership interest, for any loss caused by the prohibited act.

V. PROFITS/LOSSES AND DISTRIBUTIONS

5.1 Net Profits/Losses shall be determined in accordance with good accounting principles and shall be as finally determined for federal income tax purposes.

5.2 Net Profits/Losses shall be apportioned pro rata among the Partners' capital account according to each Partner's interest.

5.3. Distribution shall be made upon the affirmative vote of the Partners as provided for in paragraph 3.1. herein.

VI. ADDITIONAL PARTNERS/DISSOLUTION

6.1 The Partnership may admit additional Partners upon the affirmative vote of the Partners, as provided for herein. Additional Partners shall then be admitted upon payment of a contribution to capital as determined by the Partnership and each Partner's interest in the Partnership as provided for in paragraph 2.1 shall be redetermined.

6.2 In the event of the dissolution of the Partnership for any reason, the affairs of the Partnership shall be wound up and the proceeds of the Partnership distributed in accordance with the terms of this Agreement and the laws of the State of ____[14]____.

VII. MISCELLANEOUS

7.1 Arbitration. If any controversy or claim arising out of this Agreement cannot be settled by the Partners, the controversy or claims shall be settled by arbitration in the City of ____[15]___, State of ____[15]___, in accordance with the rules of the American Arbitration Association then in effect, and judgment on the award may be entered in any court having jurisdiction.

(Document continued on next page)

16. The state whose laws will govern the Agreement, typically the state in which the Partnership is located.

17. The name of each partner printed directly below the line, with each partner to sign above the line.

7.2 Governing Law. This Agreement shall be enforced and construed under and shall be subject to the laws of the State of ____[16]___. If any provision of this Agreement shall be unlawful, void or unenforceable, that provision shall be deemed separate from and in no way shall affect the validity or enforceability of the remaining provisions of this Agreement.

7.3 Notices. All notices required to be given under this Agreement shall be either (i) personally delivered to the party to whom addressed or (ii) sent by U.S. Mail, postage prepaid, Certified Mail, Return Receipt Requested, addressed to the Partner at the last address for that Partner as maintained by the Partnership.

7.4 Entire Agreement. This Agreement contains the full and complete understanding of all of the Partners with reference to the Partnership and supersedes all prior agreements and understandings, whether written or oral. This agreement may not be amended except in writing and upon the consent of all of the Partners then existing of the Partnership.

7.5 Successors. This Agreement shall be binding on and inure to the benefit of the respective successors, permitted assigns, executors, administrators, personal representatives and beneficiaries of the Partners.

7.6. Subject Headings. The subject headings used in this Agreement are for convenience only and shall not be deemed to affect the meaning or construction of any of the provisions of this Agreement.

Executed by the Partners as of the date first above written.

____

[17]

____

[17]

____

[17]

JOINT VENTURE AGREEMENT (5-02)

A Joint Venture Agreement is typically used for a single business situation, in contrast to a Partnership, which is a continuing relationship. Partners intend to remain together—for better or for worse. Joint Venturers intend to stay together only until the completion of a particular project. The Joint Venturers may limit their liability to a stated contribution (cash or services). The Venture Manager may be one of the Joint Venturers, an outside agent, or an employee with expertise in the area.

This form assumes that there are two parties (Venturers) in the Joint Venture. More may be added by changing the appropriate sections below.

JOINT VENTURE AGREEMENT

Joint Venture Agreement made the __[1]__ day of ________, 19__ by and between ________[2]________ *[3][, a ________ corporation]* and ________[4]________ *[5][, a ________ corporation]* (individually the "Venturer" and collectively the "Joint Venturers").

In consideration of the mutual terms, conditions and covenants hereinafter set forth, the Joint Venturers agree as follows:

1. The Joint Venturers hereby form a "Joint Venture" for the purposes of __________[6]__________ and shall conduct business under the name ________[7]________ at __________[8]__________.

2. The term of the Joint Venture shall be _____[9]_____.

3. The Joint Venturers shall execute the necessary documents to register the Joint Venture with the proper governmental offices in the County of _____[10]_____, State of _____[10]_____.

4. The Capital of the Joint Venture shall consist of $_____[11]_____. ________[2]________ shall contribute $_____[12]_____ and ________[4]________ shall

(Document continued on next page)

1. The date the Joint Venture Agreement is signed.

2. The name of the first party to the Joint Venture (the Venturer).

3. If the first Venturer is a corporation, insert the state in which incorporated. Otherwise delete.

4. The name of the second Venturer.

5. If the second Venturer is a corporation, insert the state in which incorporated. Otherwise delete.

6. The purpose for which the Joint Venture is formed.

7. The name of the Joint Venture.

8. The location at which the Joint Venture will conduct business.

9. The term of the Joint Venture, for example "three years" or "from January 1, 1991 to December 31, 1993."

10. The county and state from which the Joint Venture will conduct business.

11. The total amount of capital, in numbers, for the Joint Venture.

12. The amount, in numbers, to be contributed by the first Venturer.

13. The amount, in numbers, to be contributed by the second Venturer.

14. The bank where an account will be maintained for the benefit of the Joint Venture.

15. The name of the person or entity who will manage the Joint Venture (the Venture Manager).

16. The salary of the Venture Manager, in numbers.

17. The frequency with which the salary will be paid, for example "per month."

contribute $_____[13]_____, which shall be deposited in ________[14]________ and shall be disbursed only upon the signature of the Joint Venturers.

5. The profits and losses of the Joint Venture shall be determined in accordance with good accounting practices and shall be shared among the Joint Venturers in proportion to their respective capital contributions.

6. ________[15]________ shall have the sole discretion, management and entire control of the conduct of the business of the Joint Venture as the "Venture Manager."

7. As compensation for his services the Venture Manager shall be paid $_____[16]_____ per ____[17]____ during the duration of the Joint Venture and shall be reimbursed for all reasonable expenses incurred in the performance of his duties as Venture Manager.

8. Each Joint Venturer shall be bound by any action taken by the Venture Manager in good faith under this Agreement. In no event shall any Joint Venturer be called upon to pay any amount beyond the liability arising against him on account of his capital contribution.

9. The Venture Manger shall not be liable for any error in judgment or any mistake of law or fact or any act done in good faith in the exercise of the power and authority as Venture Manager but shall be liable for gross negligence or willful default.

10. The relationship between the Joint Venturers shall be limited to the performance of the terms and conditions of this Agreement. Nothing herein shall be construed to create a general partnership between the Joint Venturers, or to authorize any Venturer to act as a general agent for another, or to permit any Venturer to bind another other than as set forth in this Agreement, or to borrow money on behalf of another Venturer, or to use the credit of any Venturer for any purpose.

11. Neither this Agreement nor any interest in the Joint Venture may be assigned, pledged, transferred or hypothecated without the prior written consent of the Joint Venturers hereto.

12. This Agreement shall be governed by and inter-

(Document continued on next page)

18. The state whose laws will govern the Joint Venture, typically the state in which the Joint Venture is located.

19. The city and state where arbitration is to take place, typically the state in which the Joint Venture is located

20. The name of the first Venturer if a corporation. Otherwise delete the line.

21. If the first Venturer is an individual, delete "BY" and print the Venturer's name directly below the line, with the Venturer to sign above the line. If the Venturer is a corporation, print the name and title of the individual acting for the corporation directly below the line, with that person to sign above the line.

22. The name of the second Venturer if a corporation. Otherwise delete the line.

23. If the second Venturer is an individual, delete "BY" and print the Venturer's name directly below the line, with the Venturer to sign above the line. If the Venturer is a corporation, print the name and title of the individual acting for the corporation directly below the line, with that person to sign above the line.

preted under the laws of the State of _____[18]_____. Any controversy or claim arising out of or relating to this Agreement, or the breach thereof, shall be settled by arbitration in accordance with the Commercial Arbitration Rules of the American Arbitration Association in the City of _____[19]_____, State of _____[19]_____, and judgment upon the award rendered by the arbitrator(s) may be entered in any court having jurisdiction thereof.

13. Any and all notices to be given pursuant to or under this Agreement shall be sent to the party to whom the notice is addressed at the address of the Venturer maintained by the Joint Venture and shall be sent Certified Mail, Return Receipt Requested.

14. This Agreement constitutes the entire agreement between the Joint Venturers pertaining to the subject matter contained in it, and supersedes all prior and contemporaneous agreements, representations, warranties and understandings of the parties. No supplement, modification or amendment of this Agreement shall be binding unless executed in writing by all the parties hereto. No waiver of any of the provisions of this Agreement shall be deemed, or shall constitute, a waiver of any other provision, whether similar or not similar, nor shall any waiver constitute a continuing waiver. No waiver shall be binding unless in writing signed by the party making the waiver.

The parties hereto, intending to be bound, have signed this Agreement as of the date and year first above written.

__________*[20]*__________

*BY*______________________
[21]

__________*[22]*__________

*BY*______________________
[23]

TERMINATION NOTICE (5-03)

The preceding forms, Partnership Agreement and Joint Venture Agreement, provide for Termination by written Notice. This form fulfills the Notice requirement for those Agreements.

Note that the Notices should be sent via Certified Mail—Return Receipt Requested.

TERMINATION NOTICE

1. The name and address of the party to whom the Termination Notice must be sent.

2. The date of the Termination Notice.

3. The name of the party to whom the Notice is addressed, or use "Gentlemen" if it is not an individual.

4. Insert either "Partnership" or "Joint Venture."

5. The date of the Agreement.

6. The name of the Partnership or Joint Venture.

7. The state whose laws govern the Agreement, as stated in the Agreement.

8. The name of the terminating party if a corporation. Otherwise delete the line.

9. If the terminating party is an individual, delete "BY" and print the terminating party's name directly below the line, with the terminating party to sign above the line. If the terminating party is a corporation, print the name and title of the individual acting for the terminating party directly below the line, with that person to sign above the line.

TO: _______[1]_______ _____[2]_____, 19__

____

____

Dear ________[3]________:

Pursuant to the terms of the _____[4]_____ Agreement dated ________[5]________, 19__ the undersigned hereby gives notice that the undersigned desires to terminate participation in the _____[4]_____, "________[6]________."

The _____[4]_____ should immediately commence to wind up its business and dissolve the _____[4]_____ as provided in the Agreement and the laws of the State of _____[7]_____. Should my assistance be required, please advise.

Very truly yours,

_________*[8]*_________

*BY*____________________

[9]

PRE-INCORPORATION AGREEMENT (5-04)

A Pre-Incorporation Agreement is used when two or more parties desire to start a business and have elected the corporate form of organization. The Agreement provides for the money needed to form the Corporation and sets forth the procedures for its operation. After the Corporation is formed, the information contained in the Agreement becomes the basis for the By-Laws and Shareholders Agreements found in this chapter. A Certificate of Incorporation, which is to be filed with the Secretary of State, has not been included in this book because each state has its own requirements that are available from the office of the Secretary of State in each state's capital.

PRE-INCORPORATION AGREEMENT

Agreement made this __[1]__ day of _______, 19__ by and between ______[2]________, _______[2]________ and ________[2]________ to engage primarily in the __________[3]__________ business, in accordance with the following:

1. The name of the Corporation shall be ________[4]________.

2. The Corporation shall be organized pursuant to the laws of and registered in the State of _____[5]_____. The authorized shares of stock shall be ___[6]___ shares of ____[7]____ value common stock.

3. The Organizers agree to purchase shares of stock within __[8]__ days after the formation of the Corporation as follows:

________[9]_________	___[10]___ shares
________[9]_________	___[10]___ shares
________[9]_________	___[10]___ shares

4. The Organizers shall be the first directors of the Corporation.

(Document continued on next page)

1. The date the Agreement is signed.

2. The name of each party who is forming the Corporation.

3. The main business in which the Corporation will be engaged, for example "restaurant," "auto-leasing," "landscaping."

4. The name the Corporation is to have. Note: the name desired by the parties may not always be available for use. It is recommended that the Organizers agree on alternative names.

5. The state in which the Corporation will be formed.

6. The number of shares authorized.

7. Insert either "no par" or "$___ par" with the value, in numbers, to be inserted. (Note: most small corporations have "no par value" shares.

8. The number of days after registering with the Secretary of State in which the shares must be purchased.

9. The names of the Organizers (the parties forming the Corporation).

10. Adjacent to each name the number of shares to be purchased by that Organizer.

11. The names of the officers of the Corporation. (Each state has separate requirements regarding the number of officers that are required. As a general rule, if there is more than one shareholder the minimum requirement is two officers, a President and a Secretary/Treasurer.)

12. The amount each Organizer will contribute to pay the expenses of forming the Corporation.

13. Depending upon whether the contribution in No. 12 is to be considered a loan to the Corporation, insert either "a loan to the Corporation to be repaid with interest at ____% per annum" and the percent, or "applied toward purchase of stock."

14. The name of each Organizer to be employed by the Corporation.

15. The corporate title of each Organizer in No. 14.

16. The salary and pay period of each Organizer named in no. 14, for example "$15,000 per year."

17. The name of each Organizer printed directly below the line, with that person to sign above the line.

5. The officers of the Corporation shall be as follows:

________[11]________ President

________[11]________ Secretary

________[11]________ Treasurer

6. The Organizers shall upon the execution of this Agreement advance on behalf of the Corporation $___[12]____ each to carry out the intents and purposes of this Agreement. Upon its formation the advance shall be deemed to be ________[13]________.

7. The following shall be employed by the Corporation and receive compensation in the amount stated. Compensation may be revised by the Board of Directors from time to time.

______[14]______ _____[15]______ ____[16]____

______[14]______ _____[15]______ ____[16]____

______[14]______ _____[15]______ ____[16]____

INTENDING TO BE LEGALLY BOUND, the parties hereto have caused this Pre-Incorporation Agreement to be executed as of the date first above written.

____
[17]

____
[17]

____
[17]

STOCK SUBSCRIPTION AGREEMENT (5-05)

The organizers of a corporation that has already been formed may determine that they need additional capital before the corporation begins operation. This Agreement is used to obligate a Subscriber to purchase the stock of a corporation when issued by the corporation and at a predetermined price. Each Subscriber executes a separate Agreement.

WARNING

It is crucial that the corporation determine if the sale of its stock is regulated by either federal or state securities laws. If the stock sale is regulated, it is recommended that an attorney specializing in securities law be engaged to prepare the Agreement and monitor the sale for compliance with the law.

1. The date the Agreement is signed.

2. The name of the purchaser of the stock (the Subscriber).

3. If the Subscriber is a corporation, insert the state in which incorporated. Otherwise delete.

4. The name of the corporation selling the stock.

5. The state in which the corporation is incorporated.

6. The date of incorporation.

7. The number of shares of stock, in numbers, the Certificate of Incorporation authorizes to be issued.

8. Insert either "no par" or "$____ par" with the value, in numbers, to be inserted.

9. The number of shares of stock, in numbers, issued to the organizers.

10. The names of the organizers.

11. The number of shares of stock, in numbers, to be purchased by the Subscriber.

STOCK SUBSCRIPTION AGREEMENT

Agreement made this __[1]__ day of _______, 19__ by and between ________[2]________ *[3][, a __________ corporation]* ("Subscriber") and ______[4]_______, a _____[5]_____ corporation ("Corporation").

The Corporation has been organized on __________[6]__________ having been authorized to issue ___[7]___ shares of ___[8]___ value common stock and has issued ___[9]___ shares of the stock to ____________________[10]____________________ as "Founders" of the Corporation.

The Corporation desires to raise additional capital by this issuance of stock.

The Subscriber desires to be a Shareholder in the Corporation and agrees to purchase shares.

AGREED

1. The Corporation will issue to the Subscriber ___[11]___ shares of the common stock of the Corporation and the Subscriber shall purchase from and pay to the

(Document continued on next page)

Corporation $___[12]___ for each share of common stock on __________[13]__________.

2. The Corporation represents and warrants, which representations and warranties shall survive the purchase date, that:

a) The Corporation has been duly formed and is in existence and has operated in conformity with all laws and regulations applicable to its operation;

b) The issuance of the shares of common stock contemplated herein is in conformance with all laws and regulations applicable to the issuance of the shares;

c) Attached hereto are true copies of the ________[14]________, By-laws and all Agreements and Resolutions of the Board of Directors or Shareholders that are applicable to Shareholders; and

d) The Corporation has duly authorized the sale and issuance of the shares to the Subscriber.

12. The price per share, in numbers, to be paid by the Subscriber. (This may be different from the price paid by the organizers.)

13. The date on which the price will be paid and the shares issued.

14. The name of the incorporation papers, a copy of which is to be attached to the Agreement. (Note: some states have a different title for the incorporation papers; i.e. "Certificate of Incorporation," "Articles of Incorporation," "Charter" etc. This title is readily ascertainable from the document itself.)

(Document continued on next page)

15. The name of the Subscriber if a corporation. Otherwise delete the line.

16. If the Subscriber is an individual, delete "BY" and print the Subscriber's name directly below the line, with the Subscriber to sign above the line. If the Subscriber is a corporation, print the name and title of the individual acting for the corporation directly below the line, with that person to sign above the line.

17. The address of the Subscriber.

18. The Federal Taxpayer Identification Number (Social Security Number if an individual) of the Subscriber.

19. The date the corporation accepts the Subscription.

20. The name and title of the officer acting for the corporation offering the stock printed directly below the line, with that person to sign above the line.

INTENDING TO BE LEGALLY BOUND, the parties hereto have caused this Agreement to be executed as of the date first above written.

__________*[15]*__________

*BY*________________________
[16] (Subscriber)

__________[17]__________
____

Subscriber's Taxpayer Identification No.:

__________[18]__________

ACCEPTED

Date _____[19]______

__________[4]__________

BY______________________
[20]

SHAREHOLDERS AGREEMENT (5-06)

When a non-publicly traded corporation is formed, it is advisable to have an Agreement among the Shareholders as to how the corporation will be organized and operate. The Agreement is used in addition to the By-laws of the corporation and should be accompanied by a Buy-Sell Agreement, also found in this chapter, governing the conditions under which a Shareholder may sell his interest in the corporation. Just as with the Buy-Sell Agreement, it is strongly urged that corporate governing procedures be established and memorialized in a written Shareholders Agreement at the time of, or soon after, the formation of the corporation when all concerned find it relatively easy to agree. Later, when matters may not be proceeding quite so smoothly, it may be less likely that agreement can be reached.

1. The date the Agreement is signed.

2. The name of each Shareholder (add or delete spaces as necessary).

3. The state in which incorporated.

4. The name of the corporation.

5. The number of shares of stock authorized to be issued, as stated in the Certificate of Incorporation or Charter of the corporation.

6. Insert either "no par" or "$____ par" with the value, in numbers, to be inserted.

SHAREHOLDERS AGREEMENT

Agreement made this __[1]_ day of ________, 19__ by and between ________[2]________, ________[2]________ and ________[2]________, all of whom are hereinafter collectively referred to as the "Shareholders" and individually as a "Shareholder."

The Shareholders have caused to be formed a _____[3]_____ corporation whose name is ________[4]________ ("The Corporation").

The Shareholders desire to provide: for the ownership of the shares, the voting of shares, the election of directors, the voting of the Board of Directors and the election of officers, among other provisions.

In consideration of the premises and the mutual covenants of the parties hereinafter set forth, it is

AGREED

1. FORMATION OF CORPORATION

1.1 The parties have caused to be formed a corporation, ________[4]________, organized under the laws of the State of _____[3]_____ and agree to execute all necessary documents.

1.2 The Corporation shall maintain a place of business within the State of _____[3]_____.

1.3 The Corporation is authorized to issue ___[5]___ shares of ____[6]____ value stock.

(Document continued on next page)

7. The name of each Shareholder and adjacent to it the number of shares each owns.

8. The name of each director of the corporation (add or delete spaces as necessary).

2. SHARES OF STOCK

2.1 The respective Shareholders shall own shares of stock in the Corporation according to the following schedule.

________[7]________ __________ shares

________[7]________ __________ shares

________[7]________ __________ shares

2.2 Any plan for an increase in the number of shares which the Corporation shall be authorized to issue shall require the unanimous consent of the Shareholders who are the parties to this Agreement, or their successors.

2.3 All shares now or hereafter owned by the Shareholders or prospective shareholders or transferors shall be subject to the provisions of this Agreement and the certificates representing same shall bear the following legend:

> The sale, transfer or encumbrance of this Certificate is subject to an agreement dated as of ____[1]____, between ________[2]________, ________[2]________ and ________[2]________. A copy of the Agreement is on file at the principal office of the Corporation. The agreement provides, among other things, for certain prior rights to purchase and certain obligations to sell the shares of stock evidenced by this Certificate, as well as for voting rights of Shareholders and Directors. By accepting this Certificate, the holder agrees to be bound by said agreement.

3. DIRECTORS

3.1 The initial Board of Directors shall consist of:

________[8]________,

________[8]________,

________[8]________,

(Document continued on next page)

9. The name of each person elected as officer of the corporation. (Note: each state has separate requirements as to the officers that are required. As a general rule, if there is more than one shareholder, the minimum requirement is two officers, a President and a Secretary/Treasurer.)

and they shall hold office until their successors are duly elected.

3.2 In all matters requiring the vote of the Board of Directors a majority shall suffice.

4. OFFICERS

4.1 The following shall serve as officers of the Corporation until their successors are duly elected:

President: ________[9]________

Secretary: ________[9]________

Treasurer: ________[9]________

5. SALE OF STOCK

5.1 Each of the Shareholders covenants and agrees that he will not sell, assign, transfer, donate or otherwise dispose of, or pledge, hypothecate or otherwise encumber any of the shares of the Corporation's stock except upon the prior written consent of the remaining Shareholders.

6. COMPENSATION

6.1 Base Compensation. The compensation of all employees shall be fixed by the Board of Directors.

7. MISCELLANEOUS

7.1 Applicable Law. This Agreement shall be construed pursuant to the Laws of the State of _____[3]_____.

7.2 Notices. All notices provided for by this Agreement shall be made in writing either (i) by actual delivery of the notice into the hands of the parties thereunto entitled, or (ii) by mailing of the notice in the United States mails to the last known address of the party entitled thereto by Certified Mail - return receipt requested. If any notice is mailed, it shall be deemed to have been received five (5) days from the date postmarked on the envelope.

7.3 Headings. The headings have been inserted

(Document continued on next page)

10. The name of each Shareholder printed directly below the line, with that person to sign above the line.

as a matter of convenience to the parties and shall not affect the constructions or meaning thereof.

7.4 Binding Effect. This Agreement is binding upon and inures to the benefit of the Corporation, its successors, and assigns, and to the Shareholders and their respective heirs, personal representatives, successors and assigns.

7.5 Amendments. No waiver, modification or discharge of the terms hereunder shall be valid unless in writing and signed by the party or parties to be charged and only to the extent therein set forth.

7.6 Severability. If any part, section, phrase or term of this Agreement be deemed invalid, by operation of law or otherwise, it is the intention of the parties hereto that the remaining parts, sections, phrases and/or terms stand and continue in effect, to carry out the intent and purposes of the parties to this Agreement, to the extent permitted by the laws of the State of _____[3]_____.

7.7 Enforcement. Each of the parties hereto and the Corporation recognizes that the corporate stock herein contemplated to be purchased is unique, and each of them for themselves, their heirs, successors or assigns agrees and consents to the specific enforcement of this Agreement.

8. CORPORATION TO BE BOUND

8.1 It is understood and agreed by and between the Shareholders that the Corporation shall be bound by all of the terms and conditions of this Agreement.

INTENDING TO BE LEGALLY BOUND, the parties hereto have caused this Shareholders Agreement to be executed as of the date first above written.

____
[10]

____
[10]

____
[10]

BUY-SELL AGREEMENT (5-07)

When a non-publicly traded corporation is formed it is advisable to have an Agreement to establish the terms and conditions under which the shares owned by each Shareholder may be sold (Voluntary Transfer), transferred due to bankruptcy of the Shareholder (Involuntary Transfer) or purchased upon the death of a Shareholder. The Buy-Sell Agreement is usually executed at the same time as the Shareholders Agreement, also found in this chapter, and the two may be combined into a single agreement. Just as with the Shareholders Agreement, it is strongly urged that Buy-Sell procedures be established and memorialized in a written Buy-Sell Agreement at the time of, or soon after, the formation of the corporation when all concerned find it relatively easy to agree. Later, when matters may not be proceeding quite so smoothly, it may be less likely that agreement can be reached.

BUY-SELL AGREEMENT

1. The date the Agreement is signed.

2. The names of the Shareholders.

3. The name of the corporation.

Agreement made this __[1]__ day of _______, 19__ by and between ________[2]________, ________[2]________ and ________[2]________, being all of the "Shareholders" of ________[3]________ (the "Corporation").

The Shareholders desiring to set forth the terms and conditions under which their shares of stock in the Corporation may be transferred,

AGREE

1. RIGHT OF FIRST REFUSAL-VOLUNTARY TRANSFER

1.1 Terms of the Offer, Offer Notice. It is understood and agreed that a Shareholder shall not be permitted to sell only a portion of his shares except as specifically provided herein. If any Shareholder shall desire to sell all the shares of the Corporation's stock owned by him (such Shareholder being hereinafter referred to as the "Offeror" and such shares being hereinafter referred to as the "Offered Shares"), then the Offeror shall give concurrent notice (the "Offer Notice") to the Corporation and to the other Shareholders (the Corporation and the other Shareholders being hereinafter referred to as the "Offerees"). The Offer Notice shall:

(a) State the name and address of the person (the "Proposed Purchaser") to whom the Offeror proposes to sell the Offered Shares and the price at and the terms upon which he proposes to sell the Offered Shares to the Proposed Purchaser (and shall have attached thereto a commitment letter setting forth the substantial terms of the sale to the Proposed Purchaser); and

(Document continued on next page)

(b) Constitute an offer to sell to the Offerees all, but not less than all of the Offered Shares at the same price and upon the same terms as the Offeror proposes to sell the Offered Shares to the Proposed Purchaser.

1.2 Acceptance of the Offer. The Offerees shall have a period of thirty (30) days after the date of the giving of the Offer Notice in which to accept the offer. Acceptance shall be made by giving concurrent notice thereof, within the thirty (30) day time limit, to the Offeror. In determining whether the Corporation shall accept such Offer the Offeror shall abstain from voting as a shareholder or director.

1.3 Priority Among Offerees. If all or any of the Offerees shall accept the offer made by the Offer Notice, then:

(a) If the Corporation shall have accepted such offer, the Offeror shall sell and the Corporation shall purchase all or such portion of the Offered Shares as it desires of the Offeror's shares, at the price, upon the terms and in the manner set forth in the Offer Notice.

(b) If the Corporation shall not have accepted such offer or it shall have accepted only as to a portion of the Offeror's Shares, the Offeror shall sell to the other accepting Offeree(s) and they shall purchase all of the balance of the Offered Shares.

1.4 Failure of Offerees to Accept. If none of the Offerees, within the required time, accepts the Offer made by the Offer Notice, the Offeror shall thereafter within sixty (60) days of giving of the Offer Notice have the right to sell all, but not less than all, of the Offered Shares, but only to the Proposed Purchaser at the price, upon the terms and in the manner set forth in the Offer Notice. If the Offeror shall not so sell the Offered Shares within such period, the Offer shall be deemed to have lapsed and the Offeror shall continue to hold the Offered Shares subject to the provisions of the Agreement. After such a lapse any offer or attempt to sell the shares shall be treated as an original offer under this article.

(Document continued on next page)

2. INVOLUNTARY TRANSFER

2.1 If, other than by reason of a Shareholder's death, shares are transferred by operation of law to any person other than the Corporation (such as, but not limited to, a Shareholder's trustee in bankruptcy, a purchaser at any creditor's or court sale or the guardian or conservator of an incompetent Shareholder), the Corporation within sixty (60) days, or the remaining Shareholders within seventy (70) days of the Corporation's receipt of actual notice of the transfer, may notify such transferee of its desire to purchase all, but not less than all, of the shares so transferred ("Notice of Intent to Purchase"). In such a case, the purchase price shall be determined in accordance with the book value of the Corporation's stock as reflected on the most recent balance sheet.

3. PURCHASE OBLIGATIONS UPON DEATH

3.1 Purchase by Corporation. Upon the death of a shareholder, his estate shall sell and the Corporation shall, as soon as practicable, purchase the shares which are owned by the deceased Shareholder at his death for the price and upon the terms hereinafter provided.

3.2 Determination of Price, Certificate of Value. For the purposes of determining the price to be paid under paragraph 3.1 hereof, the Shareholders agree to cause the Corporation to execute a Certificate of Value not less than annually, as of January 1 of each year (or such other date as may from time to time be determined by the Shareholders), computed in accordance with generally accepted accounting principles.

3.3 Alternative Purchase by Shareholders. To the extent that the Corporation is prevented by law from purchasing all or any portion of the shares owned by the deceased Shareholder's estate, the surviving Shareholders shall be entitled to purchase such shares pro rata at a price fixed in accordance with paragraph 3.2 hereof. Any shares purchased under this article by the Corporation shall then be retired or held as treasury stock as determined by the surviving Shareholders.

3.4 Freedom of Estate to Sell. If the Corporation is prevented by law from purchasing all or any portion of the shares owned by a deceased Shareholder hereunder, and if the remaining Shareholders fail or refuse to purchase

(Document continued on next page)

4. The state in which incorporated.

the remaining shares, then the estate shall be entitled to make such disposition of its shares as it may determine in its sole discretion.

4. MISCELLANEOUS

4.1 Applicable Law. This Agreement shall be construed pursuant to the Laws of the State of _____[4]_____.

4.2 Notices. All notices provided for by this Agreement shall be made in writing either (i) by actual delivery of the notice into the hands of the parties thereunto entitled, or (ii) by mailing of the notice in the United States mails to the last known address of the party entitled thereto, by certified mail, return receipt requested. If any notice is mailed, it shall be deemed to have been received five (5) days from the date postmarked on the envelope.

4.3 Headings. The headings have been inserted as a matter of convenience to the parties and shall not affect the construction or meaning thereof.

4.4 Binding Effect. This Agreement is binding upon and inures to the benefit of the Corporation, its successors, and assigns, and to the Shareholders and their respective heirs, personal representatives, successors and assigns.

4.5 Amendments. No waiver, modification or discharge of the terms hereunder shall be valid unless in writing and signed by the party or parties to be charged and only to the extent therein set forth.

4.6 Severability. If any part, section, phrase or term of this Agreement be deemed invalid, by operation of law or otherwise, it is the intention of the parties hereto that the remaining parts, sections, phrases and/or terms stand and continue in effect, to carry out the intent and purposes of the parties to this Agreement, to the extent permitted by the laws of the State of _____[4]_____.

4.7 Enforcement. Each of the parties hereto and the Corporation recognizes that the corporate stock herein contemplated to be purchased is unique, and each of them for themselves, their heirs, successors or assigns agrees and consents to the specific enforcement of this Agreement.

(Document continued on next page)

5. The name of each Shareholder printed directly below the line, with that person to sign above the line.

5. CORPORATION TO BE BOUND

5.1 It is understood and agreed by and between the Shareholders that the Corporation shall be bound by all of the terms and conditions of this Agreement.

INTENDING TO BE LEGALLY BOUND, the parties hereto have caused this Buy-Sell Agreement to be executed as of the date first above written.

____
[5]

____
[5]

____
[5]

STOCK PURCHASE OPTION AGREEMENT (5-08)

A Stock Purchase Option is granted to key employees or others who may be providing the corporation with a benefit, such as a supplier who is extending credit, a party providing services at no charge or reduced charge, or a creditor who has loaned money to the corporation.

WARNING

Consultation with a local attorney is recommended to be sure that offering Stock Options in the company does not require the company to be registered either with the state or with the Securities and Exchange Commission.

STOCK PURCHASE OPTION AGREEMENT

1. The date the Agreement is signed.
2. The name of the corporation granting the Option.
3. The state of incorporation of the corporation granting the Option.
4. The name of the party receiving the Option (the Purchaser).
5. If the Purchaser is a corporation, insert the state of incorporation. Otherwise delete.
6. The number of shares, in words, that may be purchased.
7. The number of shares, in numbers, that may be purchased.
8. The price of each share, in numbers.
9. The date by which the purchase must be made.
10. The total number of shares, in numbers, that the corporation is authorized to issue.
11. The number of shares, in numbers, issued as of the date of the Agreement.

Agreement made this __[1]__ day of _______, 19__ by and between ________[2]________, a _____[3]_____ corporation ("Corporation) and ________[4]________ *[5][, a* ________ *corporation]* ("Purchaser").

1. In consideration of Ten Dollars ($10.00) in hand paid, receipt of which is hereby acknowledged, the Corporation hereby grants to the Purchaser an Option, subject to the terms and conditions hereof, to purchase from the Corporation up to ____[6]____ (__[7]__) shares of its Common Stock at the price of $___[8]___ per share.

2. The Option shall expire at 5:00 p.m. on __________[9]__________.

3. The Option granted hereunder shall be exercisable by the giving of not less than seven (7) days' written notice of exercise to the Corporation specifying the number of Shares to be purchased with payment of the full purchase price accompanying such notice. Within fifteen (15) days after written notice from the Purchaser, the Corporation will deliver to the Purchaser a stock certificate representing the shares of stock purchased.

4. By accepting this Option, the Purchaser agrees that any and all shares purchased upon the exercise of this Option shall be subject to a Shareholders Agreement and Buy-Sell Agreement executed by the Shareholders prior to the date of this Option Agreement and on file in the office of the Corporation.

5. The Corporation represents that its authorized capital stock consists of __[10]__ shares of which ____[11]____ have been issued.

(Document continued on next page)

6. Neither the Purchaser nor Purchaser's legal representatives shall be or have any of the rights or privileges of a Shareholder of the Corporation in respect of any of the Shares issuable upon the exercise of this Option unless and until certificates representing such Shares shall have been issued and delivered.

7. In the event of the liquidation, dissolution or winding up of the Corporation, a notice of such anticipated liquidation, dissolution or winding up shall be mailed to the Purchaser in which event this Option shall expire on the service of such notice. Failure to give such notice or any defect therein shall not affect the legality or validity of the liquidation, dissolution or winding up, or any distribution in connection therewith.

8. All notices provided for by this Option shall be made in writing, either (i) by actual delivery of the notice into the hand of the party entitled or (ii) by mailing of the notice in the United States mails at the last known address of the party entitled thereto, by Certified Mail, return receipt requested.

9. Except as otherwise herein provided, this Option and the rights and privileges conferred hereby may not be transferred, assigned, pledged or hypothecated in any way (whether by operation of law or otherwise) and shall not be subject to execution, attachment or similar process. Upon any attempt to transfer, assign, pledge, hypothecate or otherwise dispose of this Option or any right or privilege conferred hereby, contrary to the provisions hereof, or upon the levy of any attachment or similar process on the rights and privileges conferred hereby, this Option shall immediately become null and void.

(Document continued on next page)

12. The name of the corporation granting the Option.

13. The name and title of the individual acting for the Corporation printed directly below the line, with that person to sign above the line.

14. The name of the Purchaser if a corporation. Otherwise delete the line.

15. If the Purchaser is an individual, delete "BY" and print the Purchaser's name directly below the line, with the Purchaser to sign above the line. If the Purchaser is a corporation, print the name and title of the individual acting for the corporation directly below the line, with that person to sign above the line.

INTENDING TO BE LEGALLY BOUND, the parties hereto have caused this Stock Purchase Option Agreement to be executed as of the date first above written.

__________[12]__________

*BY*____________________
[13]

ACCEPTED:

_________*[14]*__________

*BY*____________________
[15]

NOTICE OF ORGANIZATIONAL MEETING OF INCORPORATORS (5-09)

The laws of most states provide that when there are two or more Incorporators the Organizational Meeting may be called at the request of any Incorporator upon written Notice given to the other Incorporators. The time required and the method of delivery of the Notice varies, so the corporation laws of your state should be consulted. For example, New York requires at least five days' notice by mail to each of the other Incorporators.

NOTICE OF ORGANIZATION MEETING OF INCORPORATORS

PLEASE TAKE NOTICE that the organizational meeting of the incorporators of ________[1]________ will be held on ________[2]________ at __[3]__ *[4][A.M.]* ***OR*** *[P.M.]* at __________[5]__________, ______[6]______.

The purpose of the meeting will be the adopting of By-Laws for the governing and operation of the corporation, the election of directors to hold office until the first annual meeting of shareholders, _________[7]_________ and such other business as may regularly come before the meeting.

The meeting is open to all incorporators or their designees.

Dated ________[8]________

____
[9] (Incorporator)

1. The name of the corporation.
2. The date of the Meeting.
3. The time of the Meeting.
4. Choose one.
5. The address where the Meeting will be held.
6. The city and state where the Meeting will be held.
7. A brief description of any other matters that will be considered by the Incorporators, such as the issuance of stock certificates and the like.
8. The date of the Notice.
9. The name of the Incorporator calling for the Meeting printed directly below the line, with the Incorporator to sign above the line.

WAIVER OF NOTICE OF ORGANIZATIONAL MEETING (5-10)

Scheduling problems may prevent timely notice of the Organizational Meeting from being sent so as to give each person sufficient notice. If each incorporator or subscriber waives such notice in writing, the Meeting can still be held as scheduled.

1. The name of the corporation.

2. The time of day and date of the Meeting.

3. The address, city and state where the Meeting will be held.

4. The date of signing the Waiver.

5. The name of the incorporator or shareholder printed directly below the line, with that person to sign above the line.

WAIVER OF NOTICE OF
ORGANIZATIONAL MEETING
of
________[1]________

The undersigned incorporator/subscriber for shares of stock of ________[1]________ agrees and consents that the organizational meeting of ________[1]________ be held as stated below and does waive all notice of the meeting and of any adjournment.

Time/Date of Meeting:__________[2]__________

Location of Meeting: __________[3]__________

__________[3]__________

Dated: ________[4]________

____
[5]

MINUTES OF ORGANIZATIONAL MEETING— SOLE INCORPORATOR (5-11)

The most important benefit of forming a business as a corporation (as opposed to a sole proprietorship or a general partnership) is the protection of limited liability offered to the participants. With rare exception, a participant's potential loss is limited to his investment in the corporation. While offering the flexibility needed to accommodate large numbers of participants, a corporation need not have a cast of thousands, or even hundreds or tens. Most states recognize that a corporation can be formed by just one person. This form is used to record the Minutes of the Organizational Meeting of the Sole Incorporator.

Even though the sole incorporator effectively is the corporation, clear, concise and complete Minutes are still essential.

Note that the Sole Incorporator is likely to be the sole shareholder and is permitted to hold several officer's positions. Whatever the number of directors, the authors strongly urge that the number be an odd one because experience has taught that an even number of directors invites deadlock.

WARNINGS

The laws of most states give the power to recognize a corporation to the state alone and not to the town, city, county or federal government. Therefore, to be recognized and valid, the Charter/Articles of Incorporation/Certificate of Incorporation must be filed with the state government. The terms "Charter," Articles of Incorporation," and "Certificate of Incorporation" designate the same thing. All refer to the incorporating document whose name varies from state to state.

By filing the Charter/Articles of Incorporation/ Certificate of Incorporation with your state government, you have created a legal entity which the law will regard as perpetual unless formally dissolved. The creation of a corporation and its filing with your state government should not be undertaken lightly.

A word about taxes. Just as you have a Social Security number or Taxpayer Identification Number, under which your income tax returns are filed, so too your new corporation, your new legal entity, must also obtain a Taxpayer Identification Number by filing "Form SS-4—Application for Employer Identification Number" (even if you do not have, or plan to have, employees). This form can be obtained from any Internal Revenue Service office.

MINUTES OF ORGANIZATIONAL MEETING
of
__________[1]__________

1. The name of the corporation.

The undersigned, as the sole incorporator and shareholder of __________[1]__________, held an organizational meeting at the place and on the date stated below. At the meeting action was taken and it was:

(Document continued on next page)

“RESOLVED, that a copy of the *[2][Charter]* ***OR*** *[Articles of Incorporation]* ***OR*** *[Certificate of Incorporation]* setting forth the permitted corporate purposes *[3][, and the filing receipt issued by the Secretary of _______[4]_______ of _____[5]_____ showing the payment of the filing or organization fee or tax as fixed by law and the date of payment of such tax or fee]* be annexed to these Minutes.”

“RESOLVED, that the By-Laws stating the regulations and rules adopted by the Corporation for its governing and operating, *[6][as prepared by ________________, as counsel for the Corporation]* are adopted in the form annexed to these Minutes.”

“RESOLVED, that the persons whose names appear below were nominated and appointed as directors of the Corporation and by their signatures adjacent to their respective names, accepted such appointment:”

_________[7]_________ _________[8]_________

_________[7]_________ _________[8]_________

_________[7]_________ _________[8]_________

“RESOLVED, that the principal office of the Corporation be located at __________[9]__________.”

________[10]________ ____________________
[11]

Dated: ________[12]________

2. Choose the appropriate name for the incorporating document depending on the name given to such document by the state in which the document is filed.

3. Delete if the state of filing merely accepts the document for filing but does not issue a receipt.

4. The name of the particular department of the state government in which the corporate documents are filed, typically but not necessarily the Department of State.

5. The state of incorporation.

6. The name of the attorney(s) who prepared the By-Laws. Delete if an attorney did not prepare the By-Laws.

7. The name of the each director who has accepted the appointment, printed above the line. (Note the commentary above as to the number of directors.)

8. The signature of each director.

9. The address, city and state of the principal office of the corporation (where the books and records will be kept).

10. The city and state where the Meeting was held.

11. The name of the sole incorporator printed directly below the line, with the sole incorporator to sign above the line.

12. The date of the Meeting.

MINUTES OF ORGANIZATIONAL MEETING— TWO OR MORE INCORPORATORS (5-12)

The most important benefit to forming a business as a corporation (as opposed to a sole proprietorship or a general partnership) is the protection of limited liability offered to the participants. With rare exception, a participant's potential loss is no more than his investment in the corporation. While offering the flexibility needed to accommodate large numbers of participants, a corporation need not have a cast of thousands, or even hundreds or tens. This form is used to record the Minutes of the Organizational Meeting of two or more Incorporators.

The authors urge that the number of directors of a small (in terms of number of shareholders) or closely held corporation should be an odd number. Experience has taught that an even number of directors invites deadlock.

WARNINGS

The laws of most states give the power to recognize a corporation to the state alone and not to the town, city, county or federal government. Therefore, to be recognized and valid, the Charter/Articles of Incorporation/Certificate of Incorporation must be filed with the state government. The terms "Charter," Articles of Incorporation," and "Certificate of Incorporation" designate the same thing. All refer to the incorporating document whose name varies from state to state.

By filing the Charter/Articles of Incorporation/ Certificate of Incorporation with your state government, you have created a legal entity which the law will regard as perpetual unless formally dissolved. The creation of a corporation and its filing with your state government should not be undertaken lightly.

A word about taxes. Just as you have a Social Security number or Taxpayer Identification Number, under which your income tax returns are filed, so too your new corporation, your new legal entity, must also obtain a Taxpayer Identification Number by filing "Form SS-4—Application for Employer Identification Number" (even if you do not have, or plan to have, employees). This form can be obtained from any Internal Revenue Service office.

MINUTES OF ORGANIZATIONAL MEETING
of
_________[1]_________

The organizational meeting of the incorporators of _________[1]_________ was held at ___[2]___ *[3][A.M.]* ***OR*** *[P.M.]* on ________[4]________ at ___________[5]___________, ________[6]________.

1. The name of the corporation.
2. The time of the Meeting.
3. Choose one.
4. The date of the Meeting.
5. The address where the Meeting was held.
6. The city and state where the Meeting was held.

(Document continued on next page)

MINUTES OF ORGANIZATIONAL MEETING— TWO OR MORE INCORPORATORS *continued*

7. The names of all the people present at the Meeting. Add or delete lines as necessary.

8. The name of the incorporator who called the meeting to order.

9. The name of the the incorporator elected to act as Chairman of the Meeting.

10. The name of the the incorporator elected to act as Secretary of the Meeting.

11. The name of any incorporator attending by proxy. Delete if there were no proxies submitted.

12. Choose the appropriate name depending on the name given to such document by the state in which the document is filed.

13. The name of the particular department of the state government in which the corporate documents are filed, typically, but not necessarily, the Department of State.

14. Delete if the state of filing merely accepts the document for filing but does not issue a receipt, then skip to No. 18.

15. The state of incorporation.

16. Delete if No. 14 was deleted.

17. The name of the attorney(s) who prepared the By-Laws. Delete if an attorney did not prepare the By-Laws.

The following incorporators were present:

________[7]________ ________[7]________
________[7]________ ________[7]________
________[7]________ ________[7]________
________[7]________ ________[7]________

Incorporator ________[8]________ called the meeting to order. Upon motion duly made, seconded and carried, ________[9]________ was elected as Chairman of the Meeting and ________[10]________ was elected Secretary of the Meeting and each accepted his respective office.

The Secretary then read the form of Waiver of Notice of Organizational Meeting duly signed by all of the incorporators. Upon motion duly made, seconded and carried, the Secretary was directed to attach a copy of each executed Waiver to these Minutes. *[11][The Secretary examined and approved the proxy submitted by Incorporator ______________. Upon motion duly made, seconded and carried, the Secretary was directed to attach a copy of each approved proxy to these Minutes]*. The Secretary noted that the incorporators attending either in person or by proxy constituted a quorum.

The Chairman read the *[12][Charter]* ***OR*** *[Articles of Incorporation]* ***OR*** *[Certificate of Incorporation]* setting forth the permitted corporate purposes and noted that said document was filed with the Department of ________[13]________ *[14][, and that the filing receipt was issued by the Secretary of ________[13]________ of _____[15]_____ showing the payment of the filing or organization fee or tax as fixed by law and the date of payment of such tax or fee]*. The Secretary was directed to attach a copy *[16][of each]* to these Minutes.

The Chairman then presented the proposed By-Laws stating the regulations and rules for the governing and operating of the Corporation, *[17][as prepared by ________________, as counsel for the Corporation]*. The By-Laws were read and discussed article by article. Upon motion duly made, seconded and carried, the By-Laws were adopted as the By-Laws of the Corporation and the Secretary was directed to attach a copy to these Minutes.

(Document continued on next page)

18. The name of each director. (Note the commentary above as to the number of directors.)

19. The signature of each director who has accepted the appointment signed above the line adjacent to his printed name.

20. The address, city and state of the principal office of the corporation (where the books and records of the corporation will be kept).

21. The time of adjournment of the Meeting.

22. The name of the Secretary of the Meeting printed directly below the line before the word "Secretary," with that person to sign above the line.

23. The name of the Chairman of the Meeting printed directly below the line before the word "Chairman," with that person to sign above the line.

The Chairman stated that election of directors was then in order. Nominations were called for and each person nominated was seconded. Upon motion duly made, second and carried, the following were elected as directors of the Corporation and by their signatures adjacent to their respective names, accepted their election and agreed to serve the term provided in the By–Laws of the Corporation:

________[18]________ ________[19]________

________[18]________ ________[19]________

________[18]________ ________[19]________

The Chairman then stated that certain incorporators had previously signed subscriptions for shares of stock of the Corporation when issued. Upon motion duly made, seconded and carried, the directors were authorized to direct the officers of the Corporation, upon their appointment to issue shares of stock of the Corporation in the respective amounts to the subscribers and to direct the Secretary to prepare and keep a shareholders' list and transfer journal.

Upon motion duly made, seconded and carried the principal office of the Corporation was determined to be located at ______________[20]______________.

There being no further business, on motion duly made, seconded and carried, the Meeting was adjourned at ____[21]____.

____
[22] Secretary

Approved:

____
[23] Chairman

Operating a Corporation 6

Once a corporation is formed, certain procedures must be followed to keep it running smoothly. The owners of the corporation, the shareholders, must meet at least annually. One purpose of the shareholders' meeting is to elect directors.

Directors typically meet monthly, their function being to make the financial and other policy decisions necessary to operate the corporation in the best interest of all of the shareholders. Additionally, the directors appoint officers to make the day-to–day business decisions. The discussions at both the shareholders' meetings and the directors' meetings are preserved in the corporate minutes. The actions of both shareholders and directors taken at these meetings are set forth in resolutions which are contained in these minutes.

Notices and Minutes of Shareholders' and Directors' Meetings These sections provide forms for giving proper notice of meetings of shareholders and directors plus forms for minutes of those meetings.

Corporate Resolutions These forms provide guidance in preparing resolutions that deal with some of the more common organizational issues corporations encounter. Those that are used are to be inserted into the book of corporate minutes.

Stock The last section of this chapter deals with issues related to stock certificates, such as the endorsement of a stock certificate when it is sold or transferred (a stock power), how stock is voted by a shareholder who cannot personally attend a shareholders' meeting (a proxy), and how corporations and shareholders can protect themselves if a stock certificate is lost (by affidavit of lost certificate).

NOTICE OF ANNUAL MEETING OF SHAREHOLDERS (6-01)

The by-laws of most corporations provide that specific Notice of Annual Meetings must be given in writing to each Shareholder, typically (if time allows) by mail. The Notice should state the time, location and the matters that will be presented to the Shareholders, for example: the election of Board members or the like. Most states mandate minimum and maximum times for Notice. Your state's corporation law should be consulted to determine the applicable time required. For example, New York law requires that Notice be given not less than 10 nor more than 50 days before the scheduled date of the Meeting.

NOTICE OF ANNUAL MEETING OF SHAREHOLDERS
of
________[1]________

PLEASE TAKE NOTICE that the annual meeting of shareholders of ________[1]________ will be held on ________[2]________ at __[3]__ *[4][A.M.]* ***OR*** *[P.M.]* at ________[5]________, ________[6]________.

The purpose of the meeting will be ________________[7]________________ and such other business as may regularly come before the shareholders.

The meeting is open to all shareholders of record, or their designees, as of the close of business on ________[8]________.

Dated:________[9]________ ________[1]________

BY:____________________
[10]

1. The name of the corporation.

2. The date of the Meeting.

3. The time of the Meeting.

4. Choose one.

5. The address where the Meeting will be held.

6. The city and state where the Meeting will be held.

7. A brief description of the purpose of the Meeting.

8. The last day by which shareholders must be "of record" for attendance at the Meeting.

9. The date of the Notice.

10. The name and title of the officer (typically the Secretary) giving the Notice printed directly below the line, with that person to sign above the line.

NOTICE OF SPECIAL MEETING OF SHAREHOLDERS (6-02)

During the life of any corporation events may arise that must be brought to the attention of the shareholders and that require their vote, but that cannot wait until the next regularly scheduled or annual meeting. Such events may require that a Special Meeting be called, the Notice of which must be in writing.

Since a Special Meeting is usually called in response to a specific, unique set of circumstances, the Notice should state the specific purpose.

Most states mandate minimum and maximum times for Notice. Your state's corporation law should be consulted to determine the applicable time required. For example, New York law requires that Notice be given not less than 10 nor more than 50 days before the scheduled date of the Meeting.

1. The name of the the corporation.

2. The date of the Meeting.

3. The time of the Meeting.

4. Choose one.

5. The address where the Meeting will be held.

6. The city and state where the Meeting will be held.

7. A brief description of the purpose of the Meeting.

8. The last day by which shareholders must be "of record" for attendance at the Meeting.

9. The date of the Notice.

10. The name and title of the officer (typically the Secretary) giving the Notice of the Meeting printed directly below the line, with that person to sign above the line.

NOTICE OF SPECIAL MEETING
OF SHAREHOLDERS
of
________[1]________

PLEASE TAKE NOTICE that a special meeting of shareholders of ________[1]________ will be held on ________[2]________ at __[3]__ *[4][A.M.]* ***OR*** *[P.M.]* at ________[5]________, ________[6]________ for the purpose of ____________________[7]____________________.

This special meeting is open to all shareholders of record, or their designees, as of the close of business on ________[8]________.

Dated: _______[9]_______ __________[1]__________

BY:____________________
[10]

AFFIDAVIT OF MAILING OF NOTICE OF MEETING OF SHAREHOLDERS (6-03)

The Secretary (or other officer) of the corporation responsible for mailing a Notice of a Meeting should give a statement under oath as to the date of mailing and the name and address of each shareholder to whom Notice was sent.

AFFIDAVIT OF MAILING OF
NOTICE OF *[1][ANNUAL]* ***OR*** *[SPECIAL]* MEETING
OF SHAREHOLDERS
of
________[2]_________

STATE OF _____[3]_____)
COUNTY OF _____[4]_____) ss.:

________[5]________ being duly sworn deposes and says:

I am the _____[6]_____ of ________[2]________, that on ________[7]________ I deposited in an official depository maintained under the exclusive care and custody of the United States Postal Service located in the State of _____[8]_____, a true and complete copy of the Notice of *[1][Annual* ***OR*** *[Special]* meeting of the shareholders of ________[2]________, each enclosed in a sealed, postage paid wrapper to each shareholder whose name appears on the attached list at the respective address adjacent to each name.

____
[9]

Sworn to before me this

__[10]__ day of _______, 19__

____
Notary Public

1. Choose one.
2. The name of the corporation.
3. The state in which the statement is given.
4. The county in which the statement is given.
5. The name of the person giving the statement.
6. The title of the person giving the statement.
7. The date of mailing the Notices.
8. The state in which the Notices were mailed.
9. The name of the person giving the statement printed directly below the line, with that person to sign above the line.
10. A Notary Public fills in the date, and signs and seals the form by affixing his stamp or seal.

WAIVER OF NOTICE OF MEETING OF SHAREHOLDERS (6-04)

Circumstances such as scheduling or even clerical oversight may prevent Notice of a regular or special meeting of Shareholders from being sent so as to give Shareholders the advanced notice required by either the corporate by-laws or state law. If each Shareholder waives such notice in writing, the Meeting can still be held as scheduled.

1. The name of the corporation.
2. Choose one.
3. The time of day and date of the Meeting.
4. The address, city and state where the Meeting will be held.
5. The date of signing the Waiver.
6. The name of the shareholder printed directly below the line, with the shareholder to sign above the line.
7. The number of shares held by the person signing.

WAIVER OF NOTICE OF
MEETING OF SHAREHOLDERS
of
________[1]________

The undersigned shareholder of ________[1]________ agrees and consents that the *[2][regular]* ***OR*** *[special]* meeting of shareholders be held as stated below for the purpose of such business as may lawfully come before such meeting and does waive all notice of the meeting and of any adjournment.

Time/Date of Meeting:____________[3]____________

Location of Meeting: ____________[4]____________

____________[4]____________

Dated: ________[5]________ ____________________
[6]

Number of shares: ________[7]________

MINUTES OF SHAREHOLDERS' MEETING (6-05)

The purpose of taking Minutes at a Shareholders' Meeting is to provide a lasting record of the proceedings, to record the people present (to ensure a quorum), and to record the actions (the "resolutions") taken. The wise Secretary of the Meeting will take the time necessary to make notes in order to be able to reconstruct, for the Minutes, the background discussion and comments concerning the matters discussed. Such complete Minutes may prove invaluable in the future. Because of this, the duties of the Secretary of the Meeting are not to be taken lightly.

While there is no required or correct form for recording proceedings of Shareholders' Meetings, history and tradition have developed a recognized, consistent approach. The particular style, length and depth of Minutes will depend on the needs and desires of the corporation and its Shareholders.

MINUTES OF SHAREHOLDERS' MEETING
of
__________[1]__________

MINUTES of *[2][annual]* ***OR*** *[special]* meeting of the shareholders of __________[1]__________, held at *[3][the office of the Corporation,]* ____________[4]____________, on _________[5]_________ at _____[6]_____.

The meeting was called to order by the President who stated the purpose of the *[2][annual]* ***OR*** *[special]* meeting. The _____[7]_____ of the Corporation acted as Chairman of the Meeting. The _____[8]_____ of the Corporation acted as Secretary of the Meeting.

Upon noting the presence of shareholders, either in person or by valid proxy, the Secretary stated that a quorum of shareholders was present. [9][The Secretary submitted the form of Notice of Meeting and the Affidavit of Mailing of Notice of Meeting together with the list of shareholders attached and then read the roll of stockholders as they appear on the books of the Corporation. Upon motion duly made, seconded and carried, the Secretary was directed to attach a copy of the Notice and Affidavit to these Minutes.] ***OR*** *[The Secretary then read the form of Waiver of Notice of Meeting duly signed by all shareholders. Upon motion duly made, seconded and carried, the Secretary was directed to attach a copy of the Waiver of Notice of Meeting to these Minutes.]*

Upon request by the Chairman, the Secretary read the Minutes of the Meeting of the Shareholders held on _________[10]_________, which were approved.

1. The name of the corporation.

2. Choose one.

3. Delete if the Meeting is held at a location other than the office of the corporation.

4. The address, city and state where the Meeting was held.

5. The date of the Meeting.

6. The time of the Meeting.

7. The title of the person acting as Chairman of the Meeting (typically, but not necessarily, the president of the corporation).

8. The title of the person acting as Secretary of the Meeting (typically, but not necessarily the secretary of the corporation.)

9. Choose one. If a Waiver of Notification of Meeting was issued, choose the second alternative.

10. The date of the last Shareholders' Meeting.

(Document continued on next page)

11. The names of the people elected as directors of the corporation. (The form provides five spaces; however care should be taken to review the by-laws of the corporation since the by-laws will state the number permitted for that corporation.)

12. List all other matters discussed at the Meeting, who initiated each discussion, the substance of each discussion, the recommendations made and by whom, and any resolutions voted upon (even if rejected).

13. The time of adjournment of the Meeting.

14. The name of the Secretary of the Meeting printed directly below the line, with that person to sign above the line. (Note: It should be the same as No. 8.)

Upon request by the Chairman, the Treasurer presented his report. After discussion, the report was approved and on motion duly made and seconded, the Secretary was directed to attach a copy of the report to these Minutes.

The following were duly nominated and were, upon affirmative vote, elected as directors of the Corporation to serve the term set forth in the By-Laws of the Corporation or until their successors are elected:

________[11]________ ________[11]________

________[11]________ ________[11]________

________[11]________

After discussion and due deliberation by the shareholders, upon motion duly made, seconded and carried by affirmative vote it was

"RESOLVED, that all of the decisions made and acts and action taken by the Board of Directors and the officers of the Corporation since the last meeting of the shareholders are ratified and approved."

______________________[12]______________________

____

____.

There being no further business, on motion duly made, seconded and carried, the Meeting was adjourned at ____[13]____.

____

[14] Secretary

NOTICE OF MEETING OF DIRECTORS (6-06)

Generally the shareholders of a corporation are absentee owners. They elect Directors to operate the business in their absence but on their behalf. The elected Directors determine policy. The Directors in turn appoint officers as the day-to-day managers of the corporation to carry out the policy decisions made by the board.

Directors meet regularly, perhaps as frequently as monthly but certainly no less than annually (and usually immediately after the annual Stockholders' Meeting). Notices of Meetings of Directors should be in writing, as this form provides.

NOTICE OF MEETING OF DIRECTORS
of
________[1]________

1. The name of the corporation.

2. The date of the Meeting.

3. The time of the Meeting.

4. Choose one.

5. The address where the Meeting will be held.

6. The city and state where the Meeting will be held.

7. The date of the Notice.

8. The name and title of the officer (typically the Secretary) giving the Notice printed directly below the line, with that person to sign above the line.

PLEASE TAKE NOTICE that a regular meeting of the Board of Directors of ________[1]________ will be held on ________[2]________ at __[3]__ *[4][A.M.]* ***OR*** *[P.M.]* at ________[5]________, ________[6]________, for such business as may properly come before the Board.

Dated: ________[7]________ ________[1]________

BY: ________________
[8]

NOTICE OF SPECIAL MEETING OF DIRECTORS (6-07)

Just as unforeseen events may require the attention of and vote by shareholders, so events which cannot wait for the next regularly scheduled meeting may require the attention of and vote by the Directors. Such an event may require calling a Special Meeting. Notice of this meeting must be in writing to the Directors.

Since a Special Meeting is usually in response to specific, unique circumstances, the Notice should state the specific purpose for the Meeting.

NOTICE OF SPECIAL MEETING
OF DIRECTORS
of
_______[1]_______

PLEASE TAKE NOTICE that a special meeting of the Board of Directors of ________[1]________ will be held on ________[2]________ at __[3]__ *[4][A.M.]* ***OR*** *[P.M.]* at ________[5]________, ________[6]________, for the purpose of ________________[7]________________.

Dated: ________[8]_______ __________[1]__________

BY: ____________________
[9]

1. The name of the the corporation.

2. The date of the Meeting.

3. The time of the Meeting.

4. Choose one.

5. The address where the Meeting will be held.

6. The city and state where the Meeting will be held.

7. A brief description of the purpose of the Meeting.

8. The date of the Notice.

9. The name and title of the officer (typically the Secretary) giving the Notice of the Meeting printed directly below the line, with that person to sign above the line.

WAIVER OF NOTICE OF MEETING OF DIRECTORS (6-08)

Circumstances such as scheduling problems or even clerical oversight may prevent Notice of a regular or special meeting of the Board of Directors from being sent so as to give the Directors sufficient advanced notice required by either the corporate by-laws or state law. If each Director waives such Notice in writing, the Meeting can still be held as scheduled.

1. The name of the the corporation.

2. Choose one.

3. The time of day and the date of the Meeting.

4. The address, city and state where the Meeting will be held.

5. The date of signing the Waiver.

6. The name of the director printed directly below the line, with the director to sign above the line.

WAIVER OF NOTICE OF
MEETING OF DIRECTORS
of
________[1]________

The undersigned director of ________[1]________ agrees and consents that the *[2][regular]* ***OR*** *[special]* meeting of the Board of Directors of ________[1]________ be held as stated below for the purpose of such business as may lawfully come before such meeting and does waive all notice of the meeting and any adjournment.

Time/Date of meeting: ____________[3]____________

Location of meeting: ____________[4]____________

____________[4]____________

Dated: ________[5]________ ____________________
[6]

MINUTES OF DIRECTORS' MEETING (6-09)

The purpose of taking Minutes at a Directors' Meeting is to provide a lasting record of the proceedings, to record the people present and the actions (the "resolutions") taken. The wise Director or Secretary of the Meeting will take the time necessary to make notes in order to be able to reconstruct, for the Minutes, the background discussion and comments concerning the matters discussed. Such complete Minutes may prove invaluable if, in the future when a particular Director may no longer be associated with the corporation, the corporation needs to establish the "business judgment" behind a particular resolution or to establish the fiduciary obligations of any individual Director to the corporation. Because of this, the duties of the Secretary of the Meeting are not to be taken lightly.

Resolutions are recorded in the Minutes of the meeting. The Corporate Resolutions later in this chapter contain resolutions for commonly encountered situations.

While there is no required or correct form for recording proceedings of Directors' Meetings, history and tradition have developed a recognized, consistent approach. The particular style, length and depth of Minutes will depend on the needs and desires of the corporation and its Directors.

1. The name of the corporation.

2. Choose one.

3. Delete if the Meeting is held at a location other than the office of the corporation.

4. The street address, city and state where the Meeting was held.

5. The date of the Meeting.

6. The time of the Meeting.

7. The name of each director attending the Meeting. (The form provides five spaces; however the number of directors for a particular corporation is determined by its by-laws.)

8. Choose one depending on whether all directors were present.

9. If any other person attended, state his name and any title such as "accountant," "legal counsel" or the like. Otherwise delete.

MINUTES OF DIRECTORS' MEETING
of
________[1]________

MINUTES of a *[2][regular]* ***OR*** *[special]* meeting of the Board of Directors of ________[1]________, held at *[3][the office of the Corporation]*, ____________[4]____________, on ________[5]_______ at ____[6]____.

The following directors were present:

________[7]________ ________[7]________

________[7]________ ________[7]________

________[7]________

being *[8][a quorum in accordance with the By-Laws of the Corporation]* ***OR*** *[all of the directors of the Corporation]. [9][Also present by invitation of the Board:*

____

____*.]*

(Document continued on next page)

10. The name of the person acting as Chairman of the Meeting (typically, but not necessarily, the president of the corporation).

11. The corporate title, if any, of the Chairman of the Meeting, such as "Director," "President" or the like.

12. The name of the person acting as Secretary of the Meeting (typically, but not necessarily, the secretary of the corporation).

13. The corporate title, if any, of the Secretary of the Meeting.

14. Choose one depending on whether a Waiver of Notice of Meeting was issued.

15. Choose one depending on whether Waivers of Notice were received.

16. The date of the last Meeting of the Board.

17. The name of the director who initiated any discussion.

18. List any other matters discussed by the Board, the substance of each discussion, the recommendations made and by whom, and any resolutions voted upon (even if rejected).

19. Fill in the name of each officer elected.

20. The time of adjournment of the Meeting.

21. The name of the Secretary of the Meeting plus the title "Secretary" printed directly below the line, with that person to sign above the line. (Note: it should be the same as No. 12.)

________[10]________, _____[11]_____ of the Corporation, acted as Chairman of the Meeting.

________[12]________, _____[13]_____ of the Corporation, acted as Secretary of the Meeting. The Chairman noted the presence of a quorum.

The Secretary *[14][presented the form of Notice of Meeting and proof of mailing of the Notice to the Directors.]* ***OR*** *[presented written Waivers of Notice signed by all directors of the Corporation.]* On motion duly made and seconded, the Secretary was directed to attach the *[15][Notice of Meeting and proof of mailing]* ***OR*** *[Waivers of Notice]* to these Minutes.

The Secretary read the Minutes of the Meeting of the Board held on ________[16]________ which were approved.

The Treasurer presented his report. After discussion, the report was approved and on motion duly made and seconded, the Secretary was directed to attach the report to these Minutes.

Upon motion made by Director ________[17]________, seconded and carried, the Board opened a discussion concerning the issue of

________________________[18]________________________

____

____.

The following were duly nominated and were, upon unanimous vote, elected as officers of the Corporation to serve the term set forth in the By-Laws of the Corporation or until their successors are elected:

[19] President: ______________________________

Vice President: ______________________________

Secretary: ______________________________

Treasurer: ______________________________

There being no further business, on motion duly made, seconded and carried, the Meeting was adjourned at ____[20]____.

____

[21] Secretary

RESIGNATION OF DIRECTOR OR OFFICER (6-10)

While a verbal exchange of "I quit"/"You're fired" is common, tradition, custom and simple courtesy require a written letter of Resignation, particularly if the person resigning is a Director or Officer of a business. A Resignation should be kept simple. The date on which the Resignation becomes effective (either immediately or on some particular date in the future) is the most important element.

RESIGNATION OF DIRECTOR OR OFFICER

1. The name and address of the business.

2. The date of the Resignation letter, which may or may not be the same as the date the Resignation becomes effective.

3. The name of the individual to whom the Resignation is to be directed.

4. The name of the company.

5. Choose one.

6. The resigning person's title.

7. Choose one.

8. The date the Resignation is to take effect.

9. The name and title of the person resigning printed directly below the line, with that person to sign above the line.

________[1]________ ______[2]______
____
____
____

Attention: ________[3]________

Gentlemen:

Please be advised that I hereby tender my resignation from ________[4]________ *[5][as a Director]* ***OR*** *[and the office of ________[6]________]* effective *[7][immediately]* ***OR*** *[as of ________[8]________]*.

Very truly yours,

____
[9]

CORPORATE RESOLUTION—AMENDING THE ARTICLES OF INCORPORATION OR CORPORATE BY-LAWS (6-11)

This Corporate Resolution is to be used in the Minutes of Directors' Meeting.

Over its life, a corporation may determine that its interests can be better served by doing things differently or doing different things. Such changes may require amending the corporation's Articles of Incorporation (its charter) or its By-laws—or both. Typical of the changes would be a change in the corporate structure such as the kind of stock it issues or the number or term of its directors, the corporations permitted purpose or powers, or even its name.

The recognition of the need for such change may originate either with the shareholders or with a director, but the directors must recommend the changes. If a change is such that the Articles of Incorporation (also called Certificate of Incorporation) or the By-laws must be amended, a vote of the shareholders will be necessary. If, and only if, the directors determine that the proposed change is in the best interests of the corporation, the directors must propose a specific resolution and direct that it be submitted to the shareholders, either at the next regular meeting or at a special meeting.

Note: an Amendment of the Articles of Incorporation will require a filing with the appropriate state agency (typically, the Secretary of State), because it is considered a public document. On the other hand, an Amendment of the By-laws will not require such a filing because By-laws are not public documents.

CORPORATE RESOLUTION—AMENDING THE ARTICLES OF INCORPORATION OR CORPORATE BY-LAWS

1. The name of the director making the motion.
2. The issue or change to be discussed.
3. The substance of the discussion.
4. The name of the director making the motion.
5. Choose one.
6. A description of the proposed change.
7. Choose one.
8. The date of the meeting.

Upon motion made by Director _______[1]______, seconded and carried, the Board opened a discussion concerning the issue of _____________[2]_____________.
____________________[3]____________________
____
_______________________________________.

Upon motion made by Director ________[4]________, seconded and carried, it is

"RESOLVED, that the Board recommend to the shareholders that the *[5][Articles of Incorporation]* ***OR*** *[By-Laws]* be amended to provide: ___[6]___
____
_______________________________________,
and further

RESOLVED, that such recommendation be presented to the shareholders at the next *[7][special]* ***OR*** *[regular]* meeting of the shareholders to be held on ________[8]________."

CORPORATE RESOLUTION—SMALL BUSINESS CORPORATION (SUB-CHAPTER S CORPORATION) (6-12)

This Corporate Resolution is to be used in the Minutes of Directors' Meeting.

Certain corporations which, among other requirements, have less than 35 stockholders, have only one class of stock, and whose stockholders are individuals, estates or certain trusts, none of whom are non-resident aliens may, together with their shareholders, derive tax benefits from treatment as a "small business corporation" (also referred to as an "S Corporation" or a "Sub-Chapter S corporation").

Note: this election for treatment as a small business corporation is valid only if made upon the consent of all the shareholders on the day the election is made.

CORPORATE RESOLUTION—SMALL BUSINESS CORPORATION (SUB-CHAPTER S CORPORATION)

1. The name of the director making the motion.
2. The name of the director making the motion.
3. The name of the tax authority of the state in which the corporation files its state tax returns.
4. The state in which the corporation files its state tax returns.

Upon motion made by Director ______[1]_______, seconded and carried, the Board opened a discussion concerning the issue of an election by the Corporation to be treated as a "small business corporation" for income tax purposes. The Secretary noted that the holders of all of the issued stock of the Corporation have consented to such election and presented forms of written consent to such an election. The Chairman directed that the forms of written consent be attached to these Minutes. The Treasurer of the Corporation advised that such election was also recommended by the accountant for the Corporation. Upon motion made by _______[2]______, seconded and carried, it was

> "RESOLVED, the appropriate officers of the Corporation are hereby authorized and directed to take all reasonable and necessary action to comply with the rules and regulations of the Internal Revenue Service and the ________[3]________ of ______[4]______ to make the election for treatment as a Sub-Chapter S Corporation pursuant to Internal Revenue Code, Sec. 1361, et seq."

CORPORATE RESOLUTION—INTERNAL REVENUE CODE SEC. 1244 STOCK (6-13)

This Corporate Resolution is to be used in the Minutes of Directors' Meeting.

Every stockholder of a new corporation would like to believe that the new venture will become a huge success. He would rather not think that its shares may, in the future, be sold at a loss. Unfortunately, that can happen. With advanced planning, a corporation may ease the pain and at the same time make itself significantly more attractive to investors if it can offer beneficial tax treatment on the investors' personal tax returns in the event of sale of the stock at a loss.

This form is included for the purpose of alerting the reader to the need for advanced planning. It provides the by-laws provision necessary to set up the corporate mechanism so that some tax benefits may be realized in the event of a future sale at a loss. However, since this book is not meant to be a tax treatise, it is strongly urged that the reader consult his own accountant or tax preparer for a further discussion of Internal Revenue Code Sec. 1244.

CORPORATE RESOLUTION—INTERNAL REVENUE CODE SEC. 1244 STOCK

1. The name of the director making the motion.

2. The name of the director making the motion.

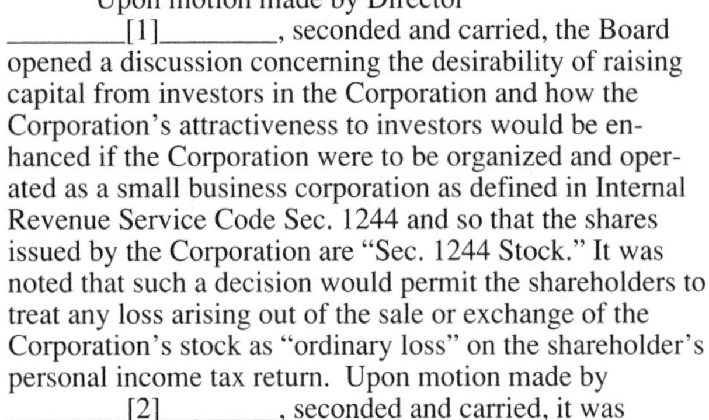

Upon motion made by Director ________[1]________, seconded and carried, the Board opened a discussion concerning the desirability of raising capital from investors in the Corporation and how the Corporation's attractiveness to investors would be enhanced if the Corporation were to be organized and operated as a small business corporation as defined in Internal Revenue Service Code Sec. 1244 and so that the shares issued by the Corporation are "Sec. 1244 Stock." It was noted that such a decision would permit the shareholders to treat any loss arising out of the sale or exchange of the Corporation's stock as "ordinary loss" on the shareholder's personal income tax return. Upon motion made by ________[2]________, seconded and carried, it was

"RESOLVED, that the sale and issuance of stock of the Corporation be made in compliance with Internal Revenue Code Sec. 1244 such that the shareholders of the Corporation receive the benefits of such tax treatment and to that end, the appropriate officers of the Corporation are hereby authorized and directed to take all reasonable and necessary action to comply with the rules and regulations of the Internal Revenue Code Sec. 1244 and to issue stock in the Corporation such that the amount of money and other property received by the Corporation for stock, as a contribution to capital and paid in surplus, does not exceed $1,000,000 at the time of issuance of the stock, and it is further

RESOLVED, that the appropriate officers of the Corporation are authorized and directed to place any appropriate legends or notations on all such stock certificates if required."

CORPORATE RESOLUTION—MEDICAL CARE COST REIMBURSEMENT PLAN (6-14)

This Corporate Resolution is to be used in the Minutes of Directors' Meeting.

High medical costs are a fact of life that must be faced by any individual or corporation. Competent, skilled employees have come to expect that, in addition to their salary or wages, they will be assisted in meeting these high costs. The corporation that can offer such assistance is more likely to attract better qualified and motivated employees. This form sets up the corporation's authority to offer such assistance.

CORPORATE RESOLUTION—MEDICAL CARE COST REIMBURSEMENT PLAN

1. The name of the director making the motion.

2. The name of the director suggesting.

3. The name of the director suggesting.

4. The length of employment required, for example "one year."

5. The name of the director suggesting.

6. The name of the director suggesting.

7. The dollar amount, in numbers, of the upper limit to be reimbursed.

8. The dollar amount, in numbers, of the upper limit to be advanced.

9. The name of the director suggesting.

Upon motion made by Director ________[1]________, seconded and carried, the Board opened a discussion noting the high cost of adequate medical care and concerning the desirability of attracting and benefitting employees of the Corporation by the ability to reduce employee concerns over such high costs. Director ________[2]_________ acknowledging the high costs, stated that in his opinion the best interests of the Corporation might be better served by not offering unlimited reimbursement, but rather imposing an annual cap or ceiling and conditioning any reimbursement on reasonable eligibility standards. Director _________[3]_______ suggested that eligibility be limited to directors, officers and full-time employees with _____[4]_____ of service to the Corporation. Director _________[5]_________ questioned whether eligibility be extended to dependents of directors, officers or eligible employees as well. Director _________[6]_________ suggested that costs below a certain amount be reimbursed only and that costs above such amount would, upon written request, be advanced and that in either event, an annual limit of a certain amount per person be imposed. The Board agreed on $ _____[7]_____ and $ _____[8]_____ for the limits on reimbursements and annual advances respectively. Director _________[9]_________ suggested that any advance or reimbursement also be limited to amounts not provided by any health, accident or disability insurance covering any director, officer, eligible employee or dependent regardless of ownership of such policy. Upon motion made by

(Document continued on next page)

10. The name of the director making the motion.

__________[10]__________, seconded and carried, it was

"RESOLVED, that the Secretary be authorized and directed to take all reasonable and necessary steps to devise, approve and implement a plan of medical care cost reimbursement within the guidelines established by the Board, for all directors, officers and eligible employees having _____[4]_____ of service to the Corporation and all dependents, as defined in Internal Revenue Code Sec. 152, of the directors, officers and eligible employees. It is the intention of the Corporation that any benefits payable shall be excluded from the gross income of the recipient of such benefit."

CORPORATE RESOLUTION—INSURANCE PLAN (6-15)

This Corporate Resolution is to be used in the Minutes of Directors' Meeting.

A corporation may realize that the death of a particular (key) corporate officer would threaten its very existence or that it might be required to pay a large sum to the widow of an officer. The corporation may elect to take out a life insurance policy on that officer. This form provides the authority to do so.

CORPORATE RESOLUTION—INSURANCE PLAN

1. The name of the director making the motion.

2. The title of the corporate officer to be insured.

3. The name of the corporate officer to be insured.

4. The name of the director making the motion.

5. The type of insurance, for example: term, straight or whole life or the like.

6. The dollar amount of the insurance, in numbers.

Upon motion made by Director __________[1]_________, seconded and carried, the Board opened a discussion concerning the benefit received by the Corporation from the past and future services and contribution made by its __________[2]__________, __________[3]__________, and the loss to the Corporation that would result from the death while in office of __________[3]__________. Upon motion made by __________[4]__________, seconded and carried, it was

"RESOLVED, that the Corporation apply for, own, pay all premiums as and when due and be the irrevocable beneficiary of a policy of _______[5]_______ life insurance on the life of __________[3]__________ which will provide benefits payable to the Corporation upon the death of __________[3]__________ in the amount of $ _____[6]_____. __________[3]_________ is directed to make himself available and to submit to such medical examination as may, from time to time, be required."

CORPORATE RESOLUTION—CHANGE OF BANK AND OTHER BANKING MATTERS (6-16)

This Corporate Resolution is to be used in the Minutes of Directors' Meeting.

Banking matters such as writing checks and borrowing money are vital to every business. Every corporation needs to establish clear and concise policies concerning the number of officers necessary to sign checks and the authority to borrow money. This form accomplishes those purposes while providing protection to the corporation by requiring that checks and loans in excess of a predetermined limit must have more than one signature.

1. The name of the director making the motion.

2. The name of the director making the motion.

3. The name of the present bank.

4. The name of the new bank.

5. The address of the new bank.

6. The dollar amount, in numbers, for checks below a certain limit (for example $500) requiring the number of signature(s) specified in No. 7 (typically only one).

7. The number of signatures required, in numbers.

8. The dollar amount, in numbers, for checks above a certain amount (for example $500) requiring the number of signatures specified in No. 9 (typically two).

CORPORATE RESOLUTION—CHANGE OF BANK AND OTHER BANKING MATTERS

Upon motion made by Director ________[1]________, seconded and carried, the Board opened a discussion concerning the growth of the Corporation having exceeded the capabilities of its present bank to serve the financial needs of the Corporation. Discussion continued as to the present banking needs of the Corporation and the authority needed by the officers to operate and manage the Corporation. The services offered by several competing banks were then discussed. Upon motion made by ________[2]________, seconded and carried, it was

"RESOLVED, that the Treasurer or other appropriate officer of the Corporation is authorized and directed to close and terminate all accounts maintained at __________[3]__________ as soon as practicable and open and maintain such accounts in the name of and for the benefit of the Corporation as the Treasurer may determine to be necessary at __________[4]_________, with offices located at ___________[5]___________, which is hereby designated as the depository of funds of the Corporation. The officers and agents of the Corporation are authorized and directed to deposit any monies of the Corporation in _________[4]_________, and it is further

RESOLVED, that any draft, check and other instrument or order for the payment of money drawn against any accounts of the Corporation with the depository for amounts not to exceed $ ____[6]____ shall be signed by any __[7]__ of the following officers of the Corporation and for amounts in excess of $____[8]____ shall

(Document continued on next page)

9. The number of signatures required, in numbers.

10. List by title all officers, assistants and others who may sign the corporation's checks.

11. The dollar amount, in numbers, for loans below a certain amount (for example $5,000) requiring the number of signature(s) specified in No. 12 (typically only one).

12. The number of signatures required, in numbers.

13. The dollar amount, in numbers, for loans above a certain amount (for example $5,000) requiring the number of signatures specified in No. 14 (typically two).

14. The number of signatures required, in numbers.

15. List by title all officers, assistants and others who may obligate the corporation by borrowing money for its needs.

be signed by any __[9]__ of the following officers of the Corporation:
____________________[10]____________________
____
____,
and it is further

RESOLVED, that the depository is authorized to place to the credit of the Corporation funds, drafts, checks or other property that may be delivered to the depository for deposit to the accounts of the Corporation, endorsed with the name of the Corporation, whether by stamp, facsimile, manual or mechanical or other signature, except that if any such item shall bear or be accompanied by direction for deposit to a specific account of the Corporation maintained at the depository, the deposit shall be to the credit of that specific account, and it is further

RESOLVED, that the Corporation borrow from time to time from the depository and that any drafts, notes, agreements, trust receipts or other similar documents for amounts not to exceed $ ____[11]____ shall be signed by any __[12]__ of the following officers of the Corporation and for amounts in excess of $ ___[13]___ shall be signed by any __[14]__ of the following officers of the Corporation: ________[15]________
____
____,
and it is further

RESOLVED, that the appropriate officers are authorized and directed to execute such resolutions, signature specimen cards and the like as may be reasonable and necessary to implement these resolutions of the Board."

CORPORATE RESOLUTION—RATIFICATION OF OFFICERS' ACTS (6-17)

This Corporate Resolution is to be used in the Minutes of Directors' Meeting.

Periodically, the Officers of a corporation may undertake acts which are beyond the scope of their authority or are properly the responsibility of the Board of Directors. If such acts are in the best interests of the corporation, the directors wisely may choose to ratify the acts rather than reject them. This form provides the Directors' resolution to do so. If the Officers' acts are subsequently ratified by the Board of Directors, the granting of authority is done retroactively to the time of the transactions. Therefore, Ratification absolves the Officers from liability for the acts and transfers that liability to the corporation. This form is set up to provide Ratification of either disclosed acts by specific Officers or all acts by all Officers.

CORPORATE RESOLUTION—RATIFICATION OF OFFICERS' ACTS

1. The name of the director making the motion.
2. The title or name of the officer or officers who undertook the specific act(s).
3. The name of the director making the motion.
4. Choose one depending on whether certain specific acts, or all acts since the last meeting, are to be ratified.
5. The title or name of the officer or officers who undertook the specific act(s).
6. The specific act(s).
7. The titles of all officers whose act(s) the Board of Directors wishes to ratify.

Upon motion made by Director __________[1]__________, seconded and carried, the Board opened a discussion concerning certain acts having been undertaken by __________[2]__________. Discussion of certain specific acts prompted the Chairman to point out that while these acts properly may have required the affirmative vote of the Board of Directors, they were nevertheless undertaken as being in the best interests of the Corporation. Upon motion made by __________[3]__________, seconded and carried, it was

> "RESOLVED, that *[4][the actions of __________[5]__________ taken with regard to ________________[6]________________]* ***OR*** *[all acts and transactions of __________[7]__________ taken or made since the last meeting of the Board of Directors which have been disclosed to the Board at this meeting]* are hereby ratified and approved as actions of the Board of Directors."

CORPORATE RESOLUTION—
AUTHORITY OF OFFICER (6-18)

This Corporate Resolution is to be used in the Minutes of Directors' Meeting.

Since the primary responsibility of the Board of Directors of every corporation is to establish policy and then to appoint Officers to implement that policy, the directors must give Officers sufficient authority to act. This form provides either broad, general authority or specific authority.

CORPORATE RESOLUTION—
AUTHORITY OF OFFICER

1. The name of the director making the motion.

2. The title of the officer to be given authority.

3. The name of the director making the motion.

4. Choose one depending on whether general or specific authority is to be given.

5. The title of the officer to be given authority.

6. The name of the other party to a specific contract.

7. The terms of a specific contract, such as "entering into an agreement for the sale of the Corporation's widgets in Europe."

Upon motion made by Director __________[1]__________, seconded and carried, the Board opened a discussion concerning the authority of the __________[2]__________ to transact business on behalf of the Corporation. The Chairman pointed out the need to give the officers of the Corporation authority so that they could best manage the affairs of the Corporation. Upon motion made by __________[3]__________, seconded and carried, it was

"RESOLVED, *[4][that the __________[5]__________ is authorized to negotiate, enter into and execute and deliver in the name of and on behalf of the Corporation, any contract or agreement which said officer deems to be reasonable and necessary for the business of the Corporation without further or prior act of the Directors of the Corporation]* ***OR*** *[that the ________[5]________ is authorized and directed to execute and deliver in the name of and on behalf of the Corporation a contract with _________[6]_________ for ____________________[7]____________________]* and the Secretary is authorized and directed to affix the corporate seal thereto if so ordered by the officer executing the contract and without further or prior order of this Board."

CORPORATE RESOLUTION—
INDEMNIFICATION OF DIRECTORS (6-19)

This Corporate Resolution is to be used in the Minutes of Directors' Meeting.

Despite acting in the best interests of the corporation and in their honest exercise of business judgment, and properly exercising their fiduciary duties without any self-dealing, one or more of the Directors of a corporation may be sued, perhaps by a shareholder. Other shareholders of the corporation may decide that such a law suit is baseless and determine that the Directors should not have to "reach into their own pockets." The shareholders can resolve to indemnify the Directors for the amount of any judgment or settlement against the Directors, including their legal fees.

Note that the Directors cannot resolve to indemnify themselves. Rather the shareholders, as the owners of the corporation and on whose behalf the Directors run the corporation, must do so.

CORPORATE RESOLUTION—
INDEMNIFICATION OF DIRECTORS

1. The date of the Shareholders' Meeting.

2. The names of the directors to be indemnified.

3. The circumstances giving rise to the law suit.

Whereas, the shareholders of the Corporation at the meeting held on ________[1]________ were advised that a legal action has been commenced against the Corporation and _____________[2]______________ as Directors of the Corporation on account of certain actions of the Board of Directors, and

Whereas, the shareholders determined that said Directors were acting in their respective capacities as Directors of the Corporation, acting in the best interests of the Corporation, acting on the basis of their legitimate exercise of business judgment, and acting in accordance with the fiduciary duties imposed on them by law, and

Whereas, after due deliberation by the shareholders determined to constitute a quorum present at the meeting, upon motion duly made, seconded and carried by the affirmative vote of the shareholders, it was

> "RESOLVED, that _____________[2]_____________ shall be indemnified by the Corporation for all reasonable, actual and necessary expenses, including attorneys' fees, which have or may be incurred by them or any of them in connection with the defense of a lawsuit commenced against them and the Corporation, whether by judgment, settlement or upon and after appeal, and arising out of ______________[3]______________
> ____
> ____."

STOCK POWER (6-20)

A Stock Power is used whenever a stockholder sells shares of stock. A stock certificate is "negotiable" (that is, can be sold, assigned or transferred) only when accompanied by a Stock Power. The Stock Power is to a certificate for stock as the endorsement (on the back of a check) is to a check.

WARNING

In order for the Stock Power to be accepted by the transfer agent designated by the corporation, the Seller's signature must be *guaranteed* by an officer of a commercial bank or a licensed stock broker. This is *not* the same as having the Seller's signature notarized by a Notary Public, which will result in the Stock Power being rejected by the transfer agent.

1. The name of the Seller of the stock. (Note: the name on the Stock Power must be exactly the same as it appears on the stock certificate.)

2. The Seller's social security or taxpayer identification number.

3. The name of the Purchaser (if known). Otherwise, leave blank.

4. The Purchaser's Social Security or Taxpayer Identification number (if known). Otherwise, leave blank.

5. The number of shares being sold, in words.

6. The number of shares being sold, in numbers.

7. The type of stock, i.e.: common, preferred, etc.

8. The name of the corporation whose stock is being sold.

9. The certificate number(s) of the stock being sold.

10. The transfer agent will fill in this portion.

11. The date of the sale.

12. The name of the Seller printed directly below the line, with the Seller to sign above the line.

STOCK POWER

FOR VALUE RECEIVED, I, _________[1]_________ (my social security/taxpayer identification no. is: ______[2]______), hereby sell, assign and transfer unto ________[3]_________ (whose social security /taxpayer identification no. is: _______[4]______) _________[5]________ (___[6]___) shares of the _______[7]______ capital stock of __________[8]_________ standing in (my)(our) name(s) on the books of said Corporation represented by Certificate(s) No(s) __________[9]_______________, and do hereby irrevocably constitute and appoint _________[10]__________ as attorney to transfer said stock on the books of the Corporation with full power of substitution in the premises.

Dated:______[11]______

____

[12]

PROXY (6-21)

A shareholder of a corporation might not be able to attend a shareholders' meeting but might nevertheless wish his vote to be counted. A Proxy provides written notice to the corporation that the shareholder has designated another to attend the meeting and authorizes that person to cast the shareholder's votes. The Proxy also requires the corporation to permit the attendance of the designee (the Proxy holder) at the meeting and to accept and record the designee's vote.

PROXY

KNOW ALL MEN BY THESE PRESENTS that the undersigned shareholder of _____[1]_____ shares of ________[2]________ does hereby appoint ________[3]________, of ___________[4]___________, or the bearer of this proxy, to be his true and lawful attorney-in-fact and agent to vote as proxy at the meeting of shareholders of ________[2]________ to be held on ________[5]________ at ___________[6]___________ or any adjournment of such meeting and to act as fully as the undersigned could do if personally present at such meeting. By this proxy the undersigned does hereby revoke any proxy previously given.

Dated: ________[7]________

WITNESS:

______________________ ______________________
[8] [9]

___________[10]___________
___________[10]___________

1. The number of shares owned by the shareholder.

2. The name of the corporation.

3. The name of the designee (the Proxy holder).

4. The address of the designee.

5. The date of the shareholders' meeting.

6. The location of the shareholders' meeting.

7. The date of the Proxy.

8. The name of the witness printed directly below the line, with the witness to sign above the line.

9. The name of the shareholder giving the Proxy printed directly below the line, with the shareholder to sign above the line.

10. The address of the shareholder.

AFFIDAVIT OF LOST STOCK CERTIFICATE (6-22)

Stock certificates sometimes get lost despite the best efforts to safeguard them. The Uniform Commercial Code provides that the issuing corporation must replace a stock certificate: 1) when the registered shareholder requests a replacement AND 2) before the issuing corporation receives notice that the security has been acquired by a bona fide purchaser (someone who has bought the stock certificate and does not know that the certificate had been lost). The owner may be required to file a sufficient indemnity bond with the issuing corporation (which usually can be obtained through the issuing corporation) and satisfy any other reasonable requests of the issuing corporation. This form provides written request to the issuing corporation.

An Affidavit is a statement made under oath before a Notary Public or similar person authorized by the laws of that state to administer oaths. The Affidavit must be signed in the presence of the Notary.

AFFIDAVIT OF LOST STOCK CERTIFICATE

STATE OF _____[1]_____)
COUNTY OF _____[2]_____) ss.:

________[3]________, being duly sworn, deposes and says:

I am *[4][the lawful owner]* ***OR*** *[the executor, administrator, representative or fiduciary of the Estate of ________[5]________ who at the time of death was the lawful owner]* of ___[6]___ shares of _______[7]_______ registered in the name of _______[8]_______.

I believe the original certificate(s) representing said shares has been lost, stolen, destroyed or misplaced because I have made a diligent search of all available records and have been unable to locate the certificate(s). I believe that said certificate(s) were not endorsed, that said certificate(s) have not been sold, transferred, assigned, delivered, hypothecated, pledged or otherwise disposed of and that no person or entity other than the undersigned has any right, title, equity, claim or interest in or to said certificate(s) or the ownership interest represented by said certificate(s).

I agree that if said certificate(s) ever come into my custody or control, I will immediately, and without consideration, surrender and return said certificate(s) to ________[7]________ for cancellation.

This affidavit is made for the purpose of inducing and requesting ________[7]________ and its transfer agents to issue new certificate(s) in substitution and

1. The state in which the requesting owner of the lost certificate is located and in which he will make the Affidavit.
2. The county in which the requesting owner of the lost certificate is located.
3. The name of the person giving the Affidavit.
4. Choose one.
5. The name of the deceased owner of the lost certificate.
6. The number of shares represented by the lost certificate(s).
7. The name of the issuing corporation.
8. The name of the owner of the lost certificate.

(Document continued on next page)

9. The name of the company which will issue the indemnity bond (usually selected by the issuing corporation).

10. The name of the person giving the Affidavit printed directly below the line, with that person to sign above the line.

11. A Notary Public fills in the date and signs and seals the form by affixing his stamp or seal.

replacement of the lost certificate(s) and for the purpose of inducing ________[9]________ to issue an indemnity bond assuming liability.

____
[10]

Sworn to before me this

_[11]_ day of _______, 19__

____
Notary Public

Buying and Selling A Business 7

Just as the goods or services produced by a business can be bought or sold, so too can a business *itself* or its parts be bought or sold.

Buying There are two basic ways to buy a business. One is to buy the assets of the company and the other, if the business is a corporation, is to buy its stock. The methods differ in terms of the legal consequences. In an asset purchase, the buyer assumes only those liabilities of the seller to which the buyer agrees. In a stock purchase, however, the buyer assumes *all* of the liabilities of the seller. Forms for both asset and stock purchases are found in this section.

Bulk Transfers This section provides the necessary forms to protect the buyer and the seller from the seller's creditors if the sale of the business is a sale of assets.

AGREEMENT FOR THE PURCHASE/ SALE OF A BUSINESS/ASSETS (7-01)

Essentially, there are two ways to purchase an existing business. The Assets, including goodwill, can be purchased or its stock, if a corporation, can be purchased. The determination should be made in consultation with a tax advisor as there are tax consequences to both the Buyer and Seller depending on the method chosen. Legally, the differences are that in an Asset Purchase the Buyer assumes only those liabilities of the Seller that the Buyer agrees to; in a Stock Purchase the Buyer assumes all of the liabilities and Assets of the Seller. (See also the Agreement for the Purchase/Sale of Corporate Stock which follows.)

Note: the Agreement requires that Schedules A, B and C be prepared listing the assets, accounts receivable and promissory notes respectively. To prepare these, create three separate sheets each headed with the proper schedule names (for example, "Schedule A") and list the required information on each. Follow the style shown at the end of this form. Further, the sale of assets may be considered a Bulk Transfer. See the Bulk Transfer forms later in this chapter, which are required for such a sale.

AGREEMENT FOR THE PURCHASE/
SALE OF A BUSINESS/ASSETS

1. The date the Agreement is signed.

2. The name of the Seller.

3. If the Seller is a corporation, insert the state in which incorporated. Otherwise delete.

4. The name of the Buyer.

5. If the Buyer is a corporation, insert the state in which incorporated. Otherwise delete.

6. The name under which the Seller conducts business.

7. The address at which the business is operated.

AGREEMENT made this __[1]__ day of __________ ,19__ by and between ________[2]________ *[3][, a _________ corporation]* ("Seller") and _____[4]______ *[5][, a ________ corporation]* ("Buyer").

Seller is the owner and operator of ________[6]________ located at ________[7]________ and desires to sell certain of the assets of ________[6]________ ("Business").

Buyer desires to purchase from the Seller the aforesaid Business, as a going concern free of all obligations and liabilities and exclusive of cash and receivables.

In consideration of the mutual terms, conditions and covenants hereinafter set forth Seller and Buyer agree as follows:

1. Seller shall sell to Buyer the Business owned and operated by the Seller as a going concern. Such sale shall include the assets as shown on Schedule A attached hereto, which shall include but not be limited to: goodwill; assignment of trade names, trademarks and copyrights, if any; assignment of the lease for the premises at ________[7]________; all furniture and fixtures, supplies and equipment located in the premises on the date of closing; all records pertaining to the operation of the Business; all contracts between the Business and third parties;

(Document continued on next page)

8. The total price, in numbers, for the sale of the business.

Note: Nos. 9, 10 and 11 should be arrived at in consultation with a tax advisor as there are specific tax consequences regarding the allocation which may change according to the current federal and state tax laws.

9. The amount, in numbers, attributed to the physical assets of Schedule A.

10. The amount, in numbers, attributed to the intangible assets, i.e. goodwill.

11. The amount, in numbers, attributed to the restrictive covenant (the non-compete provision).

12. The amount, in numbers, to be paid on signing the Agreement.

13. The amount, in numbers, to be paid on the closing date.

14. The amount, in numbers, to be paid by promissory notes.

all other assets necessary to the operation of the Business, and pre-paid expenses.

2. This sale does not include any cash on hand or in banks at the date of closing. This sale does not include any accounts receivable due to Seller at the date of closing or those that accrue after the date of closing attributable to acts that occurred prior to or on the date of closing.

3. All proceeds received by Buyer in payment of accounts receivable due to Seller as listed on Schedule B, attached hereto, shall upon receipt be immediately turned over to Seller in the form in which they are received. Seller covenants that these funds shall be deposited in a separate account and shall be first used to pay all accounts payable incurred by Seller in the conduct of the Business prior to the closing date.

4. All accounts payable, liabilities and obligations incurred by Seller in the conduct of the Business up to the date of closing shall be paid by the Seller, and Seller shall hold the Buyer harmless against such amounts. Buyer is not acquiring, directly, any of Seller's liabilities by operation of law or otherwise.

5. The purchase price for the assets transferred pursuant to the Agreement and Schedule A is $_____[8]_____ of which $_____[9]_____ is attributable to the physical assets on Schedule A, $_____[10]_____ is attributable to goodwill, trade name, and other intangible assets of the agency, and $_____[11]_____ is attributable to the restrictive covenants of paragraph 7 herein. Payment shall be made: $_____[12]_____ upon the signing of this Agreement; $_____[13]_____ in cash or certified check upon the closing date; and $_____[14]_____ represented by promissory note(s) as attached hereto as Schedule C.

6. Until the closing date Seller agrees to conduct the Business in the same manner in which it has heretofore been conducted and shall not without the written consent of the Buyer increase the compensation or employee benefits to any employee or employees.

7. Seller shall not for a period of two (2) years from the closing date through any entity in which Seller has an ownership or management interest or control:

(Document continued on next page)

(a) Compete, either directly or indirectly, with the Business for the products and services provided by the Business within the geographic areas in which the Business operates as of the date of closing.

(b) Solicit any individuals or businesses who were customers of the Seller prior to closing or disclose any information about said customers to any person, company or other legal entity.

(c) Directly or indirectly induce, or attempt to influence, any employee of the Business to terminate their employment.

8. Seller represents and warrants to Buyer:

(a) All assets transferred pursuant to this Agreement, except as otherwise noted in Schedule A, are free of any and all liens, security interests, claims and encumbrances.

(b) Seller is not in breach or default of any contract, lease or other commitment to be assigned pursuant to this Agreement and will not commit a breach or act of default to the date of closing.

(c) Seller makes no representation or warranty as to the future conduct of the Business and the continued relationship with the customers of the Business.

(d) Other than those attached to this Agreement there are no outstanding leases; employment agreements; employee pension, retirement or union agreements.

(e) Seller has not engaged a broker for the sale represented by this Agreement. Each party hereto agrees to indemnify and hold the other harmless from any broker's or finder's fee or alleged broker's or finder's fee incurred by the other party, or any claim by any party that the other entered into an agreement calling for a broker's or finder's fee.

(f) All inventory transferred herein is merchantable.

(Document continued on next page)

(g) All furniture, fixtures and equipment transferred by the Seller are in good condition and repair and free from any defect or condition that would materially affect their operation, excepting normal wear and tear.

(h) No special consents are required to carry out the transactions contemplated by this Agreement.

(i) Seller has complied with all applicable provisions for Bulk Transfers, U.C.C. Article 6.

The above representations and warranties shall survive closing.

9. Buyer hereby agrees to assume the lease(s) for the premises at __________[7]__________ and hereby indemnifies and agrees to hold Seller harmless from any liability thereunder.

10. Buyer agrees to indemnify and hold Seller harmless from any liability arising out of any agreement or commitment initiated by Seller and which is continued by Buyer after the date of closing.

11. The closing shall take place on ________[15]________ at ____[16]____ at the offices of ___________[17]___________.

IN WITNESS WHEREOF, the parties have executed this Agreement.

__________*[18]*__________

*BY*______________________
[19] (Seller)

__________*[20]*__________

*BY*______________________
[21] (Buyer)

(Document continued on next page)

15. The date of the closing.

16. The time of the closing.

17. The location of the closing, typically the office of the Seller's attorney.

18. The name of the Seller if a corporation. Otherwise delete the line.

19. If the Seller is an individual, delete "BY" and print the Seller's name directly below the line, with the Seller to sign above the line. If the Seller is a corporation, print the name and title of the individual acting for the corporation directly below the line, with that person to sign above the line.

20. The name of the Buyer if a corporation. Otherwise delete the line.

21. If the Buyer is an individual, delete "BY" and print the Buyer's name directly below the line, with the Buyer to sign above the line. If the Buyer is a corporation, print the name and title of the individual acting for the corporation directly below the line, with that person to sign above the line.

SCHEDULE A

LIST OF ASSETS

PHYSICAL ASSETS

Quantity	Description and Location	Lien, Security Agreement,etc.

INTANGIBLE ASSETS

Description

SCHEDULE B

ACCOUNTS RECEIVABLE

Account Name	Date Due	Invoice No.	Amount

SCHEDULE C

PROMISSORY NOTES

Lender	Date Due	Amount

AGREEMENT FOR THE PURCHASE/ SALE OF CORPORATE STOCK (7-02)

This Agreement is used when the Stock of an existing corporation is purchased. In a Stock purchase, the Purchaser buys the existing company as a going concern with all of its assets and liabilities. The method of purchase chosen (Stock versus Assets) should be made in consultation with a tax advisor since each method has different tax consequences to both the Seller and Purchaser. This Agreement also requires a Stock Power which is found elsewhere in this book. (See also the preceding Agreement for the Purchase/Sale of A Business/Assets.)

Note that the Agreement also requires that any promissory notes be listed on Schedule A. Follow the style shown at the end of this form.

1. The date the Agreement is signed.

2. The names of the Sellers. This form assumes two Sellers (referred to in the singular as "Seller" in the form). Add or delete spaces as required to accommodate the actual number of names.

3. The name of the Purchaser.

4. If the Purchaser is a corporation, insert the state in which incorporated. Otherwise delete.

5. The name of the corporation whose stock is being sold.

6. The state of incorporation of the corporation whose stock is being sold.

7. The numbers of the stock certificates representing the shares of stock.

8. The total number of shares being sold, in numbers.

AGREEMENT FOR THE PURCHASE/
SALE OF CORPORATE STOCK

AGREEMENT made this __[1]__ day of __________ ,19__ by and between ________[2]________ and ________[2]________ (collectively the "Seller") and ________[3]________ *[4][, a ________ corporation]* ("Purchaser").

Seller is the owner of all of the outstanding shares of stock of ________[5]________, a _____[6]_____ corporation ("Corporation") and is desirous of selling its shares; and

Purchaser is desirous of purchasing all of the outstanding shares of the Corporation.

In consideration of the mutual terms, conditions and covenants hereinafter set forth Seller and Purchaser agree as follows:

1. Seller hereby sells to the Purchaser and the Purchaser hereby purchases from the Seller all of the outstanding shares of stock of the Corporation, represented by Certificates Numbers ____________[7]____________, totaling ____[8]____ shares of the Common Stock of the Corporation.

2. Seller warrants and represents that he is the owner of the shares of stock referred to in paragraph 1 above; that such shares constitute all of the outstanding shares of stock of the Corporation; that he owns all of the shares of stock free and clear of all mortgages, pledges, liens, encumbrances, charges and claims; that he has the right, power and authority to enter into this Agreement, and to transfer and deliver the shares of stock heretofore owned by him to

(Document continued on next page)

9. The price, in numbers, per share of stock being sold.

10. The price, in numbers, of all of the shares of stock being sold. (Note: the purchase price is usually arrived at by valuing the assets and adding an amount for the value of an ongoing, profitable business.)

11. The amount, in numbers, to be paid on signing the Agreement.

12. The amount, in numbers, to be paid on the closing date (the date the transaction is to be completed).

13. The closing date.

14. The amount, in numbers, to be paid by Promissory Note.

15. The name and address of the Escrow Agent who will hold the shares of stock and Stock Power, typically the attorney for the Seller.

the Purchaser; and that there are no actions, suits, claims or litigation pending or threatened against or affecting the ownership by him of the shares transferred or delivered to the Purchaser. He further warrants and covenants that the delivery by him of the Certificates for such shares accompanied by a Stock Power, as hereinafter provided for, is sufficient to and does transfer and convey full and clear title to all of the shares reflected by the Certificates to the Purchaser, and that he will make, execute and deliver such further instruments as may be required to confirm said transfer.

3. The purchase price for the shares shall be $__[9]__ per share for a total of $_____[10]_____. Payment shall be made: $_____[11]_____ upon the signing of this Agreement; $_____[12]_____ in cash or certified check upon the closing date, ________[13]________; and $_____[14]_____ represented by promissory notes as attached hereto as Schedule A.

4. To secure the payment of the purchase price to the Seller by the Purchaser the shares of stock shall be delivered to ________________[15]________________ ("Escrow Agent"), to be held in escrow, together with a Stock Power executed by Seller with his signature guaranteed by the Escrow Agent.

5. The Escrow Agent shall hold the shares in escrow and shall deliver them to the Purchaser upon payment to the Seller of the last payment. In the event that the Purchaser fails to make any of the above payments on the due date or within 60 days of demand thereafter, the Escrow Agent shall deliver said shares to the Seller. Upon delivery in either instance the Escrow Agent shall be relieved of all responsibility and liability.

6. Seller shall have the right, and may delegate such right to anyone of his choice, to inspect the books and records of the Corporation to verify any and all statements upon which the purchase price was based. Said inspection shall be on 48 hours' notice and is to be conducted during normal business hours at the Corporation's place of business.

7. Seller (and each of them if more than one), has heretofore been employed by the Corporation, and acknowledges that he has been paid and received all pay-

(Document continued on next page)

AGREEMENT FOR THE PURCHASE/ SALE OF CORPORATE STOCK *continued*

16. The most recent tax year for which the Sellers state that corporate taxes have been paid.

17. The most recent tax year for which the Sellers will protect the Purchaser from the payment of any taxes.

ments and compensation of any kind or character at any time due to him by reason thereof. He further warrants, represents and acknowledges that: (a) he has no claims of any kind whatsoever, whether as an employee, stockholder or otherwise, against the Corporation, or any of its officers, directors or stockholders; (b) he has not since the termination of his employment by the Corporation incurred any obligation for which the Corporation may be liable; (c) he knows of no fact which could justify or sustain the imposition of a liability on the Corporation other than the liabilities reflected on the Corporation's balance sheet.

8. Seller holds harmless and indemnifies the Purchaser for and on account of any loss, damage and expense incurred by the Purchaser by reason of the assertion by the Seller or on his behalf of any claim contrary to the terms of this Agreement, any breach of any of the foregoing warranties or any misrepresentation of the foregoing facts.

9. Seller confirms that as far as he is aware, all corporate taxes have been fully paid up to and including the calendar year __[16]__, and there is no reason for the imposition of any additional tax or penalty. In any event, Seller will indemnify and hold Purchaser harmless against any cost, expense or liability by reason of the imposition upon the Corporation of any additional income or other taxes and penalties (including interest) for the years up to and including __[17]__.

10. Seller agrees to cooperate with the Purchaser for an orderly transition of the business. Seller shall, simultaneously with the execution of this Agreement, deliver to Purchaser its resignation as officers and directors of the corporation.

11. Any notices to be delivered under the terms of this

(Document continued on next page)

18. The address where the Sellers are to receive notices.

19. The address where the Purchaser is to receive notices.

20. The name of the Escrow Agent printed directly below the line, with that person to sign above the line.

21. The name of each Seller printed directly below the line, with each Seller to sign above the line. Add or delete lines as required to accommodate the actual number of names.

22. The name of the Purchaser if a corporation. Otherwise delete the line.

23. If the Purchaser is an individual, delete "BY" and print the Purchaser's name directly below the line, with the Purchaser to sign above the line. If the Purchaser is a corporation, print the name and title of the individual acting for the corporation directly below the line, with that person to sign above the line.

Agreement shall be sent certified mail, return receipt requested to:

If to Seller: __________[18]__________

____

____

If to Purchaser: __________[19]__________

____

____

12. This Agreement shall be binding upon the successors, heirs, executors, administrators and assigns of the parties hereto.

IN WITNESS WHEREOF, the parties hereto have executed this Agreement as of the date first above written.

ESCROW ACCEPTED:

____
[21] (Seller)

____
[20] (Escrow Agent)

____
[21] (Seller)

________*[22]*________

*BY*__________________
[23] (Purchaser)

SCHEDULE A

PROMISSORY NOTES

Lender	Date Due	Amount

INTRODUCTION TO BULK TRANSFERS

A Bulk Transfer is a sale or transfer in bulk—meaning a sale or transfer: 1) of a major portion (more than 50%) of the materials, supplies, merchandise or other inventory of the seller, and 2) which is NOT in the ordinary course of the Transferor's (the seller's) business. If, for example, it is customary to sell off a wholesaler's entire inventory of summer merchandise before receipt of fall merchandise, such a sale is not a Bulk Transfer because it is in the ordinary course of the seller's business.

The purpose of the law of Bulk Transfers is to protect creditors from unknowingly losing rights in a debtor's assets by advising creditors that a Bulk Transfer is to take place. The following forms must be used to comply with the provisions of the Uniform Commercial Code. Failure to do so makes the buyer (Transferee) responsible for the seller's (Transferor's) debts related to the transferred assets.

The Bulk Transfer (also called Bulk Sale) of the assets is governed by the Uniform Commercial Code (the "U.C.C."), a set of uniform laws adopted by all states (except Louisiana and the Commonwealth of Puerto Rico). There are, however, slight variations from state to state and it is advisable to determine if the following forms are applicable for your state or if other forms are required. For example, New York State requires the filing of a form with the state tax authority (the New York State Department of Taxation and Finance) advising of a Bulk Transfer. Check with your tax advisor concerning such additional requirements.

There are statutory provisions exempting certain sales or transfers: (1) transfers given as security for the performance of an obligation; (2) general assignments for the benefit of creditors; (3) transfers made because of a security agreement or lien; (4) sales by executors, administrators, receivers, trustees in bankruptcy, or any public officer under court order; (5) sales made in the course of judicial or administrative proceedings for the dissolution or reorganization of a corporation in accordance with notice to all creditors and an order of the court or administrative agency; (6) sales or transfers to a person or corporation within the state who agrees to pay the debts of the transferor in full, and who gives public notice of that fact and is financially solvent; (7) transfers to a new business organized to take over and continue the old business, if public notice is given and the new business assumes the debts of the old business; and (8) transfers of property which are exempt from execution.

Note: the Agreement for the Purchase/Sale of a Business/Assets in this chapter may be a Bulk Transfer requiring the use of Bulk Transfer forms (however, see exemptions 6 and 7 above).

BULK TRANSFER— SCHEDULE OF PROPERTY (7-03)

A Schedule of Property is required in a Bulk Transfer so that creditors who may have a lien or security interest in certain assets can be made aware of the assets being transferred. The party to whom the assets are to be transferred is required to keep the schedule for six months from the date of the transfer and must permit all creditors to inspect and/or copy the schedule. See the Demand for List of Creditors and Known Claimants that follows.

BULK TRANSFER— SCHEDULE OF PROPERTY

1. Choose one.

2. The name of the party receiving the assets.

3. The name of the party selling, transferring or assigning the assets.

4. The date the transfer is to occur, which must be at least 10 days subsequent to delivery.

5. Choose one. If more space is required to list the items being transferred, on a separate sheet headed "Schedule A" list the items (see the example in No. 7 below) and then skip to No. 9.

The full and detailed inventory, including quantity, description and cost, so far as possible with the exercise of due diligence, of the assets to be *[1][sold]* ***OR*** *[transferred]* ***OR*** *[assigned]* to ________[2]________ by ________[3]________ on ________[4]________ is *[5][as is more fully set forth on the annexed Schedule A.]* ***OR*** *[as follows:* ____ ____.*]*

(Document continued on next page)

BULK TRANSFER— SCHEDULE OF PROPERTY *continued*

6. Choose one.

7. The quantity and description of the assets. Note: the description must sufficiently identify the goods depending on the type of business. For example, "30 gross, screws" would be insufficient for a machine shop or hardware store (which has vast quantities of assorted screws) but probably would be sufficient for a textile business. "30 gross, 1 1/4" No. 8 flat head screws" would be sufficient for a hardware store.

8. The cost of the assets to the party selling, transferring or assigning.

9. The city and state where the schedule is signed.

10. The date the schedule is signed.

11. If the sale, transfer or assignment is being made by a corporation, the name of the corporation. Otherwise delete the line.

12. If the sale, transfer or assignment is being made by an individual, delete "BY" and print the seller's name directly below the line, with the seller to sign above the line. If the seller is a corporation, print the name and title of the individual acting for the corporation directly below the line, with the individual to sign above the line.

QUANTITY	*DESCRIPTION*	*[6][COST TO [SELLER]* ***OR*** *[TRANSFEROR]* ***OR*** *[ASSIGNOR]*
[7]	*[7]*	*[8]*
[7]	*[7]*	*[8]*
[7]	*[7]*	*[8]*
[7]	*[7]*	*[8]*
[7]	*[7]*	*[8]*
[7]	*[7]*	*[8]*

Dated: ________[9]________

______[10]______, 19__ ________*[11]*________

*BY*__________________
[12]

BULK TRANSFER— LIST OF CREDITORS AND KNOWN CLAIMANTS (7-04)

In a Bulk Transfer, the party selling, transferring or assigning assets is required to provide to the party receiving the assets a complete List of Creditors and Known Claimants (people who have made a claim but which the selling, transferring or assigning party disputes). This document is typically prepared and served by an officer of the corporation, an accountant from the corporation, or another party having knowledge of the Creditors.

1. The state where the document is signed.
2. The county where the document is signed.
3. The name of the individual signing the document.
4. Delete through No. 6 if the party selling, transferring or assigning the assets is an individual and skip to No. 7.
5. The title of the corporate officer signing the document.
6. The name of the corporation selling, transferring or assigning the assets.
7. The name of the party receiving the assets.
8. The name of the individual or corporation selling, transferring or assigning the assets.
9. The name of the creditor.
10. The business address of the creditor.
11. The amount of the creditor's claim.
12. The name of the claimant.
13. The business address of the claimant.
14. The amount of the disputed claim.

BULK TRANSFER—
LIST OF CREDITORS AND
KNOWN CLAIMANTS

STATE OF ______[1]______)
COUNTY OF _____[2]______) ss.:

________[3]________, being duly sworn, deposes *[4][and states that he is the _____[5]_____ of ________[6]________]* and certifies to ________[7]________ and to all whom it may concern:

The following is a full, accurate and complete list of the creditors of ________[8]________ and the indebtedness to each, to the best of the information and belief of deponent as they appear on the books and records of ________[8]________, and all other persons known to assert a claim against ________[8]________:

CREDITOR	BUSINESS ADDRESS	AMOUNT OF INDEBTEDNESS
[9]	[10]	[11]
[9]	[10]	[11]
[9]	[10]	[11]
[9]	[10]	[11]
[9]	[10]	[11]
[9]	[10]	[11]

CLAIMANT	BUSINESS ADDRESS	AMOUNT OF DISPUTED CLAIM
[12]	[13]	[14]
[12]	[13]	[14]
[12]	[13]	[14]
[12]	[13]	[14]

(Document continued on next page)

BULK TRANSFER— LIST OF CREDITORS AND KNOWN CLAIMANTS *continued*

15. Choose one.

16. The date of sale, transfer or assignment of the assets.

17. The name of the person in No. 3 printed below the line, with that person to sign above the line.

18. The Notary Public completes this part of the form, and signs and seals it by affixing his stamp or seal.

This certificate is made and intended to comply with Section 6-104 of the Uniform Commercial Code in connection with the *[15][sale]* ***OR*** *[transfer]* ***OR*** *[assignment]* of assets by ________[8]________ to ________[7]________ on ________[16]________, 19__.

____
[17]

Sworn to before me this

_[18]_ day of ________, 19__

____
Notary Public

BULK TRANSFER—
DEMAND FOR LIST OF CREDITORS AND KNOWN CLAIMANTS (7-05)

It is recommended that the party receiving the assets from a Bulk Transfer make a formal written request for the names of all the creditors and claimants. The purpose of this Demand is to assure the buyer that he has the names of all Creditors and Known Claimants.

BULK TRANSFER—
DEMAND FOR LIST OF CREDITORS AND
KNOWN CLAIMANTS

1. The name and address of the party selling, transferring or assigning the assets.

2. The name of the party receiving the assets.

3. The date of the Demand.

4. If the Demand is being made by a corporation, the name of the corporation. Otherwise delete the line.

5. If the Demand is being made by an individual, delete "BY" and print the individual's name directly below the line, with the individual to sign above the line. If a corporation, print the name and title of the person acting for the corporation directly below the line, with that person to sign above the line.

TO: ________[1]________
____
____

PLEASE TAKE NOTICE that pursuant to Section 6-104 of the Uniform Commercial Code the undersigned, ________[2]________, hereby demands a list of your creditors and known claimants, together with their last known business address and either the amount of the indebtedness or claim (even if disputed) of each. Said list is to be certified, under oath as provided for by statute.

Dated: ________[3]________

__________*[4]*__________

*BY*____________________
[5]

BULK TRANSFER—
NOTICE TO CREDITORS AND KNOWN CLAIMANTS (7-06)

This form should be sent to all Creditors and Claimants of the party selling, transferring or assigning the assets in a Bulk Transfer. If the Notice is not sent to each Creditor and known Claimant, the Bulk Transfer will not be binding on them and each may sue for payment from both the party selling, transferring or assigning the assets and from the party receiving the assets. The Notice should be delivered personally or sent by Certified Mail—Return Receipt Requested at least ten days before possession of the goods or payment for the goods, whichever occurs first.

BULK TRANSFER—
NOTICE TO CREDITORS AND KNOWN CLAIMANTS

1. The name of the party selling, transferring or assigning the assets (the Transferor).

2. The name of the party receiving the assets (the Transferee).

3. The date the transfer is to become effective.

4. A general description of the assets.

5. The address where the Schedule of Property and list of creditors will be kept.

6. The address of the Transferor.

7. The address of the Transferee.

8. Any other name or address used by the Transferor. Note: if there is none, insert the word "none."

9. Choose one.

10. The name and address where creditors are to send their bills for payment.

TO: Creditors and Claimants of ________[1]________, Transferor:

PLEASE TAKE NOTICE that you and each of you are HEREBY NOTIFIED pursuant to Sections 6-105 and 6-107 of the Uniform Commercial Code as follows:

1. The Transferor, ________[1]________, is to transfer to ________[2]________, Transferee, on ________[3]________, in bulk the ________[4]________, all of which are listed and described in a Schedule of Property which, with a list of the creditors and claimants, is available for inspection and copying by any creditor or claimant during normal business hours at the office of the Transferee located at __________[5]__________.

2. The name and business addresses of the Transferor and Transferee are:

Transferor:	Transferee:
_____[1]_____	_______[2]______
_____[6]_____	_______[7]______
______________	________________

3. All other business names and addresses of the Transferor used within the past three (3) years are: ______________________[8]____________________.

4. *[9][All of the debts of the Transferor are to be paid in full as they fall due as a result of this transaction and creditors should send their bills to: _______[10]_______ _________________.]* ***OR*** *[The debts of the Transferor are not to be paid in full as they fall due as a result of this transaction.]* ***OR*** *[The Transferee is in doubt if the debts of*

(Document continued on next page)

BULK TRANSFER—
NOTICE TO CREDITORS AND KNOWN CLAIMANTS *continued*

11. The location where the assets are to be found and a general description of the assets.

12. The dollar amount, in numbers, of the estimated total of the Transferor's debts.

13. The location where the Schedule of Property and the list of creditors is to be kept.

14. Choose one. If "is not to pay existing debts" is chosen then delete the remainder of the paragraph through No. 16.

15. The name of each creditor who will be paid.

16. The dollar amount of the claim to be paid, in numbers.

17. Choose one. If no payment (new consideration) is to be made, skip to No. 21.

18. The dollar amount, in numbers, of the payment being made upon the transfer.

19. The date the payment will be paid.

20. The location where the payment will be made.

21. The date of the Notice.

22. If the Notice is being sent by a corporation, the name of the corporation. Otherwise delete the line.

23. If the Notice is being sent by an individual, delete "BY" and print the individual's name directly below the line, with the individual to sign above the line. If a corporation, print the name and title of the person acting for the corporation directly below the line, with that person to sign above the line.

the Transferor will be paid in full as a result of this transaction.]

(a) The location and general description of the assets to be transferred is
__________________[11]____________________
____
and the estimated total of the Transferor's debts is $______[12]______.

(b) The Schedule of Property and List of Creditors and Known Claimants is located at:
__________[13]__________.

(c) The Transfer *[14][is not to pay existing debts.]* ***OR*** *[is to pay existing debts and the amount of such debt and to whom owing is:*

CREDITOR	*AMOUNT*
[15]	*[16]*
[15]	*[16]*
[15]	*[16]*

(d) The Transfer *[17][is not for new consideration.]* ***OR*** *[is for new consideration of $_____[18]_____ to be paid on ______[19]______ at _________[20]__________.]*

Dated: ______[21]_____ __________*[22]*_________

*BY*____________________
[23]

BULK TRANSFER—
NOTICE OF INTENDED BULK TRANSFER
BY AUCTION SALE (7-07)

If a Bulk Transfer is made by sale at Auction, the Auctioneer must send notice to all creditors and claimants. The failure to do so will result in the Auctioneer being liable to the creditors up to the amount realized at the auction even if the money generated by the Auction is to be paid to the Transferor. A separate notice must be sent to each creditor or claimant, either by personal delivery or by Certified Mail—Return Receipt Requested at least ten days before the Auction.

1. The name and address of the creditor or known claimant.

2. The name of the Auctioneer.

3. The name and address of the Transferor.

4. Any other name or address used by the Transferor. If there is none, insert the word "none."

5. The address of the location of the auction.

6. The city in which the auction will be held.

7. The county in which the auction will be held.

8. The state in which the auction will be held.

9. The time of the auction.

10. Choose one.

11. The date of the auction.

12. The location of the assets being auctioned.

13. A general description of the assets to be auctioned.

BULK TRANSFER—
NOTICE OF INTENDED BULK TRANSFER
BY AUCTION SALE

TO: ________[1]________
____
____

PLEASE TAKE NOTICE that pursuant to Section 6-108 of the Uniform Commercial Code:

1. ________[2]________, Auctioneer, will sell at public auction certain property of ________[3]________, Transferor.

2. To the best of Auctioneer's knowledge, the Transferor has not used any business name or address, except as above, during the past three (3) years other than: ______________________[4]______________________.

3. The auction will be held at __________[5]__________, City of _____[6]_____, County of _____[7]_____, State of ____[8]_____, at ___[9]___ *[10][A.M.]* ***OR*** *[P.M.]* on _____[11]____, 19__.

4. The property to be sold is located at __________[12]__________ and is described as follows: ______________________[13]______________________
____.

(Document continued on next page)

BULK TRANSFER— NOTICE OF INTENDED BULK TRANSFER BY AUCTION SALE *continued*

14. The estimated dollar amount, in numbers, of the Transferor's debts.

15. The location of the Schedule of Property and the List of Creditors and Known Claimants.

16. The date by which creditors and known claimants must file their claims.

17. The name and address where claims are to be filed.

18. The date of the Notice.

19. If the auctioneer is a corporation, the name of the corporation. Otherwise delete the line.

20. If the auction will be conducted by an individual, delete "BY" and print the individual's name directly below the line, with the individual to sign above the line. If the auction will be conducted by a corporation, print the name and title of the person acting on behalf of the corporation directly below the line, with that person to sign above the line.

5. The estimated total of Transferor's debts is $_____[14]_____.

6. The Schedule of Property and list of creditors and known claimants may be inspected at _____________[15]_____________.

7. Creditors of the Transferor must file their claims in writing on or before ________[16]________ with ______________________[17]______________________.

Dated: ________[18]________

__________*[19]*__________

*BY*______________________
[20]

General Contract Clauses 8

This chapter contains general clauses that are advisable to include in most contracts. The clauses deal with issues that are not specific to any particular kind of transaction but rather are applicable to most transactions. These clauses should be reviewed to determine which should be included in a contract. Without the so-called "boilerplate" provisions contained in this chapter, problems may arise after a contract has been signed.

CONTRACT CLAUSE—INDEMNIFICATION/ HOLD HARMLESS (8-01)

In many types of agreements one party will agree to indemnify and hold the other party harmless (not responsible) in the event of a lawsuit or claim by a third party (any person who is not a party to the agreement) relating to the subject of the agreement. An agreement to Indemnify/Hold Harmless can be either a free-standing agreement (such as the form found elsewhere in this book) or it can be made part of an agreement.

CONTRACT CLAUSE—INDEMNIFICATION/ HOLD HARMLESS

[1] INDEMNIFICATION/HOLD HARMLESS - ________[2]________ irrevocably covenants, promises and agrees to indemnify ________[3]________ and to hold ________[3]________ harmless from and against any and all losses, claims, expenses, suits, damages, costs, demands or liabilities, joint or several, of whatever kind or nature which ________[3]________ may sustain or to which ________[3]________ may become subject arising out of or relating in any way to ________[4]________ including, without limitation, in each case attorneys' fees, costs and expenses actually incurred in defending against or enforcing any such losses, claims, expenses, suits, damages or liabilities.

1. The number of this paragraph when inserted into a contract.

2. The name of the party giving the Indemnification.

3. The name of the party being indemnified.

4. Insert either "the subject matter of this agreement" or describe what the Indemnification is for; i.e. "the sale of widgets."

CONTRACT CLAUSE—AUDIT OF BOOKS AND RECORDS (8-02)

In a partnership or joint venture agreement, or in an agreement that involves payment of commission or royalty, it is important to have the ability to inspect and Audit the Books to verify the condition of the business and to insure proper payments.

CONTRACT CLAUSE—AUDIT OF BOOKS AND RECORDS

[1] AUDIT OF BOOKS AND RECORDS - The books, records, reports and accounts of the __________[2]__________ shall be kept at all times so as to accurately reflect the business and financial condition of the __________[2]__________. Said books, etc. shall be kept at ___________[3]____________ or at such other location as may be mutually agreed upon in writing. Upon _____[4]_____ written notice, given to the other(s), any party may audit and inspect said books, records, reports and accounts during normal business hours.

1. The number of this paragraph when inserted into a contract.
2. The name of the company, partnership, joint venture, etc.
3. The address where the books, etc. are to be kept.
4. A time period, in words and numbers, i.e. forty-eight (48) hours, three (3) business days, etc.

CONTRACT CLAUSE—NOTICE PROVISION (8-03)

Almost every agreement requires notification to one or the other of the parties regarding specific events (for example, the change of address for the sending of payments). Such notification is referred to as giving Notice.

CONTRACT CLAUSE—NOTICE PROVISION

1. The number of this paragraph when inserted into a contract.

2. A number of days, in words and numbers, that is reasonable for Notice sent by mail to be received, i.e. five (5).

3. The name and address of each party who would be entitled to receive Notice under the agreement.

[1] NOTICE PROVISION - All notices required or permitted to be given hereunder shall be in writing and may be delivered personally or by U.S. Mail, postage prepaid. Receipt of notice shall be deemed to have been given upon receipt if personally delivered or within ____[2]____ (__) days after being deposited in the U.S. Mails. Notice shall be addressed:

If to: __________[3]__________

__________[3]__________

__________[3]__________

If to: __________[3]__________

__________[3]__________

__________[3]__________

CONTRACT CLAUSE—ARBITRATION
(Covering the Entire Agreement) (8-04)

The parties to a contract may decide that in the event of a dispute, resolution through the usual means (lawyers and the court system) would take too long and be too costly. The alternative is an agreement to submit disputes to the American Arbitration Association.

The decision by the parties to submit any dispute to Arbitration must be clearly spelled out in the contract. Because Arbitration will eliminate a party's opportunity to have his day in court, the law will insist on a clear, unequivocal written expression of this wish in the agreement.

This is the standard Arbitration clause recommended by the American Arbitration Association for commercial Arbitration. For a list of regional offices and a copy of the Commercial Arbitration Rules contact:

American Arbitration Association
140 West 51st Street
New York, NY 10020-1203
Tel: (212) 484-4000
Fax: (212) 765-4874

CONTRACT CLAUSE—ARBITRATION

1. The number of this paragraph when inserted into a contract.

[1] ARBITRATION - Any controversy or claim arising out of or relating to this contract, or the breach thereof, shall be settled by arbitration in accordance with the Commercial Arbitration Rules of the American Arbitration Association, and judgment upon the award rendered by the arbitrator(s) may be entered in any court having jurisdiction thereof.

CONTRACT CLAUSE—ARBITRATION CLAUSE
(Covering Specific Parts of the Agreement) (8-05)

This Arbitration clause is specific as to what portions of an agreement are subject to Arbitration. It also requires the Arbitration to be in a specific location. For example, if you are in Philadelphia and the other party is in Los Angeles, it would be to your advantage to have the Arbitration in Philadelphia.

For a list of regional offices and a copy of the Commercial Arbitration Rules contact:

American Arbitration Association
140 West 51st Street
New York, NY 10020-1203
Tel: (212) 484-4000
Fax: (212) 765-4874

CONTRACT CLAUSE—ARBITRATION

[1] ARBITRATION - Any controversy or claim arising out of or relating to __________[2]__________ of this contract shall be settled by arbitration in ____________[3]____________, in accordance with the Commercial Arbitration Rules of The American Arbitration Association, and judgment upon the award rendered by the arbitrator(s) may be entered in any court having jurisdiction thereof.

1. The number of this paragraph when inserted into a contract.

2. A list of the paragraphs of the contract that are to be subject to Arbitration.

3. The city and state where Arbitration will take place, typically the location of one of the parties.

CONTRACT CLAUSE—GOVERNING LAW (8-06)

If the parties to an agreement are from different states, the agreement should contain a clause setting forth which state's laws should control the legal interpretation of the contract.

CONTRACT CLAUSE—GOVERNING LAW

1. The number of this paragraph when inserted into a contract.

2. The name of the state whose laws will govern.

[1] GOVERNING LAW - This Agreement shall be construed in accordance with and governed by the laws of the State of ______[2]______, irrespective of the fact that a party hereto may not be a resident of or maintain a place of business in that State.

CONTRACT CLAUSE—JURISDICTION FOR COURT ACTION (8-07)

The purpose of this provision is to set forth where any lawsuit or action will be filed. It prevents one party from commencing a suit or action in a state that is inconvenient to the other.

CONTRACT CLAUSE—JURISDICTION FOR COURT ACTION

1. The number of this paragraph when inserted into a contract.

2. The state in which the suit or action is to be filed.

3. There may be more than one federal district court in a state; therefore name the city and state to eliminate any doubt.

[1] JURISDICTION FOR COURT ACTION - The court and authorities of the State of _____[2]_____ or the federal district court having venue for __________[3]__________ shall have jurisdiction over all controversies that may arise with respect to this Agreement, the parties hereby waiving any other venue to which they might be entitled by virtue of domicile or otherwise. Should either party initiate or bring a suit or action before any other courts, it is agreed that upon application any such suit or action shall be dismissed, without prejudice, and may be filed in accordance with this provision. The party bringing the suit or action before a court not agreed to herein shall pay to the other party all the costs of seeking dismissal including reasonable attorneys' fees.

CONTRACT CLAUSE—TRADE SECRETS (8-08)

If the subject matter of an agreement requires divulging information that would be regarded as a trade secret, i.e. a customer list, method of manufacture or the like, this clause should be considered.

CONTRACT CLAUSE—TRADE SECRETS

1. The number of this paragraph when inserted into a contract.

2. The name of the party who will be restricted.

3. The name of the business to be protected.

4. A number of years, in words and numbers. It has to be reasonable in duration, i.e. two (2) or three (3) years.

[1] TRADE SECRETS - ________[2]________ shall not divulge to any person, firm or firms, corporation or corporations, any trade secret having to do with the business of __________[3]__________ that shall come to the knowledge of ________[2]________ by reason of this Agreement and the relationship of ________[2]________ and __________[3]__________ created by this Agreement, during the term of this Agreement and for _____[4]_____ (__) years after the termination of this Agreement.

CONTRACT CLAUSE—CORPORATE AUTHORITY TO ENTER INTO AGREEMENT (8-09)

If a corporation is a party to an agreement and the agreement contemplates an act that would require approval of the Board of Directors, then this clause should be part of the agreement. This would include such matters as the sale of an asset or hiring a consultant, but not an act in the normal course of business, such as the sale of manufactured goods.

Note: most extraordinary matters, such as a merger, would require shareholder approval in addition to Board authorization.

CONTRACT CLAUSE—CORPORATE AUTHORITY TO ENTER INTO AGREEMENT

1. The number of this paragraph when inserted into a contract.

2. The name of the corporation.

[1] CORPORATE AUTHORITY - ________[2]________ has the full corporate power, authority and right to enter into this Agreement and to perform the acts contemplated herein. The Board of Directors of ________[2]________ has taken all necessary action to duly authorize the execution, delivery and performance of this Agreement which actions are reflected in the minute book of the corporation.

CONTRACT CLAUSE—WAIVER NOT TO BE CONSTRUED AS WAIVER OF SUBSEQUENT DEFAULTS (8-10)

The concept of a Waiver refers to a person giving up rights to which he would otherwise be entitled. The inclusion of this provision permits the Waiver of a breach or default of an agreement without setting a precedent as to future breaches or defaults. If, for example, a contract provides that the other party is to make monthly payments to you by a certain date, and you choose not to object if a payment is late, this clause will prevent the other party from using your lack of objection as an indication that future late payments will be acceptable under the contract.

CONTRACT CLAUSE—WAIVER NOT TO BE CONSTRUED AS WAIVER OF SUBSEQUENT DEFAULTS

1. The number of this paragraph when inserted into a contract.

[1] NO WAIVER OF DEFAULTS - No waiver of any term, provision or condition of this Agreement, the breach or default thereof, by conduct or otherwise, in one or more instances shall be deemed to be either a continuing waiver or a waiver of a subsequent breach or default of any such term, provision or condition of this Agreement.

CONTRACT CLAUSE—FORCE MAJEURE (8-11)

In agreements where performance may be affected by events beyond the control of a party, for example a fire at a manufacturing plant, this provision will afford protection.

CONTRACT CLAUSE—FORCE MAJEURE

1. The number of this paragraph when inserted into a contract.

2. The name of the party agreeing to the Force Majeure.

3. The name of the party being protected.

[1] FORCE MAJEURE - ________[2]________ agrees that ________[3]________ shall not be liable for: any (i) losses; (ii) damage, including consequential damages; (iii) detention; (iv) delay or failure to perform in whole or in part resulting from causes beyond the control of ________[3]________ including but not limited to: acts of God; acts or omissions of ________[2]________; fires; strikes; insurrections; riots; embargoes; delays in transportation; inability to obtain supplies; or requirements or regulations of the United States government or any other civil or military authority. Delays or non-performance excused by this provision shall not excuse payment of any amount due hereunder owed at the time of the occurrence.

CONTRACT CLAUSE—ASSIGNMENT (8-12)

Agreements based on the personal contribution or expertise of one party should not be assigned (transferred) to someone with whom the other party might not want to do business. On the other hand, an agreement to sell a specific item would not normally require this type of protection.

CONTRACT CLAUSE—ASSIGNMENT

[1] ASSIGNMENT - This Agreement and any rights granted hereunder shall not be assigned by ________[2]________ to any person, firm or corporation without the prior written consent of ________[3]________, ________________[4]________________.

1. The number of this paragraph when inserted into a contract.

2. The name of the party to be prohibited from assigning; i.e. licensee, agent.

3. The name of the party to be protected; i.e. licensor.

4. Insert either: "which consent shall not be unreasonably withheld" or "at the sole discretion of ______[2]______," depending on whether the party to be protected wishes absolute control over the party to be assigned.

CONTRACT CLAUSE— ENTIRE AGREEMENT/MODIFICATIONS TO BE IN WRITING (8-13)

It is recommended that this clause be a part of every agreement. It prevents one party from claiming that there were "side" agreements, either written or oral, or subsequent verbal changes to an agreement.

CONTRACT CLAUSE— ENTIRE AGREEMENT/MODIFICATIONS TO BE IN WRITING

1. The number of this paragraph when inserted into a contract.

[1] ENTIRE AGREEMENT - It is agreed between the parties hereto that there are no other agreements or understandings between them relating to the subject matter of this Agreement. This Agreement supersedes all prior agreements, oral or written, between the parties and is intended as a complete and exclusive statement of the Agreement between the parties. Neither this Agreement, nor its execution, have been induced by any reliance, representation, stipulation, warranty, agreement or understanding of any kind other than those herein expressed. No change or modification of this Agreement shall be valid unless the same be in writing and signed by the parties.

CONTRACT CLAUSE—HEADINGS/CAPTIONS (8-14)

If an agreement contains Headings or Captions to introduce provisions, i.e. such words as TERMS, ROYALTIES, TERMINATION, etc., this clause should be included, indicating that the Headings or Captions are merely labels and have no impact on the meaning of the contract.

CONTRACT CLAUSE—HEADINGS/CAPTIONS

1. The number of this paragraph when inserted into a contract.

[1] HEADINGS/CAPTIONS - The headings and captions contained in this Agreement are for convenience purposes only and are not determinative nor are they to be considered in construction of the terms or provisions herein.

Employees and Representatives 9

In a perfect world, we could conduct business as we do personal relationships, relying on verbal agreements and handshakes. But business cannot be conducted in this manner. An area where misunderstandings can occur with frequency is in employer-employee relationships. It is because of this possibility that it is especially critical to put everything in writing.

Hiring This section provides an Employment Application form which asks the applicant for his work history and other information. The Request for Employee Verification and Authorization enables an employer to verify the information and history submitted by the applicant.

Employment Agreements Employee contracts, compensation and tuition reimbursement forms are presented. In addition, protection for the employer in the form of non-competition and and non-disclosure agreements are offered.

Employment Notices Any employer who must deal with a problem employee will find the warning and termination notices in this section particularly helpful.

Independent Contractors This section relates to the hiring of sales representatives, consultants and others as independent contractors.

EMPLOYMENT APPLICATION (9-01)

This form has been designed to comply with state and federal fair employment laws which prohibit discrimination in employment. The form is self-explanatory.

EMPLOYMENT APPLICATION

1. The name of the company.

________[1]________ is an Equal Opportunity Employer.

Date:___________

Last Name________ First Name______ Middle Initial___
Address ______________ Social Security No. __________
______________ Phone # (___)_______________

Are you 18 years or older? Yes ___ No___

The Age Discrimination in Employment Act of 1967 prohibits discrimination on the basis of age with respect to individuals who are at least 40 years of age.

Are you a U.S. Citizen or an alien authorized to work in the United States? Yes___ No___

What type of work are you applying for? ______________
____

What skills or qualifications do you have?______________
____

What (office) (factory) machines can you operate? _______
____

EDUCATION:

	School	Course	Did you Graduate? If Yes, Year
Grammar	_________	_______________	__________
High	_________	_______________	__________
College	_________	_______________	__________
Other	_________	_______________	__________

(Document continued on next page)

EXPERIENCE:

(The last two companies worked for)

Company ____________________________________
Address ____________________________________
Phone # (____)__________
Supervisor ____________________________________
Dates Employed: From ______ To ______
Reason for leaving ______________________________

Company ____________________________________
Address ____________________________________
Phone # (____)__________
Supervisor ____________________________________
Dates Employed: From ______ To ______
Reason for Leaving ______________________________

MILITARY SERVICE:

Branch_________ Discharge Date_____
Rank____________
National Guard/Reserve Yes____ No___
Date Obligation Ends ____________

REFERENCES:

Name ____________________________________
Company ____________________________________
Address ____________________________________
Phone # (____)__________

Name ____________________________________
Company ____________________________________
Address ____________________________________
Phone # (____)__________

I acknowledge that the Company is relying on the information given and I certify that the information in this form is true to the best of my knowledge. I authorize the company to obtain information from any person named above, and I release all concerned from any liability in connection with obtaining and releasing such information.

Signature of Applicant ________________ Date______

REQUEST FOR EMPLOYMENT VERIFICATION AND AUTHORIZATION (9-02)

This form should be completed by each prospective employee being considered for Employment. It requests and authorizes the release of prior Employment information.

The Request should be printed on company stationery.

1. The date of the request.

2. The name and address of the former employer.

3. The name of the employee.

4. The employee's social security number.

5. Choose one.

6. The position the employee held at the former company.

7. The dates of the former Employment.

8. The name and title of the person sending the letter printed directly below the line, with that person to sign above the line.

9. The name of the employee printed directly below the line, with the employee to sign above the line. (Note: while a release by the employee is not necessary, it puts the employee on notice that his Employment history is likely to be verified and gives the prior employer comfort in knowing that he can release to the proposed new employer the truth, "warts and all.")

REQUEST FOR EMPLOYMENT
VERIFICATION AND AUTHORIZATION

__________[1]__________

TO: ________[2]________
____
____

Re: Employment of ________[3]__________
Soc. Sec. No. ___________[4]___________

Gentlemen:

________[3]________ has applied for a position with our company and has advised us that *[5][he]* ***OR*** *[she]* was employed by you as __________[6]__________ from ________[7]________ to ________[7]________. It would be appreciated if you would verify the employment and provide the final salary. Additional comments regarding your evaluation of this applicant would be most helpful.

Very truly yours,

____
[8]

I hereby authorize the release of all information regarding my employment.

____
[9]

EMPLOYMENT AGREEMENT (9-03)

This Employment Agreement is for use with middle management employees. As the level of management increases, the Employment Agreement becomes more sophisticated to deal with increasingly complex issues. The language should be carefully worded so that there can be no misunderstanding as to its intent. Wherever possible, examples should be used, as in paragraph 4 where the present language could be followed by "as an example: a private corner office, desktop computer and a private secretary." Also see the Non-competition Agreement, the Non–disclosure Agreement and Employee Invention forms in this chapter, which may be used as separate agreements or incorporated into this Agreement.

1. The date the Agreement is signed.

2. The name of the Employer.

3. If the Employer is a corporation, insert the state of incorporation. Otherwise delete.

4. The name of the Employee being hired.

5. The beginning and ending dates of the Employment period.

6. The amount of the salary and time period it will cover, in numbers, for example "$5,000 per month."

7. The frequency with which the salary is to be paid, for example "weekly" or "semi-monthly."

8. A description of the Employee's duties and his title, if any.

9. The agreed upon number of weeks of paid vacation, in numbers.

10. Delete if there is to be no reduction in salary during a prolonged illness and renumber the remaining paragraphs.

EMPLOYMENT AGREEMENT

Employment Agreement this __[1]__ day of ________, 19__ by and between ________[2]________ *[3][, a ______ corporation]* ("Employer") and ________[4]________ ("Employee").

Employer employs the Employee and the Employee accepts employment, upon the terms conditions and covenants as follows:

1. The term of employment shall be from _____[5]_____ to _____[5]_____.

2. Employee shall receive, for all services rendered, a salary of $_____[6]_____ per ___[6]___, payable ____[7]____. Salary payments shall be subject to withholding and other applicable deductions.

3. The duties of Employee shall be ________ [8] ________ ____.
The Employee shall devote his full and entire time and attention to the Employer's business.

4. Employee shall have an office, facilities and services that are suitable to the position and appropriate for the performance of Employee's duties.

5. Employer shall reimburse Employee for all reasonable expenses incurred in the performance of Employee's business, e.g. entertainment, travel, etc. Employee will be reimbursed upon submission of an itemized account of such expenditures with receipts where practicable.

6. Employee shall be entitled to __[9]__ weeks of paid vacation each year.

[10][7. If Employee is unable to perform Employee's

(Document continued on next page)

11. The number of weeks of paid sick leave, in numbers.

12. The reduced salary during a prolonged illness, in numbers, and the period it will cover.

13. Since no Employer can continue to pay an Employee indefinitely when the Employee is unable to work, determine and insert a cut-off time. Note: if the Employee is female, be sure to consult your State Department of Labor as to state law regarding maternity leave and make reference to such law in this paragraph as follows: "This provision is subject to _____ regarding pregnancy and maternity leave" and insert the appropriate statutory reference, for example "New York Executive Law, Section 296."

14. The number of days' notice, in words and numbers, upon which either party may cancel the Agreement.

15. If there is to be severance pay, insert the amount, for example "one week of salary for every year of employment." If not, delete the last two sentences of the paragraph and replace with: "Employee shall receive salary up to the last day of employment and under no circumstances shall there be severance pay."

16. If there is to be a death benefit, insert the amount, in numbers. If not, delete from "and as a death benefit..." to the end of the sentence.

17. The city and state where arbitration is to be conducted, typically the location of the Employer.

duties by reason of illness or incapacity for a consecutive period of more than ___[11]___ weeks, the compensation payable after the aforesaid period shall be $____[12]_____ per _____[12]_____. Upon return to full employment, full compensation shall be reinstated.]

8. Notwithstanding any provision in this Employment Agreement to the contrary, if Employee is unable to perform or is absent from employment for a period of more than __[13]__ months, Employer may terminate this Employment Agreement, without further cause, and all obligations of Employer hereunder shall terminate.

9. This Employment Agreement may be terminated, at will, at any time and without cause, by either party upon ____[14]____ (__) days' written notice to the other. *[If Employer elects to terminate, Employer shall pay to Employee on the last day of employment severance pay of _______________[15]______________, subject to withholding and deductions. If Employee elects to terminate, Employee shall receive salary up to the last day of employment but no severance pay.]*

10. In the event Employee dies during the term of Employment, Employer shall pay to Employee's estate the salary that would otherwise be payable to the end of the month in which the Employee died *[and as a death benefit a sum equal to $_______[16]_______].*

11. Any controversy or claim arising out of, or relating to this Employment Agreement, or the breach thereof, shall be settled by arbitration in the City of ____[17]____, State of ____[17]____, in accordance with the then governing rules of the American Arbitration Association. Judgment upon the award rendered by the arbitrator(s) may be entered in any court of competent jurisdiction.

12. Any notice required to be given shall be either: (i) personally delivered, or (ii) sent by U.S. Postal Service, postage pre-paid, Certified Mail, Return Receipt Requested to the Employer at the place of employment and to the Employee at the last residence address given to and on file with the Employer.

13. A waiver of a breach of any provision of this Employ-

(Document continued on next page)

ment Agreement shall not operate or be construed as a waiver of any subsequent breach.

14. The services of Employee are personal and unique and therefore Employee may not assign this Employment Agreement nor delegate the duties and obligations hereunder except in the normal course of business.

15. This Employment Agreement contains the entire understanding of the parties, except as may be set forth in writing signed by the party against whom enforcement may be sought, simultaneously with or subsequent to the execution of this Employment Agreement.

INTENDING TO BE LEGALLY BOUND, the parties have executed this Employment Agreement as of the date first above written.

__________*[18]*__________

*BY*____________________
[19] (Employer)

____
[20] (Employee)

18. The name of the Employer if a corporation. Otherwise delete the line.

19. If the Employer is an individual, delete "BY" and print the Employer's name directly below the line, with the Employer to sign above the line. If the Employer is a corporation, print the name and title of the person acting for the corporation directly below the line, with that person to sign above the line.

20. The name of the Employee printed directly below the line, with the Employee to sign above the line.

INCENTIVE COMPENSATION AGREEMENT (9-04)

This Agreement provides for the payment of a cash bonus by an Employer to an Employee. It may be incorporated into the Employment Agreement found in this chapter.

A stock option provision was not not made part of this Agreement for two reasons. First, the Stock Purchase Option Agreement elsewhere in this book may be used. Second, consultation with a local attorney is recommended to be sure that offering stock options does not require the company to be registered either with the state or with the Securities and Exchange Commission.

INCENTIVE COMPENSATION AGREEMENT

Agreement made this __[1]__ day of ______, 19__, by and between ________[2]________ *[3][, a ________ corporation]* ("Company") and ________[4]________ ("Employee").

Company desires to grant to Employee an incentive for the performance of Employee's duties. Company hereby grants to Employee as follows:

[5][In addition to Employee's regular salary, Employee shall receive compensation equal to _____[6]_____ (__[7]__%) percent of the Company's pre-tax profits, as determined by the Company's accountants, in accordance with generally accepted accounting principles. Such additional compensation shall be determined, and paid to Employee within __[8]__ days of the end of the Company's fiscal year.] ***OR*** *[In addition to all other compensation, Employee shall receive bonus compensation in such form and amounts and at such times as the Company shall determine in its sole discretion, but in any event no less than $ _____[9]_____ per ____[10]____.]*

(Document continued on next page)

1. The date the Agreement is signed.

2. The name of the Company.

3. If the Company is a corporation, insert the state in which incorporated. Otherwise delete.

4. The name of the Employee.

5. Choose one. If the second alternative is chosen skip to No. 9.

6. The percentage of pre-tax profits, in words.

7. The percentage of pre-tax profits, in numbers.

8. The number of days, in numbers, after the close of the company's fiscal year by which the Incentive Compensation will be paid.

9. The minimum amount of Incentive Compensation to be paid, in numbers. (Note: if no minimum amount is promised, end the paragraph after the words "sole discretion.")

10. The time period for which Incentive Compensation is paid, for example "per month."

11. The name of the Company if a corporation. Otherwise delete the line.

12. If the Company is not a corporation, delete "BY" and print the individual's name directly below the line, with the individual to sign above the line. If the Company is a corporation, print the name and title of the person acting for the corporation directly below the line, with that person to sign above the line.

13. The name of the Employee printed directly below the line, with the Employee to sign above the line.

INTENDING TO BE LEGALLY BOUND, the parties hereto have caused this Incentive Compensation Agreement to be executed as of the date first above written.

__________*[11]*__________

*BY*________________________
[12] (Company)

____
[13] (Employee)

TUITION REIMBURSEMENT AGREEMENT (9-05)

To encourage the development of an Employee, a company may assist the Employee in obtaining additional education (either for general educational purposes or for specific purposes relating to job performance) and to provide tuition reimbursement. This Agreement permits the Employer to monitor the Employee's performance both at school and on the job to determine if the Tuition Reimbursement should continue.

TUITION REIMBURSEMENT AGREEMENT

1. This Agreement should be on Company stationery.

2. The name of the Company.

[1] [COMPANY STATIONERY]

________[2]________, believing that it is to the benefit of the Company to further the formal eduction of its employees, agrees with the undersigned Employee as follows:

1. The Company shall reimburse the Employee for tuition expenses incurred by the Employee for educational courses taken at a recognized learning institution leading to a high school diploma, high school equivalency certificate, associate degree, college degree or graduate degree or as otherwise approved by the Company, provided the Employee:

(A) submits to the Company a program of study from the learning institution indicating the courses to be taken and the diploma, certificate or degree that will result; and

(B) submits to the Company paid receipts for tuition; and

(C) maintains a satisfactory work record with the Company; and

(D) maintains a passing grade average for all courses taken under this program.

2. Reimbursement shall be made at the commencement of each course, provided however, that if reimbursement has been made for prior courses, the Employee has received passing grades for those courses.

3. Employee agrees that the cost of books, transportation and other incidental expenses shall be borne by the Employee.

(Document continued on next page)

3. The name of the Company if a corporation. Otherwise delete the line.

4. If the Company is not a corporation, delete "BY" and print the individual's name directly below the line, with the individual to sign above the line. If the Company is a corporation, print the name and title of the individual acting for the corporation directly below the line, with that person to sign above the line.

5. The date the Agreement is signed by the Employee.

6. The name of the Employee printed directly below the line, with the Employee to sign above the line.

4. The Company reserves the right to terminate this program at will except as to courses for which the Employee shall have paid tuition prior to the termination date.

__________*[3]*__________

*BY*______________________
[4]

ACCEPTED

Date: ________[5]________

____
[6] (Employee)

NON-COMPETITION AGREEMENT (9-06)

Non-competition Agreements are common when an Employee is hired for a sensitive position and a change of employment to a competitor would prove injurious to the Employer's business. Non-competition agreements have usually been upheld by the court if they meet two criteria: they must be reasonable in length of time and reasonable in geographic area. For example, an Employer cannot prevent a former Employee from ever working throughout the entire United States.

WARNING

Some states, for example California, prohibit Non-competition Agreements. Therefore, be sure to check your state's employment laws before using this form.

1. The date the Agreement is signed.

2. The name of the Employer.

3. If the Employer is a corporation, insert the state of incorporation. Otherwise delete.

4. The name of the Employee being hired.

5. The period of non-competition. As a general rule this should not exceed three years.

6. The geographic area to be prohibited, such as "in the state of Illinois." As a general rule this should not go beyond the states bordering the state in which the company is located.

7. The name of the Employer if a corporation. Otherwise delete the line.

8. If the Employer is an individual, delete "BY" and type the Employer's name directly below the line, with the Employer to sign above the line. If the Employer is a corporation, print the name and title of the person acting for the corporation directly below the line, with that person to sign above the line.

9. The name of the Employee printed directly below the line, with the Employee to sign above the line.

NON-COMPETITION AGREEMENT

Agreement made this __[1]__ day of _______, 19__ by and between ________[2]________ *[3][, a _______ corporation]* ("Employer") and ________[4]________ ("Employee").

Employee has this day accepted employment offered by Employer and in consideration of the employment agrees as follows:

1. During the period of employment, Employee shall not engage in any other business activity, directly or indirectly, regardless of whether it is for profit, gain or otherwise that is similar to the business activity of Employer.

2. In the event of the termination of employment, whether voluntary or involuntary, Employee agrees that Employee will not for a period of _____[5]_____ from the effective date of termination engage in a business activity similar to that of Employer ________[6]________.

INTENDING TO BE LEGALLY BOUND, the parties have executed this Agreement as of the date first above written.

__________*[7]*__________

BY ______________________

[8] (Employer)

____

[9] (Employee)

NON-DISCLOSURE AGREEMENT (9-07)

A Non-disclosure Agreement is similar to a Non-competition Agreement but it is not limited in scope or geographic location. As its name implies, the Agreement prevents an Employee from disclosing information learned on the job to the Employer's competitors.

NON-DISCLOSURE AGREEMENT

1. The date the Agreement is signed.

2. The name of the Employer.

3. If the Employer is a corporation, insert the state of incorporation. Otherwise delete.

4. The name of the Employee being hired.

5. A description of the information to be protected, for example "customer lists," "product development information," "computer software," etc.

Agreement made this __[1]__ day of _______, 19__ by and between ________[2]________ *[3][, a _______ corporation]* ("Employer") and ________[4]________ ("Employee").

Employee has this day accepted employment offered by Employer and in consideration of the employment agrees as follows:

1. During the course of employment, Employee shall become aware of certain methods, practices and procedures with which Employer conducts its business, including but not limited to: __________[5]__________, all of which Employer and Employee agree are proprietary information and as such are trade secrets.

2. Employee will not at any time, either during his/her employment or thereafter divulge, furnish, or make available, either directly or indirectly, to any person, firm, corporation or other entity any proprietary information used by Employer. Employee agrees that all such matters and information shall be kept strictly and absolutely confidential.

3. Employee, upon the cessation of his/her employment, irrespective of the time, manner or reason of termination, will immediately surrender and deliver to Employer all lists, books, records, memoranda and data of every kind relating to all proprietary information and all property belonging to Employer.

4. Employee acknowledges that a breach of any of the provisions of this Agreement may result in continuing and irreparable damages to Employer for which there may be no adequate remedy at law and that Employer in addition to all other relief available to Employer shall be entitled to the issuance of an injunction restraining Employee from committing or continuing any breach of this Agreement.

(Document continued on next page)

6. The state whose laws will goven the Agreement, typically the state in which the Employer is located.

7. The name of the Employer if a corporation. Otherwise delete the line.

8. If the Employer is an individual, delete "BY" and print the Employer's name directly below the line, with the Employer to sign above the line. If the Employer is a corporation, print the name and title of the person acting for the corporation directly below the line, with that person to sign above the line.

9. The name of the Employee printed directly below the line, with the Employee to sign above the line.

5. Wherever used "Employer" shall mean ________[2]________, its subsidiaries and/or affiliates.

6. If any provision of this Agreement shall be determined, by a Court having jurisdiction, to be invalid, or illegal or unenforceable, the remainder of this Agreement shall not be affected but shall continue in full force and effect as though such invalid, illegal or unenforceable provision were not originally a part of this Agreement.

7. This Agreement shall be construed in accordance with and governed by the laws of the State of _____[6]_____, irrespective of the fact that a party hereto may not be a resident of that State.

INTENDING TO BE LEGALLY BOUND, the parties have executed this Agreement as of the date first above written.

__________*[7]*__________

BY ____________________
[8] (Employer)

____
[9] (Employee)

EMPLOYEE INVENTION/ "WORK FOR HIRE" AGREEMENT (9-08)

This Agreement gives to an Employer ownership of anything an Employee creates during the term of his Employment or while "on company time" that relates to his employment. For example, a new computer software program that facilitates doing a particular task within the company is a "work created for hire" and the Employer should not have to involuntarily or additionally compensate the Employee for its creation nor should the Employee be permitted to claim ownership of it.

EMPLOYEE INVENTION/ "WORK FOR HIRE" AGREEMENT

1. The date the Agreement is signed.

2. The name of the Employer.

3. If the Employer is a corporation, insert the state of incorporation. Otherwise delete.

4. The name of the Employee being hired.

5. Change or expand these categories to suit the particular business. As a general rule they can be anything that can be patented or copyrighted.

Agreement made this __[1]__ day of _______, 19__ by and between ________[2]________ *[3][, a ________ corporation]* ("Employer") and ________[4]________ ("Employee").

Employee has this day accepted employment offered by Employer and in consideration therefore agrees as follows:

1. Employee agrees that *[5][all inventions, computer programs and products]* created by Employee either for use by Employer or which could be used by Employer in furtherance of Employer's business activity, which are created or conceived during the course of employment by Employer, shall be considered as Works Made For Hire and all rights to said Works shall and do vest in Employer.

2. Employee further agrees that said Works are proprietary information not to be divulged, furnished or made available, either directly or indirectly, to any person, firm or corporation or any other entity. Employee agrees that all such proprietary information shall be kept strictly and absolutely confidential.

3. Employee, upon the cessation of his/her employment, irrespective of the time, manner or reason of termination, will immediately surrender and deliver to Employer all data, information and models of every kind and in any stage of progress relating to the Works.

4. Employee acknowledges that a breach of any of the provisions of this Agreement may result in continuing and irreparable damages to Employer for which there may be no adequate remedy at law and that Employer, in addition to all other relief available to Employer, shall be entitled to the issuance of an injunction restraining Employee from committing or continuing any breach of this Agreement.

(Document continued on next page)

EMPLOYEE INVENTION/ "WORK FOR HIRE" AGREEMENT *continued*

6. The state whose laws will goven the Agreement, typically the state in which the Employer is located.

7. The name of the Employer if a corporation. Otherwise delete the line.

8. If the Employer is an individual, delete "BY" and print the name of the Employer directly below the line, with the Employer to sign above the line. If the Employer is a corporation, print the name and title of the person acting for the corporation directly below the line, with that person to sign above the line.

9. The name of the Employee printed directly below the line with the Employee to sign above the line.

5. Wherever used herein "Employer" shall mean ________[2]________, its subsidiaries and/or affiliates.

6. If any provision of this Agreement shall be determined, by a Court having jurisdiction, to be invalid, illegal or unenforceable, the remainder of this Agreement shall not be affected thereby but shall continue in full force and effect as though such invalid, illegal or unenforceable provisions were not originally a part of this Agreement.

7. This Agreement shall be construed in accordance with and governed by the laws of the State of _____[6]_____, irrespective of the fact that a party hereto may not be a resident of that State.

INTENDING TO BE LEGALLY BOUND, the parties have executed this Agreement as of the date first above written.

__________*[7]*__________

BY ____________________
[8] (Employer)

____
[9] (Employee)

EMPLOYEE WARNING NOTICE (9-09)

To avoid charges of discrimination, unfair dealing or the like, it is advisable to record Warnings given to an Employee for improper conduct. The matter should be discussed with the Employee and a notation made of the date and topic discussed. When the conduct has reached the level where a written Warning must be made, this Notice should be used. The Notice should be prepared in duplicate with one copy given to the Employee and the other to be signed by the Employee to acknowledge receipt and then retained by the company in the Employee's personnel file.

1. The Notice should be on company stationery.

2. The name of the Employee.

3. The date of the conversation with the Employee in which the charges were discussed.

4. A detailed statement of the charges by category and specifics, for example "Lateness, April 1, 1990 arrived 10:15, April 2, 1990 arrived 11:30."

5. The name of the Employer if a corporation. Otherwise delete the line.

6. If the Employer is not a corporation, delete "BY" and print the Employer's name directly below the line, with the Employer to sign above the line. If the Employer is a corporation, print the name and title of the individual acting for the corporation directly below the line, with that person to sign above the line.

7. The date the Employee receives the Notice.

8. The name of the Employee printed below the line, with the Employee to sign above the line.

EMPLOYEE WARNING NOTICE

[1] [COMPANY STATIONERY]

TO: ________[2]________

This will confirm our conversation of ________[3]________ and will constitute a formal written notice concerning ________________[4]________________.

The above practice is not acceptable to the Company and its continuation may result in suspension from or termination of employment.

This notice is being made a part of your permanent employment record.

__________*[5]*__________

*BY*______________________
[6]

RECEIVED

Date: ________[7]________

____
[8] (Employee)

EMPLOYEE SUSPENSION NOTICE (9-10)

This form should be used after sending an Employee Warning Notice or used in its place if the conduct is serious enough to warrant immediate suspension. The Employee Suspension Notice becomes part of the record justifying a subsequent termination. The Notice should be prepared in duplicate with one copy given to the Employee and the other to be signed by the Employee to acknowledge receipt and then retained by the company in the Employee's personnel file.

EMPLOYEE SUSPENSION NOTICE

[1] [COMPANY STATIONERY]

TO: ________[2]________

You have received informal notices that your conduct has been found to be unsatisfactory. On ________[3]________ a formal Warning Notice was placed in your permanent employment record. The unacceptable conduct was continued by you in that ______________________[4]______________________.

You are herewith suspended from work for a period of ____[5]____ commencing ________[6]________. Suspension shall be without pay; however, your health benefits shall continue during the suspension providing you return to work immediately following the suspension period.

YOU MAY BE SUBJECT TO TERMINATION IN THE FUTURE IF YOU CONTINUE TO VIOLATE COMPANY POLICY.

__________*[7]*__________

*BY*______________________
[8]

RECEIVED

Date: ________[9]________

____
[10] (Employee)

1. The Notice should be on company stationery.

2. The name of the Employee.

3. The date of the warning notice, or if there was no warning notice, delete the paragraph and replace with: "On __(date)__ you __(describe the incident)__. This conduct is not acceptable and warrants suspension from employment." Then skip to No. 5.

4. A description of the incident in detail.

5. The period of suspension, for example "one week."

6. The date suspension is to begin.

7. The name of the Employer if a corporation. Otherwise delete the line.

8. If the Employer is not a corporation, delete "BY" and print the Employer's name directly below the line, with the Employer to sign above the line. If the Employer is a corporation, print the name and title of the individual acting for the corporation directly below the line, with that person to sign above the line.

9. The date the Employee receives the Notice.

10. The name of the Employee printed below the line, with the Employee to sign above the line.

EMPLOYEE TERMINATION/ INVOLUNTARY DISCHARGE NOTICE (9-11)

There are many reasons for terminating the employment of an Employee. This form deals with two possible causes: employee misconduct or layoff due to poor business conditions. Choose the paragraph that applies.

EMPLOYEE TERMINATION/ INVOLUNTARY DISCHARGE NOTICE

[1] [COMPANY STATIONERY]

TO: ________[2]________

[3][On ________[4]________ we discussed your employee performance record, [________[5]________,] and you were advised that your performance was not satisfactory for continued employment.

Your employment will be terminated on ______[6]______ and you shall receive all compensation due to you at that time. In accordance with Federal Regulations you shall be notified of your options to continue in the Company health plan.]

OR

[On ________[4]________ we discussed your continued employment with the Company and the market conditions under which the Company is now operating. Under the circumstances your position has been necessarily eliminated.

Your employment will be terminated on ________[6]________ and you shall receive all compensation due to you at that time. In accordance with Federal Regulations you shall be notified of your options to continue in the Company health plan.]

Very truly yours,

__________*[7]*__________

*BY*____________________
[8]

1. The Notice should be on company stationery.

2. The name of the Employee.

3. Choose one, depending on why the Employee is being terminated.

4. The date the Employee was personally notified that he was terminated.

5. Insert if appropriate: "and issued a warning notice and/or suspension to you on ______" and state the dates. Otherwise delete.

6. The date employment ceases.

7. The name of the Employer if a corporation. Otherwise delete the line.

8. If the Employer is not a corporation, delete "BY" and print the Employer's name directly below the line, with the Employer to sign above the line. If the Employer is a corporation, print the name and title of the individual acting for the corporation directly below the line, with that person to sign above the line.

SALES REPRESENTATIVE AGREEMENT (9-12)

Rather than hire employees to sell its products (thereby obligating the company to pay salary, benefits, social security, etc.), a company may instead hire independent Sales Representatives who work strictly on a commission basis. This Agreement contains the necessary elements for maintaining Sales Representatives as independent contractors rather than as employees.

1. The Agreement should be on company stationery.

2. The name and address of the Sales Representative.

3. The name of the Sales Representative.

4. A description of the products to be sold.

5. A description of the geographic limitations of the sales territory, for example "The New England states and Pennsylvania."

SALES REPRESENTATIVE AGREEMENT

[1] [COMPANY STATIONERY]

________[2]________

____

____

Dear ________[3]________:

The purpose of this letter is to set forth our agreement with respect to the terms and conditions upon which you agree to act as a direct seller of products distributed by the undersigned:

1. Effective as of the date of execution of this Agreement, you are engaged by the undersigned as a non-exclusive direct seller for _______[4]______ in __________[5]__________.

2. In such capacity, you will pursue such leads as you may obtain or that we may supply to you for the sale to such individuals who are interested in purchasing the undersigned's products. All sales will be at such purchase price as shall be mutually agreed upon by you and the undersigned.

3. You will use your best efforts to promote the sales and obtain orders for the undersigned and shall at all times maintain the good will between the undersigned and its customers.

4. You will determine the methods of carrying out your obligations hereunder and the number of hours that you will work. At all times you will maintain standards of performance and behavior established by the undersigned and will conduct your activities in accordance with standards and directions of the undersigned. You may employ such individuals as

(Document continued on next page)

6. On a separate sheet headed "Schedule A" state the commission structure.

7. Typically, the state in which the company has its place of business.

you may desire on such terms and conditions that you may establish, and you alone will be solely responsible for the payment of salaries and/or other compensation to your employees and for the payment of federal, state and local tax obligations with respect to such payments.

5. In consideration for the services to be rendered by you, you will receive commissions in accordance with the Schedule which is attached hereto and is set forth as Schedule A [6]. Such Schedule of Payment is subject to change by the undersigned upon prior written notice. Such commissions will be payable upon delivery of the products sold.

6. It is agreed that you will not be treated as an employee of the undersigned for federal and state tax purposes. Rather, you will be an independent contractor and will be solely responsible for payment of all federal, state and local tax obligations with respect to all amounts paid to you by the undersigned.

7. This agreement will continue until terminated by either of us at will.

8. Any controversy or claim arising out of or relating to this Agreement, or the breach thereof, shall be settled by arbitration in accordance with the then obtaining rules of the American Arbitration Association in the State of ____[7]____, and a judgment upon any award rendered by the arbitrator(s) may be entered in any court having jurisdiction thereof.

If the foregoing accurately contains the terms and conditions of our Agreement, kindly execute the enclosed

(Document continued on next page)

8. The name of the company if a corporation. Otherwise delete the line.

9. If the company is not a corporation, delete "BY" and print the name of the individual sending the letter directly below the line, with the individual to sign above the line. If the company is a corporation, print the name and title of the individual acting for the corporation directly below the line, with that person to sign above the line.

10. The date the Sales Representative signs the Agreement.

11. The name of the Sales Representative printed directly below the line, with the Sales Representative to sign above the line.

copy of this letter Agreement where indicated and return it to the undersigned.

Very truly yours,

__________*[8]*__________

BY ______________________
[9]

ACCEPTED

Date ______[10]_______

____
[11]

SALES AGENCY AGREEMENT (9-13)

This Agreement is similar to the preceding Sales Representative Agreement but is broader in application, covering a wider range of products and giving the Agent more latitude.

SALES AGENCY AGREEMENT

1. The date the Agreement is signed.

2. The name of the Principal (the party contracting with the Agent).

3. If the Principal is a corporation, insert the state in which incorporated. Otherwise delete.

4. The name of the Agent.

5. If the Agent is a corporation, insert the state in which incorporated. Otherwise delete.

6. Insert either "exclusive" or "non-exclusive."

7. On a separate sheet headed "Schedule A" list the products, with their prices, to be sold by the Agent.

8. A description of the territory in which the Agent may sell, for example "the New England states and Pennsylvania."

Agreement made this __[1]__ day of ______, 19__, by and between ________[2]________ *[3][, a ________ corporation]* ("Principal") and ________[4]________ *[5][, a ________ corporation]* ("Agent").

In consideration of the mutual terms, conditions and covenants hereinafter set forth, Principal and Agent agree as follows:

1. Principal appoints Agent as its _______[6]_______ sales representative to sell the products of the Principal as listed in the attached Schedule A [7].

2. Agent accepts the appointment and agrees to promote, market and sell the products of the Principal at the prices set forth in Schedule A.

3. The parties agree that the list of products and/or prices may be amended from time to time. Principal may unilaterally remove products from the list or change prices. Additions to the product list shall be by mutual agreement.

4. Agent's territory to sell products shall be ________[8]________ (the "Territory"), which may be amended by mutual written agreement.

5. With Principal's prior written consent, Agent may attempt to sell product outside Agent's Territory or at prices different from those on Schedule A. Principal's consent shall be on an individual sale basis only and shall not be construed to expand Agent's territory or to amend Schedule A.

6. Principal shall furnish to Agent all sales material for the products listed on Schedule A and shall keep the material up-to-date.

7. Agent shall use its best efforts to promote, market and sell the products of Schedule A within the allocated territory, devote such time and attention as may be reasonably necessary, and abide by the Principal's policies.

(Document continued on next page)

9. The number of years, in numbers, after the Agreement ends, during which the Agent will not compete with the Principal. It is advisable not to exceed three years. (Note: in some states, for example California, non-competition restrictions are prohibited by law. Check your state's law before including this provision.)

10. On a separate sheet headed "Schedule B" list the commission schedule. Include sales quotas if desired.

11. The number of years, in numbers, of the Agreement.

12. The number of days, in words and numbers, of advance notice of termination.

8. Agent agrees that during the term of this Agreement and for a period of __[9]__ years thereafter, Agent, either directly or indirectly, shall handle no products that are competitive with those products listed in Schedule A within the Territory.

9. Agent shall obtain, at its own expense, all necessary licenses and permits to permit Agent to conduct business as contemplated herein. Agent represents and warrants that Agent shall conduct business in strict conformity with all local, state and federal laws, rules and regulations.

10. Principal agrees that Agent may employ representatives in furtherance of this Agreement and Agent agrees that Agent shall be solely responsible for the payment of wages or commissions to those representatives and that under no circumstances shall Agent's representatives be deemed employees of Principal for any purpose whatsoever.

11. Principal shall pay to Agent a commission on the sale of products as set forth on Schedule B [10], which commission may be amended from time to time by mutual agreement. Principal shall be responsible for the granting of credit to customers and shall pay commissions to Agent on the 15th date of the month for all merchandise shipped by Principal in the preceding month.

12. This Agreement shall be for a period of __[11]__ years unless sooner terminated by either party upon _____[12]_____ (__) days' written notice, without cause.

13. Upon termination Agent shall be entitled to receive commissions for all orders accepted by Principal prior to the date of termination. Payment to be made upon shipment.

14. Agent is an independent contractor and nothing contained in this Agreement shall be deemed or interpreted to constitute the Agent as a partner or employee of the Principal, nor shall either party have any authority to bind the other in any respect, it being understood and agreed that all orders submitted by Agent are subject to acceptance by Principal in its sole discretion.

15. It is agreed between the parties that there are no

(Document continued on next page)

other agreements or understandings between them relating to the subject matter of this Agreement. This Agreement supersedes all prior agreements, oral or written, between the parties and is intended as a complete and exclusive statement of the agreement between the parties. No change or modification of this Agreement shall be valid unless the same be in writing and signed by the parties.

16. This Agreement shall not be assigned by Agent without the prior written consent of Principal.

17. All notices required or permitted to be given hereunder shall be in writing and may be delivered personally or by Certified Mail - Return Receipt Requested, postage prepaid, addressed to the party's last known address.

18. This Agreement shall be construed in accordance with and governed by the laws of the State of _____[13]_____.

INTENDING TO BE LEGALLY BOUND, the parties hereto have caused this Agreement to be executed as of the date first above written.

_________*[14]*_________

*BY*____________________
[15] (Principal)

_________*[16]*_________

*BY*____________________
[17] (Agent)

13. The state whose laws will govern the Agreement, typically the state in which the Principal is located.

14. The name of the Principal if a corporation. Otherwise delete the line.

15. If the Principal is an individual, delete "BY" and print the Principal's name directly below the line, with the Principal to sign above the line. If the Principal is a corporation, print the name and title of the person acting for the corporation directly below the line, with that person to sign above the line.

16. The name of the Agent if a Corporation. Otherwise delete the line.

17. If the Agent is an individual, delete "BY" and print the Agent's name directly below the line, with the Agent to sign above the line. If the Agent is a corporation, print the name and title of the person acting for the corporation directly below the line, with that person to sign above the line.

AGENCY AGREEMENT (9-14)

An Agency Agreement is used to appoint an Agent as a Venture Manager (see the Joint Venture Agreement elsewhere in this book) or for other types of business situations where an "employee" or "consultant" arrangement is not desirable.

AGENCY AGREEMENT

Agency Agreement made this _[1]_ day of ________, 19__ by and between ________[2]________ *[3][, a ________ corporation]* (the "Company") and ________[4]________ *[5][, a ________ corporation]* (the "Agent").

The Company is engaged in the business of _________________[6]_________________ and desires to engage the Agent in furtherance of that business.

In consideration of the mutual terms, conditions and covenants hereinafter set forth, the parties agree as follows:

1. The Company engages the Agent for the purposes of _________________[7]_________________.

2. The duties of the Agent shall be ____________[8]____________ and the Agent shall devote ________[9]________.

3. This Agreement shall continue in full force and effect until ________[10]________ but may be terminated by either party upon __[11]__ (__) days' written notice to the other, Certified Mail, Return Receipt Requested.

4. For the services performed hereunder the Agent

(Document continued on next page)

1. The date the Agreement is signed.

2. The name of the party granting the Agency (the Company).

3. If the Company is a corporation, insert the state of incorporation. Otherwise delete.

4. The name of the Agent.

5. If the Agent is a corporation, insert the state of incorporation. Otherwise delete.

6. A description of the business in which the Company is engaged, for example "the purchase and resale of souvenirs commemorating Custer's Last Stand."

7. A description of the purpose for which the Agent is being engaged, for example "managing the Joint Venture known as Custer's Commemorative."

8. A description of the duties of the Agent, for example "design, have manufactured and conduct wholesale sales of souvenirs commemorating Custer's Last Stand."

9. The amount of time the Agent is to devote to the agency, for example "such time and efforts as is required," "___ hours per week," "all of its time and effort."

10. The termination date of the Agreement.

11. The number of days, in words and numbers, for Notice.

12. The commission rate agreed upon, in numbers.

13. The name of the Company if a corporation. Otherwise delete the line.

14. If the Company is not a corporation, delete "BY" and print the individual's name directly below the line, with the individual to sign above the line. If the Company is a corporation, print the name and title of the individual acting for the corporation directly below the line, with that person to sign above the line.

15. The name of the Agent if a corporation. Otherwise delete the line.

16. If the Agent is an individual, delete "BY" and print the individual's name directly below the line, with the individual to sign above the line. If the Agent is a corporation, print the name and title of the individual acting for the corporation directly below the line, with that person to sign above the line.

shall receive compensation at the rate of __ [12]__% of wholesale sales, net of freight, discounts and returns. Commissions shall be deemed earned when goods are shipped and invoices paid.

5. The Agent shall not represent any company or product engaged in the same business as the Company during the lifetime of this Agreement nor for a period of twelve (12) months thereafter if the Agent terminates this Agreement prior to its expiration date.

6. The Agent may employ any employee it deems necessary to accomplish the purposes of this Agency but such employee(s) shall not be deemed to be employee(s) of the Company and they shall look only to the Agent for compensation.

7. Nothing contained in this Agreement shall be construed to constitute the Agent as a partner, joint venturer, principal or employee of the Company, it being intended that the Agent is an independent contractor responsible for its own actions.

INTENDING TO BE LEGALLY BOUND, the parties have signed this Agency Agreement as of the date first above written.

__________*[13]*__________

*BY*______________________
[14] (Company)

__________*[15]*__________

*BY*______________________
[16] (Agent)

CONSULTING AGREEMENT (9-15)

A Consultant typically is called upon when special skills are required for a specific period of time or for a specific project. This Consulting Agreement covers the basic issues in contracting for the services of such a party.

CONSULTING AGREEMENT

1. The date the Agreement is signed.

2. The name of the Company employing the Consultant.

3. If the Company is a corporation insert the state in which incorporated. Otherwise delete.

4. The name of the Consultant.

5. If the Consultant is a corporation, insert the state of incorporation. Otherwise delete.

6. The starting date of the Agreement.

7. The ending date of the Agreement.

8. The number of days, in words and numbers, of advance notice of termination.

9. The amount, in numbers, to be paid to the Consultant.

10. The time period for which the amount in No. 8 is to be applied, for example "per month."

11. The frequency of payment, for example "quarterly."

12. A description of the services to be performed by the Consultant.

Agreement made this __[1]__ day of _______, 19__ by and between ________[2]________ *[3][, a ________ corporation]* ("Company") and ________[4]________ *[5][, a ________ corporation]* ("Consultant").

Consultant is an independent contractor willing to provide certain skills and abilities to the Company that the Company has need for.

In consideration of the mutual terms, conditions and covenants hereinafter set forth, Company and Consultant agree as follows:

1. The Company hereby employs the Consultant as an independent contractor, and the Consultant hereby accepts employment.

2. The term of this Agreement shall commence on ________[6]________ and shall terminate on ________[7]________. After the first thirty (30) days of the term, either party may, without cause, terminate this Agreement by giving _____[8]_____ (__) days' written notice to the other.

3. Company shall pay to Consultant and Consultant shall accept from the Company as compensation for all services to be provided pursuant to this Agreement, the sum of $_____[9]_____ per _____[10]_____ payable ____[11]____.

4. Consultant shall provide on an "as needed" basis the following services: ______________[12]______________. Consultant shall devote such time, attention and energies as required.

5. Consultant is an independent contractor and may engage in other business activities provided, however, that Consultant shall not during the term of this Agreement solicit Company's employees or accounts on behalf of Consultant or another entity.

(Document continued on next page)

13. The state whose laws will govern the Agreement, typically the state in which the Company is located.

14. The name of the Company if a corporation. Otherwise delete the line.

15. If the Company is not a corporation, delete "BY" and print the individual's name directly below the line, with the individual to sign above the line. If the Company is a corporation, print the name and title of the person acting for the corporation directly below the line, with that person to sign above the line.

16. The name of the Consultant if a corporation. Otherwise delete the line.

17. If the Consultant is an individual, print the Consultant's name directly below the line, with the Consultant to sign above the line. If the Consultant is a corporation, print the name and title of the person acting for the corporation directly below the line, with that person to sign above the line.

6. If Consultant becomes unable to perform services pursuant to this Agreement by reason of illness, incapacity or death, compensation shall cease upon the happening of the event.

7. Neither party may assign this Agreement without the express written consent of the other party.

8. Consultant is an independent contractor and nothing contained in this Agreement shall be deemed or interpreted to constitute the Consultant as a partner, agent or employee of the Company, nor shall either party have any authority to bind the other.

9. It is agreed between the parties that there are no other agreements or understandings between them relating to the subject matter of this Agreement. This Agreement supersedes all prior agreements, oral or written, between the parties and is intended as a complete and exclusive statement of the agreement between the parties. No change or modification of this Agreement shall be valid unless the same be in writing and signed by the parties.

10. All notices required or permitted to be given hereunder shall be in writing and may be delivered personally or by Certified Mail - Return Receipt Requested, postage prepaid, addressed to the party's last known address.

11. This Agreement shall be construed in accordance with and governed by the laws of the State of _____[13]_____.

INTENDING TO BE LEGALLY BOUND, the parties hereto have caused this Agreement to be executed as of the date first above written.

_________*[14]*_________

*BY*______________________
[15] (Company)

_________*[16]*_________

*BY*______________________
[17] (Consultant)

Releases, Powers of Attorney and Notary Statements 10

This chapter contains legal forms that are used in a broad range of situations.

Releases These forms should be used whenever a person or a business is asked to give up a right it may have. There are General Releases (giving up the right to sue in court), for both individuals and corporations, a Model/Photographer's Release (giving up the right to prevent others from using your photo), and a Customer Testimonial Release (giving up the right to prevent others from using your testimonial).

Powers of Attorney This section provides a Power of Attorney and related forms used to authorize others to act for an individual when he is not present to act.

Notary Statements A Notary Public attests to the authenticity of a signature through the use of a Notary Statement. Two such statements are presented in this section, one for an individual's signature and the other for the signature of a person signing on behalf of a corporation.

GENERAL RELEASE (From an Individual) (10-01)

The General Release is one of the most commonly used legal documents. This form and the one following, General Release (From a Corporation), are used whenever a dispute is resolved between two parties. The type of dispute can include the amount of a bill, an employment contract, an exchange of merchandise, the termination of a contract, etc. The rule to follow is: exchange releases whenever you resolve a dispute.

GENERAL RELEASE (From an Individual)

1. The name of the person giving the Release in exchange for receiving money or other consideration (the RELEASOR).

2. The address of the RELEASOR.

3. The dollar amount, in words, being paid. If there is no money being paid, or the consideration is the promise not to sue, enter "Ten."

4. The dollar amount, in numbers.

5. The name of the party paying the money and getting the Release (the RELEASEE).

6. Identify the RELEASEE by entering his address if an individual, or if a corporation by entering the state in which the RELEASEE is incorporated and its current office address; i.e. "a __________ Corporation with offices at ______________________."

7. A description of the facts that gave rise to the dispute; i.e. "a purchase order dated ________,19__," "contract of employment between __________and__________ dated _______,19__."

__________[1]__________ residing at __________[2]__________ as RELEASOR, in consideration of the sum of ______[3]______ Dollars ($____[4]____) and other good and valuable consideration received from __________[5]__________, __________[6]__________ as RELEASEE, receipt whereof is hereby acknowledged hereby agrees to release and discharge the RELEASEE, RELEASEE'S heirs, executors, administrators, successors and assigns from any and all actions, causes of action, suits, charges and obligations, debts, dues, sums of money, accounts, reckonings, bonds, bills, specialties, covenants, contracts, controversies, agreements, promises, variances, trespasses, damages, judgments, extents, executions, claims, and demands whatsoever, in law, admiralty or equity, which against the RELEASEE, the RELEASOR, RELEASOR'S heirs, executors, administrators, successors and assigns ever had, now have or hereafter can, shall or may have for, upon, or by reason of any matter, cause or thing whatsoever from the beginning of time to the date of this RELEASE, more specifically:________[7]__________ ____.

Wherever the sense of this RELEASE requires, a singular number shall be construed to be plural and vice versa, and words of the masculine gender shall be construed to be feminine and vice versa.

This RELEASE may only be changed in writing signed by both RELEASOR and RELEASEE.

(Document continued on next page)

8. The date the Release is given.

9. The name of the WITNESS printed directly below the line, with the WITNESS to sign above the line.

10. The name of the RELEASOR printed directly below the line, with the RELEASOR to sign above the line.

11. The Notary Public completes this part of the form, and signs and seals it by affixing his stamp or seal.

IN WITNESS WHEREOF, the RELEASOR has executed this RELEASE on the __[8]__ day of _______, 19 __.

WITNESS:

____________________ ____________________

[9] [10]

STATE OF ____[11]____, COUNTY OF ___[11]___, ss.:

On _________[11]________, 19__ before me ______[11]______ personally came _______[11]_______ to me known, and known to me to be the individual(s) described in, and who executed the foregoing RELEASE, and duly acknowledged to me that (t)(s)he(y) executed the same.

____

Notary Public

GENERAL RELEASE (From a Corporation) (10-02)

The General Release (From a Corporation) is the companion to the preceding General Release (From an Individual.). The General Release (From a Corporation) should be used whenever a dispute is resolved by a corporation giving the Release.

GENERAL RELEASE (From a Corporation)

1. The name of the corporation giving the Release in exchange for receiving money or other consideration (the RELEASOR).

2. The state in which the RELEASOR is incorporated.

3. The address of the corporation.

4. The dollar amount, in words, being paid. If there is no money being paid, or the consideration is a promise not to sue, enter "Ten."

5. The dollar amount, in numbers.

6. The name of the person or entity paying money or giving other consideration and getting the Release (the RELEASEE).

7. A brief description of the facts giving rise to the dispute, i.e. "a purchase order dated ______," "a contract between______and______."

__________[1]____________, a corporation organized under the laws of the State of ______[2]______ whose principal place of business is located at _______________[3]______________, as RELEASOR, in consideration of the sum of ________[4]________ Dollars ($____[5]____) received from ___________[6]__________, as RELEASEE, the receipt of which is hereby acknowledged, agrees to release and discharge the RELEASEE, RELEASEE's heirs, executors, administrators, successors and assigns from any and all actions, causes of action, suits, charges and obligations, debts, dues, sums of money, accounts, reckonings, bonds, bills, specialties, covenants, contracts, controversies, agreements, promises, variances, trespasses, damages, judgments, extents, executions, claims and demands whatsoever, in law, admiralty or equity, which against the RELEASEE, the RELEASOR, RELEASOR's heirs, executors, administrators, successors and assigns ever had, now have or hereafter can, shall or may have for, upon or by reason of any matter, cause or thing whatsoever from the beginning of time to the date of this RELEASE, and more specifically:_______________[7]_______________
____.

Wherever the sense of this RELEASE requires, a singular number shall be construed to be plural and vice versa, and words of the masculine gender shall be construed to be feminine and vice versa.

This RELEASE may only be changed in writing signed by both RELEASOR and RELEASEE.

(Document continued on next page)

8. The date the Release is given.

9. The name of the WITNESS printed directly below the line, with the WITNESS to sign above the line.

10. The name and title of the person acting for the corporation printed directly below the line, with that person to sign above the line.

11. The Notary Public completes this part of the form, and signs and seals it by affixing his stamp or seal.

IN WITNESS WHEREOF, the RELEASOR has executed this RELEASE on the __[8]__ day of ____________, 19__.

WITNESS:

________[9]__________ ________[1]______

BY_______________
[10]

STATE OF ___[11]___, COUNTY OF ___[11]___, ss.:

On _________[11]________, 19__, before me _______________[11]_____________ personally came __________[11]___________ to me known, who duly sworn, did depose and say that (s)he resides at _____________[11]________________, that deponent is the _____[11]_______ of _________[11]________, the corporation described in and which executed the foregoing RELEASE, that deponent knows the seal of the corporation, that the seal affixed to the RELEASE is the corporate seal, that it was affixed by order of the Board of the corporation, and that deponent signed (his)(her) name thereto by like order.

____
Notary Public

MODEL RELEASE (10-03)

This form should be used by a photographer to secure the right to use the likeness (the photograph) of any model whose picture will be taken.

1. The name of the MODEL.

2. The fee paid to the MODEL.

3. The name of the PHOTOGRAPHER taking the pictures.

4. Indicate the length of time of the permission being granted to use the photographs, and if such period is other than "unlimited" or "one year," check the last box and insert the expiration date of the permission.

5. The date the photographs are taken.

6. The name of the MODEL printed directly below the line, with the MODEL to sign above the line.

7. The address of the MODEL.

8. The name of the WITNESS printed directly below the line, with the WITNESS to sign above the line.

9. The name of the MODEL's parent or legal guardian (to be used if the MODEL is a minor). If the MODEL is not a minor, delete.

10. The name of the parent/legal guardian printed directly below the line, with that person to sign above the line. If the MODEL is not a minor, delete.

MODEL RELEASE

__________[1]__________, the MODEL, in consideration of the sum of $______[2]______, the receipt of which is hereby acknowledged, sells, assigns and grants to ________[3]________, PHOTOGRAPHER, the right and permission to use photographs of me taken this day. This right is granted for art, advertising, trade or any similar lawful purpose, except the following which are subject to separate negotiations and written consent of the model: television, motion pictures, billboards, posters, product packaging and point-of–purchase displays.

This right shall expire on (check one):

( ) unlimited; ( ) one year from today; ( ) ____[4]____

Accordingly, I hereby release and discharge the PHOTOGRAPHER and persons acting for or on behalf of PHOTOGRAPHER from any liability by virtue of any blurring, distortion, alteration, optical illusion or use in composite form that may occur or be processed in the taking of these photographs or in the processing of these photographs through the completion of the finished product.

I hereby warrant that I am of full age, or that if I am a minor that I and my legal guardian have every right to contract in my name in the above regard. I further state that (I)(we) have read this RELEASE prior to its execution, and that (I)(we) are fully familiar with its contents.

DATED:_____[5]________ ____________________
[6]

WITNESS: ADDRESS:____________________
[7]

__________________ ____________________
[8]

I, _________[9]_________, am the guardian of the above named MODEL and I do hereby consent to the execution of this RELEASE and agree to all of its terms.

____
[10]

CUSTOMER TESTIMONIAL/ENDORSEMENT RELEASE (10-04)

This form is used to secure permission to use customer testimonials or endorsements of a product or service.

CUSTOMER TESTIMONIAL/ENDORSEMENT RELEASE

1. The name of the person or business seeking the permission to use the Testimonial or Endorsement.

In consideration of the payment to me of TEN DOLLARS ($10.00) and other valuable consideration received by me, I hereby give _______[1]_______ (the "PUBLISHER"), the absolute and irrevocable right and permission, with respect to any photograph(s) taken of me or in which I may be included with others, direct quotes or portions of direct quotes made by me or all or any portions of statements, details, events or recountings of events in which I participated (the "MATERIAL"): (a) to copyright the same in PUBLISHER'S own name or any other name that the PUBLISHER might choose; (b) to use, re-use, publish and re-publish the same in whole or in part, individually or in conjunction with other similar MATERIAL, in any medium and for any purposes whatsoever, including (but not by way of limitation) illustration, promotion and advertising, and trade; and (c) to use my name in conjunction therewith if PUBLISHER so chooses.

I hereby waive any right that I may have to inspect or approve the finished product or products or the advertising copy or printed matter that may be used in connection therewith or the use to which it may be applied.

I hereby release PUBLISHER from any liability by virtue of any blurring, distortion, alteration, optical illusion, or use in composite form that may occur or be produced in the reproduction, use, processing, printing or publication of the MATERIAL.

This authorization and RELEASE shall also inure to the benefit of the legal representatives, licensees, and assigns of the PUBLISHER as well as the photographer(s) and others who compiled the MATERIAL.

I hereby warrant that I am of full age, or that if I am a minor that I and my legal guardian have every right to contract in my name in the above regard. I further state that

(Document continued on next page)

2. The date the permission is granted.

3. The name of the customer giving the Testimonial or making the Endorsement printed directly below the line, with the customer to sign above the line.

4. The address of the customer.

5. The name of the WITNESS to the signing of the Release printed directly below the line, with the WITNESS to sign above the line.

6. The name of the customer's parent or legal guardian (to be used if the customer is a minor). If the customer is not a minor, delete.

7. The name of the parent/legal guardian printed directly below the line, with that person to sign above the line. If the customer is not a minor, delete.

(I)(we) have read this RELEASE prior to its execution, and that (I)(we) are fully familiar with its contents.

DATED:__________ [2]

____________________ [3]

WITNESS:

ADDRESS:____________________ [4]

____________________ [5]

____________________ [4]

I,_________[6]_________, am the guardian of the above named minor and I do hereby consent to the execution of this RELEASE and agree to all of its terms.

____

[7]

POWER OF ATTORNEY (10-05)

A Power of Attorney is used to give another person or entity (attorney-in-fact) authority to act for you if for some reason you cannot be present to act (for example, you have moved to California from New York and you need someone to be present at the sale of your home in New York).

You may at some time need to use a Power of Attorney while outside the United States. Should it be necessary, consult that country's diplomatic mission in the United States before you leave for that country's "notarial" requirements. Conversely, you may be outside the United States at a time you need to give a Power of Attorney. In that event, have the form "notarized" by the the U.S. Consul in that country's United States consulate.

While a Power of Attorney generally relates to delegating authority to act with respect to property, some states, New York for example, specifically permit the use of a Power of Attorney to authorize the attorney-in-fact to provide such things as medical care for a spouse or child. The laws of your state should be consulted before using this form for that purpose.

POWER OF ATTORNEY

I, ________[1]________, residing at ____________[2]____________, do hereby appoint ________[3]________, of ____________[4]__________, my attorney(s)-in-fact to act in my name, place and stead in any way which I myself could do if I were personally present, with respect to ____________[5]_____________, to the extent I am by law permitted to act through an agent.

This Power of Attorney shall not be affected by my subsequent disability or incompetence.

To induce any third party to act under this Power of Attorney, I agree that any third party receiving an executed copy or facsimile of this Power of Attorney may act hereunder and that no revocation or termination of this Power of Attorney shall be effective as to any third party unless and until such third party shall have received actual notice or knowledge of such revocation or termination. I and for my heirs, executors, legal representatives and assigns, do indemnify and hold harmless any such third party from and against any and all claims that may arise against such third party by reasons of such third party having relied on this Power of Attorney.

(Document continued on next page)

1. The name of the person giving the Power of Attorney.

2. The address of the person giving the Power of Attorney.

3. The name of the party (attorney-in-fact) who will act for you.

4. The address of the party who will act for you.

Note: you may name more than one party. If you want these parties to act together, enter the word "jointly" after the word "act." If you want these parties to act independent of one another, enter the word "severally" after the word "act."

5. The area in which you are granting authority. It may be general, for example "Banking Transactions" or specific, "Banking transactions regarding Bank Account No. 124-8976 at New York Trust and Savings." If the Power of Attorney is to be used for a person, describe the authority being given such as "medical, surgical and hospital treatment and care" and identify the person to receive the care by full name and date of birth.

6. The date you grant the Power of Attorney.

7. The name of the person giving the Power of Attorney printed directly below the line, with that person to sign above the line.

8. The Notary Public completes this part of the form, and signs and seals it by affixing his stamp or seal.

I have hereunto signed my name this __[6]__ day of _______, 19__.

____
[7]

STATE OF ____[8]____, COUNTY OF ____[8]____, ss.:

On _______[8]_______, 19__ before me ______[8]______ personally came ________[8]________ to me known, and known to me to be the individual(s) described in, and who executed the foregoing, and duly acknowledged to me that (t)(s)he(y) executed the same.

____
Notary Public

AFFIDAVIT—POWER OF ATTORNEY IN FULL FORCE (10-06)

When a Power of Attorney is presented for use, the attorney-in-fact (the one authorized to act) may be asked to sign an Affidavit stating that the Power remains valid and effective and has not been revoked or terminated. It is to be signed before a Notary Public.

AFFIDAVIT—POWER OF ATTORNEY IN FULL FORCE

1. The state and county where the Affidavit is signed.

2. The name of the attorney-in-fact.

3. The name of the person who gave the Power of Attorney.

4. The date the Power of Attorney was given.

5. A description of the document or transaction for which the Power of Attorney is being used.

6. The date on which the Power of Attorney is being used.

7. The name of the party accepting the Power of Attorney.

8. The name of the attorney-in-fact to be printed directly below the line, with the attorney-in-fact to sign above the line.

9. The date of the Affidavit.

10. The signature and stamp of the Notary Public taking the signature of the attorney-in-fact.

STATE OF ___[1]___, COUNTY OF _____[1]_____ ss.:

________[2]________, being duly sworn, deposes and says that: The Power of Attorney granted to me by ________[3]________, on ______[4]______, a true copy of which is annexed hereto is in full force and effect; that at the time of the execution of ___________[5]___________, on __________[6]__________, I had no knowledge of or actual notice of the revocation or termination of the Power of Attorney by death or otherwise.

I make this affidavit for the purpose of inducing ________[7]________ to accept the above described instrument as executed by me as attorney-in-fact knowing that in accepting the aforesaid instrument they will rely upon this affidavit.

____

[8]

Sworn to before me this

__[9]__day of ______________

__________[10]__________

Notary Public

REVOCATION OF POWER OF ATTORNEY (10-07)

Because a Power of Attorney permits another person or entity to act for you, the Revocation and termination of that Power of Attorney should be documented. It would be wise not only to communicate the Revocation verbally but to confirm it by the use of this form sent to the attorney-in-fact by Certified Mail—Return Receipt Requested.

REVOCATION OF POWER OF ATTORNEY

I, ________[1]________, residing at ____________[2]____________, do this date ________[3]________, hereby revoke and terminate the Power of Attorney granted by me to ________[4]_______, of ____________[5]____________ on _______[6]_______ and declare that it is no longer in force or effect.

I have advised ________[4]________ of this revocation and termination on ________[3]________, by __________________[7]______________________.

____
[8]

STATE OF ____[9]____, COUNTY OF ___[9]___, ss.:

On _______[9]_______, 19__ before me _________[9]_________ personally came ________[9]________ to me known, and known to me to be the individual(s) described in, and who executed the foregoing, and duly acknowledged to me that (t)(s)he(y) executed the same.

____
Notary Public

1. The name of the person who gave the Power of Attorney.

2. The address of the person who gave the Power of Attorney.

3. The date of the Revocation.

4. The name of the attorney-in-fact.

5. The address of the attorney-in-fact.

6. The date of the Power of Attorney.

7. How the notice of Revocation was given, i.e. "in person" or "telephone to (212) 555-1234."

8. The name of the person who gave the Power of Attorney printed directly below the line, with that person to sign above the line.

9. The Notary Public completes this part of the form, and signs and seals it by affixing his stamp or seal.

INDEMNIFICATION/ HOLD HARMLESS AGREEMENT (10-08)

If there is a risk that you might be sued in the performance of an act for another, it would be advisable to use an Indemnification Agreement to protect yourself.

1. The name of person who will be indemnified.

2. A description of what the Indemnification is for, i.e. "sale of widgets to XYZ Company," "transportation of car from ______ to ______."

3. The date the Agreement is signed.

4. The name of the WITNESS printed directly below the line, with the WITNESS to sign above the line.

5. The address of the WITNESS.

6. The name of the party giving the Indemnification if a corporation. Otherwise delete the line.

7. If the party giving the Indemnification is an individual, delete "BY" and print the individual's name directly below the line, with that person to sign above the line. If the the party giving the Indemnification is a corporation, print the name and title of the individual acting for the corporation directly below the line, with that person to sign above the line.

8. The address of the party giving the Indemnification.

INDEMNIFICATION/ HOLD HARMLESS AGREEMENT

The undersigned does hereby irrevocably covenant, promise and agree to indemnify ________[1]________ and to hold (it)(them)(him)(her) harmless from and against any and all losses, claims, expenses, suits, costs, demands, damages or liabilities, joint or several, of whatever kind or nature which ________[1]________ may sustain or to which (it)(they)(he)(she) may become subject arising out of or relating in any way to ____________[2]____________, including without limitation in each case attorneys' fees, costs and expenses actually incurred in defending against or enforcing any such losses, claims, expenses, suits, damages or liabilities.

Dated: ________[3]________

WITNESS:

________[4]________	________*[6]*________
________[5]________	*BY*________________ [7]
________[5]________	________________ [8]
	________________ [8]

NOTARY STATEMENT (ACKNOWLEDGEMENT)—INDIVIDUAL (10-09)

Many of the documents used throughout this book, and others from banks, government agencies, etc. require that the people who sign them have their signatures notarized by a Notary Public. Not all states use the title Notary Public. For example, in Pennsylvania this person is called a Prothonatory. But whatever name is used, it is always an individual who is licensed by the state to authenticate signatures.

NOTARY STATEMENT (ACKNOWLEDGEMENT)—INDIVIDUAL

1. The state and county where the Acknowledgement is being taken.

2. The date of the Acknowledgement.

3. The title of the person notarizing the Acknowledgement, i.e. Notary Public.

4. The name of the person whose signature is being notarized.

5. A description of the document that has the signature, i.e. General Release, Power of Attorney, etc.

6. The signature, stamp or seal of the Notary Public.

STATE OF ___[1]___, COUNTY OF ____[1]____, ss.:

On _______[2]_______, 19__, before me ________[3]________ personally came ________[4]________, to me known, and known to me to be the individual(s) described in and who executed the foregoing _________[5]_________, and duly acknowledged to me that (he)(she)(they) executed the same.

____
[6]

[SEAL]

NOTARY STATEMENT (ACKNOWLEDGEMENT)—CORPORATION (10-10)

This Acknowledgement is used in the same manner and for the same purpose as the preceding Notary Statement (Acknowledgment)—Individual, except that this form is used when a corporation must have the signature of one of its officers notarized.

NOTARY STATEMENT
(ACKNOWLEDGEMENT)—CORPORATION

STATE OF ___[1]___, COUNTY OF ____[1]____, ss.:

On _______[2]_______, 19__, before me ________[3]________, personally came ________[4]________, to me known, who by me duly sworn, did depose and say that deponent resides at ___________[5]____________, that deponent is the ______[6]_______, of _________[7]_________, the corporation described in and which executed the foregoing ________[8]______, *[9][that deponent knows the seal of the corporation, that the seal affixed is the corporate seal, that the seal was affixed by order of the Board of _______[10]_______ of the corporation]*, and that deponent signed his name to the foregoing by order of the Board of _________[10]_________.

____
[11]

[SEAL]

1. The state and county where the Acknowledgement is being taken.

2. The date of the Acknowledgement.

3. The title of the person taking the Acknowledgement, i.e. Notary Public.

4. The name of the person whose signature is being notarized (the Deponent).

5. The address of the person whose signature is being notarized.

6. The corporate title of the person in No.4, i.e. President, Controller, etc.

7. The name of the corporation.

8. A description of the document signed by the person in No. 4, i.e. General Release, Power of Attorney.

9. Delete if the document does not have the corporate seal and skip to No. 11.

10. The name of the governing body of the corporation, i.e. Directors, Trustees.

11. The signature, stamp or seal of the Notary Public.

Glossary

Acknowledgement A formal declaration made in the presence of a Notary Public that the statements contained in a document are true and that the signing of the document is the free act of the person making the statement. Also called a Notary Statement.

Affidavit A statement made under oath before a person, such as a Notary Public, qualified in that state to administer oaths.

Agent One who is authorized by another, called the "Principal," to act for or on behalf of the Principal.

Arbitration The process for resolution of dispute by one or more private, unofficial (non-governmental) persons whose selection is agreed to by the parties to the dispute, and which is outside of the judiciary processes (the courts). As used in this book, and as typically used, the word implies the use of the rules and regulations of the American Arbitration Association.

Assignee One who receives the title of ownership, right or interest from another who is the owner of that title, right or interest.

Assignment The act by an Assignor of transferring the Assignor's title of ownership, interest or right in real or personal property to another. The Assignor relinquishes his rights to, and his liabilities and responsibilities for, the property. The recipient of this transfer is called the Assignee.

Assignor One who transfers his title of ownership, right or interest to another.

Balloon Payment Loan A type of loan in which payments of either principal or interest do not pay off the loan completely by the maturity date, resulting in a single payment (a "balloon") on the maturity date.

Bankruptcy Loosely "insolvency," the inability to pay one's debts because one's debts and liabilities exceed one's income and assets. Also, legal proceedings brought in the United States Bankruptcy Court, which administers distribution of a bankrupt's assets to his creditors.

Beneficiary One who has or will receive a benefit, such as a person for whose benefit a trust has been created; any person entitled to all or any part of the estate of a deceased person under the terms of a will.

Breach An intentional or unintentional violation of an obligation, contract or promise.

Bulk Transfers (Also known as Bulk Sales) The transfer or sale of a major portion (more than 50%) of the materials, supplies, merchandise or other inventory of a business which is not in the ordinary course of the transferor's or seller's business, as governed by Article 6 of the Uniform Commercial Code.

By-Laws The rules and regulations establishing the governing structure of a corporation or association.

Closing (or Closing Date) The settlement date of all obligations of the seller and the buyer to each other, at which time title to property passes from the seller to the buyer.

Codicil A written supplement, modification or alteration of an existing Will, which must be signed and witnessed with the same formality as a Will.

Collateral Property given, designated or pledged as security or guaranty for the fulfillment or discharge of an obligation.

Consideration Any benefit given to one by another as an inducement to enter into a contract.

Consignee A merchant who receives goods for sale on a commission basis but who does not actually take ownership of the goods.

Consignment Sale A form of sale in which goods are deposited by the owner (the Consignor) with a merchant (the Consignee), with the merchant to receive a commission on each item actually sold. The Consignee does not own (take title to) the goods.

Consignor The owner of goods who leaves the goods with a merchant for sale on a commission basis.

Corporation An artificial entity created or recognized by a state, acknowledging an association of one or more people, which is separate and distinct from those people. Generally, individual shareholders enjoy the protection of limited liability in that each is liable and "at risk" only to the extent of his investment to purchase the stock of the corporation.

Custodian One who is entrusted, either by law or agreement, with the care, keeping, control or possession of a thing or person.

Damages Monetary compensation paid to a person who has suffered loss, detriment or injury to his person, property or rights through an act or omission of another.

Decedent A deceased person.

Declarant One who makes a declaration, generally not under oath and out of court.

Deed The term for any one of several types of documents signed by the seller (also known as the grantor or vendor) establishing the transfer or ownership (title) of real estate to the buyer (also known as the grantee or vendee).

Deed of Trust A document used in several states, in place of a mortgage, in which title to real estate is transferred to a trustee (who may be either the seller or a third party). The holder of the Deed of Trust cannot further encumber the property or make any improvements to the property without the consent of the buyer. If the buyer defaults in repayment, the holder of the Deed of Trust is entitled to take immediate possession of the property (see also Mortgage).

Default A failure or omission to meet a legal obligation.

Deponent A person who gives testimony under oath, which is then, typically, put in writing. (See also Affiant).

Designee One who has been designated by another.

Director (of a corporation) A person, appointed or elected by the shareholders of a corporation, who is authorized to direct and oversee the affairs of the corporation.

Domicile One's "home," the place where one ultimately intends to return. A person's domicile and residence may be, but are not always, the same. A person may have more than one residence but only one domicile.

Donee A person who receives a gift from another.

Donor A person who makes a gift to another.

Due On Sale A mortgage or loan provision requiring that the principal amount borrowed, and all interest accrued to the date of a sale of property, must be paid in full on or before the closing date of the sale.

Easement Permission or license, granted by the owner of real estate to another, to cross, trespass or use that property for a specific purpose.

Encumbrance A claim, charge, lien or interest in property, especially real estate.

Equity In real estate, the value of property over and above the total amount owed on any mortgages, liens or the like. The term is also used to refer to a legal doctrine of fairness—doing to others what one would want others to do to them.

Escalation (or Escalator) A contract clause permitting or providing for increases or decreases in price based upon fluctuations in underlying costs. It is is most commonly used in leases.

Escrow The delivery of money, a document or property by a buyer to a third person (typically referred to as the "Escrow Agent") to be held by that third person until a specific event occurs, and upon that occurrence, delivery to the seller. If the event does not occur, the money, document or property is returned to the seller.

Estoppel A legal doctrine which holds that one should be stopped from denying, disavowing or repudiating one's own statements or acts.

Estoppel Certificate (Mortgage Estoppel Certificate) A document in which a lender or holder of a mortgage (the Mortgagee) certifies the amount of unpaid principal and interest, the date of maturity and the rate of interest.

Exclusive Agency (Real Estate Brokerage Agreement) A form of real estate brokerage agreement in which the property owner agrees that a particular broker will be paid a commission in the event of any sale of the property, regardless of whether the buyer was procured by another broker. See also Exclusive Right to Sell and Open Listing.

Exclusive Right to Sell (Real Estate Brokerage Agreement) A form of real estate brokerage agreement in which the property owner agrees that a particular broker will be paid a commission in the event of any sale of the property, regardless of whether the buyer was procured by another broker *or even the property owner himself.* See also Exclusive Agency and Open Listing.

Execute To complete or make a document valid by signing and delivering it.

Executor The representative of the estate of a deceased person who has been approved by a court of probate and who is responsible for collecting the deceased person's assets, arranging for the payment of the deceased person's debts and estate taxes and for distributing the deceased person's property in accordance with his Will.

Executrix The feminine form of Executor.

Finder A "middle-man" engaged to locate an outside source of capital for a business venture or to locate a purchaser or seller for a business or personal property.

F.O.B. See Free On Board.

Force Majeure A force, event or occurrence which is beyond the control of the parties to a contract, such as a fire or strike.

Foreclosure Termination of a mortgage, in which the mortgage holder takes possession of the property by order of the court upon default by the borrower.

Free On Board A term meaning that the goods or subject matter of a sale is to be loaded for shipment without expense to the buyer.

Gift The act of transferring ownership of property or money to another, in which the person making the gift (the Donor) receives no payment or other consideration. Note that there must be "donative intent" (the Donor intends to make a gift, as opposed to making, for example, a loan) and there must be actual delivery of the gifted property to the person receiving the gift (the Donor).

Goodwill (Also Good Will) The intangible value added to a business resulting from its reputation among its customers and the market place.

Grant A transfer of property by gift, sale or lease.

Grantee One to whom a grant, especially of real estate, is made; the buyer of real estate.

Grantor One who makes a grant, especially of real estate; the seller of real estate.

Guarantee One to whom a guaranty is made or given.

Guarantor One who makes or gives a guaranty.

Guaranty A promise to be responsible for the debt of another in the event the other defaults.

Guardian One who has been lawfully charged with the duty to care for and to manage the property and affairs of another who, because of age or law, is considered to be incapable of managing his own property and affairs.

Hold Harmless See Indemnify.

Incumbrance See Encumbrance.

Indemnify The act of holding another not responsible for loss or damage. Also, the agreement to reimburse another for loss or damage from a third person's act or refusal to act.

Intangible That which cannot be touched. Intangible property means property which has no intrinsic or marketable value, such as goodwill or a trademark.

Intestate A person who dies without leaving a valid Will, or the condition of the estate of that person.

Irrevocable That which cannot be withdrawn, repealed, cancelled, annulled or changed.

Joint Venture A voluntary agreement between two or more people to conduct business for profit in a specific business situation and for a limited or fixed period of time. Typically, a Joint Venture is managed by a "Venture Manager" or "General Partner" who is liable for losses, and one or more other investing partners, referred to as "Limited Partners," each of whom is liable for losses only to the extent of his respective capital contribution to the Joint Venture.

Judgment The final decision of a court, which determines the rights and claims of the parties to a law suit.

Jurisdiction In the legal sense, the authority by which courts hear and decide cases and exercise their legal authority. The term also is used to refer to the sphere of territorial range of authority (usually divided along political boundaries such as towns, cities or states).

Last Will and Testament See Will.

Lease An agreement between the owner of property and another in which the owner retains title (ownership) of the property but grants to the other exclusive use and possession of the property for a fixed period of time and for a fixed fee. In a lease of real estate, the owner is usually referred to as "landlord" and the person receiving the rights of use and possession is usually referred to as "tenant." In a lease of personal property (property other than real estate), the owner is usually referred to as "lessor" and the person receiving the right of use and possession is usually referred to as "lessee."

Lessee See Lease.

Lessor See Lease.

Letter of Credit A promise by a bank, financial institution or other lender to pay a specific amount of money at the request of, and in accordance with, the instructions of its customer to a third party (such as a supplier or manufacturer of merchandise), provided that the required documentation is presented; usually used with regard to shipment of goods between countries.

Liability A comprehensive term referring to any and every hazard or responsibility.

License A permission or authority granted to another, or the certificate or other document which notes or attests to the granting of a permission or authority.

Lien A claim, charge, security or encumbrance upon the property of another as security for a debt.

Lien Holder One who owns or holds a lien upon the property of another.

Lienor See Lien Holder.

Liquidated Damages An agreed upon amount of damages (money) an injured party will be entitled to receive upon default or breach of an agreement by the other party, so that the injured party does not have to establish the exact amount of his actual damages in any subsequent lawsuit.

Litigant A party to a law suit.

Living Will A document used by an individual to clearly express his intentions regarding medical care and treatment during his lifetime in the event that he becomes unable to make or participate in the making of such decisions himself.

Metes and Bounds The exact legal description of a parcel of real estate which locates and defines the boundaries of the property in distance (in feet and inches) and compass direction (in degrees, minutes and seconds) and which is usually found on the deed.

Mortgage An interest given by the owner of real property (the Mortgagor) to secure repayment of a loan made by another (the Mortgagee). Despite making such a loan, title (ownership) remains in the name of the owner of the property and, in the event of a default in repayment, the lender must bring a legal proceeding known as "foreclosure" in order to sell the security to receive repayment of the loan. (See also Deed of Trust).

Mortgagee A lender who agrees to accept a lien on real estate as security for the repayment of a loan made to the owner of that real estate.

Mortgagor The owner of real estate who pledges his property as security for the repayment of a loan or debt.

Negligence The omission or failure to do something or to perform some act which a "reasonable man," guided by ordinary considerations, would do in the same or similar circumstances.

Notarize The acts performed by a Notary Public or other official authorized to administer oaths, especially the acts of signing and affixing his stamp or seal to a document.

Notary Public A person authorized by the laws of a state to administer an oath and witness signatures. A Notary Public attests only to the fact that the statements were made to him under oath on a certain date and place; he does not attest to the truth of those statements. See also Acknowledgement.

Notation Letter of Credit A type of Letter of Credit in which the running (declining) balance is recorded ("notated") on the back of the Letter of Credit.

Notice A formal declaration of intent, usually in writing, required to be given under the terms of an agreement, such as notice of a contract breach; also, the manner, method or means of communicating some fact or information to another.

Obligee The person in whose favor some act or obligation must be performed by an Obligor.

Obligor One who is required to perform some act or obligation.

Officer (of a corporation) A person appointed or elected by the directors of a corporation in accordance with the by-laws of the corporation and who is authorized to manage the day-to-day operations of the corporation (typically, the president, vice-president, secretary and treasurer).

Open Listing (Real Estate Brokerage Agreement) A form of real estate brokerage agreement in which the property owner is free to list the property with other brokers or to sell the property himself. The property owner is required to pay a brokerage commission only to the broker who procures the actual buyer. See also Exclusive Agency and Exclusive Right to Sell.

Option A contract in which the owner of property (the "Optionor") gives to another (the "Optionee") the exclusive right to purchase the property during a specific time period and on terms which have been agreed upon. The Optionor cannot revoke the Option and is required to sell the property if the Option is exercised. The Optionee can elect to purchase the property or not.

Optionee A person who receives an Option to purchase property.

Optionor The owner of property who gives an Option to purchase the property.

Over-tenant See Sub-lease.

Partner One who has formed a partnership with one or more others.

Partnership A voluntary agreement between two or more people or companies to conduct business for profit on a continuing basis as co-owners. Profits as well as losses are to be shared proportionally and each partner (and his assets) is liable and "at risk" for any losses incurred by the partnership.

Party A person or entity in a transaction, matter or proceeding who is obligated, as in a party to a contract, or is directly influenced by its outcome, as in a party (plaintiff or defendant) to a law suit.

Per Capita A formula for estate distribution in which all heirs divide property equally on a "per head" basis.

Personal Property That which can be moved, as distinguished from real property, which is land.

Per Stirpes A formula for estate distribution in which beneficiaries of the same degree of kinship are each to receive equal shares of the estate if each survives the Testator, but in which the children of each pre-deceased beneficiary divide only their parent's share.

Pledge The use of goods or other tangible property as security for a debt or other obligation. Possession of the goods is delivered to the creditor or lender who has a lien on the goods, but legal title (ownership) remains with the debtor or borrower.

Power of Attorney A document establishing the granting of authority to another person (called the "Attorney-In-Fact") to act in place of and on a behalf of a person if that person cannot be present to act for himself.

Pre-deceased One whose death precedes that of the maker of a Will or who dies before the probate of that Will.

Principal Any person or entity who grants authority to an agent or attorney-in-fact to act in its behalf.

Probate The act, process or court proceedings for proving or receiving official recognition that a document is, in fact, the Will of the deceased.

Proxy The person appointed to represent and act for another. The term also refers to the document establishing such appointment.

Purchase Money Mortgage A loan given by the seller of real estate to the buyer of the real estate to enable the buyer to purchase the property.

Quorum The number of members of a board, committee or the like which must be present at a meeting in order for the actions and resolutions of that meeting to be binding (to be "official") on all members; typically, a simple numerical majority of the total number of such members.

Ratify To approve, sanction, confirm or make valid.

Real Property Land, as distinguished from personal property.

Realty See Real Property.

Release The giving up of a right, claim or privilege, such as the right to sue, which one has or may in the future have against another. A "General Release" is the giving up of any and all rights, claims or privileges against another.

Releasee One who pays money or gives other consideration in order to be released.

Releasor One who gives a Release in exchange for money or other consideration.

Resolution A formal written statement or expression of opinion adopted by an official body or assembly, such as a Board of Directors.

Revocation The cancellation, annulment or repeal of some power or authority previously given or granted.

Rule Against Perpetuities With respect to Wills, a legal rule recognized in most states which prohibits holding property (the "alienation of property") in trust for a period longer than a "life in being plus 21 years" as measured from the date of the Testator's death (not the date of signing the Will).

S Corporation A "small business corporation" defined by Internal Revenue Code Sec. 1361 as a certain type of corporation which has no more than 35 shareholders, has no shareholders who are not individuals (except for a trust), has no shareholders who are nonresident aliens, has only one class of stock, and fulfills other requirements as well.

Security The pledge of property to guarantee payment of a loan (see Collateral).

Self-amortizing Loan A type of loan which by its terms provides that if all payments are made on time, principal and interest will have been repaid in full by the last scheduled payment (also known as a self-liquidating loan).

Shareholder An owner of all or a part of a corporation in whose name stock certificates are issued (also referred to as a "stockholder").

Signature Guarantee The certification of a signature as attested to by an officer of a commercial bank or stock exchange-registered stock brokerage firm. This is not the same as a Notary Statement (Acknowledgement).

Stock Power The endorsement of a stock certificate (whether on the back of the certificate itself or by a separate document) which allows the certificate to be sold or transferred. A stock power is to a stock certificate as an endorsement is to a check.

Sub-lease The transfer to another (known as "under-tenant") of all or part of one's interest in real property for a period of time ending no later than the ending date of one's own lease. The tenant, as "over-tenant," reserves for himself any rights to get the lease back and also remains ultimately liable to the landlord for performance of the terms of the original lease (also referred to as the "over-lease").

Subscriber A person or entity who agrees to purchase shares of stock of a corporation at a predetermined price on an indeterminate date in the future when the stock is issued.

Tangible That which can be touched, as opposed to intangible. Tangible property is property which has intrinsic value.

Term Length of time. When used in connection with a lease, term refers to the length or duration of permitted occupancy or possession, measured from the date of first permitted occupancy or possession (not the date of signing the lease).

Termination An end, severance or cessation of something, such as the termination of a contract.

Testator A person who makes a Will.

Testatrix The feminine term for a person who makes a Will.

Title Ownership or a claim of right of ownership, especially of real estate; a document proving ownership.

Transferee The buyer of property or rights, or the one to whom a transfer of property or rights is made.

Transferor The seller of property or rights.

U.C.C. See Uniform Commercial Code.

Under-Tenant See Sub-lease.

Uniform Commercial Code A body of uniform laws (with only slight variations) governing business, banking and commercial relationships, which have been adopted by all states (except Louisiana).

Vendee One who pays money or gives other consideration in order to receive title (ownership) of property. The buyer of real estate is usually referred to as the Grantee.

Vendor One who transfers or sells property to another; the seller. The seller of real estate is usually referred to as the Grantor.

Waive The act of exercising a waiver (see Waiver).

Waiver The voluntary, intentional relinquishing or giving up of some known right.

Warrantee One to whom a warranty is given.

Warranty A promise that a statement of fact is true.

Will A document signed during a person's lifetime which directs the disposition of that person's assets and property after his death.

Witness One who signs his name to a document, not as a party to the agreement, but rather for the purpose of establishing the authenticity of the signature of a party to the agreement.

Index by Title

A

B

C

D

E

F

G

I

J

L

M

N

O

P

R

S

Subject Index

Numbers in parentheses are document numbers found at the top of each document. They are followed by page numbers.

A

B

C

D

E

F

G

H

I

J

L

M

N

O

P

R

S

T